The Journey of a Modern Mystic

The Journey of a Modern Mystic

The Battle for the Kingdom of God

Volume I

Edward Rasor

iUniverse, Inc.

New York Lincoln Shanghai

The Journey of a Modern Mystic
The Battle for the Kingdom of God

iUniverse books may be ordered through booksellers or by contacting:

iUniverse
2021 Pine Lake Road, Suite 100
Lincoln, NE 68512
www.iuniverse.com
1-800-Authors (1-800-288-4677)

ISBN-13: 978-0-595-38858-5 (pbk)
ISBN-13: 978-0-595-67649-1 (cloth)
ISBN-13: 978-0-595-83237-8 (ebk)
ISBN-10: 0-595-38858-2 (pbk)
ISBN-10: 0-595-67649-9 (cloth)
ISBN-10: 0-595-83237-7 (ebk)

Printed in the United States of America

For Sarah and Jessica

B'Ism al Lah, al Rahman, al Rahim
(In the name of God, the Compassionate, the Merciful)

Contents

▼

PART IV: AN END IN MEDITATIONS

Acknowledgments

I wish to express my deepest thanks to the "unmentioned" herein. I remember.

My deepest thanks to Chip and Maureen, and Mike S.

Micky, so much would not have been possible without you. Thank you for knowing God. You are the reason life is beautiful.

My deepest love and thanks to the "girls" in New York; Barbara, your patience, love, and expertise has been invaluable.

Tim, my "brother," I can add no words to the obvious.

To my small train of lovers past, thank you for instructing me in love. I remember.

Mother, thank you. The ways and means we are instructed in love are many. You took me when none would. You gave me life when none would. Thank you.

Marilyn, you are my breadcrumbs in the dark night.

To Michele, you are the clock with which I have measured the passing of time. You are a princess and a friend.

I had only ever gone to Jenchinan in my dreams. Sophia resides therein. There is wisdom in Jenchinan. Amidst this fertile ancient soil an unbroken line of queens reign still.

For no other in the entire world is this book written than for Sarah and Jessica. May your years and grace be abundant. May your hearts always hear the song of life and my supporting refrain. I remember, Sarah. I remember, Jessica.

Preface

"He who drinks from my mouth will become as I am and I shall be he."

—(The Christ, The Gospel of Thomas)

Why is a life's story worth telling? Literature is populated by the archetypes of the vast landscape of the humanities. In their varied forms, the complete story of the human condition has been penned in totality long ago. Yet we never seem to tire of peeking behind the curtain to take note of the minutes of other's lives. When biographies are contemporary, they appear applicable to our lives, our times. We make personal that attraction that prompted us to remove the book from the shelf. When well penned, we are moved to the moment to live within such lives. When raw and graphic, we are deported with visceral sympathy.

We take flight in the exploits of others and refuge in their redemption. We cower in the safety of our darkened nights, a voyeur to the travails of others. We lapse in passion in the poet's lament, the sculptor's construction, and the artist's tempura. We live vicariously in precarious times. In the seclusion of our frenetic worlds, we note only topically the passing of possibilities—the myriad possibilities in the lives all around us. We are often encapsulated in the routines and restrictions of our choices and conditions. Thus our lives pass, and we only measure our season's solstice by others'.

This is a story in which little reading between the lines is necessary. However, some is required. In all areas where violence and related bloodshed are referenced in this book you are to presume there was a great deal more. Violence is primarily the only thing that has been repeatedly edited out of this text. The most audacious and provocative examples of living on the streets have also been removed. These examples including such things as contract killing, armed raids on coke-houses, drug overdoses, armed robbery, sniping, and numerous other horrific expressions of the dark side of life. Many of these stories appeared gratuitous after a certain point and detracted from the larger point I aim to make.

I assert this story is very different from other stories. This life is very different than other lives. While all will see elements of their own lives reflected at various times throughout this work, it is in the conclusions reached that I hope others would consider their own lives with renewed circumspection. My life has a beginning, and middle, and one day will end; all lives end. My story, however, appears to have a beginning and a middle, but it is otherwise timeless. My life is, in many ways, our life. When we look closely at the triggers and experiences contained in this book, we understand that all life is choice, all outcomes are of our own choosing, and our destiny is crafted every moment by our intention.

What follows is my arduous climb up Jacob's Ladder. There is no flight from Eden; rather, a story follows of exodus from pandemonium. In the savage years of my youth, I survived the mean streets of New York City to excel at the craft of my childhood—violence and survival.

Instead of a life of indiscriminate violence, crime, and victimization, I sought and received sanction by my government in the most elite Special Forces in the world. From the battlefields of New York to the killing fields of Iraq, Cambodia, Afghanistan, and other far-flung dying places, this story follows the painful and vivid recollections of a life in search of meaning and purpose in a world increasingly lacking both.

This is not the story of death and loss in the war on terror; that story is part of the medium in which another, more unbelievable and inspiring story is told. This is not a military story either. This story is about God. This story is about Love. This story is about beauty. This is a story of not only taking control of our internal world but manifesting those findings upon the external world. This story takes this to the profound extreme.

This story is about affirming a better world—one of charity, of compassion, of ascent, of clarity and unity of life—of hope. As such, this is a story about the search for God in the bloodbaths of youth and war, crime and punishment, grace and redemption. This is the story of the Holy Breath of God blowing through the world of a man who would not be a victim.

It will remain for the reader to decide if the circumstances of this life motivated the outcome. Often we are the product of our environment; a classic nature versus nurture result. However, when the outcome of a life is so profoundly contrary to what is expected, we are compelled to ask how such a thing is possible. While traditional humanists will suggest that the product of my life is simply the result of deprivation and willpower, I assert that the story contained within these pages demonstrates the latent, tangible, and awesome power of spirit. I assert that spirit clocks toward God irrespective of the circumstances of the flesh. So, two stories clearly unfold within these pages. The circumstances of this life are simply the vehicle in which the spirit of a soul clocking toward God is increasingly revealed as the distance is closed to the Prize.

In *The Journey of a Modern Mystic: The Battle for the Kingdom of God, Volume I*, I relate the disturbing, sometimes hilarious, and often poignant account of the raw and graphic life that created, or otherwise accommodated, the impulse to quantum-leap beyond the flesh and the mind, the impulse to God. In *The Journey of a Modern Mystic: The Age of Consciousness, Volume II*, the means to fully deconstruct the illusory world and secure passage to spiritual vision, material fulfillment, and mastery of human intercourse is explained in practical and applicable discourse. We have the choice, always, to rationally consider the insightful condition of our mind nearer to God, or we can endeavor to secure for ourselves the Light itself and experience this world beyond the appearance. Would you be a voyeur? This book is autobiographical. It is my hope that *Volume II* will be more useful to secure that which I describe in these pages.

As evidenced in the following pages the graduated projection of my internal world eventually gained a critical mass and began uncontrollably expressing and clocking toward God. Eventually, the entire manifest world has become no more then the backdrop on which my internal findings are projected. This life has been spent tediously deconstructing the entire world. Every intercourse, every moment, every coincidence has been painfully disassembled, considered, and made contextual by the internal—exclusively. The result is a breathtaking approximation of the nature of reality, God, and the ultimate mystery of life.

"I shall relate to thee without omission both theoretical wisdom and that wisdom which can be known only by intuitive realization—knowing which, naught in this world will remain unknown to thee."

—(Bhagavad-Gita)

PART I

▼

An Uninspired Life

CHAPTER 1

▼

Upon the Altar

Hear my prayer, Lord. Grant to me thy light; I am needy and seek of thy bounty. Grant me your Love, your Truth, your Compassion, and the stillness of my soul wherein I might better hear your echoes and see your reflections, Blessed Mother. Grant me your light, dear God.

I was born into this world one time. I have four mothers. I have two sisters. I have six sisters. I have no fathers. I have five fathers. Such was the welcome I received upon my grand entrance forty years ago. I was born to a fifteen-year-old child who betrayed the Irish American values of her family and slept with a boy who wooed her more than he loved her.

Her mother was so convinced that God would strike her with lightning to scramble the egg that was me that when my mother started to show, she was "put away." She was sent to live with an aunt in North Carolina. When she came to term, she made her way on her own to New York City by train where, in the confines of a sterile and unfamiliar hospital, this uneventful life was born. The year was 1963 and people were beginning to ask the question, "Is God dead?" John F. Kennedy was crafting his little-known "Freedom from War" document, which sought to define the glue that bound nations to war. JFK was inserting teams of Special Forces into the national nightmare that would become Vietnam.

It was a watershed moment. The old landmarks that had previously defined the landscape of American life and values were falling away, and in its place was the Age of Angst. To this age I came, and by all subsequent accounts I would suggest unwillingly.

Though it was out of the norm, my mother was not only permitted to breast-feed me for a week or so, but a birth certificate was issued. She named me Paul Richard after Pope Paul and Cardinal Richard Cushing. She was a Catholic. It was good that she gave the new pope-child up on a Friday. By Saturday afternoon, she would be able to take the train to Boston where she could still make confession, take mass on Sunday, and if things went wrong, or right, be in heaven on Monday.

FROM CRADLE TO CRADLE TO CRADLE

She had been told that a wealthy doctor and his family from upstate New York would be adopting me, that I would have a great life, and that she should take comfort in her decision. Perhaps a doctor had adopted me. It makes no matter. I have no recollection of it. The following was pieced together many years later from Mrs. Wu of The Children's Aid Society:

I was adopted and returned as broken goods. How this oversight, that I was broken, could have happened has never been explained, though there are often kernels of truth in the stories that get passed on. I was taken home with a family and kept there for some time. They returned me because I was circumcised. This seems an entirely unlikely happenstance. In any event, it seems an odd thing to bring a baby back to the store due to the physical appearance of an appendage that should not otherwise be of any use to any but the bearer, and not until much later in life. But this is just one of the many stories in the world of adoption, in the halls and archives of the New York City Children's Aid Society. I was placed in an orphanage.

Later, as the storyteller relayed it, I was adopted and brought to the home of a mean sister who beat me incessantly. Apparently, my new mother thought so, too, and in an effort to ameliorate the problem she also returned me as broken goods. I was placed in an orphanage.

The final "home trial" took some many months later. While the woman who raised me swears I was only eighteen months old when she brought me home, I later viewed photos of me in captivity, and I was well over twenty-four months. Pictures were dated then also. Besides, "Mom" never even knew I was Paul. She was obviously going to be a poor historian. Good thing for history that she waited tables.

FROM PARENT TO PARENT TO PARENT

Mom was married to Bill, and by all later accounts it was an uninspired marriage. So many of the institutions that would mark my days could only be called such: uninspired. Life, in fact, was to prove to be a series of dark vignettes with profound punctuations of light. She maintained in later years that Bill lost himself in his work, refused to grow up, and cheated on her. She was, of course, correct. Bill would be for me that which I would not become. Bill maintained that she demanded so much of life—a house, suburbia, and more—that he had to work more and more often, later and later hours, just to provide her the life to which she became accustomed. In the end he created no more than a middle-class niche in fantasy. They both cheated on each other.

Mom increasingly took solace (and the occasional appliance being repaired) from the man across the street as the *material to fill her emptiness*. Knowing that my little sister was born of this affair, I cannot help, in the absence of more information, to assume that it was on one of these newly repaired appliances that Michele was made. As a man now, I am thrilled for her that she would have such escape in the emptiness that must have been her life. At the same time, I am somewhat repulsed to picture the woman I would know as mother having sex near my playroom on the now properly seated washing machine.

Tom was as unhappy as a man could be in his marriage to Marie. His behavior clearly showed this. He already had nearly grown children by the late 1960s. Madeline wanted children. Bill hated Italians. Madeline was told that she could not have children. However, it was later found that Bill could not have children. Tom was Italian. When my mother brought me home and gave me my first bath, it was likely my first bath ever. She recalled that Bill would not even rise from his paper in the living room. The water turned black, and, surprise, my skin was not brown or olive;—it was white. My hair was not black; it was blond. I was not Italian, but the damage had been done because Bill thought I was. When Bill would come home late from work and I would see his headlights on the wall of my room, I would get up and run to the landing where the staircase descended to the front door. It was here that Bill would greet me at night when the house and the world slept, and beat me.

He would take me by the heels and hold me up over the drop to the basement. This was considerable height for a little man. The stairs from the upstairs descended to the front door landing, and then a flight of stairs descended from the landing to the basement. "Bill, stop it," my mother responded to my wailing. I would run off to my room and sit in the corner looking at the now lifeless space on the wall above my bed where just recently his headlights shone.

Bill drank and gambled. Many times he beat me and told my mother that I flushed his money down the toilet. This may explain how I grew to despise money. My mother was in the middle of the great leap of faith. She was planning on leaving Bill, and Tom was going to leave Marie. They would create a new life from the rubble of their choices. They both stood at the line in life where marks the familiar and the abyss. She jumped. Tom did not.

My grandmother still lived in the family home in Queens, New York. My aunt, having never married, still lived with her and my grandfather, "Uncle" Jack. My great-grandparents were either dead or dying at this time. Margie, whom everyone called Nana, took her bi-annual trips with Uncle Jack to Florida without fail each year. She took me to Florida on this trip, along with my twin cousins, Jackie and Louie. Many years later I was to find out that she did not want to take me. Instead, my mother had to pay her. This is the grandmother who still told my mother when I was thirteen years old that it was still not too late to give me back.

FROM HOME TO HOME TO HOME

I remember this trip like no other in my life. It was a time of misery and joy, road trips, and boating. I was beat the whole way to Florida and back. I resented my mother for having sent me away, but she had "work to do." I had Nana's favorites on either side of me in the back seat. Nana most certainly had favorites her whole life, and she lacked the remotest degree of sophistication or class to conceal this fact. One of my cousins would hold his hand over my mouth and the other my nose, until I puked in my own mouth and it sprayed through the vice-grip on my face. I would then gasp for air and get smacked for being noisy. She would then give a nickel to one of the boys as they took turns. Again the game would start: "Who Could Keep Quiet the Longest." And again it was me who, gasping for air, broke the silence. I got smacked, and Louie got a nickel this time.

Understand that this would go on for hundreds of miles at a time. At one point when I had to pee, my Uncle Jack pulled to the side of the road in the backwater of South Carolina; the "boys" also declared that they had to pee. As they were older, each one had a door, and I was always in the middle. They did not have to pee; rather they waited 'til I was by the wood line and jumped back in the car telling my grandmother we were done. They left me. I ran back to the road with my pants falling down to my ankles as I watched the car get smaller and smaller. I vaguely recall the lonely wait, but when they returned I was right where they left me, and I got beat.

As all boys are wont to do, I had fun the only way a boy could, and it is only in the retrospection that I find these memories intrusive. I do not recall that I had any sense then that life was unkind. It just was. In Florida the boys took me out in a boat some far distance from the imaginary line where bathers go no further. That line is approximately where water is over one's head. As I was just a little boy, the line was considerably closer. They sank the boat till water came in over the sides and swam away. I screamed for help and watched the water fill the little blue boat. I remember no more. Apparently, a man that heard my screams swam out to pull me from beneath the surface of the water, the little blue boat already claimed by Poseidon. He was kissing me, or so I thought when I woke and puked water. My grandmother was there by this time. When I stood up, she smacked me. I was punished and forced to remain in the hotel room the remainder of that day and the next. That night when all gathered after showers and dinner to play Kismet, I was not permitted to have white chocolate, a favorite treat that my mom never gave me. I loved white chocolate. My mother was back in New York making plans; she had work to do. Whether she knew it or not, she was about to become a single mother of two…correction, three.

The world is often much more secure when we consider well our demons past. The things that gave rise to fear, comfort, and security are often amazingly simple and obtainable for a child. Yet, I had no sense of security and was not by this age smitten with the whole childhood thing. We drove that afternoon from Laurelton to Howard Beach, New York. I am confident she must have wrestled with the language to use in describing the coming changes in our lives, but she could not have known that I would recall the details thirty-five years later.

"Edward, we no longer live at our old home. Mommy is not going to be married to Daddy anymore. You will still see him at times, but he will not live with us. You are going to have a baby sister. You are going to have a new father."

I stared out the window and watched the busy life of traffic and people. We were driving into the city. We arrived in a place where every house was on top of each other; there were so many doors, so many cars. *There were people and families in all these little places*, I thought. Across the street from where we parked the car there was a building with thousands of windows and little balconies. There were many buildings like this. This was my home on 85th Street. I could not possibly know that the concrete jungle that was to be my home would become the fertile fields I would plough en route to Elysium. The initial casting was complete. The scenes were being constructed to make my world stand in stark contrast to what I found on internal examination. I began to rely internally for succor.

CHAPTER 2

▼

Education in Poverty

Suffering is not the possession of the doomed alone. Suffering is like a virus that spreads through the greater community of the world until such a point as it loses is momentum in subjectivity. Yet, some-where beyond you perhaps, like waves extending from the center of a pond, the reverberations of this suffering will idle into the great body of water that carried the impact of the loss.

There in the middle of the world, on a blue planet in the Milky Way, in an old apartment in Queens, I would build the memories of this unremarkable life. The lessons I would have in love, in family, in community, in faith, and in life would all be born of what I did not have.

Mom told me the following story much later in life. She said that after just two weeks of attending kindergarten; she got a call to meet with my teacher. The teacher said Mom was going to have to have a talk with me because I wanted to be the teacher and of course she could not have that. Mom says that when I got on the bus the first day of school, I turned around just atop the steps and opened and closed my fingers on my hand, smart and rapidly saying "Bye-bye, Mommy." She said she knew my childhood ended that day. I would later consider it ended on arrival.

EARLY LESSONS

All I ever learned in school I learned by second grade. Mrs. Bibilo was my second-grade teacher at PS 232, Queens. She taught me to read, and the rest I did myself. From the moment I learned to read, I only ever read to learn. My mother would later admonish me, "Young man, you think you have all the answers." I would later discover two very important things in life: first, I did think I had all the answers, and second, I did have all the answers.

At least I did insofar as my own life and my own journey was concerned. Mom also frequently told me, "You cannot fight City Hall!" She was right on this point, but because of her admonishment about my having all the answers, I thought I could fight City Hall. Throughout my life I never let slip the opportunity to bleed on the altar of my convictions, City Hall or not. Convictions? For some people convictions are born in the absence of example.

I always hated John Gotti. When very young, I did not realize there were two of them, senior and junior. I later hated both of them. When I realized exactly how sick they were, I thought to kill one or the both of them; in fact, I planned it. When I again considered how sick they were, I came to the realization that if I failed, my family would be murdered. I never hated another human being again. This period of time was a discovery for me in my life, as it enabled me to consider and place my hands around the sources and motivations for hatred and revenge—in my life and in others. I considered early that Life itself consumes that which is antithetical to Life, in Life's own time. This may have originally been an opinion of resignation, as I was impotent to act on my disdain for Gotti. I was, however, remarkably accurate for a seedling of a man. Life does plough anti-life back into the soil if it fails to yield crop.

The Gotti clan was that thing that exists on the ass of society in one form or another, in all places, in all times, by varying names. In the new world, they were mafia. In New York City, they were mafia. John Gotti, Jr., would go on to injure me so badly I had to be hospitalized in early 1976. But this is not what I so detested—not really. Above all things, I despised how they humiliated people. Honor is their greatest heist. Gotti, Sr. was ultimately related to my world in what he represented regarding my mother and Tom. People like him embody the *concept* of evil, and "evil" stole from my home.

THE MAFIA'S LONG ARM

My playground was a place called "The Hole." This no-man's land between Brooklyn and Queens is where the mafia was reported to bury their enemies. Bad and secret things happened there at night. This is where we made our forts. This is where we stole away to escape our homes. There were a few homes in The Hole, but mostly it was just…a hole.

I lived on 85th Street, across the highway from one of the most dangerous neighborhoods on earth: East New York. John Gotti lived on 85th street. My mother lived on 85th Street; Tom did not. His wife was supposedly the daughter or niece of Funzi Tieri, next boss of the Genovese crime family (1972–1981). Tom was told that if he disrespected Marie and divorced her they would kill his girlfriend's children. They had his job ruined at Tenneco and reduced him to denying my mother—in essence, but not in practice. Tom spent the remainder of his life only visiting twice a week, though an unnatural family-in-absentia relationship existed nonetheless. My mother spent the rest of her life accepting only seconds. In a life denied she came to accept this as, I thought, the price of love. I had simply thought she loved him, and thus she did what she did. I had always thought that it was a relationship that was so structurally flawed that I would be loath to ever duplicate it in my life. When I aged I realized that love imprisoned would seek to feed itself regardless of the obstacles. Now I have come to see that my childhood impressions were correct, love commands irrespective of the obstacles to love's fulfillment. If she never did love him, then I cannot condone her choice as it renders poisoned the well from which we drank.

Every Tuesday and Thursday this fantasy took place where dinner would be served promptly, as always, at 5 PM. Tom—a.k.a. "Papo"—would come "home" at 4:30 PM, and Michele would beam. This was her father. It was always clear; it was always distinct. Early on it was apparent to Marilyn and I that Michele was my mother's even before we fully understood what that meant. Operationally, I was given my own room in a three-bedroom apartment since I was the only boy (thank heaven for the penis). Marilyn and Michele's room was a fiction. Michele slept with my mother. Years later I would come to understand the attachment to a child—the desire to be close to, to dream with (and for) your own flesh and blood. But my mother kept Michele in the bed with her until I left home. Of course, I was thirteen when I left home for good, so it is debatable if her behavior was pathological or not. I think it was. This might explain also why no one ever looked for me to bring me home; Michele finally had her own room when I left.

Papo arrived twice a week. He was gracious and kind—never mean, never drinking, never cursing. In many ways, he embodied the things I would aspire to possess when I became a man. I really had no idea since I was too young to understand anything but the most topical of impressions. After the dishes were cleaned, we would sit, talk, go out and play, or watch TV. Often Mom and Tom would also watch TV; sometimes they went into the bedroom to "talk." Papo left every Tuesday and Thursday no later than 10 PM.

FIRST KISS LOVE

Recently, I was waxing nostalgic with my mother about the incredible feelings that new love provided. I explained to her how I can taste, even now, the incredible magic of a first kiss, how love consumes, how it compels you to have no other thoughts but thoughts of your love, how love—having found you worthy—makes you feel that *this* love, *this* grace was created only for the two of you before the beginning of the world. I told her that I have known this thing in my life and believed it would never occur again with such intensity and force. I spoke humbly before her.

She just stated at me and said, "I never had that, Edward."

"You never had that?" I asked, surprised.

"Didn't you have this with Papo?" I implored.

She responded she did not, not like I had described. My very forehead was crinkling just processing this inside my head.

"What do you mean you never had this sort of love?"

"I have never loved like that." She added, "People from my generation never loved like that, Edward."

I was stunned. What this meant was that this perverted acceptance of this second-hand love that was in my home was not love at all. All these years I rationalized in my heart that she was required by love's demands to display this perverted partial love of have and have-not. We spoke quite clearly on what love was and was not; she did not love like this, or worse, she did and slipped into the place where she redefined something so beautiful as not being love. If she did not love this deeply, and he did not love her, then the only example I had of love in my life, however dysfunctional, was an aberration. While my mother and I have come to talk easily and freely of such things, it is still possible that time clouded her recollection and that loss glazed her memory.

My mother had her moments of frailty, and on one such occasion she loaded the three of us in the car and drove. I vaguely recall the scenes and certainly do not know the motivations. I only know that she drove to another neighborhood and dropped my sister and me off on the side of the road with a note and my name pinned to me. Marilyn, always my dutiful and loving sister, held my hand, and in her other hand a duplicate note. My mother was crying. My little sister, her real daughter, stared at Marilyn and me through the glass. My mother drove off and left us there. She had had enough. My life seemed to always be marked by this. I was still but a boy. I could not have been out of first grade. I do not recall the events and how something so terrible is reconstructed in damaged lives. Nevertheless, life continued, and she apparently returned to us (or we were returned to a found *her*).

Growing up in a fairly tough neighborhood was made even more difficult by my mother walking us back and forth to school those first years. This was not the neighborhood to be walked back and forth to school. As she recalled it years later, "they" were threatening her still, and at times she would be followed the whole length of the three-block walk to the school by the "black cars." It is likely that "they" sought to intimidate her, and time has made worse her recollection. "They," of course, were apparently the people related to Marie. I suspect that it was not as constant as Mom implied, either. Rather, there was likely a time when the issue was emotional for Marie, and she had her stooges scare Mom. Even mobsters take no real pleasure in harassing mothers and children.

In the end, Tom died before Marie did, and my mother knew thirty years of emotional and physical seconds. Michele knew her father in this manner. I did not like men who exerted power to hurt, or to deny others. I did not then and still do not. Marie's family was like this. Yes, Marie was like this and the same applies. The Gotti folks were like this. Much of the playground of my childhood was like this. This is the personal impact of a bully's actions where something much greater is taken from the innocent: dignity. In the end, the satellite relationship that my mother and Tom had could only have been justified for so long by "them" in the black cars. Tom settled into a life of convenience and my mother to seconds.

DEMONS: REAL AND IMAGINED

We would have our little Christmases in the little new apartment in Queens, just up the street from the Gotti family, right across the highway from the most dangerous neighborhood on earth, East New York, then drive across Queens to my aunt and Nana's home on Christmas morning. It was nice at my grandmother's house; it seemed always ancient and mysterious, though. It was also a house of the decaying and the dead. It was a museum. There were old paintings and pictures of people from long ago on the walls. There were many marble statues that cast alarming shadows at night when I sneaked downstairs for candy. There was death here, too. My mind knew that the very bottom of the house was dead. Grandma and Grandpa had died there, and when there was reason to have to get a snack or something late at night when Nana was babysitting me I would have to carefully trace my steps from the third floor to the basement turning on each light along the way. There could be no mistake returning. If I missed a switch on the return run through the house and up the stairs, I would have to return to get the switch, and the dead now knew I was down there where they do dead things.

The far corner of the bottom of the house, in the basement, is where they likely slept. In my pockets, in my hand, went the snack that imperiled me so dearly on nights like these. It must never be both hands, though. There must always remain a free hand to manage the light switches. Deep breath. "Go!" I was off deftly navigating the place where the carpet turns to hard floor and hitting the switch. Faster now. It got complicated at this point where the hard floor turns back to carpet and the staircase begins, because there was a turn and a light switch as well. This was "the corner." No one ever told me so, but I knew that the opening to the next room is where my dead grandmother could rise any moment from the chair. She did not want to hurt me. I do not think so. But she did want to show me she was dead. She did not know I already knew.

Click. The switch went to the off position. I had tricked them once; they would not be fooled on my way upstairs unless I was fast. I would already be on the first floor before they realized I had tricked them again. I would later chuckle, but not now; it was too soon. The last part was the trickiest because the room before the first floor stairs had statue heads of people and huge mirrors on the far wall. This was the big, cavernous living room. In the dark I was never able to tell at speed which heads belonged and which were new.

Click, click, click went the light switches as I maintained speed. Done. I could now sneak into my aunt's Mallomar cookies undetected by anyone. I was safely back in Uncle Jack's room seated in the oversized recliner. The hand from "Creature Feature" was just returning on the television show, and I was safe once again from Nana and the dead. The "hand" always returned after a word from the sponsors. In clay animation, the hand ate the words "Creature Feature." I just had to be back in the chair before the appearance of the "hand." This favored show always knew what was in my Nana's house. Secure in the oversized chair, the monsters were again in the box before me.

GOTTA LOVE CHRISTMAS

I had strangely few Christmas memories before this time. I recall only one complete Christmas memory from the old house. Bill's parents, Grandma and Grandpa Rasor, came to visit. This wonderful Christmas they brought me a beautiful red Volkswagen car. It was quite large. It must have been the size of a small dog. It was shiny, and the lights worked on the front and the rear bumpers. It had a lazy-Susan-like turntable beneath the chassis where the real work of moving the car across the floor was accomplished. While it had four black wheels visible on the sides beneath it, on the turntable were two aggressive rubber wheels, much smaller, but driven by the little battery-operated engine. It would go forward until it hit an object and then go backward until it hit another. In this fashion it would move about the house hitting chair legs and so forth. I took such pleasure in this. Grandma and Grandpa Rasor always got the best gifts. Though I rarely saw these two people, they would continue to send me some expression of a Christmas gift each year throughout their lives.

The adults, having taken some measure of joy in Edward and his new toy, retired to the kitchen where they were likely talking and having Christmas morning coffee. It seemed like a good enough time to do a little exploring into how my new car exactly worked. Sitting alone in the living room amid all the Christmas morning debris I noticed that there was a large hole on the bottom of my shiny, red Volkswagen. This hole seemed to have no purpose. Though I was only three or four years old, I decided this was a good place to put my penis. I can scarcely imagine the thinking that went into this fearless exploration, but it marked the turning point in a life ready to explore putting my penis into other places.

With my pants around my ankles and my penis inserted in my shiny, red Volkswagen, I thought my new toy could only be further improved upon by turning it on. "Rrrrrghhhh" the engine protested. The lights flashed brilliantly and then dimmed. Unseen cogs, wheels, and pieces of steel went to work biting into my penis and cinching the shiny, red Volkswagen firmly into my lap. The wail that I emitted must have been horrific as all the grown-ups raced into the living room where they found me crying and fucking my shiny, red Volkswagen with my pants around my ankles. This would not be the last time I overlooked the price tag for such action. This is my very earliest memory of Christmas morning.

Christmas mornings at the new place were just Mom, Marilyn, Michele, and me. I cannot remember a time when I believed in Santa Claus, but simultaneously I recall that I had always *wanted* to believe in Santa. I had always believed in something more than what was given me. When I got older I would revisit my mother's admonishment about having all the answers and realize that here I was correct, too; there is always something in which to believe. There was more, and I was keenly aware of this, even as a child.

I had discovered Christmas gifts in the living room closet, and when I asked my Mom why they were there before Santa came, she surrendered without a fight. She told me they were from her, not Santa, and not to tell Michele that there was no Santa. Of course, I would have discovered her stash. This closet was my closet; it was my secret place in the new house where no one could find me, and I could steal the world in dreams and books. It was in this place where no one would ever find me. Apparently, Santa could not, either.

This was the secret place I eventually ran a wire, concealed from the socket, to a bulb and built a library behind the vacuum cleaner. I built a false wall out of World Book Encyclopedias (minus the "R" volume) and secreted pillows for comfort. While the kids were in class learning ABCs, I was in the libraries stealing and reading encyclopedias and other books. When the kids were reading Dr. Seuss, I was reading Dickens, and Josephus' *Antiquities of the Jews*. When they were doing arithmetic, I was entombed in the closest in the corner of the living room exploring the Sphinx, Plato, and non-canonical scriptures. I built an entire world in my closet and would often squirrel away snacks and an emergency flashlight. I had to be careful that my mother did not discover the flashlight missing else her search might lead her to my "secret place."

The secret place was not just a closet, it was *my* closet. Also, I could not be found when my mother wanted to lock me in my room each night after 5 PM. I hid other things in my secret place when Mom was angry with me. My mother was in constant search of wooden ladles and wooden spoons for cooking. They had the oddest way of disappearing. Of course these were the very instruments of torture that she beat me with each day. These were not teaspoons. These were the large, pasta-cooking, stir-the-bottom-of-the-cauldron utensils. She finally got wise and got plastic cooking utensils. Blood could be washed off them, and she rarely used them to cook, rather they had a special use. These utensils beat me to near death for years.

MY GUARDIAN ANGEL

I started cutting school in the fourth grade. In the wintertime we would play hooky from school and shovel snow for the janitors in the apartment buildings for twenty-five cents. This was often enough to buy a pack of Winchester cigarettes. We started smoking. I was ten years old. I began playing hooky regularly, and when the school would call home my sister would take the call, pretending to be my mother. Then she would beat me up a bit. It was always the case that she could kick my butt for most of my life, although when she beat me she did it to protect me. When she forged my mother's signature or took a call, she did it to protect me, and to limit the bloodshed that would follow if my mom found out I was in trouble. It never mattered what the complaint was from school, or if it was true. My mom yelled at me nearly every day of my life, and she beat me more frequently than a typical child receives affection. Her response to my being in trouble was always less motivated by corrective action than retaliation that she was soiled outside the home by my behavior.

I began having nightmares like any other boy. It was not the nightmares that I remember as much as the times when I would come to my mother's bed afraid and crying from the bad dreams. Sometimes I would ask her if I could sleep with her if I was really distraught. She had a large bed, and it was just she and Michele. She would always tell me no and to go back to my bed. I do not remember a time when she took me back to bed. I do not even remember her telling me a story in my life. It is possible she did. It is more telling that I do not recall. I digress.

It is not that I had many nightmares, though I would understand if I had. It is just that these moments stand out in my memory as palpable. I took to the occasional stealing of her safety by crawling into her big bed anyway when I was scared. I just would not ask her. If I were scared, I would kneel at the foot of her bed and slowly raise one leg below the throw blanket that rested at the foot of the bed. Then I would secure a further bite with my waist. I listened to their breathing for an indication I had roused either of them. Over a long period of time in the dark I would have half my body on the bed and support my other half with my hand on the floor. Slowly, very quietly, I would push the rest of myself on to the bed. All the while the cats' eyes would be watching me in the dark. They would initially get alarmed, as my behavior was sneaky. Cats know sneaky. I was with someone now. It was safer than my own bed where the fear was.

If I was discovered, I was scolded and sent back to my room. From a very early age I stopped looking toward my mother for comfort and protection and instead sought refuge where I would for the remainder of my days—in the comfort and protection of Marilyn. Marilyn never questioned me, never scolded me, and never denied me. Marilyn would reluctantly rouse herself from sleep, move over, and pat the bed for me to lie beside her. As I got older, I still had occasional bad dreams and would simply lie beneath her bed where she would let her hand hang over the side and I would embrace it while I slept. I never had another nightmare again after twelve years of age.

There are those to whom grace is given freely and before the foundations of the world were cast. Marilyn is among these pillars. She was born to Mary Kearns a few years before I was born. While I do not know the details of her birth, I had always known more than even she did about her adoption. Marilyn is the single greatest and most constant blessing in my life. She has loved me with uncommon grace and unconditional faith. She was also the early darling of Bill as he thought she was Irish, and not Italian. Later in life, I found out *my* real mother's name was McDonough.

THE HAND THAT ROCKS THE CRADLE

My mother called me in living room of the "museum" that was my Nana's house when I was eight years old and explained she had something to tell me. She said, "Edward, I love you very much but I am not your mommy."

"I know," I told her and asked if I could go out and play. In this manner another of my life's uninspired moments passed; often, the value of these moments could only be measured in retrospect. I had intuitively known my mother was not my Mother for some time and had years earlier told her so. This "talk" in the museum was not the first time we had such a talk. The first time we had such a talk I had raised the subject when just an adolescent.

"Mom, do not feel bad. Your job is to just feed and clothe me," I had told her out of the clear blue. "You do not have to love me. You are not my mommy; please take care of me, though." I was six years old when I told her this. I do not have any clue why I told her this, what prompted it, or what I meant by it. This may not be mysterious at all. It may just be the insightful and candid comments of an abused child. It is revealing, however. I recall the talk but not the details. Mom later filled in the blanks.

My mother beat me. She beat me hard, and she beat me often. To this day my sister Marilyn does not forgive her, though they get along. Marilyn simply does not pardon Mom's actions, whereas I do. Where Marilyn and I differ is that I forgave my mother for everything she did to me and did so in real time. I needed her and came to love her, and through this I learned a facet of unconditional love. It is true that many abused children make excuses for their parents and predicaments. This is not what has happened in this case. I am not a victim, nor was I then. Well beyond the love of need-love, I later came to see her as frail and susceptible to all the things that make us all human. However, Marilyn is also right in many regards. While she beat me and chose to love me least, she loved Marilyn only in second place, and this had to be more difficult for Marilyn. I had accepted from the beginning that I was not loved; Marilyn never did.

My mother worked hard. It is a difficult thing to weigh in the balance, if she was a good mother or not. It is in many ways relative or the opinion of the observer. Marilyn does not think our mom was such a good mother, and we have had words over this. I often argue to her what loss is there for me to remember something that was not. She flatly holds her hand up in the faddish "talk to the hand" motion, shakes her head, and walks away. I do not reconstruct the past; rather I only consider that had my mother known any better she necessarily would have conducted herself differently. As she did not, were I to lament something I did not have, I would be enabling victimization and stagnation.

My mother was the only constancy I had. She never drank and did not carouse with men, date, or flirt. She never indulged herself, missed a day's work, or stole away to the movies. She did not lend to excess in anything she did. She was modest, polite, kind to others, engaging, and considerate, but she was somewhat different when she was away from the eyes of the world. Every holiday was marked by decorating with the appropriate foodstuffs and banners—witches, ghosts, and bats in late October; turkeys, pumpkins, and pilgrims in November; a Christmas tree, baby Jesus, and snowmen in December; and Easter bunnies, eggs, and chocolate in April. We were a family of marginal Catholics. I have since noted the world is replete with marginal faith and occasional reverence.

My mother, Madeline, was by all appearances a good mother. I wrestle with the obvious. She did beat me badly and often, and I came to believe even as an adult that I either deserved it for things I'd done, things I got away with, or things I might have done. In truth, her beating did nothing to change the course of any decision I made. There was never a day in my life when I thought, *Gee, I might get beat for this. I better not do it.* Not one time. There was simply no way I could ever know for what I would be beaten. The rules always changed.

Many today have a watered-down understanding of what "beat" means. I do not talk of the "Take time out in the corner, mister" beating. I am not talking of the hand paddling of a child's bottom beating. I am talking about the "Ma'am, I'm sorry. We are going to have to arrest you and send you to jail for killing your child" beating—every single day of my life. I went to sleep with a stuffed nose and puffy eyes for most of my childhood.

I was acclimated to the seasons of not-love and would leave home for good when I was still a nearly a baby. I increasingly became a difficult boy and took to hanging around with the wrong crowd. But in my defense, everyone was the wrong crowd—just varying degrees of bad.

MY ONLY REGRET

While one might think that a childhood like mine would have ample resources of regret, there is really only one time in my life was I terribly disappointed in myself for doing something awful, and that was humiliating an old man. It is always the oddest things that provoked my circumspection. It was not the blood-shed or the violence of my youth—though it would later be that, too. It was in humiliating someone where I felt I had taken their dignity.

One day in the middle of a bitter winter, we were making snowballs and throwing them at buses, cars, and people.

"Why not dip them in the freezing water?" we asked each other. And we did. What better way to improve a snowball? The only winter arms escalation greater than the iced snowball was the snowball iced with a rock inside.

He was an older man, and he wore a long, black woolen coat. He stood in the bitter cold waiting for the bus. It was a nearly impossible shot from across the street. I threw a nearly impossible shot. It cleared the street and the park, and hit the old man smack on the back of his neck. As we ran away, my friends were laughing. I looked over my shoulder. I lingered. I became paralyzed of thought and movement. I began to cry. He was emasculated, vulnerable, and old. He was unable to respond to the terrible thing that was done to him. He removed his jacket in the bitter wind. I saw the gray now that marked his years. In that moment I imagined him storming the beaches of Normandy, young and afraid. I saw him with a wife and kids, with dreams and values. I saw him now undressing and trying to ward of the chill and the painful realization of his frailty as he sought the ice that settled in his shirt. I had done this to him. I had taken some-thing from this man that no other may have ever injured in all his years. My friends asked me what was wrong with me and wrestled me to not return to apol-ogize. I have never forgotten what I had done to him and the weight of it has never left my heart.

A TYPICAL DAY

If I had done something wrong, or if a call had come in from school that slipped past my sister, I would know about it with swift and exact justice. My mother would raise the window from the third-floor apartment and call to me, "Edward." "Edward." And she would keep calling without end until I came home or was within earshot to sound back with the refrain, "Coming!" The difficulty lie in the fact that every day at 5 PM if I were not home for dinner, I would hear the tell-tale sound of the window going up—click, click, click—as it passed each indent. She would then call my name non-stop until…you know. If I were on the other side of the neighborhood, people would tell me "Eddie, your mother's calling." Not only was this routine embarrassing, but I came to associate the call to dinner with the call to pain.

"I gotta go, guys," I offered as I began the run toward 85th Street, toward home. As I got closer, I could hear her. I was so embarrassed that I would slow to a walk well within earshot in case any one saw me running. I did not want it to be obvious that I was the "Edward" being called, though of course everyone knew I was Edward. When I was only a few houses away, and she could see me as she continued calling, I would look around quickly and respond, "Coming." It was almost a plea. She never seemed to figure out that this was humiliating. If I were in trouble, she would round the corner at the top of the stairs just as I committed to the landing and start beating me. I would be crying, and she would remove entire tracks of hair with one hand while beating me with the other. If I was late, she would perhaps just yell and threaten me rather than beat me; this would often be accompanied by the slamming of pots, pans, or the plates to the table while Marilyn and Michele looked on sympathetically. If she was tired, or it was going to be a "session," she just got out the plastic cookware and beat me as I ran from room to room desperately hoping the landscape would somehow be different and afford me cover. These instruments had a much longer life span than wood. My mother embraced some of the novelties of the modern age quite readily. I will only use wooden utensils in my home now.

I was eleven years old when we all chipped in and bought our first nickel bag of pot from some chick at the school park named Sam. She was from the "older" guys who hung out there. She ripped us off, and we did not get the pot, but we learned the valuable lesson of *caveat emptor*. The streets of my world were filled with the people who made it out of the 1960s, and some who should not have. The park was filled with drug dealing, and the corner of my street had a gang who hung out there. They were not the type that is found today; rather, they were the kind seen in the movies about Brooklyn in the 1950s—Italian, over-sized hair brushes in back pockets, packs of Marlboros rolled up in a white t-shirt sleeve. They were punks, but they were not the worst of the lot. They all came from upper-middle-class families. They were all older, carried knives, and fought for turf. They were our friends.

The crew that hung out at the PS 232 park were somewhat different, rougher, and more prone to drug use. Some hung out in both places, and they all were friends. On a given weekend night there could be up to 150 people, maybe 200 in both places. One late afternoon, a friend of mine, Luke, who later spent some considerable time in prison, was sitting on the park steps with me when car after car after car of guys—and girls—with bats, chains, and knives poured out the vehicles and started attacking the people in the park. We saw Jimmy run past us like the wind, and two people were in hot pursuit, their knives up in the air waiting to bring their arms down. We quickly ran to the 85th Street gang, and within moments a hundred people were en route—including Jimmy's brother, Chucky. But the damage was done, and the bleeding and the injured lay everywhere. They were from Old Howard Beach and did not even find who they wanted to find that day—Tommy. Tommy was the biggest and baddest SOB in the ville. No one fucked with Tommy. On the weekends, he was the only one who was able to leave his orange bottle of methadone right out in the park, and none would dare touch it. It was a time for dead-ends. It was a time where the new age of violence and drugs was being born in the places left vacant by the 1960s.

BLACKS AND BLOODSHED

My neighborhood bordered the Jamaica Bay Preserve on the one side and Brooklyn East New York on the other. Jamaica Bay is the area around JFK International Airport, Rockaway Beach, and the mob's "refuse" disposal locale. East New York is the jurisdiction of the 75th Precinct, one of the most violent places in the world. I was ice-picked in my chest in East New York. This brush with death was even more eventful because I wore the same white shirt a week later when I was stabbed while I slept. He failed in his goal. I shot him with a Browning Hi-Power, 9mm. It was the first time I shot someone with a pistol, though not the last. It was also the first time I shot a Browning. It is a reliable weapon and devastating at close range. I was a child. The blood on my shirt looked brown when washed. I continued to keep it because the holes were small, and it seemed lucky, in some absurd way.

Within the same month, I had it on a third time when Denis came up behind me in a store and slashed at me with a knife from behind. It was only seeing his approach in the Indian clerk's eyes that enabled me to turn around at the last minute and deflect the blade from puncturing my lung. I stopped wearing that shirt at this point because it was now apparent that it was not a lucky shirt. For the longest time it hung on the wall in whatever new place I was living. Yes, East New York had a reputation, but I think it was mostly due to the fact that all the black people lived there, and we grew up in a time where forced busing and racial affairs were quite real and a threat to many. No, most of the real trauma in my early days came not from East New York but from other hot vacation spots nearby. East New York was also the location of my first job at eleven years old—"booting" junkies with heroin.

The blacks used to lie in wait in the Jamaica Bay area and steal dirt bikes from the wealthy white kids. We were not the wealthy kids, so we would lie in wait for the black kids on their new dirt bikes with a rope or cable across the path. When they rode by, we would jump up and "take them out." We would then ride off with their stolen dirt bikes. This was the area between them and us. The older guys would sometimes have us cross the distance to Times Square Stores, East New York, where the blacks gathered in the hundreds. We had to shout obscenities to make them chase us into the weeds. As they closed the gap, our guys would jump up and start firing at them. One time I remember well, I was racing back as fast as I could flee. Over a hundred of them chased my friends and me when an arrow from a crossbow (or bow) drilled right into a telephone pole I was passing. I remember thinking how that would hurt. Then we would hear the deafening roar of the rifle and pistol volleys. Crouching behind everyone, we would see masses of people fleeing, some limping and others carrying injured people. In this world, you made your bones daily, and there was no room for weakness.

I hated it. I despised the place I lived. I never had a sense that anything was right. I was increasingly turning inward, while outwardly I rebelled against family, society, school—everything. I was being raised in madness, and none of it seemed to me to be the enlightened world that I was coming to know was possible from the safety of my "secret place" in the closet. I did not like this place. I did not like being beaten. I did not like being yelled at. I did not like the love-less-ness. I wanted to flee. In early 1976, I was ready to flee. In the summer of 1976, when the United States was celebrating her bicentennial, I left home for what would be, in effect, the remainder of my life. I never really returned. But 1976 was still a few years away, and I just barely survived the passing of time.

▼

Near Death

When we die there is a falling away. Much of what I will explain is
very difficult to put into words because there is simply no equivalent
in our experience. It is a dissipation of membranes that depart and
allow something akin to a drop of water landing in the ocean; an
all-embracing storm of images and "sensations" of thought pervade
us at the same time. It is self-limiting and transient. This process is
the unsheathing of our physical form and its facilities.

By my twelfth year, I was changing in profound ways. I was beginning to
interrogate the world much differently than those around me. Strange and
unusual understandings were incited within me. There was a point where I, the
viewer in my unfolding drama of childhood, changed so dramatically that I was
no longer the person I was when I earlier set the stage of my days. Increasingly I
would have remarkable childhood epiphanies that I could not share with any
other person. There was a breathlessness to my life, and living often seemed
futile. For there was an increased knowing and understanding of things sublime,
but the battle of my life was leaving me so bloodied that I continued in doubt to
process my realizations and insights through the human filters I was given. I was
not convinced *this* was correct. I was not convinced anything I was given was correct. The motivation to second guess even the manner in which my mind was

instructed to operate was born out of the observation that no one around me had a clue what he was doing, thinking, or believing.

My heart, my mind, or whatever characters made up my being were each called singularly out upon the stage of my young mind and asked to justify their character. Each in turn was undressed and turned around for my consideration. "This is not the play I desire, and I am recasting the drama." They each protested and declared their employment; no less than their livelihood was at stake. In this manner I began the early process of considering my world, my mind, and how I related to the world. Thus began my young experiment with taking my entire world apart. Since this time in childhood my life became my laboratory. I continued to examine, undress, and repopulate my mind with only the things I wanted in there.

All the literature of the sages, seers, and prophets past could no more put a string of words together to describe what I describe above than could I or any other understand their words without our hearts and souls hearing first. Our souls and hearts were awash in our tears at our world falling away. I could no better describe this early motivation than in the manner I offer above, and I am the subject. It is the case, though, that one must read without his mind, see without vision, and hear without ears to fully understand what I am telling you.

I have since battled my entire life with the sense that "*this*" is all wrong. It is not the community of family, neighbors, and nations that is wrong. What has always seemed so wrong to me is the sense that there is more—much more. I had been aware from a very early age that there were chains upon me. The restrictive luggage that was not mine, was quite heavy and cumbersome, and increasingly wore me down. I began to notice these chains, more or less, on others. I developed the ability to see into myself and into others. I sensed acutely things that were not discussed, not openly, in the hearts of others. I entombed myself necessarily as I was not cast so readily for the stagecraft that was the larger human drama. I turned inward from the age of twelve.

I ventured into the recesses of the places that language fails all, save poets and prophets, the places wherein only the language of the Gods or theologians could describe. In this place, where the chains of my mortal life so bitterly rebelled, the backdrop of the angst of my life was set.

A Time for Birth and a Time for Death

"Mom, I'm going out to play," I shouted through the apartment. As was often the case on days like this, I was returning to find friends who did not have any checkpoints in their days, or any accounting. No one in the world cared whether most of the kids that were my friends were in any place or another through the course of the day. To my mother's credit, she always insisted on dinner at 5 PM. She was good about this. I would often have to break away from some critical crime or "hanging-out" period to return home to the place where relative normalcy (if it could be called that) contrasted the little-known world of crime and delinquency that was the playground my mother purchased for me. She either had no idea or ignored the fact that everyone used drugs, committed crimes, and exacted violence on one another.

I found Scooter and Luke in the little park in between the many apartment buildings. There were tens of thousands of lives in the little brick holes and windows of these buildings.

"What's up," I asked?

"We're going to steal that car over there and go for a ride. You up?"

To my right was the parking lot, and I followed his direction to a Ford station wagon. I would later find out was owned by the plaintiff, Rita Silowitz. I was reluctant, but apparently not enough.

We walked over and, in the fashion learned from numerous Hollywood movies, cast a glance left and right, and "popped" the hood.

These Fords were the best. All that was needed was a screwdriver or some other metallic object to jump the distance on two of the poles of the solenoid on the firewall above the tire. Later, carmakers would install a number of other theft-prevention measures that would require us to also use a "slap-hammer," or dent puller, to remove the ignition module. This enabled the steering column to traffic freely through its orbit.

Rita Silowitz's Ford did not yet have this. It would not have mattered this night, in any event. We had been stealing cars since I was ten and had had numerous joyrides, car chases, and other experiences. It would not have mattered. This night was a collision in destiny. It was Christmas Day, 6 PM, 1975, and I was about to die.

We hot-wired the car, and when we went to all pile in I changed my mind, said "Later," and left them. I really knew better each time the guys did something like this, but I often folded as I never wanted to go back home as the alternative.

More often than not I refused many of the escapades of youth. The ability to at least know right from wrong eventually saved my life—perhaps many times over.

Only a few minutes later, Scooter pulled along side me as I was walking back to 85th Street.

"Come on, don't be a pussy. Luke had to go home," Scooter dared me. Though it was not a dare obvious to adults or people with a normal childhood, "Don't be a pussy" means no less. If you did not respond with capitulation or some other really good come back, you *were* a pussy. I got in. It was 6:15 PM. I was not a pussy.

We drove to Ozone Park, Queens, which was only on the other side of the highway that separated Howard Beach from the remainder of Queens, *and the rest of the world*, I thought. On Pitken Avenue was a little store where many of the kids hung out. We both knew some of them; they all knew Scooter. Scooter and his terrifying family were known to most people on the streets. Susan, Scooter's mother, was feared as badly as his sister, Diane. They were people who, if they even *thought* you'd wronged them, would beat your head in—in front of your home, in your home, in a store, in front of the police—whatever it took. If they *knew* you wronged them, the consequences were worse. They would hunt you, hunt your sister, beat your ten-year-old brother, handcuff your mother, and set the house on fire. They would force their way into your home and beat your mother to near death in front of her husband with a baseball bat. There was no end to the madness of this place. They had done these things many times. They were feared. Scooter's family sold drugs right out of their home on 89th Street. The police would often raid their house but it only curtailed their activities for a short time. They would be back at it in a few days.

Susan had previously been married to someone related to organized crime, or so it was rumored. Most people were related to the mob in one form or another in Howard Beach. She made her money the old fashioned way—she stole it, extorted it, and sold escape in the form of pot, downers, acid, speed, mescaline, valium, and numerous other things. She and Diane were the brains behind the operation on 89th Street. They had a little plastic desktop organizer whose original intent was to conceal paperclips, rubber bands and the like in little drawers. Their desk organizer was filled with the escape pods of anesthesia and death. Many people wanted to hurt them. Many of them really were knee-deep in organized crime. Tonight, her son was an easier target.

Scooter and I departed the little hangout and were about to head down to Cross Bay Boulevard when I noticed Donna Blue, a girl I knew from the neighborhood.

"Donna, hop in," I invited. She declined. This would prove to be a very wise choice.

We drove off. Scooter could not have been going very fast. I noticed the large sycamore trees that lined the rise on either side of the street as we descended from the old cemetery to the busy thoroughfare of the boulevard that dissected Queens. At this point I cannot even recall the events in real time as they seemingly happened in slow motion. Isn't it always like this when wounded of flesh or heart?

I was sitting in the passenger seat, and neither of us had on our safety belt. They were simply not used by many people back then. From behind a tree a man stepped out, leveled a shotgun, and blasted the front of the car. When I saw the man, I turned toward the back seat, desiring to clear the front bench. Scooter's left hand was steering from atop the steering wheel. As he attempted to duck, his body pulled to the center of the car, turning his left hand with this motion. The car careened toward the right side of the street, ascended the embankment, and hit the tree. It was so instantaneous, so immediate. It was devastating.

I was turning sideways in the seat when the impact occurred. The entire front of the car collapsed as an accordion. The car stopped at the firewall. I kept going. I went through the windshield but could not continue as the tree stopped me. The tree was right up to the firewall. There was only blackness. It was all so incredibly slow. My mind has been unable to even speed it up on replay.

It Is All So Amazing

I was so warm. I was so cold. I was wet. I was not aware of where I was or what was happening. I looked up and saw a crowd of people standing over me. I saw Donna Blue. I called to her. In my mind, I was stretching out my hand to her. In reality, my arm was broken and could not have been reaching out to her. I was sure I called out to her, though. I was so afraid. I was sobbing. I was dying. Donna turned from me and walked away. She, too, was crying. It was all rather sad in a sort of detached way. One more life was ending on a little street in Queens in the 1970s. The meaning and value placed on this life seems so strange and powerful as it ebbs away.

I heard the sound of sirens, but I had no sense of time. It may have been hours. It may have been minutes. I knew nothing else. I was effused with warmth, and it coursed though me. If I had any pain, I do not recall. I was the most comfortable I have ever been in this body. I was shrouded in darkness but I no longer had any fear. This point always stood out to me above other recollections. I was simply not afraid. It is not as if there is something of which to be afraid, and then it is gone and we can measure the contrast. It is fearlessness that, in and of itself, announces presence. I was aware that I was aware of all things. I was so warm and safe. I heard the tremendous sound of air. Only years later, when I jumped from airplanes at 20,000 feet or more, would I again hear sound that so resembled this earlier time on that bloody street in Queens.

I was floating, and I was alive. I was most certainly floating above my body. I was aware that I was lying on the ground on Pitken Avenue in Queens, on the third blue planet from the sun, in an obscure corner of the Milky Way. I saw the people gathered about me and saw the ambulance come to collect me. I saw the wrecked car. This was the only time I saw the car, and later, I was exactly correct in the condition the car rested. What I was viewing was from an entirely different perspective than my asphalt bed would have allowed. I was seeing from above, and this point is most clear even now. I was bathed in light. The light was in my eyes, in my vision, as if electricity was humming from within me. There was an aurora around, within everything. I was overwhelmed with joy. I was quickly approaching the intensifying light. I was being drawn to it, but it was not someplace else. The sound of the rushing air seemed coordinated with increasing awareness of brilliant light. I then saw nothing else on the ground. I was consumed.

The light was at once everywhere and a single point at the same time. It seemed *I* was sucked into me, folded into myself like a sword craftsman might forge steel. There was an apparently audible "pop" launching me into darkness (similar to a champagne cork), but it was light. This confusion of light and dark would reoccur many times in my life thereafter. I was just sure this was of my mind and that I did not actually hear this sound. However, this is really an afterthought. I did not reason anything in the moment. I was then in total darkness, save for the light that seemed to be behind me, casting upon my back in the void. Then there was no sound at all. It was an incredible silence. In my mind I was crying. I was sobbing. It seems superfluous to assign the physical action of sobbing to the mind alone, but there truly is such a sense. When one notes some trite declaration as "I was crying inside," what is really being said? Stating such a thing is the simplest vehicle to describe an experience, but the experience is beyond words. It is an emotional or mental lamentation of grievous wounding or joy. Perhaps, in accordance with maturity and capacity, the same event having taken place in an older me may have yielded very different impressions, very different observations. Yet, at twelve years old the only thing my mind could process was the sense that I was in a state of utter joy. I was overwhelmed with peace and contentment.

I have thought and believed for many years since that I was "kicked out" of this place. It is hard to describe, but I have always felt as if I was denied admission of some sort. I have since learned many people describe a similar impression when mortally injured. Why? Because the only common ground to interpret such an experience is that of being admitted or not, it is that simple. The immediate problem for me in the years that followed was that I *wanted* admission more than I had ever wanted anything before or since. My mind thought I was being told to go, but I honestly have no idea if I ever actually heard this. The only sound of which I am sure was the sound of tremendous air.

In almost the exact fashion in which I had pierced into this place, I felt like I was being sucked back. In my mind's eye I still see the countless images all around me, but I do not recall what any of them were in detail. I later read that people see their lives "flash before their eyes." Whatever that means, I do not know. This is not what happened to me. Besides, by that time I would have had no life sufficiently worthy of recall. Of course, this is debatable. It is not the passing of years that lessens my memory. There simply were no discernable images or immediately recallable memories. However, I was aware of more than just me. What I was viewing was considerably different than the images upon my mind-screen, which I would come to know so intimately. I also never concurred with the religion of science that informs us that these are the biological chemical discharges of the brain as it expends its life force. I was me and there was something else. What else there was occupied the whole of the environment I occupied, and its constituent parts.

One thing of which I am certain above all else is that what I experienced was not the creation of my mind. There was an overwhelming sense of "me" and "not me" at the same time. The two were distinct, and were not the same. I have since noted many accounts of such experiences, and what is most noteworthy is that these accounts span all lands in all ages. Whether a person is educated or uneducated, rich or poor, Christian, Muslim, Hindu or other, there is a commonality in this experience which serves to inform us of a greater totality than we perceive in our waking life. When the vagaries of the accounts are distilled to the core events, the commonalities cannot be dismissed as merely biological.

While the parts of this experience remained vague, the deportment of the whole event left me with an indelible understanding or awareness. It was as if all of my sensory and rational faculties were bypassed, and a virus seeded in my mind. From the moment of this event onward I was aware of an opening inside of me from which I could enter and return at will. I was already in the process of analyzing my young world. This experience synergized my internal quest. From this point in my life onward, I was aware of a presence in my life that was awesome and terrible, omnipotent and tender. I have conducted my life since decidedly convinced that a portal existed within me from which I communed directly with God. I learned early that human language and institutions failed on every count to enable what I would now experience intimately. *Jacta alea est.* Thus began my battle for the Kingdom of God.

CONCUSSIONS AND REPERCUSSIONS

I heard a man declare, "He is alive. Hit the lights." Sirens wailed through the cold night. I was vaguely aware of being in an ambulance that was now picking up speed. The man was busy around my head. I knew I was in an ambulance now. I knew that I was alive. I knew that I was just recently not. I was aware of what was happening. I was, contrary to what might be assumed, happy. I was even then at a loss for what transpired. In the confines of that ambulance I felt I had just been born for the second time in twelve years. I just no longer had any veil.

I lay in the ambulance and later in the hospital, only partially interested in all the fanfare. I was baffled and overwhelmed. I was now in pain and was somewhat frightened, but only in the sense that I was in trouble. I was, after all, in big trouble. I was keenly aware that something just happened to me that was not supposed to happen. As the attendants busied themselves about my injuries I was thinking on the most splendid experience of my life. From that moment on, my whole life was to be an observer. I never really returned.

The details of all the busy things that happened following my entrance into Jamaica Hospital are vague. As Shakespeare observed in Hamlet, "Time [was] out of joint." This would later be a refrain to describe so many of the perceptions that would mark my world. My mother had been driven to the hospital by one of her regular patrons at the King's Castle Restaurant on Long Island. When she was notified, she was too shaken to drive. My mother got regularly sick at the sight of blood. Tonight she would be very sick.

She came to the gurney where I awaited surgery in the hallway. I was in and out of consciousness. To my regret I was lucid when she came to the side of the gurney. My face and head bled freely. The bandages were a reflection of the reputation Jamaica Hospital had at that time—shitty. My skull was distorted where the frontal bone was pushed in. Lacerations were all about my face and over my right eye and cheek. Much of the skin that covered my forehead was obliterated. For lack of a better landmark on which to declare her shock, she grabbed my right hand and begin patting it, asking "My God, Edward. Your eye! What happened to your eye?" I screamed and remembered no more. My arm was broken in seventeen places from wrist to elbow.

I was aware of people sitting around me. One was a stranger. He was a detective and had gotten to know my mother and older sister well over the past nine days. The light bathing the sterile, lime-green hospital room revealed how poor of a color choice lime green really is. *Who would have chosen lime green?* I thought. *It is so nasty.* The twisted steel that held the curtains and lined so many contraptions really accented the green. I was not focused on anything. I realized that lime green sucks.

"Edward?" I looked up and saw my mother crying gently when she noted my lucidity. The man approached and told her he had a few questions to ask me.

"Edward, what happened?" he asked me.

I was not really sure where I was but I started to recall how I got here. *This must be a hospital*, I thought.

"I was walking along," I began with my well-practiced innocent voice, "and a shiny metal thing came off a car. I bent to pick it up, and they threw me in the car." I do not recall if they bought this or not, but I was not really sure what happened—only that, as usual, I had probably done something wrong and was going to get beat and punished for it. Besides, *she* was right here. It never mattered what my answers were but I always thought it better, as a rule, to admit nothing, deny everything, and make counter-accusations if necessary.

"Edward, what happened?" The interrogation continued. What I did not know was that this was a different day. I had previously returned to the deep-sleep place.

"I was hitchhiking," I began with some new authority, "and I do not remember anything else." I had the sense to know less said was better. By this time I was well aware that I was in trouble. What I did not know was that I lay in a bed that was all too big for my little broken body, and my head was wrapped in bandages. I had a cast on my right arm and visible stitches on my face where they could not wrap me. I had some total 150 sutures. I did know I now hurt—a lot. What I did not know was that Scooter was in the bed next to me, behind the curtain. To my credit, Susan and Diane smirked each time I was questioned and I did not give anyone up.

Ratting someone out was a big deal in my world. People died for this. Here I was, not even aware that they were there, and I was passing my street test. I was "making my bones." The policeman who had the uneventful duty of wrapping this case up for Rita Silowitz was not moved by my lies.

"Edward, Scooter is right beside you in the other bed," he told me. I knew vaguely that Scooter was present but it did not register. They pulled back the curtains, and I saw first Susan with her way-out-of-date beehive hairdo like Marge Simpson, but red, and too much makeup on her fat, cherub face.

"Oops," I realized silently.

My mother leaned forward and whispered in my ear how I was in a lot of trouble. She scared me. She always scared me. Basically, she was letting me know what she thought inappropriate to say out loud. She was going to beat my ass and batter my body and it would start as soon as the room cleared out if I did not answer the questions. What appears inappropriate is that she whispered to me because she knew that threatening physical harm to a hurt child would seem terrible. However, what she saw as inappropriate were others hearing that she would do this to me, not the actual pending action. Therefore, she whispered.

She told me that I was dead. I would be punished for the rest of my life (she could never know how the rest of my life would be changed with or without her) and that she would beat my ass right now if I did not tell the policeman what he wanted to know.

I knew my mother. She felt dirty being around Scooter's family for weeks. She likely made small talk as the hours wore on, and hated me for every minute that she was sullied by their street-like Brooklyn deportment.

The cop leaned over and told me that after the car crashed, Scooter ran away.

"He just left you there to die," he told me. Some people tried to chase him, and he jumped from backyard to backyard. Finally, he ran into a yard that had the blue plastic pulled over the pool for the season. Scooter did not realize that it was a pool as there were felled leaves all over the tarp and he ran right onto it, collapsing into the pool, the plastic tarp his water shroud.

They pulled him from his watery grave and brought him back for medical treatment. I always felt that he got the better end of the bargain as he had fewer injuries. He only had minor lacerations here and there. In the end, however, I am certain I got the better end of the bargain, though I have had to live the remainder of my life with the terrible scars across my face. I always, always kept quiet about what really happened. Neither of us ever spoke about the shotgun blast. For years after that event, I would pull little pieces of shrapnel from my head as time and growth motivated them to the surface. In 1989 the last little piece of metal or glass worked itself free of its fibrous casing.

I was punished. I was aware even then that the enormity of what I had done would call for cruel and unusual punishment. She was up to the task, however. I think her approach to this great event in both of our lives lacked even a modicum of care or love. What had happened was so significant in my life, the lives of my sisters, and her own life that she should have taken at least some investigative approach into what was happening in my life that left her so unawares that her only son was mixed up with some really bad players—and that I was nearly very dead. Instead, she restricted me to my room for the rest of my life, yelled at me no less than other times, but reminded me constantly that my life was over. She would have beaten me; she always did, but I was physically too broken already. Even she knew that it was pointless. As she never really beat me to affect a positive outcome, but rather as a release for her own frustrations, this must have been a terrible blow for her not to be able to hit me. There would still be more time for her, though, but the window was closing.

CHAPTER 4

▼

Solitude

Not only do people expect God to make new the world and keep us safe from the dark, but the only time we implore God is under threat or duress. How could we possibly see God under duress when we cannot see God lying in a hammock drinking iced tea on a lazy Sunday afternoon? People do not see God when things are bad for the same reason they do not see God daily—they choose not to see!

My life was forever changed in 1975. I have never been able to find the words to describe what it was that changed. More importantly, I was never able to describe what happened to me. There has only ever been one other time when such a watershed change in me took place—a change that seemed to alter my very DNA. That time is the recent few years.

I slept and learned to sleep. I suppose most people take for granted the natural passage of sleep as some default setting, inexplicable and mysterious, familiar yet foreign. However, my dream world began to take on the character of an interrogatory. I was actively learning and interacting in dreams. Rarely came the time when I did not know I was dreaming. In time I was able to comprehend the framework of my dream world and willfully manifest at will within this state. The very *texture* that supports the cast and props of my dreams became palpable in my waking state. The texture framing the landscape of my dream world began to insinuate into my waking window on the world. The two states, awake and asleep, blended together over time with the only constant being the enabling *texture*, the framework in which both existed.

What most people recall as the vivid ability to fly in dreams, alter outcomes, or see objects differently and at will was now mixing with my waking world. My dreams were increasingly lucid. My waking state became lucid in a way that is more real than words can describe. I never believed in anything again as long as I lived.

Many do not know the tender mercy it is to *believe* in God and aspire to survive the body. Most declare they seek to *know* God, and want to go to heaven when their labors are completed. In the place where they *believe*, most never *know* that their faith is all that makes the absurdity of this life tenable. When their rational faculties can go no further, it is their faith that fills in the place where hope and promise abide. Belief makes all things possible, and makes life doable. They have, whether they realize it or not, taken a leap where their experience can go no further. This belief is a pearl. When one *knows* the landscape beyond the flesh life can seem interminable. There is madness in *knowing* and being! There is security and ignorance in belief.

I no longer believed that I would survive the body after 1975—I *knew* I would. It makes no matter that any other can have this knowingness imparted to them or not—I know. Contrasted with a fairly miserable childhood, my body became a prison. I know longer believed; I knew!

I was just a boy and was already not very impressed with this whole life thing. It just did not seem like such a good idea after all. I had the very real and overriding sense that I was not supposed to be here. I thought this well before Christmas Day, 1975. Now I was certain that there was a mistake. Some many years later, when I had finally found my biological mother, among the first sensitive questions I asked her was if she had been raped. As unpleasant as this question was, I was surely convinced that some upstart to the fabric of time had forcibly ripped me from the neterworld into the flesh. I was as certain of this just as surely as I knew I would be beaten for the slightest infraction in my life—whether justified or not. There simply had to be a mistake. My conception was consensual.

SINNER AND SAINT

I was no saint and had not a saintly trait about me. I was a cunning and very smart young man who simply thought everyone was missing something very vital. I have since allowed myself that I was, in many ways, also the influences of my environment, and much of my behavior would not have been had I been somewhere else and raised differently. I was right. As the years passed I found I was singularly able to define a proper state of rightness and wrongness, absent any of the information that was provided me in my childhood. I keep returning in my thoughts to the sense that all I ever formed that was worthy in this life was formed in the absence of guidance, rather than the guidance itself. I became, literally, what was not in my life. In that regard, I am immensely blessed.

I prayed. From an early age I communed with God intimately. Even before I was twelve years old I was developing a personal relationship in a way that was contrary to the Church but self-evident to me. In the confines on my room, in the inner sanctum that was my mind—my *sanctum sanctorum*—I sought refuge and prevailed. God was revealed to me, in me, and no gods of the Romans or of others could ever replace this again. God became intimate and experiential for me. I was aware of God in all things, in my life, in real time. Yet, my irreconcilable life on the streets had only begun.

In the seventh grade it was attempted to reintegrate me in both public and Catholic schools. The former administered placement tests at which I excelled, and I was promoted through the next grade without ever having to be there. The latter had me queried by priests, and I was subsequently promoted ahead of my peers and confirmed in the Roman Rite. I lived in a world that was both magic and tragic.

I was what can only be described as a truant. I often avoided school and hung out with other juvenile delinquents. I became increasingly taken to not going to school and just doing my own thing. While it was peer pressure that first persuaded me to be truant, the times changed. Other kids got caught and had to go back to school, or moved away. The seasons passed and other events changed the nature of why I first played hooky—diversion, fun, excitement, change, and adventure. Eventually not going to school was the only choice I had. There came a certain point where I had been out of school so long that even the idea of going back was preposterous.

I stole away increasingly to the libraries and stole books. My mother was often at work during the day, and when I was not able to get into the house, for lack of keys, I would climb the fire escape, pass Mrs. Taravella's bedroom window, and take to the roof where I would sneak into the house from the interior fire escape. I would then make myself something to eat and go to the closet. I would idle away many hours reading. Sometimes, when I had a girl over as company for the day, we would sunbathe nude on the roof. This was unlike sunbathing anywhere else in the world as the final approach to JFK International Airport was directly overhead. By this point on final approach the planes were close enough for us to see the faces of the passengers in the windows. It was an endless parade of laughter and young sensuality. In the end, my entire education was self-taught. The confines of modern public academia seemed pointless when there were worlds to be discovered.

When it was time for school to get out, I would retrace my truant steps and head back where the kids gathered at the end of the day to forge homework, link up with brothers or sisters for the walk or ride home, or wait for their parents to pick them up. I no longer played hooky by peer pressure. I played hooky because it was the smartest thing to do. Yes, I enjoyed not being in school. It was all so absurd. There was a whole other world to discover, enjoy, or just be in, in my own peace. During the time of the day when I was supposed to be in school, the school did not care where I was, and no one bothered me. I had peace. There was a time early on, in grade school, where I went through the note forging business and the notes home. My fourth-grade report card had forty-two red "U" marks for unsatisfactory. There were only forty-five spaces. After sixth grade, no one seemed to care—including me.

On Wednesday afternoons, public school let out early so the Jewish kids could go to synagogue and the Catholics to religious classes. There may have been children of other faiths, but I never knew them. My neighborhood had a great mixture of those who were Jews and those who are going to heaven—just ask. I did not know a Protestant where I grew up. You were either Roman Catholic, pagan, or a murderer. On this afternoon I left Saint Helen's, having actually spent the afternoon in school. I had not earlier attended the public school. I just showed up for the afternoon session at church. I had learned further that day how I could not get to God except through Man and that God was merciful—if I listened to my Roman masters. Was I a young cynic? Yes, I was.

LA COSA NOSTRA

From the corner of my eye I saw them approach, and they began taunting me. I was not one of the kind of kids who was usually taunted but there was a food chain and, deny it as I might, I was in it. My head was still swathed in the white of the recently wounded, small areas of brownish blood marking the points most tender beneath. I may as well have been a limping gazelle on the periphery of the herd or a bleeding diver in the Gulf Stream. I was thrown against the wall of

Saint Helen's Church. As they took my broken arm and started beating it into my own head, I wondered where Saint Helen was. I wondered who she was. My body was held by the larger of the two, at that time, John Ruggerio, while John Gotti torqued me so I could not move and beat me with his own punches (but found the cast a more useful weapon). Ruggerio was the punk cousin to Gotti. Even his father was underling to the would-be Gambino Capo. That is how it was with all the stooges that were pretenders to organized crime, or in this case those that actually were mafia. They were thieves, but they stole that which is far more precious and intimate then society is able to safeguard. They stole dignity. I didn't mind having my ass beaten. We all got our asses beat growing up. Something else was beat out of me that day.

I do not even know who Saint Helen was, I thought again as my face felt the all-too-familiar wet. Wet—especially hot-wet—was the increasingly well-known sense that my body was spilling out of me. Even though my body was near perfect in its original design, the circumstances of my childhood had people continually improving upon it with holes God forgot to make. How thoughtful.

I wondered if Saint Helen could see me, if anybody could see me. I wanted so badly for someone to see me, to help me. No one did. Like all things, the beating eventually ended, and they left me in the bushes from where they dragged me, between the only Jewish Synagogue and the Holy Mother Church. This is the busiest intersection in Rockwood Park, Howard Beach. I do not know what it is like now but back then you just stayed in your car and waited for the light to change. People minded their own business. I lay there for some time. What I remember most was not how hurt and broken I was, but that I wanted some time to pass for the other kids that left the church building to leave; they were hanging around outside the bushes, some were at the bus stop only a short crawl away. I did not want anyone to see me like this. I was more embarrassed than beaten. I was ashamed. I limped home in the allies, behind buildings, and waited for streets to clear for dinner before crossing to my home. Occasionally people would stare at me with shock and compassion. This only made me nearly cry. I was so sad and humiliated.

Some years later a young Frank Gotti was riding his motor dirt bike to his home from the Jamaica Bay area when the Gotti's next-door neighbor of many years, John Favara, turned the corner, arriving home after an exhausting and honest day's work as a department store manager. Many people do not realize that when you buy a home, craft a life, and lead an honorable existence, you do not necessarily have a choice in your neighbors. In Howard Beach it was often the case that the blessed lived side by side with the wretched. You just minded your own business and remained, above always, polite. There is an unspoken code amongst people like this. Of course, they make it up as they go along, so they control the rules. This day was to be a day where Gotti's neighbor did not control the rules—or the road—and it may have cost him his life, and the life of an innocent young boy.

Turning toward his home, John was unable to see well as the setting sun was right before him. Who can know what circumstances had his car taking the life of the next Gambino crime boss's youngest son? It is suggested that Favara was speeding and blew a stop sign. It is a sad and tragic affair. As one who does not hold to the notion of corruption of blood, it could not be willed upon any child what happened to this young man. The young Gotti died. The family, the sycophants, the vine-climbers, and the pretenders to rage all mourned. The blinds were pulled tightly, and the Favara family remained (un)safe in their home.

Compounding such tragedy, the idiot neighbor never repaired his automobile, sent condolences, or otherwise expressed remorse. This idiot left this death-car parked beside the Gotti's house for quite a while. An old part of me inside understands the desire to exact vengeance for what was increasingly appearing to be callous behavior by the lack of contrition on Favara's part. I understand why, at this point, Frank's mother, reportedly clubbed the neighbor with an aluminum bat and hospitalized him. What history will recall is John Favara as victim only, but I maintain Favara could not have been too clean in any event. When aware of the gravity of his predicament, Favara supposedly went to his childhood friend, Anthony Zappi. Zappi's father, Ettore, had been a Capo in the Gambino family. They could do nothing for him but the point remains few were clean in this world at this time. Favara was recast squeaky clean to make Gotti appear even dirtier; I am not convinced. How many of us can seek counsel with a Godfather when trouble knocks on our door? What does not sit with me is what this event did to my world, on the other side of life. The Butterfly Effect was threading my world.

BLOODBATH

John Gotti, Jr., Pete S., and other associates gathered at a local bar in Howard Beach following the wake and did what people do when grieving—they drank and loosened up. They likely recounted tales and comforted John Gotti, Jr. (Curiously, first hand accounts suggest all were not necessarily comforting John Gotti, Jr. In fact, it has been suggested that he was not even liked by his peers that day. Nearly all the locals preferred instead to solicit the patronage of John Gotti, Sr.).

Frank Gotti was a child, irrespective of his family's affairs. The tragedy was terribly real for many, and hysterically real for others who feigned sympathy as supporters. Perry, my sister's boyfriend (and future husband), walked into this place for unrelated reasons. He lived just across the street on 79th Street. His timing sucked. Everyone knew Perry, and Perry was not like them, or even my group of friends. Perry was basically a good kid, and everyone knew it. He was not a punk. He was not a fighter. He bothered no one and got along with all. Pete reached out and asked him what was on his keychain. Perry was wisely leaving. Pete looked at it and sprayed the little can of mace that was part of the key ring. He handed it back to Perry and turned his attentions elsewhere. As there is a slight delay from the time Mace (CS gas) is sprayed in a room to the time people start crying and gasping. The keychain was on Perry's hip, and he was on the way out the door when someone asked, "What the fuck is that shit?"

"Who sprayed that shit?" asked one of the sycophants.

"Perry sprayed it," said Pete.

They proceeded to beat the living shit out of Perry in the way that only my childhood neighbors could. (It is unclear if Gotti, Jr., actually participated). Pete would not be outdone and, likely in an effort to further distance himself from his own stupidity, took his walking crutch (his leg was casted) and beat Perry with it until the crutch broke over Perry's back. He then took the fractured crutch and used it to carve Perry into a bloody, unconscious piece of meat. Perry was brutally beaten, stabbed, and sliced that day—and his dignity, stolen—for no other reason than "Because." They loaded him into a car, drove to a hospital, threw him out, and told the attendants "niggers did this." They then drove off.

Mourning. It is such a sad affair in Howard Beach, Queens.

Rewinding back to my own mourning, Gotti and Ruggerio damaged me so badly outside the church I had to return to the hospital. My head was reopened, and my arm needed to be reset. The bloodied material of the casting was coiled up like a snake as it had mostly unwound, leaving only the cloth gauze beneath holding my shattered arm. When I had the emergency surgery the night of the injury, they had to use what amounted to a hook to pull my frontal plate back out. They told me that because it was fractured along the suture line of the natural bone separation this was possible, and I was lucky. This day, the reluctant suture line of my skull was again invited to mend elsewhere.

I am sure that Gotti and Ruggerio do not recall my name from youth, though they may recall this event—maybe; who cares? They taught me more by their actions than they could have ever imagined. It was not the bleeding or the beating. I had so many of those throughout my life that I had lost count. It was above all else the notion that there is something greater that can be taken away from a man, something that community and law enforcement cannot protect against, nor can they return—dignity. If you were not a part of "this thing of [ours]" you were not worthy of respect. It was that simple.

Years later the adage that the apple does not fall far from the tree was proven true in reverse when the older Gotti was taking drinks in a bar made famous in *Goodfellas*. It is on Rockaway Boulevard, Queens, across from Aqueduct Racetrack. Some poor "Joe" was just stopping off to have a drink after cashing his weekly paycheck. I do not suggest he was a saint, but what happened to him was so illustrative of the younger Gotti's upbringing. The man had double-parked his car or some other infraction and was told to move it because Mr. Gotti needed him to do so. The name apparently did not ring a bell because the man said he did not know who Mr. Gotti was and to tell him to "Wait a fucking minute." *Wrong answer, buddy.* They dragged him outside, and Gotti, Sr., and crew personally beat the shit out of him. Is that the moral of the story? No. This happens all the time. It is always something further that is of interest for me.

John Gotti, Sr., reportedly, proceeded to reach down and take his entire paycheck, just cashed. This could have been for no further purpose than to inform him that they can take his dignity as well. The man went to the police. The guy still did not "get it" when the police tried to talk him out of filing charges. I am sure the federal organized task force watching Gotti was getting a kick out of all this. The man filed charges. It was all over the papers the next day in only the way the New York daily newspapers can sleaze something. Likely his wife packing her bags, the neighbors pulling the blinds, and the boss telling him, "Stay home today…uh, this week" was all the encouragement he needed to be quoted in the papers the very next day as saying, "There was some mistake. It was not Mr. Gotti. I never meant to offend Mr. Gotti." They stole his dignity, and when he was confronted by what they had taken from him he collected any battered remnants and offered the rest up for sale. Such was the world that these people created as they moved through the circles of their parasitic fantasy—*La Cosa Nostra*.

DOING TIME

My wounds were leaking both blood and not-blood when we came back from the hospital. Not-blood is stuff that is clear and *not* clear. It is ooze, and it has stains of blood in it to remind you that while it looked innocent it was still your life force in the shiny clear water. My body was mostly healed of the numerous aches and pains from the accident save for the head and the arm. It was right and proper that I got my ass beaten by my mother for getting my ass beaten at church. I was doubly punished for this. It was not because I did anything wrong or even that I lost a fight; it was "Because." In getting badly beaten I necessitated her having to spend money, take me to the hospital, and tend to me further; it exacerbated the original insult from Christmas. Man, this shit sucked.

I am not sure where punished, doubly punished, or downright fucked have their lines drawn, but I was now frequently locked in my room for long stretches—not hours upon hours, mind you, but months. I recall with such misery standing in place crying inside my door that I had to use the bathroom. I would hold my penis and squeeze tightly the more I had to go. This seemed to help. I would often slip to the floor crying because either no one heard me or they were not coming. When I did get let out to go to the bathroom I would immediately be escorted back to my cell by the warden. They took shifts, my mother and Marilyn, as my mother was not always home. It never escaped me once that my sister had unimaginable compassion and empathy for me during my times of imprisonment; actually, she was always kind to me. She was caught in the middle of it. Though I do not recall it now, she apparently feels she was also not well treated. I suppose no one wants to be alone. I had no sense of it then, though. Neither of us ever recalls Michele being beaten a day in her life. It may have happened, but I doubt it. It is not important. However, it is suggestive. I was doing time.

I was let out for meals and, of course, my big court day. While I do not recall the exact details of this court stuff, I recall how much my mother hated me for making her be there. She hated that she had to spend hours with Susan and her family. She hated a lot of things. I only recall that the judge admonished me for getting into Rita Silowitz's car and said I should be thankful to have a mother who loved me so very much. And then it was time for more of the after-bleeding. I came to despise the life into which I was born. I hated then the contrasts that were this home and this life. It must be understood that this punishment was not the first time I was locked in my room. My mother had been doing this for years. I despised my life. When out of doors, the contrast was crafted to appear as though all was normal. I lay in bed for years begging to die. I knew no other way to make amends for the apparent mistake for sending me here. "Take me back and we'll call it even, God."

I would lie in bed and dream. I surrendered completely to the only friend I had—myself. I spent hours inside of me and would often have to be reluctantly "brought back" by my sister shaking me and telling me it was time to eat. I was wide-awake, but I was not there at all. In the daytime I would go to school, but not to school. I had been out of school so long now that I did not even have the nerve to walk through the doors. Walking into school like I belonged there took bigger balls than I had.

I did not have many friends, close friends, though there were some people with whom I hung out. That is what we called it, "hanging out." What was a friend, anyway? As an adult I am still not certain but it is a place where there is love and it is unconditional. Friendship is a place, in a person, where respite is provided in the middle of the fray, regardless of background, faith, color, or history. I did not have many friends with each year that passed beyond my twelfth. In any event, it would not have mattered as none of my "friends" made it out of childhood. I defined all I have in this life by the things I had not. I did not have friends. I had Edward, I had me, and I loved me. Through all the years I have weathered the vacillations of life, its changes and demands, and the molding, as we become what we are to be. I have not changed very much from the little boy literally tying sheets together to scale down from the third-floor tower in which I was imprisoned. When my sister found out I was doing this when my mother went to work, she took to letting me out if I would promise to get back in before Mom came home. I did.

When my mother found out that I discovered a way to take a little object, tie it to a string, slip it under the door, and leverage it along the seam to where the eye hooked on the door to escape, she began taking my shoes and my clothes with her when she left the house. I would still escape and go out and play barefoot. When she took my clothes I went out in my underwear. She was bound to find out about the eyehook leverage technique, as I had not sufficiently mastered it to replace the catch from the inside. It was a one-shot deal if she was the one to escort me back and not Marilyn.

When she discovered that I used the phone without her permission, she placed a lock on the phone. When she then found out that I could pick the lock, she took the phone with her when she left the house. It should not be thought that my life was unhappy. It was not. It was miserable but I was wed to only what I knew. I would later realize that we might often find ourselves wed to things that are harmful, either through imposition or incremental forfeiture of other landmarks. Many willfully surrender their dreams or sense of wrong and right, their values, or their freedom for security or companionship. I was not the best-behaved boy, but I was a product of my environment.

SEEDS OF SUPER-PERCEPTION

I grew in isolation. I was in a crowd, yet stood alone. I knew my life was an aberration and had the very sense that I was unhappy, but it was also all I knew. I spent all of my young childhood learning to meditate in isolation and in crowds. I have never been instructed in any mediation. In fact, I have never been instructed in any faith, religion, method, or the like (save for my Catholic upbringing). Every single day of my youth imprisoned I learned to escape through the portal.

The days when I was not punished were punctuated with all the commonplace occurrences of other boys. I had forts. I played hide-and-seek. I climbed, and I explored. But I also shot Tommy with a pistol in the fort. I played by the beach with the guys and also participated in throwing Andy from the Cross Bay Bridge because he had wronged one of us. I played Ring-a-Leveo with the other kids, but at night I dreamed of things I could not explain. I saw the world very differently than other kids and was always in conflict with what was being fed to me and what I knew to be reality. I felt from the very beginning that I was two boys, two people, and that what was inside me was beautiful in spite of all that I saw around me. I was able to escape in my mind, in my dreams. I increasingly became able to do this in an awakened state following the accident. I was able to slowly command my dreams in a very powerful and lucid manner. I spent the remainder of my childhood daydreaming of dreaming. I went through the motions of trying to be a boy, to live and to have fun, but the world I was in was so downright violent and deceitful. The contrast with my internal was truly incredible.

Following the accident I began to have a reoccurring dream. I do not remember this dream prior to my injury.

✳   ✳   ✳   ✳

I was sailing…no, that's not right. I was floating above the city. I must have been flying as I was looking at the tops of all the houses and could see the very real stone masonry of their construction. They were unlike any houses I had ever seen. They were so small and so close to one another. There were little streets but there were no people on them, no cars, no busy activity. The scene was all very, very silent. Each little house only had one door. There were as many windows as doors—perhaps less.

Whitewashed and ancient I was sure I had been here before. I did not know how but I knew this place. The scenery was not looped. There was not just one set of scenes I saw over and over. There was newness in my vision. I was really taking aerial flight. Then I realized that this was a cemetery. Everyone here was dead. I had been here before. I was dreaming. Yes, I was now aware that I was dreaming; I looked more intently now at the scenery below me. I had now dreamed this dream over and over and I knew this was the place I had named the City of the Sleeping Dead. I was a child and named with a child's mind. I was more amazed that I knew I was dreaming than I was with seeing this dream again. Not only was I often awake in dreams, but now I was investigating repeating dreams. I was in this dream but it was different. In other dreams I was able to willfully create and change the scenery and adjust the timeline in reverse or fast-forward. In this dream the same visual message repeats over and over and is not subject to manipulation.

I saw there were few trees or anything that could be called life. I could almost make out the carvings on the "little houses," but I did not know what they said. They were all stone. I do not ever recall seeing any markers or regular monuments to the dead. It all seemed like everyone was above ground. It started to rain. I was not sure it had ever rained before.

*   *   *   *

I had once spent considerable effort looking online for cemeteries that matched the appearance of this dream. I found such a visual match in the cemeteries in New Orleans; though I did not trigger a recollection from these old above-ground cemeteries in the south. I have a greater sense of considerable sun and heat. I sense that the scene that unfolds in this dream is in the Mediterranean area. As I have aged married more and more of my internal world with the external I have dreamed less and less, in general and particular.

The darkness scared me more than the light. I was looking up at the ceiling and was holding myself. I had to pee. Leaning up against the door for sounds of life, I called out, "Mom? Mom? I have to make! Mom? Mom?" There, I heard the sound of sheets rustling and knew from experience that she was coming to let me out to go to the bathroom. It always seemed that when I knew that I would actually be able to go soon I had to go more. My hand clenched down ever more tightly around the end of my penis, my knees drawn together.

"Thank you, Mommy," I said as I made my way past her in the dark.

I sat down to pee. I had learned long ago that not setting the toilet seat back down in a house of women was met with swift judgment exacted. I sat to pee.

I often found myself lingering and would have to be called forth by my mother or sister desiring to get back to bed. Even though I had been asleep, the thought that I was not locked in was liberating. I would look at simple things like a brush or an eyelash curler with renewed interest. It was different to me when I did not have it. Everything was different and wonderful to me. I was trained in this manner early on to see the world quite differently and with an overstated sense of wonder.

"Goodnight, Mom," I said as my feet trotted past her.

"Goodnight, Edward," I would hear before the soft metallic click of the eye-hook dropping in the loop.

I slid under my covers and rubbed my feet back and forth to make them not cold. I tugged and pushed my pillow into just the right design to support me as I began to seek again my last dream.

Many people, apparently, are able (or at least desire) to pick up dreams where they left off. I am among the lucky ones who can do it at will. Where I cannot I simply reconstruct the entire set, I literally finger paint with my mind. This is not an overstatement. Though currently I have very few dreams as I have aged, I never had a nightmare again past the age of twelve—after December 25, 1975, to be exact. I am not sure why, but in every other sense there was really nothing that I was ever afraid of again.

CHAPTER 5

▼

Dark Night of the Soul

When it is suggested that all we must do is knock and it will be opened, it should not be confused with it will be opened right away. In any regard, we so remove ourselves from the natural station of being by our aimless idolatry of the material world that we literally untrain our hearts from knowing when the door is even opened.

By late January 1976, I was to reenter school and pick up where I left off. I was twelve years old. The problem was that where I left off and where my mother thought I left off were two very different places. There were so many things about my life that she just never grasped. I was growing up in the 'hood before there was a "'hood." I was gone long before I packed to leave. I increasingly became a difficult boy and took to hanging around with the wrong crowd. But in my defense, everyone was the wrong crowd. There were just varying degrees of bad.

I was a regular smoker at twelve years old. I occasionally smoked pot, but never really liked it or got much into anything stronger. I already had a difficult enough time with my waking state to scramble it further. I truly had a wonderfully altered reality already. However, nearly everyone touched drugs either by company, usage, selling, or seeing people stoned out everywhere, dying, or being arrested. There was a pronounced market in drugs and death in my childhood neighborhood.

Out of my group of friends, only two people made it out alive or without going to prison—Rocky and myself; and Rocky did not really count because he had to do seven years in prison for murdering Mikey Merlo. Perhaps, I did not make it out, after all. Mikey Merlo was a piece of rubbish, and even his parents readily admitted that it was only a matter of time. Rocky was a friend. Merlo was a dealer reputed to be associated with John Gotti, Jr. It was really such a shame what happened to Rocky, not Merlo. Rocky was a little older than I. At that time in my life he was the only male I knew who had any characteristics I would seek to emulate. We both made it to legal age. Rocky had just barely escaped New York by the time I had returned from Army leave some years later.

Rocky had dropped me off at my house one late afternoon in 1983 so I could spend some time for dinner with my family, then he would return to pick me back up around 7 PM. After dinner I fell asleep on the living room floor watching TV. At 8 PM the phone rang. The call was from his mom, Katherine. She never called. She was crying hysterically. Rocky was arrested. He had killed someone.

Apparently, during the time between Rocky dropping me off and picking me up, Merlo and some other thugs had ripped Rocky off on Jamaica Avenue. They had pistol-whipped and beaten Rocky, and stolen his money and jewelry. The story is for another place and time, but in the end Rocky went to get his money back. When they were not intimidated by the sawed off shotgun, they began chasing Rocky. Many of them had pistols and were closing the distance when Rocky held the shotgun over his shoulder and blew Merlo's head clean off. In a tragic irony a uniformed cop was making a private call on the public phone ten feet away. Rocky slowed to a stop, dropped the gun, and placed his hands above his head. He went to prison. I was the only one to make it out from my tribe.

THE FIRST ESCAPE

I ran away from home for good in 1976, though it was not the first time. The first time I ran away was with Alan. I remember Alan well. We were friends, in accordance with my previous observations about friends. We were really just two misfits who found each other in space and time. I liked Alan, but we often fought. We literally beat the shit out of each other. In this manner we most certainly perfected our street-fighting skills. When we were teamed up, we could easily take out four to six people in a street fight. Alan was spoiled, sour, and had a serious chip on his shoulder; he fit in perfectly.

It really was no wonder that Alan turned out all screwed up; his parents were all screwed up. His mother and father had been married some years before when one night they went out with a couple who were friends of theirs. They had sex that night—all of them. When the morning came, they each went home with the other's partner. Alan's father went home and married his friend's wife, and his mother went home with and subsequently married her girlfriend's husband. Alan's mother was hot to my young, horny mind, and I would frequently tell Alan that I wanted to have sex with his mother. He understood but confided in me that she was "sick." After relating to me what is mother had done recently, I agreed with him. She really was sick. I still wanted to have sex with her, though. When he was particularly annoying to me, I would tell him this.

The first time Alan and I ran away, we had enough money to get to Newport Ritchie, Florida. Alan said he had a cousin there with whom we could live and start over there. I never really understood what my young mind thought "starting over" meant. In the end, I am not sure we can ever "start over." Everything really is a continuation, no matter how hard we might like to think otherwise. I needed to start over.

We had nearly eighty-eight dollars, and we discovered this would be just enough to get us two Amtrak tickets to our new destination. We packed lightly and fled. We were both thirteen. We took the A Train into New York City and arrived at Grand Central Station. I had been here before, but I looked at it as if I would never see it again. We went to the train ticket window and discovered that the next train was in the morning and we could not buy the tickets until then. We decided to make our way to Central Park and sleep there the night. We were already hungry. We should have taken some more food with us.

Walking down 5th Avenue from 42nd Street to 59th Street was far less distance than I thought, and we had plenty of time to kill. The smells of the hotdogs and pretzels had the same effect on both of us: it made us hungry. Central Park was dangerous in those days. People were often mugged or beaten. The park just had a bad reputation. Even at night the park was alive. There were people doing mediation, running, playing, talking, and having sex. There were people using and dealing drugs, mimes, artists, and musicians. Even at night the place had its own heartbeat. We secreted ourselves away to a place where children played in the daytime. There was a little jungle-gym park with other small places where we could hide and wait for the morning to arrive.

As the hours passed we increasingly became more cold, and hungry. We agreed upon a really good idea—we would take what little money was above what the cost of the tickets were and split a hog dog. Bad idea. We left the park and ordered a hot dog from a vendor on the street. The noise and traffic was incredible. Queens was clearly not like the city.

We found a little corner and carefully cut the hot dog in half, each cautiously watching the other. We made certain that the sauerkraut was equally divided as well. I could see even then how people might take to fighting in a survival situation. I remember thinking, even as we were cutting the hot dog, how good Alan's half looked, too.

It was gone! *Maybe I should have taken smaller bites*, I thought. *Maybe it would have lasted longer.* I was not nearly full but was already missing the taste. A life spent knowing hunger would instruct me in visualization techniques that savored each and every particle while imagining it as a complete meal. I was not yet skilled in this technique. I was still hungry.

Alan was hungry, too. We returned to the little hiding place in the park. By this time there was a small group of gay people dressed as women hanging around, and we had to sneak around the bushes in the back so they would not know we were there. We took to our hiding place and watched the people outside for a while. We were cold. We tried to sleep, but this did not work. Neither of us was tired, and it was so cold.

I lay there looking up at the stars and I thought that all around me are thousands and thousands of ghosts, angels, and others watching me, perhaps. I wondered what they were thinking. What did they do? Was it like a job or a love, and did they do other things? Were they really here right now? I bet they see me when…oh, no! That is just wrong. I was increasingly to have these sorts of unrelated, intrusive thoughts regarding other worlds, thoughts that were simply not in context with my environment. It is not just that I considered such thoughts; everyone had moments where they thought of such things. I could not turn it off, though.

"Hey, Alan?"

"Yeah?" He looked to me. Someone had to say it.

"You want to split another hot dog?" I broached.

"Let's go," he offered immediately. We were off. It was clearly the blind leading the blind. Naked hunger. Damn the torpedoes. Full speed ahead.

Twenty minutes later we sat, only marginally more satiated than before, "You know, we don't have enough for the tickets now?" he offered.

"I know," I regretted. Such heroes and escape artists. Little fools.

"We might as well get some more food."

"Let's go," I agreed. Off we went but we saw no need for another hot dog. Instead we walked up the street and got two full-blown cheeseburgers at a diner.

"What do we do now?" I asked.

"I don't know," he said. We laughed at each other. We called each other idiots. We were and we knew it.

"I'm cold."

"Me, too," he replied. "Let's go home and do this again when we are really ready, when we have gotten some more money."

"Yeah, let's do it that way. This wasn't a really good idea anyway…with so little money and all," I volunteered in agreement.

"How are we going to get home?" Alan offered. We sat in the silence a long time.

We both knew by this time that we were in real trouble. Alan rationalized, on his end, that he could lessen the damage by having his father drive him home. He knew very well how to play his mother off his father by this time, and they both went along with it even though they knew Alan played them. He called his father.

RETURNING CAPTIVES

The wait on Columbus Circle seemed to take forever. It was not such a great place on 59th Street. They have since revitalized most of the area, built the Lincoln Center shopping mall, and moved the homeless people somewhere else. Tonight though, we were young and vulnerable. But if you asked us, we would tell you that if anyone tried to pull anything on us we would cut him up. We were such nice boys.

The car pulled up and his father and mother-in-law were with two other friends. They had been out drinking, and this was all highly unusual and inconvenient to have to come pick us up after failing to make good our break. We stopped at a store so Alan's father could buy sodas for everyone. He came back to the car with five and handed them all out to everyone but me. I watched as Alan just stared at his father with a nasty smirk.

"What is wrong with you?" Alan asked his father.

"What do you mean what is wrong with me?" he answered.

"There are six of us!"

"Sorry, Ed," he said to me over his shoulder, already aware who got shortchanged.

"Sorry? You would have had to pull a can out of the six-pack to get five. You counted. You knew exactly what you were doing," Alan passed his can to me.

Alan's father wasn't a bad guy. In fact, years later when I returned on leave from the Army, I looked him up. He seemed more interested in what I was doing than where Alan was. It was apparent he felt Alan had let him down. Alan was in prison in Riverhead, Long Island, on drug charges. I think he let Alan down long before.

ANATOMY OF A BEATING

Alan did not get beat when he went home. His father gave his mother the "New Age child of a divorced couple" speech. Alan's dad left, and his mom told him to come inside so she could make him something to eat and they could talk. I would never be that lucky.

I walked the 200 meters or so around the corner and considered my options; none of them were good. I waited on my front steps some time before working up the courage to go in the house. I always had to enter my house like a thief. As soon as I cracked the seal on the door I would still have to negotiate the next flight of stairs, and still another door. This door had a little chime that was sometimes working, and sometimes not. There was little chance I could just get into bed and put this all behind me. That damn chime sucked.

The upstairs door was open. We kept our dirty laundry behind the door. *Hooray for dirty laundry*, I thought, and I climbed the stairs. With Mom in bed, undisturbed, I could sneak to my bed, and hopefully the morning finds me in a different world.

I was terrified at first. I did not see her, and when I did I did not know it was her. She scared the shit out of me, and then scared the shit out of me more when I knew it was *her*.

Crack! Her hand struck my face from the empty dark of the kitchen. Having been trained extensively in the art of beating-avoidance I feigned right and launched left. Shit, she got me. She was good.

The hair, it was always the damn hair. My hair was now fully integrated with her hand. I was as screwed as Medusa would have been, and only Houdini could have gotten out of it. With one hand she pushed my head away, and when my body tried to counter she'd pull. She would have made a great master of Shaolin Temple. She already mastered the art of economy of motion and used my body, or momentum and leverage to hurt me so well.

Oh, she was good. My head now returned in space and met violently with her other hand as it came down in its arc.

"How dare you come into my house this late at night? Do you think this is a hotel, mister?" she demanded. Understand, this beating was not because I tried to run away; I was being beaten because I came in late.

No answer was always the best. There never really was a dialogue in these exchanges. Many a boy has been beaten further than was necessary in the feeble hope that his parents' interrogations were real and a different ending than the last beating might result depending on our answers. Wrong.

Smack, smack, sm—. There I broke free, but there was the sound of the kitchen drawer opening behind me. I hated that sound. To this day the sound of metallic and plastic cooking utensils crashing about in a drawer terrifies me. Of course, I also shudder when I see red Volkswagens.

The sound of utensils rattling in the draw went silent. *Damn*, I thought. *She got one.*

As always I cast my eyes about the room for a place to hide. There was none. There never was. I knew my sister Marilyn was listening and loathing this. I knew, too, that Michele was listening. My only option would be to race to the far side of the dining room table and lobby for a war of attrition.

Jeez, she was on me. There was never enough time. It is always like that with sheer terror; even when you know caution is escalating to fear, to horror, to sheer terror, it just sneaks up on you and pounces when it finally arrives. You can never escape sheer terror when it locks you in its tractor beam. You will not escape un-terrified. Where did she learn this shit?

She had long ago stopped aiming for my bottom or any other soft spots; she now just flailed wildly. She hit knuckles, bones, the bridge of my nose, my cheek, my neck, and my ear with these thick, hard, plastic utensils. These were almost novelty utensils as they were apparently for cauldrons. Few people would know this little fact but the ear has a tremendous amount of pain receptors in it. A good blow to the ear with a plastic spoon, or similar device will result in a yelp that often stops the most violent attack. However, my wails and pleas never resulted in more than continued beating. The fact that I was beaten like this every day of my life was common knowledge on 85th Street, Howard Beach, New York. My screams were heard by everyone within one square city block. The pain was only equaled by the humiliation. Everyone knew I was beaten without mercy every day.

She missed my head on the first skull blow. However, the second time she hurt herself just as she struck my ear, crushing it between the spoon and my skull. She pulled back in consideration of her own wound. This stopped me from get-ting the "Uncle" credit implied in the blow to end all blows. I was reeling, rolling, crying, screaming on the floor, and she recovered from the consideration of her hurting herself on me and leaned over to give me one more—just in case it (whatever "it" was) was not clear to me. Then silence. This second blow was not *the* second blow; it was the second *skull* blow. This beating had gone on approximately ten minutes by the time I hit the floor writhing in agony and begging to die. She never knew I ran away and failed; I was beaten for coming in late.

I ran into my little room and closed the door behind me. I cried and cried. I could hardly breathe. My nose was stuffed. My ears, my ass, my face, my back, my legs, my groin—everything was on fire. Blood ran freely in my fingers as I held my ear. I was so accustomed to the inside of me coming out.

"I'll give you something to cry about, mister," came the familiar demand to shut up from the other room. On this occasion I took to the bathroom and looked at myself in the mirror. My face was once again bruised, my eyes familiar with the swollen tears of my childhood. It always seemed that the reflection of me was red and puffy. The tears running freely down my face marked my childhood's retreat. I had spent years bruised and crying in this mirror. I now only saw emptiness when I looked at myself in the mirror in Queens. I held my breath as I crossed back to my room so she would not hear my breathing catching and heaving.

"I hate it here," I said. "I hate this whole fucking life." I started crying again silently as I sat in the dark corner of my room, behind the caddy-cornered dresser, my arms wrapped around my knees, and rocking.

"Why are you doing this to me?" I cried to the heavens over and over again.

"Why is this happening to me, God? Why?"

The post-beating euphoria of endorphins was now released. It was the peace after the "good cry" peace. My thoughts became measured and more clearly considered. Sobbing in the way that only breathing can break words in half, I cried to God, "I don't want to live anymore. Please, God. Just take me now." I cried my childhood plea.

"Why?" I asked. "Please, I am ready to die now."

I lay down in bed and wrapped the pillows around me and rocked myself to sleep. I was no longer afraid of nightmares when I slept, just when I awoke.

The recollection of time gets fragmented for the years that followed. I was in an endless bloodbath of broken lives, death, homelessness, and violence.

CHAPTER 6

▼

The Descent

Do not allow yourself to see a world where it is getting worse every day. Do not surrender. Do not surrender to the illusion that you are an impotent witness only. You are every bit a part of the solution as is everyone else, and God. Speak with the voice of God; see with the eyes of God; assert your will as the will of God.

I was never able to describe myself to anyone so I stopped trying when I was twelve years old. I was different and thought odd by most. I believed or knew things to which people paid lip service, including the Church. I was utterly convinced—even in my darkest times—that I was not abandoned by God. I soon took to living on the streets and prayed easily and with conviction before the friends of mine who, rightfully, lost every reason in the world to believe in anything. I knew I had a special relationship with God; it is a fact of my existence. I never had a sense that I was alone and never had a reason not to think that God heard me, loved me, or cared for me. During this time in my life I thought I had personal access to God. At this time in my life I know I did. One might consider why then my life was so tortured and seemingly forlorn. It was not. My life was blessed beyond comprehension.

There never seemed to be one thing that I prayed for that did not come to pass, sometimes with frightening accuracy and timing. Perhaps there are things that I prayed for in this life that have not come to pass, but there is really only one that I can recall. More importantly and objectively, other people were aware of this grace as well. God and an understanding that there was so much more here became a big deal for me. It was not a big deal in a religious sort of way, as I increasingly understood God in the absence of any doctrine or intercessory agent. I did know the occasional priest and nearly became one myself many years later. Although I did not choose that path, the calling has never ceased.

I was a boy lost in the late 1970s in a world where all my peers were being consumed and spent. I crafted for myself a vision of this life that was both beautiful and possible. My introversion was not the result of the circumstances of my life; the egg clearly came before the chicken. However, my childhood provided me lifetimes of experience in this one lifetime to enable the ascent up Jacob's Ladder.

It was a remarkably personal journey, and I realized I had embarked upon it from the first day I was born. All of our lives are personal journeys, of course. But my life increasingly secured peace, power, and grace in the contrast of my material tragedies. My life was raw with the bloodshed and spent lives of youth. It brimmed with treachery and conflict, abandonment and redemption. I had many moments of compassion and beauty that were born out of wet eyes that a comfortable life could not have yielded. I decided consciously to make my entire life a laboratory of sorts. I would endeavor to make the best of the days that were mine and transcend into that place where my dreams were born, holding tight to my pillow in that little house in Queens, New York, and all the cellars, rooftops, cars, and trains that would follow.

THE SECOND ESCAPE

I did not even pack when I left. I do not think I even cared where I wound up. I have lived an incredible life alone. It started out of need very early. I kissed Marilyn good-bye and said no more; I was gone. That year I hitchhiked to Florida. I was thirteen. I had street smarts. I was smart on many issues and had also demonstrated an ability to do some really stupid things. I was unable to hitch a ride in the city. Even then people would not pick up hitchhikers in the city. I took a taxi to the Goethals Bridge.

"You want to get out right here?" the man said incredulously.

"Yes, this is good," I mustered with some authority. I got my first ride within an hour, and within two hours I was traveling down the Jersey Turnpike in the cab of a tractor trailer.

I did not feel lonely, and I was not afraid. I was free, and only someone who has hungered for this freedom can describe it. People who know exactly what I am talking about do not need any words at all to understand my liberty. Invariably words fall short, and people just nod their heads with the "Yes, I know exactly what you mean" nod. It is freedom, if only for a time. It is dreaming, if only for a day. I have few recollections about this escape to Florida. I talked, negotiated, and manipulated my way into homes, cars, trucks, and restaurants, and acquired what I needed as I needed it. I intermittently stayed in contact with my sister. When I returned, I was somewhere in the middle of fourteen and still did not seem to grow very much. I was very small. I was four feet, eleven inches until I was sixteen years old.

LIVING ON THE STREETS

I did not go home when I returned to New York. I did not go anywhere, and it was a better place than home. At a certain time each day, everyone goes home for dinner, and the streets start to take on an emptiness. There is less traffic. People are finishing the evening dog-walk. The remaining light of day has departed.

Later in the evening the streets were able to echo my footsteps, then it was time for me to find a place to sleep. Many times the night would find me within eyesight of my house. I could see the lights on in the living room. I would wonder what my sisters were doing inside. I would follow the goings-on by the lights going on and off in various rooms. When the last light was turned off and Marilyn was in bed, I would turn into the cold to find a place to sleep.

Through friends of friends I took to spending my days and nights outside of my neighborhood and quickly found a world that operated twenty-four hours a day—a place where it was much easier to remain anonymous. There were other kids like me, too. They all had different stories but we all had one thing in common—each other. You can tell who is who as the night turns to silent night. We were in twenty-four-hour stores, parks, under the El (elevated) train stations, and other places where we warded off time—and the cold. I discovered that there were more girls than boys who had nowhere to go. After a period of time we developed leads, contacts, plans, ideas, and other contrivances to secure the means to eat, sleep, and carve out some enjoyment in our lives—or at least to survive.

Sometimes I would go to one of the apartment buildings and ring the many bells hoping someone would blindly let me in. Someone always did. As each of these buildings was a six-floor structure, I would stop by each floor and collect floor mats on my journey to the roof. On the sixth floor I would steal all the mats into the staircase and take them up the last leg to my bedroom—the landing at the roof, just inside the door from the night's cold. There I would fold all the mats around me and make a bed. The winter was particularly cold, and I tried not to sleep with my back to the door as an arctic burst always came from beneath.

In the daytime I would sneak out. It was apparent I did not live in these places. There is a peculiar look someone has when they sleep on the streets. There is no mistaking it. I do not think anyone was looking for me, but there were a lot of missing doormats on these nights. It is an indescribable feeling of no connectedness when one sleeps like this and arrives in the bright of day where the entire world is freshly washed and moves with a purpose. I would come out of my newly conquered lair and my young face would have the imprints of other people's doormats. My hair was matted off to one side and my breath less than fresh. One time I looked in the mirror in the elevator and saw the letters "W-E-L-C" imprinted across my face.

I would walk about with soiled hands, hungry, wiping the sleep from my eyes. Once Lisa and I had slept in this very fashion that I had learned so well. She, too, was on and off the streets, and she was often afraid to go home. We held each other, as the winter wind could not be stopped from beneath the door. Somewhere in the night we each found sleep. Somewhere in the night our gum found our hair. When we woke, our gum was woven through our hair such that when standing side by side both heads would have to tilt toward each other. It was awful. Lisa was taller than I was, too. The gum when warm was malleable but now cold was as cement adhesive binding us. Some of the hair came from the far side of our heads. It was truly a mess. We had to walk through the neighborhood—like "Cousin It" from *The Addams Family*—to the only place where we knew we could get help: the shopping center. Parents were sending kids to school, people were going shopping, crossing-guards were blowing whistles, and Lisa and I had to go to the drug store to cut our heads apart using a vanity mirror on aisle three.

After crawling from my previous night's lair, I would make my way to the school where other people were getting ready to *cut* school. There I could find someone's house to go to, wash up, and get something to eat. It got old, and I was keenly aware that I was out of sorts with the schedule of the world. A person never has any sense what goes on inside the microcosm of the many little worlds that make up a community until you are in the macrocosm where you can sense being detached from it. It is like looking into a fishbowl. The days were manageable, but the nights grew dark and cold; everything was more urgent and needful in the bitter dark. The streets were silent, and there were no cupboards, no beds, no pillows, no TVs, and no one to talk to. It was just lonely and miserable. But still, going home was not an option. There are worse things in life than being cold and hungry with no place to sleep.

THE ASPHALT TRIBE

I am not sure if anything I did during this time could be called enjoying life. I think I was just alive, and no more. Most of the friends I had were women, and there are many reasons for this. I think one of the most obvious reasons is most of these people needed protection, and I felt inclined, to protect them. Maybe I just do not know what drew us together, but it has remained a constant with women and me for my whole life. Dee Dee, Poco, Bernadette, Pepper, Sandra, and so many others became the friends with whom I spent my days and my nights, though there were many other people who came in and out of my life in the blindness that was these years to come. Women were less of a threat to me than men. In the end, I held them as something inherently beautiful, both in body and in their tender hearts. This was my first understanding that I could embrace wonderful conclusions in spite of the circumstances of my childhood. These women were not girlfriends or lovers, necessarily; they were friends. I never once lost compassion in all my anguish. In fact, the circumstances of my own life instructed me in simply caring for others.

While on the streets, I made money. I did not sell my body (mostly), and in the end I did not sell my soul—though I almost lost my life and my soul many times. I was keenly aware that the road I was on was treacherous. Even at fourteen, I managed to secure an apartment for myself. Prior to that, I would rent a motel room each night and two of us would enter, and then over the period of the next hour we would bring four or five more of us in to the room. Eventually we would all secure the same bed or floor each night, whether we had to lower sheets and climb up (if we were assigned a second-floor room) or slip in one at a time. The motel people did not care to whom they rented only that each person who stayed paid. We could not afford that arrangement, so we made our own. We all slept together, and we all knew each other well. We knew all of our respective pasts, save for the darkest places, and each other's sometimes-absurd dreams and expectations. I had no sense during any of this time that any of this was right, real, or meaningful. I just did not want to be where I would be otherwise. We were a tribe of nomads, bundled together with the cord of trauma, and none would note our passing. Most expected us to die, in any event.

How could we possibly afford this? It is an obvious question. Well, there are many ways to attain money, at least enough to close the night. When multiple people wake in the morning with the single focus of securing money for the night ahead, amazing things happen. Also, I lived and operated in a very bad world where I applied no ethics to thieves, junkies and drug dealers. I would often take out any combination of these dregs through deceit or outright assault and brutality. I actually got very good at this sort of existence and increasingly raised the stakes to the point where I was planning and executing elaborate cons and armed takedowns, and as a result netting vast sums of money.

The hardest part of the daily struggle came when I was afraid I would lose my grip on the place inside myself that had become a bearer of light for my days and nights. I was simply my only and closest friend and lover. Even in the middle of this lost youth, my introspection continued unabated. I never lost sight of the beauty and the mystery of Christmas Day—*my* nativity. For me Christmas Day, 1975, was such an incredible door through which I had passed. Having passed through this door I was constantly aware that I was part of so very much more than the appearances of the streets. I passed through a stage when I was just a boy to a place where there seemed to be an entire universe that opened up inside me. I could just close my eyes, and it seemed there was another dimension inside me. Eventually, I would not have to close my eyes but would willfully command my external world. I was alive in a way that I cannot explain, and this has not been lost on me—or the others I have met in my life. I am confident that some well-schooled shrink might conclude that this was the traumatic introversion of my upbringing. People like this make excuses and provide the victimization saga for those who cannot articulate their own innocence. I was not a victim and would not trade one day with any other in all time. But I did reach breaking points. Each breaking point brought me to a new threshold regarding the insanity of this world. My life was an amazing observation of the highs and lows of the human condition and I knew this. I was well aware that something quite out of the ordinary was handed to me.

THE THIRD ESCAPE

One day I felt so lost and tired I decided I had to get out. I don't remember it being significantly different from any other day, though. My tired eyes observed the families going about their daily routines of taking the kids to school, kissing good-bye, shuttling off to work, waiting for the bus, or playing in the park. For some reason, on this morning the normalcy reverberated against the hollow walls of my stomach. Today normalcy was too horrific to witness. It took what little strength I had left not to cry. I felt alone, and I was lonely. While I had befriended myself in a rich and unusual way, at times like this I was aware of just how alone I was as a boy. I walked along Myrtle Avenue in Brooklyn. I entered the Outreach Project.

"Good morning, Father," I said to Father McGuiness. He was a Catholic priest who collected the lost kids about him in the evening. He knew our hang-outs, and he would talk to us and ask us how we were doing. Many times he brought us food. He always tried to feed us.

"Eddie, come in. Have something to eat," he offered. The secretary looked up and smiled. Same problem, different kid—every day.

"Thank you, Father," I said.

He sat across from me and smiled. My face was pensive, and it must have been obvious that I had tears nearly ready to burst. Some of my friends had disappeared. Some left; some died. Father knew most of them. For some reason on that day, the loss was too much to handle. I ate. Father McGuiness began to speak without my having to introduce the reason for my visit. He knew of a place on Long Island where the people would help me.

"You are wasting your life, Eddie. You are exceptionally bright but you will die if you don't get off these streets." I nodded. I was feeling so lost, so hungry, so tired, I agreed to do whatever he suggested. He called my mother. I am not sure how the conversation went but I was going to go home for a bit, and Father was putting my mom in contact with someone from a home for kids. I would latter learn it was not a home for kids; it was a home for people much older than me. I was going to be the *kids* in the Home for Kids."

These days of living on the streets opposed to living at home were arguably a choice. From the perspective of a boy who finally refused to be beaten any longer, there was no alternative. All life is merely perception, and I am sure my mother and others have varying recollections of our lives during this time. I, however, simply refuse to be a victim on any count in this life. I am utterly convinced that every single thing—good or bad—happens to or with me for a reason in the grand unfolding drama that is my life. To what extent my life and its actions or reactions have impacted on another I cannot say; nor can I say I am sorry or have regrets.

Every other life that intersects with mine is unfolding on its own path as well. To the extent that I have served as a prop in the stage show of another's life, I have done so with love and compassion, even though the actions or results may have suggested otherwise. I have never had any sense at all that anything in my life was tragic, or that I have mortally wounded another heart. Every person is an actor in every other's life. I know this smacks of ethical relativity. I cannot help this. This is what I hold to be true, and since I was a boy I have stood witness with forethought and anticipation at the unfolding drama of my life. It has been both breathtaking and terrifying. My mother had a baby boy. That is all I was. I did not need much. In the end, she had me for no more than ten or so years. In prison, they call that a "dime." Still, she knew our family was sick. And it was likely better that I was gone.

FIRST COMPROMISES

I returned home as per my agreement with Father McGuiness. There is a strange thing about the place that is home, regardless of the blessings and demons inside those walls. They are blessings and demons that you know and you take comfort in this. It is sick, but it is true. My mother was very sweet to me. As was often the case, she cried as she talked with me from across the kitchen table. My mother was crying because I was thin. I was gaunt for a child. I was dirty, though not filthy.

"Are you hungry?" she asked.

"Yes, I am," I told her. She rose from the table and made me something to eat while she talked very level-headed about her call with Father McGuiness. Having done this for years he apparently gave my mom some very clear dos-and-don'ts. She had listened. Thank goodness. When I was at the junctures of my life where the life force itself that kept me in this world was most imperiled, my mother always mustered profound sensitivity. It never lasted, but it made me love her so painfully deep. Perhaps that is just a reflection of my ability to love deeply and not a commentary on her grace at all. I always had a powerful ability to love deeply, in spite of all things.

I got up from the table, came behind her, and hugged her while she was preparing my food. I hugged her from behind and cried. She never turned around.

After a while she turned and looked at me with her hands on my shoulders. Her eyes were brimming with tears. I felt so bad for her. I was just awfully sure that I was hurting her. I was always hurting her and did not know why.

"Go take a bath, Edward," she ran her one hand through my hair as she said this. I went to the bathroom. It was like the Ghost of Christmas Past was showing me all the things I had missed. I saw my sister Michele in the hallway and said in a dejected, beaten voice

"Hi, Michele. How are you?"

"Fine," she answered, still unsure what to make of all this, whether there was a side to be on or not, or if all hell was about to break loose. Somewhere outside of my mother's power to influence, one way or the other, I was growing up and life was happening to me. She knew so many were dying out there all the time and entire tracts of our family life were now hopelessly in different spheres, different tracks in different worlds. We were, in essence, strangers.

I closed the door, sat on the toilet, and ran the water in the tub. I reached up and locked the bathroom door. I cried. I cried in that bathroom the whole time the water filled up. I smelled the scent of the powder my mother used after she took a bath. There were the hairbrushes still wrapped tightly with the hair of a thousand brushings. I counted the toothbrushes. There were three of them. I was sobbing now, and my nose was stuffed. It seemed I had been crying in this bathroom for a thousand years. I turned off the water and looked in the mirror.

I felt so damn alone.

"Why am I always alone?" I sobbed. I rolled my dirty clothes up and got into the tub. Before I turned the light off I noticed the rubber bag in the bathtub I had always played with when I was a kid. (When I was a kid? Huh!) The bag hung from the showerhead and had a hose and nozzle at the end of it. I used to fill it with water and let it hang from the showerhead and sink my boats. I laughed now. I now knew that it was a douche bag, and I now knew what women did with it. I laughed a little more. I lay there and lowered my head slowly in the water. It felt so good. I felt safe. I was in the dark again. I felt I was home but knew that I was not. I knew with certainty that I could never go home again.

The water entered my ears, and I felt it race up to my eardrums. I titled my head left and right and lowered my head further till only the tip of my nose was out of the water. The air bubbles had left my ears, and I could now hear my heart beating. The water was hot. I closed my eyes.

I had been breathing like this in darkness for many years. I closed my eyes in the darkness and thought of nothing. I felt my chest rise and fall against the water around me. I counted my breaths and then stopped. I just breathed. I was in peace. I felt myself floating. I dreamed I was somewhere else but as usual I did not picture anything else. I just floated in the tub of hot water, in the little apartment in Queens that I could only ever go back to in dreams.

"Foxy, I don't know. I am taking him out there tomorrow," my mother said to her sister on the phone.

"Who knows, Foxy?" I heard her say with her dismissive voice.

"It's all bullshit, that's what it is."

"He needs to get his fucking act together," she said as I dried off. My mother was always certain that everything I ever needed was right there at home. I could smell the food in the kitchen. I was so hungry. I opened the door and saw my little sister watching me from the other room. I quickly closed the distance to Michele and kissed her. I then crossed the hallway and opened the door to my room. The room was decorated in girl's stuff. I moved the teddy bears over and lay down on the bed. I did not want to eat. I was too spent to cry. I was empty.

I had met so many people and traveled to so many strange places recently. I had seen life from a vantage point most people will never know. Many of the people I had recently met were already dead, arrested, overdosed, or just disappeared from the streets. The drug wars, gunfights, Colombians from Corona, and Puerto Ricans from Brooklyn were just a snapshot of what was too much. I stared at the wall. The same little hole was still there. It would likely always be. It was too small for anyone else to notice. It really had no other purpose anyway except for me. I stared at it as I had done for years and slowly the world went out of focus. The wind was rustling in the room. The light was dancing in and out of the wall before me. The wall was breathing. I slept.

CHAPTER 7

▼

Deliver Us from Evil

See the nature of the divine world superimposed upon the subordinate natural world and you will have facilitated one of the most important milestones to apprehending the Kingdom of God on Earth. You are, in the end, what you see. You see, in the end, what you dream. You dream, in the end, what you dare. Dare to see God.

The ride to Long Island was silent except for my mother telling me she was missing work for me. I always made her miss work. I did get to see Marilyn last night, and I missed her already. I always talked with Marilyn when I was away. I always let her know where I was and whom I was with in case I died. For over thirty years I have been advising my sister of my last known location in case of death.

We must have driven further out than I had ever been, though it was only mid-way to the end of Long Island. People lived differently out here. They all had homes, and there were trees. I liked the trees and the grass. I was struck by how green everything was away from the city. I did not then recall that we used to live out here, only a short distance down the road from the *home for kids*. We parked in the parking lot of a building that looked more like a hospital than a house. In fact, it was a hospital during World War II, and before that it was a tuberculosis rehabilitation center. It was big. I saw a man walking outside, and he had a cardboard sign hanging from around his neck that read: I act out, ask me why. I wanted to go and ask him, but I thought better of it.

"We have an appointment with Kenny," my mother said. The really cute girl behind the desk told us to have a seat. She was older than me, but she was still within range. She was cute. *I could do this*, I thought.

"Hello, I am Kenny," the small man said taking my mother's hand. Kenny was an unassuming, gentle little man with big bug eyes. He then looked at me with that same dumb-ass smile all adults do when they patronize you.

"And you must be Edward," he declared, "or would you rather be called Eddie?"

"Edward is fine," I told him.

"Let's take a walk around the house," he suggested and began talking about all sorts of little tidbits of information regarding the house, people, and what they do there.

If it was a house, it was huge. There were many people, young men and women, busy with all sorts of unknown, but apparently urgent, errands. I would later find out that I was correct in wondering about this. Most of what was done was not urgent at all—just busy work. Also, the young men and women I saw were all older than me by at least ten years.

Kenny introduced us to Duncan. Duncan was a "resident" who had been there for many months. They explained that everyone lives there for about a year. Though there are no windows and locks, we were sufficiently far away that no one tried to leave. If I wanted to leave, no one would stop me, Duncan informed me. He also told me in front of my mother that if I left, I would die. This was a constant refrain, and it would later be a challenge only equal to, "Don't be a pussy." We know where that got me.

"This is where we grow vegetables and fruits," Kenny told us as we walked around outside. I noticed that there were other staff members here and there, and they all looked very much like the people who hung out in Forest Park, Queens. In fact, these were all former junkies.

Kenny explained that there was no physical contact, no violence or drugs of any kind, and no sex. Well, I had already seen a few girls whom I thought about that with, so I already saw that this was going to be a problem—at least in my head. It turned out not to be a problem at all, however. Kenny explained that I would meet with him twice a week, that I would have tutoring to realign my education, and that we had a regular schedule from morning to nighttime. It was all so fucking nice. It was not all bullshit but I later learned that the guy who walked out front with the sign got a little "talking to" for potentially running us off.

They simply did not want to frighten us—basically, frighten my mother. They had every intention of frightening me. They planned to frighten the hell out of me.

It was done. My mother, being the Girl Scout that she was, already had a bag packed for me of which I was unaware. How thoughtful. This was all happening too fast. I now had a meal and a bath, and this was increasingly looking like a bad idea. This phenomena would become something that I looked at very closely as I aged: the ability of the mind to inform us that an outcome that we could not otherwise expect may in fact be likely with just the addition of some food and sleep. These things never changed anything in and of themselves. Fed and bathed, my life still sucked, and I still had nowhere to go if I left this place today. Contrary to anything my mother might say, then or now, I was not welcome at her home except in passing. I was fourteen years old. Even if I chose not to stay at this place, I was definitely not going back to Queens with her tonight. They carried my bag in, and we were left alone.

"Do not be afraid, Edward," Mom said. "Just do as they ask of you, and be a good boy."

I had so many good-byes by this time I was becoming numb to them. I had not seen one other kid even close to my age in my walk around the grounds. In the end, it was a good guess. I was the youngest person they ever had.

"Good-bye, Mom."

"Good-bye Edward."

"I love you!"

"I love you, too, Edward." She was in the car and backing up.

"Mom?" I called to her as she drove away with her window rolled up. "I'm sorry." I had made her miss work again.

This, then, is the process of how we come to define love in a language alien. Through repetition, inculcation, learned responses, and time, we come to define love in our myriad ways each and saddled often to our definition of love is a very real non-love state. Love is often *not* in our exclamations asserting as much. In asserting, "I love you, Mom," I was defining love counter to my findings on inspection.

WELL, IT'S BETTER THAN JAIL!

Some threshold had been crossed when the automobile that brought me drove away. Kenny was gone, and in his place were two older guys. They waved good-bye to my mom with me and told me to follow them. The two guys took me inside and told the person at the front desk that they were taking me upstairs. Then they handed some person my bags. I would later see these two men going through my belongings, and none of my stuff would be returned to me.

"Why did you let my mother leave my bags if you were just going to just take them?" I asked. I was told I would have to earn my own clothes and personal items.

They took me upstairs to the showers. All of the showerheads were on one wall. There was no one else in the bathroom. They told me to take my clothes off.

"All of them," the larger of the two said.

I paused in shock. I was not a fool, though, and understood that they were just inspecting me. I stood there in my underwear. I dropped them and crossed my hands in front of my privates. I knew the attendants knew they were there, but I did not want to show them.

"Move your hands," the smaller ex-junkie commanded. I did.

"Lift up your nuts." I complied.

"Turn around."

"Bend over," I was told quietly.

"What?" This part pissed me off. There was something both unnatural and unhealthy at this point. This was one of those times when the mind asks if this was now for pleasure or process. Was this a secret trick where they would jump out and butt rape me?

"Just bend over," they said patiently.

"Spread your cheeks," they added in unison.

"I'm not spreading my ass cheeks for anyone. Fuck you!" I stated dismissively and went for my shorts.

"Listen, just turn back around and spread your ass cheeks. We don't want to do this any more than you do, but we have to make sure you do not have any weapons or contraband. We do this to everyone," the larger man, who was obviously in charge, explained.

"Up my ass?" I inquired. "You want to see if I have a fucking gun or a knife in my ass?"

Their silent pause convinced me this was indeed what they were looking for. I wondered, *were knife handles, triggers, or bags of coke usually detected by casual ass inspection. Did people get them in their ass, but always just barely, and they were then easily detected by visual screening?* I reluctantly complied. I guess now I can imagine what a woman feels like to go to the doctor, or even Alan's first day in jail—or Alan's every night in jail. It was such a violation. It was done.

"Get in the shower," I was told, relieved that they no longer had to badger a young, scared child. This frightened child appearance had worked for many years because of my size. However, I was cunning, ruthless, and quite dangerous by this age. Recalling my own youth I take serious the potential threat of any child with an attitude problem old enough to pull a trigger or butter bread. I was likely far more dangerous than any of the adults walking the grounds outside.

I took a shower, and they threw me some clothes that were not mine; they did not fit, and they looked stupid as hell. They were obviously charity clothes. *The people who bought these from the store originally should have had their ass kicked*, I thought. I felt dumber wearing these clothes than having my ass inspected. They brought me downstairs and introduced me to the "family."

People were now completely out of whatever holes they had been in, and I met approximately thirty people. *Where had all these people come from?* I wondered. The oldest was maybe forty or fifty; the youngest was, well, me. Most were in their early to late twenties. Many were women as well. I was still a child, and they knew it. All of them seemed to come from middle—to upper-middle-class backgrounds. They were not the stock that walked the streets of the city. Many of these people would turn out to be from the upper crust of Long Island's wealth. This place was a semi-private institution, and most of those in residence were from Long Island's wealthiest families. Apparently, my mom was able to get me in on the handout program. I could have done a lot worse, especially considering how many kids I knew who got sent to Spafford Correctional Facility—most of us were too young to go to Riker's Island. When a kid went into these places, it was over for him; his life was ruined.

They explained to me that everyone gets appointed a big brother, but that I would have a big sister, too. They had never done that before. Pat was my big brother, and another Pat was my big sister. I liked Big Sister Pat. She was always kind to me, and we grew very close.

Wherever the fortunes of my life took me, I would come to have a profound relationship with women, in general and in particular. Women were always extremely attracted to me. This is not necessarily an attraction of the senses; it is something else, and it is powerful. Invariably women sought me out, and I sought them for company, friendship, and, occasionally, more. Mostly, my relationships with women were not of a sexual nature. I am not convinced that this attraction is due to the women in my early life; that is too easy. Rather I think the proximity of women in my life is due to something else, something inexplicable.

For, as in Pat's case, I often do not control the circumstances of our engagement. It is so often the case that, against all possible odds, I am aligned with, paired with, or otherwise in the company of women, always. If I sit in a public place, slowly the seats around me will adjust to a predominantly female occupation. If any given group of mixed sexes meets repeatedly in any given location with repeated selection of seats, the women in any given forum gravitate to me. I am not unattractive, but this is not what it is at all. It is an attraction that has nothing to do with appearances. I would have it no other way.

Many people had wire clothes hangers manipulated around their heads in such a fashion that a small six-inch-by-six-inch cardboard placard hung right in front of their heads, just above their eyes. The signs all had little morsels of information and requests for aid. Some were painfully to the point.

"I am an idiot, ask me why." one sign read.

"I don't talk about my feelings," read another. There were many such placards. The people wearing them looked like idiots. Some people had shaved heads, and others were scrubbing floors with signs on them that were clearly from refrigerator packing.

There was an aluminum chair in the front hallway on which people would be sent to sit when they were bad, real bad. There they could not move or even go to the bathroom without permission. Even then someone would have to go with the person and watch his penis if the person was a man; I am not sure how the women did it. Perhaps they used one of those inspection mirrors on the little telescoping wand. There were little poems throughout this "house" admonishing the reader to some recognition of flaw or purpose. It was surreal.

I would be there a long time. I was right; I could never go home again.

HAIRCUTS

When I would do something wrong, like the ridiculous infraction of coming to the living room less than a minute late, I would have to get a "haircut." Some months after arriving at my new digs, this is exactly what happened. I arrived less than one minute late to the living room after dinner. I had to stand for a "haircut." This was not a haircut in the traditional sense of the word. Instead, I would have to go up to the furthest corner of the highest floor in this labyrinth of a house where I would have to stand in the military position of attention for an impossibly long time. Behind the designated door I could hear the conversation and laughter of my soon to be executioners. They talked of idle and unrelated things, but I was terrified, only feet away. They got silent. That was the silence before the...

"Edward!"

"Knock!" boomed the authoritative command.

I would then rap on the door three times. Too hard and it was over for me. Too soft and I would hear about that, too. Too few or too many raps and I would get it also.

I entered the room. I was always able to tell how much trouble I was in by how many people were in the room. In this instance, there was a normal amount—five or six people. At least one was always a counselor. Most of the residents, if not all but a handful, were here because of drugs or the law. I was not there for either. I was just passing time as I had nowhere to live.

"You are called here today..." they would begin from the least among them to the most important. I suppose there was an art in yelling at people, but I'd had enough of it in my years at home, which is one of the reasons why I fled.

"...so why do you think you can do anything you want? Who the fuck do you think you are?" I was asked in a near frenzy, complete with froth and saliva spewing from the first speaker's mouth.

This is absurd, I thought. I was washing dishes and was not a minute late to the meeting—it was really only seconds, and they hadn't started yet. Next in line, and more of the same: yelling and screaming at me.

"When you are told to be somewhere, *you are supposed to get your ass there on time, do you hear me?*" the voice morphed into a grotesque timbre.

"Yes, I h...," I began.

"*Shut the fuck up!*" they all jumped in. I was smiling now. It had become a cacophony of strained minds barely holding on to mutinying voices.

"*Get that smirk off your face!*" they chanted. Neck veins were equally distended on all of them, and their faces were blood red, save for their lips.

They were all in their chairs, but their knuckles were white like their lips from the blood being forced out by the handrails squeezed so tightly in their fists. *This is a fucking nightmare*, I thought. I excised and later reviewed every single detail of this scenario, as I had never seen humans behave like this. This was a marginally contained fury. I despised rage.

"Fuck you!" I left.

"Get your ass back here," they trailed off pathetically as I went to pack my shit.

"Fuck off!" I shouted resignedly over my shoulder.

THE FOURTH ESCAPE

This is where their approach, their techniques, turned into a cult-like orgy of fear.

"You're going to die out there," one of them offered sheepishly from the doorway of my room as I packed.

"Dude, I don't give a fuck where I die, as long as I do not have to hear that shit again," I responded. I walked down the stairs and out the door into the rain. Some of them walked me to the property line imploring me to save my life. They were like clergy begging me not to sail my ship past the horizon lest I fall off the world.

"You'll die."

"You'll die!" continued the mantra.

"You'll go back to shooting dope," someone added. I paused, laughed very hard, and shook my head in disbelief. This saying was used to describe anyone's return to their previous lifestyle. It was only ever amusing. However, today, standing in the rain, through with all of their shit, it sounded all the more absurd.

"Man, they were fucking out-there," I realized.

As I looked behind me I could see all of them returning to the house except Pat. She stood there crying. After a while I looked over my shoulder and could still see her standing there drenching wet in the harassing rain. It was freezing rain, and it drove into me like darts. I could now only see a few feet in front of me. Pat was gone. The ground water pooled in my sneakers and made a sick, squashing sound and feel. It only felt nasty until I was soaked to the bone. I made my way intently to the highway only a few miles away. I did not know then that it was the wrong highway. I truly applied myself to make this arrangement work. I could not help but feel that this "home" sucked every bit as much as my home in Queens. It was a different suck, though, but the same.

I did not think I would get a ride to the highway, but was sure I would get a ride once I got there. I walked for a long time, and then saw the familiar cloverleaf ahead. Or was it? I could not be sure. Maybe it was the rain. I was tired, wet, and had walked so far. It was now night and, after six hours, hardly any cars came by, and those that *did* would not even slow to give me a second glance. I walked from one highway to the other thinking this was the way my mother had driven me so long ago. It was not. After so many hours, I was sick, cold, hungry, and exhausted. I turned a corner and thought, finally, this looked familiar. It was. It was the place I had started from. It was the home. I was devastated. I had nowhere else to go. I walked back dejected and defeated.

When I came inside shock registered on the faces of those that were still awake. Some went and got the night counselor and sat me on the "chair." Life would be different. I reasoned that I would gather my strength and better prepare for next time.

FURTHER COMPROMISES

I sat there for four days. No one was permitted to talk to me, and no one could smile or say hello, though a few did. Pat smiled, and in some small way I felt good. Pat liked me and cared for me in much the same way Marilyn cared for me. I liked her. She was much older than I, but she was always so kind to me. She really believed I would have died. Wow! Maybe she was right. These people were really afraid of something out there, and some would never leave this place, even years after leaving the home. I would not be one of them. I would leave again and sooner than I expected. Probably I only needed a warm bath and a full stomach. We would see.

After four days, they took me to another haircut. I was pretty sure that they were being careful with me this time. I did not get special treatment, but I think it was now apparent I was a child. *Dear God, I was a child.* I never really considered this during the early years on the street. I wonder why no one else really considered this, either. I was now aware that I was a child. How could I not be? I was the only male present that did not shave.

No one yelled during this haircut, but they made it clear that now I was being punished for leaving. I was going to have my head shaved bald. I was going to have a specially built baby crib for me in the middle of the living room for when I misbehaved and would have to carry a baby doll every time I was out of the crib. I had to wear a baby rattle around my neck. For my special punishment I would spend eight to twelve hours a day in a little room upstairs that had been filled for years with books upon books, but was never put into any organized system for retrieval and use. I was the youngest there, and sadly, the best equipped to do the job.

I spent thirty days in a closet with books. Why does this seem so familiar? I never even hinted at my utter joy in my punishment. Being in a closet was always the only thing that made life tolerable. But I would be able to sleep in a bed at night, and I would be able to die there—not "out there" as they all feared. Plus, there was food there. And now, now there were books. I had the organization mapped out in two days, but then I left key piles of books scattered throughout the room to give the appearance of progress, but not much. In fact, it would now only take me an hour or so to place the books on the shelves and be complete. I spent the next four weeks reading sixteen hours a day.

I suffered the humiliation of the baby doll, crib, and rattle for thirty days at which time I was made a "member" of the family again. Whoopee! It was a fucking nightmare. A few weeks after I was done with this punishment, I was in the kitchen cleaning pots and pans. The others had already taken to their free time and were playing cards in the dining area or upstairs watching TV. Dave, a former Navy guy, was in the kitchen for some unrelated reason. It was a big, industrial-size kitchen with big, industrial-size pots and pans. I did not mind cleaning this stuff as I was left alone and could think and dream. Some days I planned my escape. *Next time I will not fuck up*, I affirmed. What an idiot, I laughed at myself. In fact, I was my best friend but I took no shit from me and gave myself no quarter. I really screwed up some doozies and had great fun at my own expense, laughing at myself.

THE FIRST GLIMPSE OF THE MIND'S POWER

The lights were out through the kitchen, except in the area where I was cleaning and a nightlight over by the stove work area. This is the area where the line was. The line was where the folks gathered to get their food at the meals, their bodies trailing through the kitchen and out into the hallway. It was also the area where the smaller pots, pans, and various cooking utensils hung for easy access from a thick wire, which spanned ten feet or more. Dave and I got into a heated exchange from opposite ends of the kitchen over some trivial thing. Dave was a perfectionist but no one took him seriously. With me he felt he could exercise his naval authority and get away with it. I do not know how old Dave was but nearly everyone was distinguished from me by having to shave. I did not. Hell, I was just starting to get hair on my balls. But I would not take shit from anyone, no matter how old or big. As big as Dave was, he would have likely been seriously injured were we to "get into it." I was extremely dangerous by this point in my life.

"I would not say that if I were you, Dave," I told him.

"Are you threatening me," he challenged. Threatening someone had all the infraction weight behind it that beating someone up did, or getting laid. No one ever did, or got caught, doing those two things. Of course some time later it would come out that Pete, a counselor, had orgies in his closed-door sessions.

Shit! I always got the nerd groups. Many of those around me enforcing rules were getting laid twice a week in group sex.

"I am not threatening you," I defended. But he surely pissed me off. I was nearly thirty feet away from him, the utensils, the pots and pans, and the night-light. I turned to him from across the room with my hands at my sides. At once all of the pots, pans, and cooking utensils released from their perch and flew across the room at him a few feet from where he stood. It was not a scrambled or confusing event. All of the utensils came off the wire at the same time and moved at right angles to their late perch. They moved synchronized and parallel to the floor and toward Dave. I was nowhere near them. I was fully thirty feet away from him and the metal cooking tools. Some hit Dave harmlessly and others went crashing around him and past him. A few crashed loudly into the wall behind him. The kitchen was silent. It was a brief moment of pure violence, and neither of us touched a thing. We both stood there dumbstruck. I was scared. Dave ran away telling me I was scary. Dave was scared. I went outside and sat. I was not remotely concerned with trouble or such. I was at a loss considering what I just witnessed.

I was called upstairs. Dave was definitely, and thankfully, saying I did not throw anything at him. He was telling them what happened, and people were gathering. The counselors broke it up, and a shaken Dave asked that I stay away from him. His fear and sensationalism frightened me and the others. I went to bed. I could not sleep, as I was alarmed at what had happened. *What the hell happened?* I asked myself over and over as I slipped away. The next day a meeting was called for the whole family in the living room. Dave was permitted to begin by telling everyone what happened. This whole meeting was just for me, and I had done nothing wrong. It was not really very kind. Kenny was looking intently at me the whole time. I think he knew me better than anyone there. I think he believed everything Dave said. He was not alone.

James followed Dave in the "discussion."

"I don't know, Ed. At night when I have night owl [fire watch] and come into your room, your room is bitter cold, even when everyone else's is not. Sometimes I see a light around you. I cannot describe it. It is not evil, but it scares me." So spoke Mister Helper Number Two.

What the hell is this bullshit? I wondered. *What is happening?* It was all moving too fast and I could not get a grip on anything. It is the case that at times in our lives events seem to move faster than our minds can process. We know something is happening. We know what it appears to look like, but we have no idea what is happening, and it happens too fast. I had no idea what was happening but I clearly got a naked view of what others thought about me. They did not think I was mean, an ass, snotty, cruel, stupid, or anything similar. They thought I was very unlike them. This continued to be the case throughout my life.

The counselors let these diatribes continue and I was afraid. I am not sure of what I was afraid, but I was. I think I was afraid that I did not know who I was.

Sue joined in next and said, "Ed, I don't know, either, but I get the feeling that you are not from here. You are not supposed to be here, and you know things that the rest of us do not know."

My thoughts began screaming in my head, *Is there no fucking place I belong? What the fuck does that mean? I am not supposed to be here.*

Oddly, this is the same refrain I had in all my prayers when a child. The counselors let this crap continue, which really surprised me. I did not. I got up, packed my shit, and left for good. This time the weather was nice. This time I got a ride all the way back to Queens. None of it ever made any sense. Somehow, it all made perfect sense on another level. I have always maintained that people spoke first with spirit, next with actions, and last with words. What these others were sensing made perfect sense.

THE FIFTH ESCAPE AND FURTHER COMPROMISES

Moving back to New York from the home on Long Island was an uneventful task, but any hope that there would be a different outcome, a different home in the little place that was our apartment in Queens, New York, was short lived. I became more and more detached from the world around me, though I had to sustain myself and operatively complete the tasks necessary to eat and to secure lodging. The world and my needs would not just go away only because I found life distasteful. Coming back home only took for a week or so. This time I did not look back. I headed back to the familiar education in the school of hard knocks. The time I spent in the closet that was the library would forever coalesce the language and words of the dead and the poets into the tapestry that was my private world. The final pieces fell into place for my private construction and articulation of the mechanics of my profoundly altered internal world.

Once back in Queens, my mother and I made one last vain attempt to integrate me into school. I had no infrastructure in which to lead what they thought was a normal life. The madness that was my home life and community prevented me from ever coming back to become a dutiful son and scholar. My mother tried, anyway. She met with the principal and the guidance counselor to place me.

They approximated where I should have been and decided to place me in high school, pending the results of my testing. It was discussed. I would attend classes effective that day at John Adams High School, ninth grade. I had not been to school for any period of time in well over two years. The tutoring I had out on Long Island was fairly irrelevant as I exceeded their tests and just used that time to read as I wished.

The tripartite consulted a schedule of classes and produced my first day's schedule, though classes were already under way. A note was prepared for me to hand to my first teacher, should she or he require it. I do not think anyone stopped to consider some basic organizational issues: I was not living at home, and nothing would be different in my wherewithal to dedicate myself to this task. It was simply that by the time I was fifteen, or even earlier, I had lost all sense that my life at home was tolerable. My mother saw these efforts as her remaining obligations to my "upbringing." The community of which I was a part of was not even noticed by the adult world. Outside the very windows where we sat that day were tribes of kids smoking pot, tripping, stealing for lunch, and succumbing to overwhelming peer pressure in pursuit of either just surviving, or plain malfeasance. A plan that had only the trappings that made the adults feel they had committed their best efforts, and which did not address the underlying decay of my life, was doomed to failure. My first class more aptly illustrated my realization of this than any considerations I could offer to support this point.

I opened the door quietly so as not to disturb the class. *There is Ann*, I thought. Ann was a beautiful girl from the other side of Howard Beach, where the people with money came from. I was a little insecure around girls like this, especially the ones who either knew me or knew people I knew. I was just sure they would think me dirty or inferior because of where I lived or because my clothes were often hand-me-downs from my cousins Jackie and Louie. I always wrestled with the embarrassment of wearing old clothes in a world where everyone had on the latest Jordache jeans and all the best of the best. She knew me, and I was self-conscious as I walked to the back of the room and took a seat. *This whole back-to-school thing could have gone so much better*, I thought.

The teacher stopped talking when I came into the classroom. Had she continued the whole class would likely not all be staring at me. Her silence at my entrance was an invitation to consider me, and they all did. When I sat down she finally inquired, "What the hell do you think your doing?"

I rose and told her that "I just came from the principal's office and I was instructed to come to your class." I walked up the aisle and handed her the note authorizing my placement.

"I don't care who the hell told you can come to my class. Who the hell do you think you are coming to my class in the middle of the lesson? Get your ass out of my class," she further clarified.

I was in front of the class at this point, as I had not returned to the seat where my few things were. I stood before the entire class as she yelled at me, but only saw Ann's face. We had seen each other many times, and maybe spoke once or twice. I could tell she was embarrassed for me. When talking with her friends later on the bus ride home, she would be either silent or agree that that boy got what he deserved, but she would not defend me. She could not.

I walked to the back of the classroom and collected my few things. I mumbled something like, "Fuck this shit," as I walked out. I am sure I said that more out of sheer embarrassment. It enabled me to appear as if I had a choice in this whole mess and that, yes, I agreed, "Fuck this." I was on her side then, I should just leave, free will and all.

DYING TO GO TO SCHOOL

Michael Cummings, Everton Lazarus, and I were strangers to each other. The only thing we had in common was that the paths of our lives were intersecting today in such a way that would leave Everton forever changed, Michael forever dead, and me forever through with school.

The hallways were empty except one guy and a girl at the far end of a fairly long hallway as I exited the "bitch's" class. The smells of books and erasers, waxed floors, and overused dull brains frying behind closed doors were the only triggers that alerted me that this was a school.

"Michael," she quietly called, excited to see her boyfriend. The attractive black girl closed the distance to embrace Michael. I closed the door behind me, and I heard the teacher begin to speak again. I was not loitering. Everything happened so fast.

"Yo! Motherfucker!" came the shout from elsewhere.

From the staircase to my immediate left another stocky, short black guy appeared: Everton. Michael was a tall, skinny, clean-cut black kid. Everton wore a skullcap of some sort. Apparently, it had denoted something religious. "Apparently," as the papers would inform us the following day, "Michael Cummings had knocked it off Everton's head either intentionally or not the day before."

"You gonna say sorry, motherfucker?" affirmed Everton as he got up in Michael's face. They were just five feet across the hall from me but they all ignored me as if I was not there. The girl, crying, backed a few feet away. Michael was much taller than Everton.

"Man, get outta my face!" Michael said as he backed up. But Michael could back up no further as the wall was to his back. I could see the girl starting to run now as Everton pulled out a knife and slashed first left, then right. Like all things in my life, and especially in Michael's, things tend to take forever and then all of a sudden happen too fast.

Everton turned around and ran into the stairway. *I guess he was not a good aimer*, I considered immediately, as Michael was hot on his heels screaming, "Get back here, motherfucker!" Michael decided not to pursue Everton after all. Instead he got as far as the doorway when he started to trip and stumble on his intestines. He turned around just as his girlfriend reached him. She was screaming and crying. Michael may have heard her; I cannot be sure. He leaned into the wall and slid down as he collected his intestines around his seat and died. I was still standing just outside the door not ten feet away. My hand involuntarily dropped from the doorknob in disbelief as this unfolded. It was all so fast.

"Oh, fuck this shit," I said out loud, shaking my head in disbelief, and walked out the door, and down the same stairs as Everton. For both Michael and me, school was out forever.

It turns out my test grades would later be sufficient that I was effectively graduated in absentia anyway. Whoopee! I was going to tenth grade." You gotta love the public education system. I would never make it to tenth grade on paper or person. However, my immediate concern was that I had absolutely nowhere in the world to go. It was only an hour or so ago that my mother was sitting across from me genuinely wishing me well and hoping for my future. Perhaps she thought her fifteen-year-old son would start attending school and doing his homework by the light of a fire burning in a fifty-five-gallon drum. The little house in the corner of the world where I cried for years was the only home I knew. It would be nighttime soon, and I had been gone so long from the streets that I was like a housecat without claws, locked out for the night. I left Howard Beach for my future where I would meet Sandra, Puerto Rican Steve, Danny, and others who would conspire to change and influence my life further.

CHAPTER 8

▼

Lost Souls

Many loves will remain battered upon the rocks of our past as we continue our journey through this life. We can enable all of our experiences of love to inform, educate, and elucidate the spirit within us. This may not be palliative in the moment, because surely when love departs, it makes our whole world seem to shudder and we wish for no less than death to take us. This is but a glimpse of the reason the spirit tracks incessantly toward God. It must reunite with the source of all life. Love is but a reflection in the flesh of love's longing for Love.

Women were drawn to me, and from early on it was a decision I had to make to sleep with them or not. It seems obvious but it is more complicated. For many my age, and still at this age, if a woman wants to have sex, do it. I came to realize that, for me, sex was more than the act. I knew that more was possible in the union of two people, even when I was a child. I was at a time in my life where I was exploring women as well as acquiring them. I seemed to have women around me my whole life. I began exploring "sex and my soul," as I would describe it to myself. The fact is I was infatuated with the latter before I came to know the former. Women increasingly came to symbolize the vehicle of the flesh where I could feel as well as think and project the ecstasy and the light that was inside me.

Even as a child I held aloof physical ecstasy and curiously studied it. I compared it to the sensations I had in my own internal course through prayer and such. Many may have no idea to what I allude here. I cannot help you. It occurred to me that women were inheritors of a more gentle heart. While I would explore women in general, and in particular, through the remainder of my life, I have held women aloof of great critique. I simply refuse to muddy an otherwise obvious realization with the soil of emotion or ego.

After the unsuccessful attempt in school, I picked up right where I left off. I am sure my mother would say I had a home all along, but this is not entirely correct. I may have had a house offered to me from time to time, but not a home. In any event, seeking redress of pain from that which inflicted the pain is akin to asking a primitive concept of a deity for relief from suffering or natural disasters. In both cases, people thank the warden for the jailbreak. Yes, she may have offered a house for respite, and that is questionable. But a home I did not have. I went to ground within days of hitting her "home" in Howard Beach.

FOR SALE!

Marilyn was working at the Strafford Hotel in Forest Park, Queens. I went to visit her during the day. On one day I was sitting in the bar when I noticed an older woman staring at me. She was actually quite attractive. My sister passed by and called me a slut in a low playful whisper.

"I was only looking." We both laughed. The woman asked me if I would help her carry something up the stairs for her. She lived nearby. I agreed. I walked her to her house and carried some-odd thing or another up to her apartment. She must have been very wealthy. This was a very wealthy area in Forest Hills and this was a nicer place than most homes I had seen. When she went to give me twenty dollars, she asked if I wanted $100 more. I knew exactly what she meant, though no one had ever asked me this before.

"Sure," I said. She proceeded to have me sit down on the chair. As I looked at all the old portraits of what could only have been her and her husband, she took my pants to my ankles and pulled me free of my underwear. I was somewhat disgusted but apparently not enough. I watched her and could not deny that there were worse ways to earn money.

That must be quite old, I thought, looking at an antique on the end table. Then I directed my attention back to the liver spots on her hands. *All antiques in here*, I thought. She gave me a $120 and asked me if I knew what time it was. I did not.

"Here, take this," she said. "This was my husband's and I am sure he would want you to have this."

That is sick, I thought. I took the watch. It was a solid gold watch. I left her home only certain of one thing, the time.

I returned the next day and told my sister what happened.

"You are sick," she said.

"Tell me why I am sick. Why should she not be able to do what everyone else does?" I asked defiantly.

In the end another woman who was friends with the first came over to me a short time later and asked me if I would help her carry something up to her apartment. I did. I did this for a few weeks and never felt so good and so dirty in my whole life. Apparently, word spread through the "bingo club." I had money to eat, and I always knew what time it was. When I said I never sold my body, I was referring to catching, not pitching.

A WORLD OTHERS NEVER SEE

My nights were spent in Forest Park. It was a drug haven and more. On the weekends there were countless thousands of peddlers, buyers, friends, and partiers hanging out in Forest Park, Queens. Deep in the woods there was a place that was aptly called "The Dome." This is because it was both a dome where music was likely played to normal people at various times of the year, but it also marked a central point from where many worlds intersected. People came from hundreds of miles away. There were mobs and masses of people occupying an area the size of a dozen football fields. There were literally thousands of people there on weekend nights. For those living on the streets, every night was a weekend night. But the two nights of the week that the normal world rested became a time of opportunity, just as it is for the fisherman who makes his living from only one or two seasons of the year.

"Hash."

"Reefer."

"'Ludes."

"Mescaline."

"Horse."

"Dust."

These drugs and many more were hawked to any and all who came within earshot. By the time I was living on the streets again a new phenomena was born, and it killed more people in just two years than I had ever seen over the entire span of my life. This new drug killed lives and was a predecessor to the parasitic demands that crack would later place on its slaves, causing incalculable damage to the lives of countless innocent others. Angel dust (PCP) was destroying my entire tribe like a virus.

Angel dust is some fairly-easy-to-make concoction of formaldehyde, mint, and other chemicals. It has been said it is like embalming fluid, or perhaps it was. It came in liquid form and was often transferred at the dealer level in a vanilla extract bottle. One little vanilla extract bottle might cost a thousand dollars. I cannot be sure. What I am sure of is people would buy this and do a shake and bake. They would buy mint or spearmint leaves and a Tupperware bowl with lid, and place a little bit of PCP at a time in the bowl and more and more leaves as they shook it up. They would increasingly cut it with more and more leaves until all the leaves were saturated. Then they would take pinches and place it in little strips of aluminum foil. They in turn were folded like a little letter and held in plastic Ziploc bags. A person could get 500 to 1,000 of these little foils and sell each for ten dollars apiece. The attraction was enormous. The "dust" would then be smoked by the dust-heads in rolling papers like a cigarette. The difference from a cigarette is it stopped the fucking brain—dead. It was literally called "zombie dust" as it made the people immediately and increasingly into zombies. It was the most horrible thing I ever saw sweep through a population, and through the years I had many opportunities to see viruses and diseases of malfeasance and sickness sweep through populations. This shit killed.

The cars would line up for hundreds of meters and sometimes were stacked so far back to Cross Bay Boulevard that the police would have to use the PA system to tell them to pull to the side so they could enter the park and make arrests. The police could never have even dented what was going on without the assistance of the National Guard, and they knew it. Often they would bring in riot trucks and make large, sweeping arrests. Often, no one moved at all unless police activity was directly happening to them. We would watch all of this as if it were on TV. It was all oddly detached and surreal. People would be announcing their wares at the same time that just yards away paramedics were attempting to resuscitate someone who had vomit all over their face, but now lacked the respiratory effort to even force that product up any longer. People died there every night in corners, on park benches, in parked cars, and on the way to the hospital. All of this would very often be happening at the same time that arrests, robberies, sex, resuscitation, sirens, fights, catfights, and so forth were taking place. It was truly unlike anything I have ever seen elsewhere.

AN APSARA IN THE ASYLUM

People came to this place representing all parts of New York and the surrounding states. Many drove from as far away as Vermont, Philadelphia, and Baltimore. It was typical for people in neighborhoods throughout the city to collect money and send a few people up to Forest Park to "cop" drugs for all of them. This is how I met Sandra. I was smitten with her. She was, by all accounts, tragically beautiful. She was angelic and that was fitting as she was preparing for her next life when I met her.

She came from Middle Village to buy a bunch of Quaaludes from Frank Nazi. Quaaludes are barbiturates, or downers. The name Nazi was like so many other street names people were given and likely reflected Frank's striking blond Aryan features. Frank was actually a little bit older than I. He was my sister's age, and he knew her and many of the people back in my neighborhood. Everyone was out for himself, but insofar as compassion cost nothing many people looked out for their own, people they knew, and definitely people they wanted to know. In this last instance, it was not uncommon for people to beat the shit out of someone only because of someone else whom they wished to "be in good with."

Therefore, you might never see "it" coming. It was good to know many people, and I was lucky to have so many look out for me. However, as I would see, this created a dangerous reality in which everyone began to think I was something, someone, else. Everyone began to know the name "Razor." No one knew who *he* really was. As time passed, *he* became somewhat of a dangerous person to mess with. *He* was "someone you did not want to fuck with." Often I would hear stories about *him* myself, and I would ask some little probing questions. People that knew me would also listen in silence as I reveled in this. Frank knew who I was and also knew that a reputation, however developed, was critical to survival. Frank was one of the biggest dealers in Forest Park. Frank was also unlikely to make it to adulthood. Yet, like so many of the kids out on the street, Frank was a genuinely sweet and kind heart.

"Ed?" Frank asked me. "You know that chick?"

"No," I said, "but I want to." In fact, it was one of those strange commandments "Thou shalt dwell on thee" and you know not by what thorn you had become lanced.

We were looking at the little blond from Middle Village, the one who bought a bunch of 'ludes for the people back in Brooklyn, the one who waddled slightly, the one who would be meeting Jesus soon.

"What's her name?" I asked. He told me that he does not know her name, but that she came up there often, and he had never seen her take anything back to any other place. I went over and talked with her. In fact, I spent the rest of the night with her.

A new friend of mine, Danny, had a friend, Elvis, who was just sent to Riker's Island. Riker's, by reputation, is among the worst jails on earth. Danny had the key to Elvis' apartment, and as he knew I also had nowhere to live, he invited me to stay with him there. We reasoned if Elvis paid his rent this month and they began evicting in a few more for not paying, we could conceivably stay there for six months. It was to this apartment that Sandra, Danny, and some others returned after our night in Forest Park.

I was struck by something I had not experienced before: I liked her, a lot. I really liked her and thought she was so pretty. I fell in love with her in the first ways my childish mind could comprehend love. She fell in love with me. She would be the first girl that helped me realize that two people may call love by its name, but each may have an entirely different understanding as to what that meant.

Sandra was my first love, and my last for many years. I was Sandra's last love. At that age I held that love was consumption—not mindless and destructive, but consuming in every positive attribute. Love was for me voracious, hungry, play-ful, lustful, and insatiable. I have since learned that love may be perceived in many playful and cleaver guises, but love first and foremost broadcasts itself for no other reason than to broadcast itself, consuming nothing for its need. Perhaps she did love me this way, and this love was just bested by the need to die. I had already seen how the consumption of death trumped all other consumptions of the flesh and heart. Perhaps love, too, was trumped by death? It would take me many years to know the answer to this.

Sandra and I explored many tender places of the flesh. We made love often and regularly. I simply adored her. I came to know what it is like to love someone in reverse, backward. I loved the girl that was her. I loved her childhood pictures. I soured at injustices on which I could not possibly have a vested claim. I was sad for things that made her sad, yesterday and today. Being with Sandra was the first time in my life I lived outside of my flesh, outside of my mind. In Sandra I dis-covered that my mind and heart did not necessarily exist within me only; my heart and mind was palpably coexisting inside of her. We had nomadic lives, and I realized that although she could go home, and frequently did, she was not happy there. I was never able to place it, and never met her father, but she did not want to be there when he was home.

Therefore, we would often go to her house when he was not there. We would shower there, eat, make love in a bed like we were grown-ups, and we would clean all traces of having been there before we left. We sometimes went to my mother's house in Howard Beach in the daytime. Even though I had not lived there in ages, often we would go there when no one was home and put on the air of normalcy. We would shower and play together like grown-ups, and then we would eat and watch television, nap, and make love again. We would likewise erase our traces like time travelers charged with leaving no trace, lest the fragile balance of creation come unglued. At this point, there were two of us on a collision course with destruction. I have often wondered if I was not then, as I would be later, enamored with my own capacity to love. My goodness, what I did not know of the human heart.

I was still with Sandra later that year when Dan and I actually rented our own apartment on Jamaica Avenue and 112th Street. He put that together. He was good like that. It was here that Dan would return late at night after working a shift at Consolidated Edison (ConEd). He got this job because of his father. He was just able to work with a permit, and this was a really good job. Too bad he would lose it. Too bad he lost everything. Danny had a brother. He also worked at ConEd. He lost his job, also. He lost his life, too.

APSARA'S FALL TO EARTH

I came in from the streets at ten or eleven one night. I went to the bathroom. I cannot explain exactly how shocked I was when I opened the door. Had Sandra and Danny been having sex, I could have dealt with that better. What I saw seemed worse to me. Sandra and Danny were shooting up in the bathroom. Now, I know this shit as I used to get paid money from the Horse Heads to boot them up in East New York before I was even twelve years old. I was speechless and closed the door. They came out a few minutes later obviously so high that the "good news" just had to be shared. They were elated and excited. They felt this surprise was fortuitous and now they could share with me their new discovery. I listened as they described for me something they found that could "change the world." They went on to tell me how awesome it was. I had seen it change many worlds. It was heroin.

*   *   *   *

"Drag him outside and put him in the dumpster. There's an extra ten in it for you," the women at the house told us the first time someone dropped dead right in the middle of our booting his arm with horse. It was 1974 and we were going back and forth each night across the border that separated East New York from Howard Beach. They did not pay us as much as they let the people who bought the heroin from them pay us. It was our business, and it was an incentive for their clients to keep coming back. Some dealers may not have wanted this shit near where they were selling but these people had a Fort Knox behind an armored door in an apartment building complete with inner and outer security, escape routes, dogs, and weapons. The police could never have gotten into this place and even if they had there would be no shit in there by the time they did. They had cut outs in the walls, people set up to take their stash and run, and there was always flushing. But across from the apartment was a vacant flat that was used by the druggies.

We rolled his body up in carpet, and the two of us started to carry him to the dumpster. We immediately realized we could not carry him so we started to roll him. We had him aimed the wrong way and we were unrolling him out of the carpet. There were a number of druggies enjoying their high and they just watched us; some of them offered valuable tips. Before we rolled him back up, we decided that we should probably take any money he had, as he would not need it where he was going. We went through his pockets and availed ourselves of the money and trinkets that were his world—lately.

Carrying a fully-grown man on the shoulders of two children may be possible in movies, but it is not in real life. We were taunted every step of the way by debris in the hallway, turns on the stairs, and the simple burden of the weight. In the end he spilled out of the rug and hit the stairs, sliding down to the bottom much the way a slinky toy might navigate the descent, the carpet unfurling like a flag. We again collected him up, gathered our wits, took deep breaths, and got him up and out the door to the dumpster.

From this episode we learned that there was money to be made in OD'ing (overdosing) the dopers. We also knew that we did not want to kill anyone. Was there an exact science to what we were about to do? Who knew? We knew how much got these people off, and we now knew how much got them off the world. We adjusted accordingly and regularly put them to sleep and rifled through their belongings. We never took all their money, as these people would return. We never got caught and did it to countless dozens of people thereafter.

✳   ✳   ✳   ✳

"Fuck you," I said to Danny and Sandra. "Get the fuck out of my face!" I responded to their just-discovered secret. In the end maybe I could have taken a different approach, but I doubt it. They were both going to die anyway. Not that week, but she nearly did by my own hand that night. I was devastated by what they were doing, yes. I was lost that she would do such a secret thing with another, yes. However, there was something more being communicated to me in this act. I went away alone to collect my thoughts and realized that everything between her and I had to be false. It must be. A right foundation between us would have prohibited such a thing from happening. I had already seen so much shit. It was just getting closer and closer.

Two days after this event I came home and found Sandra was at the house. I knew Danny was not screwing her, not then anyway. I fell asleep on the couch. Frank was in the kitchen stoned out of his gourd eating fruit loops with beer. I awoke near midnight and noticed "the key" on the couch. The key went to *my* closet where I kept vast sums of saved money. What caught my mind was not that key was out of my pocket, but something out of place that informed me someone was trying to get it *back into my pocket*. I went right to the closet.

There was money missing, and I was sure of it. Just as sure as Ebenezer Scrooge could tell a stack was light. I was not sure what was missing though, or how much, but I damn sure knew that money was missing. I came out to the living room. Besides Danny, Sandra, Frank, and myself, there were now a few other people. I knew who was a suspect and who was not. In the end, I suspected only Sandra.

"No one is leaving here till I have my fucking money back," I declared.

"I know exactly how much is missing and we are all sitting here till I get it back"

"The bitch got your money" Frank stated flatly. Frank was fucked up in the way that only angel dust can fuck a mind. He was too stoned to be of much use, but there was a powerful conviction in his voice. He simply knew it was her.

After some time, she said she had to leave; I said no. She offered that I could check her if I wanted. This was almost like the "You're a pussy if you don't" dare. She knew I would not check her. She knew I cared for her and was devastated at her unfolding role in my life.

"Done! Follow me to the bathroom," I told her. I should have made her undress right there, but part of me saw her as fragile, and I did not want to embarrass her. I was always a sucker for women but always continued to choose to be a sucker rather than become jaded. I would rather be screwed over each time anew, like I never had been before.

She took her clothes off, and I went through them all. Standing naked before the man that loved her she had her legs slightly parted. Even then I wanted to throw her down and ravish her body. I told her to turn around. I still did not know exactly how much she had stolen from me. With her legs parted I opened her ass cheeks slightly but I never intended on checking here. I braced her with one hand and inserted three fingers in her vagina at once. It was swift, sure, and unprepared by me. I just did it. She protested with her body by recoiling. I hit something solid.

I looked at my fingers, and they had pink goo on them. Apparently, she had wrapped the money in pink tissues. *What an absurd notion*, I considered.

"Oh, please, Ed. Please! Don't tell Danny!"

"What?" Are you out of your fucking mind?" I inquired. I could not have been kicked any lower in my young life. I was in a world of madness, drugs, violence, and crime, but at the time it was the only world I had, and the one sweet thing in it had now completely unraveled.

I am still not sure if she was fucking him or not, but it is the other pathology that exists between people that use drugs. Her pleading may have been no more than her not wanting him thinking she was "cheating" him—on drugs. How disgusting.

The obvious did scream at me. Yeah, she was screwing him. Later in life I would again miss similar signposts. I told her I would not tell Danny that she stole the money. However, she had some stuff of mine in her house that I wanted as I knew we were as over as over could be. I had to get my stuff back; much of it was gold. If I let her out of my sight, knowing she was doing drugs, I was sure I would never see my stuff or her again. I told her I would not tell Danny. She removed the money. I was immediately struck by the width of the fold that was in her. *Christ*, I thought. *If she could fit that fucking thing in her and I was having sex with her, no wonder she was shooting dope and fucking other people.* There was no way I could match the girth of this wad of twenties. There must have been three or four thousand dollars in twenties. In the end, her genius was measured by the fact that she overlooked a stack of fifty-dollar bills, which may not have felt as good but she sure as hell could have made her ass more useful.

I called a taxi. I was not old enough to drive, but Dan and I spent a great deal of money at the local taxi joint, so they took us wherever we wanted to go, without questions, 24 hours a day. Dan entered the bathroom as Sandra left. Everyone wanted to know what just happened. I winked at Dan and announced, "She's clean." I then told them we were going out. It was 2 AM.

Frank, who had for all intents and purposes ceased to exist, declared "The bitch got the money," and then went back to wherever his mind was lately. Dan had nothing to do with the theft, and I always knew this. He knew I was planning something. It was apparent to all but her. We got in the taxi. It was a surreal ending to the only sweet thing I had known. I would get one reprieve to allow more disgrace to be added to our soiled hearts.

"What are you doing," Sandra yelled at me as I slapped the handcuff on her; the other link was around my wrist.

"The key is back in Jamaica. This is so you cannot bolt on me and screw me over when we get to your house!" We drove the rest of the way to Middle Village in silence. The taxi driver smiled at me in the mirror. He had seen much in his travels with me and knew this was going to be another interesting night. There was little traffic. I looked at the window, and even though I was pissed off I laughed to myself. It really was so absurd. Even in the middle of all this I somehow never lost sight of the fact that there was nothing normal or even real about any of this. I saw other kids huddling in a doorway. It was 2:30 in the morning.

*   *   *   *

I recalled how weeks earlier this same taxi driver had taken Dan, Richie, and myself into the city for some late-night outing. From the front seat I noticed Richie in the mirror going through Dan's pockets and taking money. I did not say anything. I told the driver quietly to take us up to Harlem. When we were dead smack in the middle of one of the worst neighborhoods in New York, the taxi driver stopped and I got out. Dan was still asleep but was now just arousing. I came around the taxi, opened the door and dragged Richie out. Dan and I knew each other too well for him to have to ask any questions. As I proceeded to throw Richie to the ground, Dan joined me as I started beating the shit out of him. Kicking him in the head well after his blood was all over him, Dan asked me what happened. We both continued pounding his head into the concrete while I told Dan what I saw. Dan reached down and took all the money from his pocket.

"You fucking piece of shit," Dan told him, kicking him even harder.

When he stopped guarding himself he had enough. When his skull moved in its orbit freely to the ground, we stopped beating him.

We went through his pockets and then took what money he had, took all his clothes off him, and stood him up.

"The next time you see either one of us, just start running!" I told him.

"The next time you hear our names, you had better just hide." I added.

"If we ever see you again, we will cut your fucking throat, you piece of shit!" Dan told Richie.

I had known Richie all my life from the old neighborhood. We got in the taxi and shouted racial epithets till a crowd gathered around Richie. We drove away. Richie only had a year left to live in any event.

∗   ∗   ∗   ∗

"Just throw the rocks at the window and wake her up," I told Sandra. Her sister was asleep but would do what I asked of her. She loved her sister, but knew also that I loved Sandra. If something very strange was going on, her sister would assume Sandra did something wrong.

"What the hell?" asked her sister. "Oh, Sandra," she lamented. Moments later we were in the taxi with my bag of gold. The key was in my pocket the whole time. I could have let her out right there and been done with the whole thing, but I was not done. We got back to the house and there were still people up in the living room. We came in, and I held up my hand. Her hand followed. Everyone was interested. To her surprise, I took the key from my pocket right in front of her and undid the cuffs as I told everyone what she had done to me. I then told her to get out. She protested that she had no money to get home. How tragic. I gave her fifty cents for a bus. There was no way she could get home for fifty cents, even with a transfer ticket. Perhaps it was this act that led her to her final destination, and not the bus fare.

FOR SALE! PIMPS, PROSTITUTES, AND PORN

Within weeks of this event, Sandra was reported to be turning tricks in lower Manhattan. Danny had started seeing this Puerto Rican girl named Alicia. She was a twisted little nomad herself. They called it Spanish passion. I called it insanity. She was very much like a nasty little whore, and had the mouth and smart-ass chip on her shoulder to prove it. She and I got along fine. The whore part she would prove. In fact, she trusted me so much that when Danny was no longer able to act as her pimp in the evenings on East 14th Street, she had asked if I could collect her money in between tricks! How promising my future looked now.

This is how Danny evolved after his great discovery with dope. There is no doubt that the use of heroin immediately and drastically changed Dan and Sandra's life. In Dan and Sandra's orbit, everyone they knew got pulled in or they slowly developed new orbits. I was aware of this in real time and watched with great interest. He and Sandra did not head out into the blue and cut a rug for themselves on the Bowery, but they both wound up on the same street corner in any event. When Dan told me Alicia had been turning tricks because she wanted to, I was actually surprised. I knew he was seeing her. Alicia and Dan had been seeing each other for quite a while. I knew he went into the city each day to pull his shift—his last and final anchor to a possible future. I did not know he was pimping his girlfriend. I agreed that I would at least come into the city to see what it was all about. I began hanging out in lower Manhattan intermittently.

Though I do not recall her fee schedule exactly, she charged around twenty dollars for a blowjob. She and Dan agreed upon this little dive up the street where the johns would take her if they wanted to fuck her. She charged roughly fifty dollars for that. One day, before Dan went to work, Alicia got her ass chewed out (literally and figuratively) because she let some John fuck her in the ass and did not charge more money. This was rich, I thought. It was hilarious in only the black and empty way that everything else was. It was funny as hell watching Alicia protesting that Dan should not be yelling at her. She had been punished already for her choice as this guy's package was so big she could not sit down.

Up and down East 14th Street the tribe of this land secreted in and out of hallways, alleys, cars, and meat houses. They were as nomadic as any other place I had been, doing the same things to make money. In my case I was selling my soul; in their instance they were selling their asses. In Alicia's case, she was not even selling that. They asserted ownership on select corners and defended such places as if it were their home. They were puking or dead in the cobblestone alleys, in the corners, where the Chinese kitchen attendants emptied the buckets of hot wok water and the refuse collected. The cars, merchants, and socialites passing by would never notice the different pulse of life from these young ones who were not going home, who had no homework, and who had no future.

They collected in little groups, as individuals, and none had the stereotypical black pimp with a purple Cadillac. They moved in and out of the masses of average people going about their daily affairs. They took breaks and went to the coffeehouses for something to eat or drink. All the shop owners knew them, or what they were by their excessive make-up, youth, and provocative clothing—or lack of it. They stood on the corners, by phones, and asked people driving cars that pulled over if they would "Want a date?"

Alicia had just gotten into a car with some john, and I glanced at my watch as Danny instructed me. I noticed the Buick pull up and assumed it was some other trick ending. It was. When the door opened, I first noticed the legs. Sandra's legs were actually out of proportion to the rest of her body, thus she waddled slightly. I never saw this as anything other than adorable. It was Sandra.

"Ed," she said with a fair degree of shock and only the slightest pause as she closed the door absentmindedly. She stepped to curb then shot a quick smile and wave at the man driving away.

"Oh, this is not her first night at all," I realized.

"Hi, Sandra. What the hell are you doing here?"

"Ed," she implored. It was true. I was asking the obvious. But it needed to be asked.

"How are you, Sandra?" I changed the subject.

"I am fine. I am living in the city now," she said.

"Ed? I…" she began.

"Don't!" I stopped her from continuing, but the moment was lost at the sound of a loud screech. The car door opened and a woman stepped out using the flight of her body as leverage to slam the door to the departing car.

"Fuck you, too!" Alicia screamed. "Can you believe this shit?" she asked of no one in particular.

No, I could not believe any of this, I thought.

"Who's this bitch?" Alicia asked with the most caddy voice she could muster, her head cocking toward Sandra.

"Is this…?" Sandra began.

"No," I interrupted. "She is Danny's friend."

I introduced them. There might have been a spark of friendship possible in another world but right now, tonight, Sandra was in Alicia's spot.

"Well, I gotta go," Sandra said. Alicia kept her mouth shut.

"Maybe I'll see you around," I said.

I wanted her still. I did for years to come. Even after her death, I saw her in my mind's eye for the remainder of my life.

"Sandra, maybe I can go with you for a while…I have…"

"Ed!" she sadly interrupted. I had humiliated her with that request but I only wanted to spend time with her. She said good-bye to me and left. I would only see her one more time before she left the world for good. For Sandra, the world was such an unhappy place.

A TIME TO DIE

Sometime afterward Sandra threw herself from the fourth floor of the very building she made her home in after turning tricks with strange men. She had felt like such a failure throughout her life, and she was not even old enough to have failed at anything. However, in death, or apprehending death, she failed. She was crippled and hospitalized for some time.

A year or so later I heard from Sandra. I was still on the streets but had been talking with the Army about joining. I was hanging out with my friend, Rocky. She had met Rocky once before as had her friend, Judy. Judy would be coming with her the night we were to meet. Sandra confided in me she was embarrassed, as she could not walk very well.

We were meeting on Queens Boulevard. I had already rented a room at the Kew Motor Inn, as I flatly wanted to make love to her one more time in this life. I had loved her so deeply. I wanted to make love to my dream. This was not the last time. I was so utterly devastated by what she had done to me, what she had done to herself. My loving her through this time planted the deep-seated notion that all of us have endless possibilities of redemption with each other, and God. I simply loved her. While I would later consider that I had not known love at all with her, love having been more fully defined by later realizations. I loved her then, and she occupied a considerable place in the terrain of my heart for many years.

Rocky and I were looking forward to seeing Judy and Sandra. He wanted to have sex with Judy; it was not more complicated. They had previously met and I guess the charm passed enough between them that this seemed possible. I stared out the window of the taxi looking at the places, stores, and corners along the drive. Many places triggered memories—some good, others bad.

We passed the hospital on the corner of Woodhaven and Queens Boulevard. I was smiled as I recalled being stabbed in the chest (a different incident) on Liberty Avenue. The ambulance had taken me to this hospital and my friends had followed. I remembered the tubes and intravenous lines they placed in me. I was undressed wearing one of those silly smocks. I was ready to leave. The doctor told me that they first had to get some personal information from me and administration was en route now. I rose from the gurney while my friends collected my clothes from beneath, and we all started heading to the door. Dan was holding the IV bag above my head when the security guard told us to stop. We laughed and ran out of the hospital. I was barefoot with my ass free in the wind running down the busiest street in New York with all my medical gear still attached. Returning to someone's apartment, we stapled the IV bag to the wall until the fluid ran its course. I did not belong in a hospital. I belonged with my tribe on the streets.

Anticipating seeing Sandra had me flashback also to the time when we surprised each other—and Judy. I should have had a clue here, but I did not. There was so much I did not know about life then. I knew Sandra's father was not home at that time of the day, and while Sandra did not expect me early, she knew I would be coming to collect her that day. I had never met her father. I entered the house. When I got to the top of the stairs, I heard moaning coming from the bedroom. I proceeded with interest and caution down the hallway. I thought that it was her sister and the boyfriend. I would peek. I thought her sister was cute.

I opened the door and Sandra released her mouth vice grip on Judy's body. Judy did not. Sandra's look of shock made for a hilarious, if not distressing, scene. Since that time, I have occasioned to hear men say such things as, "If she ever cheats on me, I would rather it be with another woman." Well, I have experienced this. Though I have never actually walked in on a lover in bed with another man, I have to agree that it is probably easier to see a lover in bed with another woman. I was not as outraged as I was just surprised. As the male body is no more than a utility truck, I can easily understand the infatuation with the beauty of a woman.

I was not attracted to Judy and certainly could not see myself sleeping with her. But with Sandra I could lie in her flesh for hours like a dog rolling around on a grassy knoll on a summer's day. I would lie caressing her thighs with my young hands watching her eyes roll inside closed lids while I gently touched her. I looked at her now. She was still being "kissed." *Judy must be really into this*, I thought. She did not even know I was standing there.

"Ed, please, honey…come here," she extended her hand and patted the bed. Judy looked up. There really is a "face" that kids, and women, display when they get caught with their hand, or tongue, in the cookie jar. I sat on the side of the bed, and Judy pulled the covers up around her. Sandra did not. I realized that had she sought to conceal herself from me, I would have been devastated.

"I don't think so, honey." It was really less an announcement on the idea rather on Judy. I just did not want to touch Judy—not like this, not with Sandra. Something was spoiled that day, and I would never have it back. They say a person will eat a shit sandwich if you feed it to them one bite at a time. That was my first bite.

*   *   *   *

The taxi pulled into the motel parking lot on Queens Boulevard.

"Ed?"

"Ed?" Rocky and the taxi driver called to me. My mind was in yesterday. I did not pay the taxi driver as I was on a sort of house account.

"Just call me when you need me."

"Thanks, Johnny," I gratefully told the driver.

"Knock 'em dead for me," he said and drove away. I was about to do just that. Funny thing was he did not know if I were going to meet a woman or cap someone.

I don't recall that we did anything more special than meet for drinks. She was so self-conscious of the metal walking sticks she had to use. They did not go into her armpits. Instead, they came to a brace that fitted just behind the forearms. She had gained some weight but still had the same tender beauty I had always recalled. Her hair was dirty blonde but her eyelashes were dark. She was likely a brunette but I had only ever known her blond. It never mattered to me a bit. Sandra's skin was soft and tender. It was without blemish. She had full C-cup breasts, and her nipples always pointed to that invisible place where the ceiling met the wall, wherever she was. Her lips were full, and her eyes were piercing dark brown, almost black. The contrast was striking. Our meeting was on many levels.

Rocky and Judy could not really know the depths and secrets of the thoughts and recollections that moved through Sandra and me. I lost something but was not sure what it was. I was missing something but could not describe it. She was once my friend. We talked about little things, and we flirted the whole time. She was desperately trying to find something to hold on to. I was not enchanted. I was painfully aware that something was absent. I could not describe it, and still cannot. There is simply a place where the essence that is love flees us, past a point. I do not know that it returns. I have never had it return, and have only seen it flee twice from me. We went to the room for some beers. Rocky and Judy were getting along well enough—well enough that they knew the other bed was for them. No matter what surprises were in store for everyone, we all knew that we were going to have sex. It really did not matter that it was in the same room. We were not adults. Having each a room is the wherewithal of grown men and women.

There is a moment just past the hesitation where nothing else matters in any event, passion having seized reason hostage.

Sandra and I were trying to see…if something…In the end, it escaped both of us—the moment and that which was lost. We had sex. We did not make love. Rocky and Judy were on the other bed and Sandra and I in ours. We made love tenderly at first, searching each other, exploring in body and memory. I am sure now we were both looking and sensing if we had captured the frightened bird that flew the now vacant nest. We had not. The loving turned to raw sex. While those who love may have raw sex, it does not follow that raw sex means love.

Afterward, Sandra had the covers pulled up over her breasts. She stared out the window. Something was dead. Everything was dying. It had not died tonight, but rather a long time ago. She and I interrogated our hearts with our bodies. We did not find the answer we sought. We allowed ourselves to easily cheapen each other even further. For Sandra the stakes were even higher. She lived in constant peril of wanting to disappear, to be transparent, and this night she found her one remaining light in this life still saw through her as did the world; she was transparent.

She took her life immediately following our union.

She was finally successful.

CHAPTER 9

▼

Hell

Hell is the state of absence of awareness of inheritance. Hell is the cyclic world of illusions, which is categorized primarily by the infatuation with the physical world. Hell is the state of forlornness so aptly characterized in the madly penned words of the humble poet who has focused his kaleidoscope of observation on the state which stands in most contrast to the assimilation of inheritance—the undercurrent of the Absolute God woven into the fabric of all matter and energy. We have gleaned hell. We have gleaned heaven. Stricken weary on the fields of the flesh, we have projected with the only conceptual basis we can—and have thus concluded heaven and hell are contiguous to the cycle of life and death. Both are wed to life by the base notions of reward and punishment. Both are separated by diaphanous veil, which has these states separate and yet coexisting right here, right now. To those who have noted, "I am in hell" they are not too far from the mark. Still, others note that this "is heaven" "I am in heaven." These are both notions of analogy and truth.

I had momentarily lost my breadcrumbs in the course of my long, dark night, they, having originally been cast by me to find my way back to the light. I was in a dark land.

"I don't know, Danny. This doesn't sound so smart," I told him. I had no problem ripping off drug dealers, but I did not know this place. We had no reconnaissance. All we had was Danny's shaky assurances. By this point in my life I had made an art out of going out late at night and ripping off the dregs of society. I also rendered them incapable of further conduct and action in their chosen career field. I did not know who had this guy's "back." I had no weapon other than a blade. The whole idea had dumb ass written all over it. It was difficult. It was dangerous. It was madness. We did it.

We left early in the morning to fulfill our mission. Dan knew this park in Alphabet City, Lower Manhattan, where a dealer came from some other part of the city in the morning and sold a shit-load of twenty-five-dollar pieces of heroin to buyers who lined up in the park in the morning. I was not surprised by this time that Dan would know this. We arrived early and saw them collecting in a long line.

"Jeez, there must be a hundred of them," Steve murmured from the place in the corner of the park where we secreted ourselves. The black man came in like any other person walking the early morning streets. We had discussed that we did not want to take him out until he sold the shit, as we did not want the dope. Dan argued the merits of this. We all ignored his protests.

He stood behind a fence where none could actually touch him and passed his wares through a hole in the fence. Were anyone to approach him from the other direction he would have ample time. We watched to see who was watching him. Everyone has someone watching their back in this world of the streets. There is only one occasion where someone would not, and that is when the person in reference is someone you did not want to fuck with. In this case he had no one watching his back. In this case this was someone that no one wanted to fuck with. We missed more than a few clues that morning. We figured we could hit him for at least $25,000 and be in Queens by noon.

It was done. The line had ended, and he was not going to be just hanging around. What we should have done is watch him over a period of days. We were street smart, but barely. We were smart, but not smart enough. We followed him and created the plan as we went. Bad idea. None of us had a gun, and while each of us always talked a lot of shit I knew that when push came to shove I was often the one with the least fear. I would get stuck doing the shit work.

"I'll take him out," I offered when no one else did.

"You two track us on the other side of the street and lead us. Get ahead of us, cross the street at a right angle, and turn into us." I devised.

"Dennis, you cover my back." I itemized duties and responsibilities.

"I'll close the distance behind him and when you guys approach we'll sandwich him between us and I'll stick this in his back." I held up a Bic lighter and a brown paper bag to clarify my point.

"What the fuck is that?" Steve asked alarmed; it was black comedy at its finest.

"It's a gun, stupid," I responded.

"What a fucking idiot." Dennis was laughing and shaking his head.

"Guys, it is not important that we have a gun, only that he thinks we do. You guys sandwich him in and pull the cash." I reasoned.

We were off and paid particular attention as to whether or not he made a drop or a handoff. We were also closely watching to see if we were being shadowed. We were so smart. We had no idea how far he was walking so we had to hope we brought it all together correctly, and soon.

We were walking and closing the distance when he turned. This was unfortunate as Steve and Danny had to quicken their pace to just parallel us, let alone lead for the interception. It was maddening, and we were losing time and patience. This was a bad idea and each one of us would later recount how we became increasingly aware that it was. We now had so much invested, had walked so far, that we were taking him out no matter. He had to be stopping soon. We had walked nearly twenty blocks by now. It had to be now. I had to move.

I closed the last remaining distance and stepped up to him in the middle of a traffic interchange. I told him, "If you move, I'll blow your fucking head off," and placed the paper bag to his back with the Bic pressing into his spine. He bolted like the wind. The sandwich never worked. They were not in position. Right there in the busy morning traffic, we took chase. All of us were running down the street as fast as we could chasing a Rastafarian.

We nearly had him when he pivoted right and swung open a door. Thinking he was still fleeing, we ran right in behind him to take him out in whatever shop we had entered. The problem was he was no longer fleeing. He was at his destination. We came to a dead stop, four of us, all white, stacked in a doorway, and listened as the man screamed some words from his exhausted lungs. In the dim morning light of this smoky room we made out the shapes of dozens of the biggest, blackest motherfuckers we had ever seen. Everyone froze. Time stopped. The only sound in the room now was the sound of our breathing. Good thing we had that respite; we were going to need it. Without a command being uttered, we all turned and fled for our lives. Something should have been rehearsed, that is for sure. At least we had plenty of rehearsals in running for our lives.

As the door was closing behind our fleeing asses, a cry rose from the room we abandoned. If a war cry could be articulated in lower New York, it was that morning. We were not even sure where we were, or where we were running. Half way up the block I looked over my shoulder and saw an entire group of dread-lock-wearing brothers in hot pursuit. The screeching of tires informed us all that we only had a short amount of time before these guys would catch and kill us. They had pistols and rifles. It was sheer madness. It was utterly dangerous. We laughed our asses off as we ran calling each other fucking idiots. We had snot running from our noses as they now closed the distance on us. It was so utterly hilarious, so damn dangerous, we laughed as we fled. They were really gaining on us.

I saw a train station on the corner and made for it. I no longer looked back. They were very close by this point, and I could hear their foot falls behind me. We had run four or five blocks, and we were already exhausted from our first pursuit. These were fresh troops. I ran down the steps and jumped the turnstile. I had no idea what happened to anyone else. I did not care at this point. This was clearly an every-man-for-himself moment. The doors to the train were just closing. The train started to move with the familiar sound of cars bumping and pulling before they got to speed. I started running alongside the train and jumped into the space between the cars. I was safe. I looked back out and saw the mob just hitting the platform. The train was moving too fast. Just then it was total darkness. I yanked my head in, just missing the tunnel wall. I was safe.

I walked from car to car and found Danny. He too had gotten aboard somehow. We sat for sometime and said nothing. We looked at each other seriously and burst out laughing. We never talked about it again. Later, in the ugly morning light, we walked along the elevated tracks in Queens toward our apartment. Another night had passed in the life of a nomad on the streets of New York.

THE SIXTH ESCAPE

I was increasingly feeling the urge to flee. I needed to flee all the shit, the crime, the world of druggies, violence, Dan who screwed me over (I never forgot this), and flee the gravitational force of the streets that was claiming many of my friends. This would become a recurring theme in my life. I knew that the life I was leading was insane. It was an empty life, and it was void of any meaning at all. I had previously made a point in my heart that I would leave breadcrumbs to always find my way home to my soul in the dark night of my childhood. I seated prominent and identifiable landmarks in my consciousness and in my convictions that would always redirect me to meaning and a sense of what was meaningful should I become hopelessly lost in life. I was in the dark and once again had the sense that I had to leave or die.

I had more or less always communicated intimately with God, even during these days of my misspent youth. I do not know what means or methods have the divine attuned to a supplicant, but I am convinced that the more imperiled or despondent a life is, the more the fabric of Life Itself hears the lamentation, if for no other reason than to affect the equilibrium of existence by divine laws. God always communicated with me in a way that is indescribable and intimate. I was always informed that "God" does not talk to people, not anymore—or so I have been told by, I guess, the "experts" who affirm that God nevertheless is. Truthfully, in the manner of the prophets, God did not "talk" with me, either. Yet, there is more. I have always just known. I have always been remarkably sheltered, even over the many years and countless miles. God has simply never abandoned me, and each time my circumstances grew most desperate I would be "shaken" to flee, in the middle of the night if necessary. I left.

I got up in the middle of the night and went through all the belongings that were Danny's and mine and took, well, everything of value. I left Danny some money, but I really did not see the need to leave him much. He was always at work and all the hard work of making sure everything did not come unwound was done by me. I was the one who visited the parks, clubbed people in the alleys who had wronged one of my people, made things happen, collected monies, and so on. I was the one who made it all float, and I was sick and tired of this life and the emptiness. I did not know what was out there, but I knew it was not being around drugs, guns, sluts, and bloodshed. I took quite a bit of money, wrapped it in plastic, and buried it in Forest Park. I had done this a number of times already by this point. I took some lesser amount and walked from the park.

I went out and found Rocky that night. Rocky was as Italian as a boy could be and still speak English. He was the middle child of six boys. His mother, Katherine, was a decent and sweet woman. Their home in Ozone Park was always filled with the smell of Italian food simmering. Katherine adored me and was kind and sweet to me. For many years she would take interest in my life and extend to me her kindness and motherly love. I still think of fondly of her these many years later. To some extent I would latter be her last handhold to the recollections of a son imprisoned.

Rocky was a few years older than me. He had a motorcycle that was the envy of everyone wherever he went. He replaced the exhaust with "Kerker headers" (whatever this meant) and this gave his motorcycle a throaty sound that could be heard miles away, especially at night. I had been hanging out with Rocky for some time at one of the parks. He was always selfless to me and to this day would give anything in the world for me. I have never asked. He was like a brother to me, and our closeness was simple and right.

Rocky and I decided to leave New York together that night. He drove me to my sister's house, and in the middle of the night I entered the house while everyone slept and tiptoed to her room (I had long ago ripped the chime from the inner-door). I kneeled beside her bed and placed my head on her pillow. She would not know that I kept my head there beside her for quite some time crying. I just smelled the scents of my childhood, of safety, or the only thing I had known that was permanent. It was not, of course. But right then, for that moment, I dreamed it was. I so loved this girl.

"Marilyn. Marilyn?"

She turned over in surprise. "What are you doing here?" she asked. "Does Mommy know you're home?"

"No. Listen, I am leaving."

"Where are you going?" she asked.

"To Florida again, with Rocky," I told her

She had the look on her face that I would see many times throughout my life. It was both skeptical and alarmed. She knew I was fucked no matter what course I took, and we could only hope that time would eat the demons and leave for me something worthwhile when I was old enough.

"Do you need money?" she asked. I laughed to myself. I told her I did not. It was only a week or so earlier I had seen Marilyn for the first time in many weeks. She was at Forest Park with her perennial boyfriend, Perry. They were out on the Boulevard and Perry was being handcuffed by the law.

SPEED, SURPRISE, AND VIOLENCE OF ACTION

"Eddie, look. Isn't that your sister?" someone asked me. Sure enough, it was. Marilyn and Perry had driven up to buy a nickel bag of pot. There was one guy out there on the street pointing at Perry in front of the cops and they, following his lead, searched Perry and pulled the pot out of his pocket.

I know that cocksucker, I thought. He and his brother were dust-heads and would do anything to anyone for a dollar. A year or so later, they were both thrown in prison for stealing the antique Tiffany windows from the mausoleums of the dead at the cemetery in Ozone Park. The cops were handcuffing Perry on the hood of the car. Six to eight cops surrounded him. There were at least three squad cars. This was a lot of cops for one bust. No, they stayed constantly in large numbers arresting people and calling other cops to "book 'em." This was Forest Park.

Woodhaven Boulevard was huge and wide. At this one place it was three lanes in either directions and was always a deathtrap to cross. It was right at a bend that blinded drivers that Perry was being arrested. I had been whittling and carrying a fairly large piece of oak for some time now. It was at least four feet long. It was firmly seated in my hands as I darted out from across the boulevard toward the cops, and that dirt bag, at a full sprint.

Computer games had nothing on me as I timed every step before I launched. Traffic was processed peripherally as I closed the distance. No one saw me coming until the last second. I waded into the middle of the cops, swept the oak club across the right side of my body, and hit dirt-bag boy right across his center, collapsing him immediately. Using the force of this strike I allowed my body to pivot in place, fully spinning 360 degrees around bringing the club over my head as I turned. I brought the oak club down on his lower spine, snapping it in an audible and grotesque crunch. I was still in forward motion as I turned into my movement to continue. I saw my sister's eyes wide in shock. I saw the policemen absolutely shocked. I saw Perry's face pressed against the hood of the car, smiling. I saw dirt-bag boy sprawled out on the pavement, one of his legs was trembling. I saw all this in a flash and was gone, over the hill, into the woods, and on to Jamaica Avenue, the train station, and my day-long circuitous route back to the same place.

"Do not ever fuck with my sister" was the message. They all got it. They knew Razor did it, but no one knew who Razor was. They never saw him. I had no choice, I had to survive, and I was four feet, eleven inches until I was sixteen years old. I would have died had I taken a different approach to surviving. Every act was cumulative toward perception, reputation, and seasoning. I had to stay alive. This is how I rationalize it now. Maybe there were different choices for me. I did not know them.

I kissed Marilyn good-bye in the dark of night and sneaked back out of the house. Rocky and I pushed the motorcycle a good way down the street before we started it up and quietly drove out of town.

CHAPTER 10

▼

Running on Empty

Sliced asunder right to the bleeding, toiling earth my heart feels to be. It is no wonder part of me looks to the sky of my mind's heavens and bids farewell when another part of me takes flight for the place in the secret space between worlds and dreams. My mind lies in cerebral fields of passing silence as all the work of my mind comes to rest. It is here in the silence, where slips all thoughts, that I take flight.

We drove across the Verrazano Narrows Bridge. I could see the lights of Brooklyn stretching out toward Long Island. On my right were the Twin Towers, the Statue of Liberty, the Empire State Building, and all the lesser monuments of Gotham City. Growing up I could see the Empire State Building from my window. I could not see the rest of the skyline, just the Empire State Building. I stared at it many times for hours at a time and daydreamed about all the people who lived and worked there, what they did, and what they thought. It occupied the entire horizon between the house next door and the apartment building up the street. From the roof, however, I could see all of New York from the Twin Towers to the Chrysler Building.

The Jersey Turnpike was cold, and it started to rain. I found that if I leaned into Rocky, much of the cold passed over me. The engine helped keep us warm.

We were free. We were travelers. The truckers on the road had the same fraternity of unrolling pavement in the endless pursuit of new things, new dreams. We
joined their club tonight. We took a break some hours into our trip at a rest area.
We were soaking wet, and we were cold. We went to the restroom and dried ourselves and our clothes under the electric dryer. When people came in and saw us
in there, we were just sure that they knew we were "on the road," too. We had
something to eat and some coffee. We continued in our endless quest for the
mythical place in Florida where there was some peace to quell the madness. We
were both of the same mind that this life for us was insane and a dead end. However, we had both come to the conclusions much differently.

Rocky had what I would call a better life than I did. He had a mother and
many brothers. He was and felt loved. Though Mario had left Katherine some
years earlier and ran off with Marlene, a Jewish woman from Howard Beach,
John had all the basic plumbing of a typically dysfunctional childhood. He did
not have the profound dysfunction that marked my youth.

Mario was the one we were going to see. John assured us that it would be all
right and that we could stay there for a while, forever if we wanted. John was
right on this point, and we were warmly and openly invited into their home and
their lives.

I do not recall what happened to our money, as there seemed to be so much of
it when I recollect these many years later, but it did pass that we were on our road
trip and had none after a period. John would have to stop and sign some papers
at the tollbooths. We would have to mail it back to them. John never made a
promise in his life he did not keep, to all and any. At this time there were tollbooths all the way to Richmond, Virginia. We had an atlas with which we kept
note of all the stops, the people we met, and the things we did along the way. We
also kept a side bar note of all the little fees we owed or money people loaned or
gave us. We would later repay every dime or otherwise send thank-you notes
from Florida. In northern Virginia we ran dead into southern America; we
crossed into Dixie.

We were so cold and tired. It seemed the miles were running through the tires
and into our very bones. Often I would have to smack Rocky as I saw us drifting
off the road. I did not drive the motorcycle, though I could have. I did not have a
license and was too small in any event to safely carry both of us and our bags on
such a large bike. Riding on the back of a motorcycle does not take a lot of brains.
All you really had to do was hold on and keep your legs out of the tire spokes—
and off the pavement. However, we were not regular motorcyclists. Ours was a
weapon, a tool; our motorcycle (that is how we thought of it, though it was

Rocky's) was an expression. We had to live in symbiosis with it. We leaned into the turns with it. We cared for it like a child. We had used it as a means of egress on the mean streets of New York, and now we were taking it out for a much-needed break as well. The bike was tired, too. We decided to pull over.

The road seemed to stretch on forever. Though I had previously made this trip, it was much different when you were inches off the ground, watching the world pass by with a dual-turbocharged, Kawasaki 750 between you and the asphalt. The trip also felt brand new now that I was sharing it with someone. The only place we could find to stop was agreed upon by Rocky quickly pointing up ahead with his left hand and my returning a thumbs-up in front of his drop visor. It was an overpass. We exited our sleek craft and proceeded to stretch out. Anyone who has ever watched people stretch when they exit a motorcycle notices that they walk as if they have a can of tuna in their ass—a number 10 can of tuna. This is because it feels as if you have a can of tuna in your ass. We paced about under the bridge as we turned to avoid the sheets of water that were cast upon us when cars screamed by us. We moved the bike as far as possible to the diagonal concrete incline under the bridge and sat down to one of the snacks we had.

"I'm freezing my ass off," I told Rocky. Rocky was a man of measured words, and he did not often say idle things, or the irrelevant.

"It's fucking cold," he declared.

We then decided we needed to get some sleep, and we tried to lie as we were and sleep. We could not. We were too cold. We eventually lay on either side of the standing motorcycle and hugged each other beneath the radiating heat of the engine. We were safe from draining water but we could not turn off the road. Still we hugged as we were freezing; the miles of the road replayed over and over in our heads as we drifted lightly in and out of sleep.

SOUTHERN HOSPITALITY

We both noticed the red illumination of taillights at the same time. A car had stopped and was backing up. We rose. A little old man and lady asked if we needed help. We explained we did not.

"Why are you boys out here under the bridge in this cold?" she asked us.

"Ma'am, we are going to Florida to visit my dad," Rocky explained, "but we ran out of money."

"Oh, my," the little old lady declared. The elderly couple consulted each other and then told us they wanted us to follow them off the next exit. They said they wanted to put us up for the night. Rocky and I readily agreed and mounted up. Having had some respite from the cold and the rain, we were more sensitized to it for this short ride and it seemed this next leg sucked the most.

We followed them into the type of backwoods that only northern ignorance would fear, or any one of a million moviegoers who would shout, "Don't go down that road, asshole!" Later in life I would discover this very place and noted it was not at all backward or inbred. We had some healthy skepticism, as New Yorkers are wont to have. However, it seemed truly foreign at the time.

"Hello, Earl," began the little old lady to the motel clerk. "We spoke to Reverend Falwell, and he asks that you put these two nice young boys up for the night, and feed them if that is possible."

"Ma'am, that's not necessary," Rocky protested.

"Nonsense," she continued. "It is the Christian thing to do," she replied. And so it was. The man assigned us a room and asked if one bed would be okay. John and I must have both been thinking of hugging each other under the bridge and just laughed.

"Yes, one bed is fine," we assured him.

John assured the man, the old couple, and anyone else who would have cared to listen that it was our intent to write a check and mail it back as soon as we got to Florida. While they protested that it was not necessary, Rocky and I got an address and as soon as we arrived in Florida we wrote and mailed a check out the very next day. We each took a shower and slept deeply that night. In the early morning there was a knock on the door, and some young woman had brought us home-cooked food. We thanked the man at the desk profusely on the way out. He was not working the night before and had no idea for what we were thanking him. We knew. We continued on.

BUCKBEE

Some hours later we met Buckbee. We were taking a break at a service station and sharing some snack food behind the service area when a young black man pulled up on his motorcycle.

"Nice bike," he began. I let Rocky handle this, as I knew little about bike talk. I would go through my whole life knowing little about many of the things that were important to others. I know nothing about sports. I know nothing about cars, bikes, bands, or other hobbies or outings. I know nothing about camping, rafting, or others pastimes that mark the avocations of our lives. The only two things I would come to know well in my life were God and war.

Rocky explained to Buckbee that we were on a mission, of sorts, to get to Florida from the big city of New York. We were going to visit his dad, Mario. We also informed him we were out of money. He told us to follow him. We followed Buckbee into the 'hood—or what could only be called a rural Virginia 'hood. It was an all-black neighborhood. We were coming from a place and time in New York where racial tensions were fairly high. In fact, neither Rocky nor I had ever really made distinctions based on race, only behavior. Racial relations were drastically worse down south. We did not appreciate this then.

There were little dilapidated homes on both sides of the streets. Rocky and I followed Buckbee slowly. "This must be his home," we agreed. We were aware that this might be a set-up and stayed alert for signs of this. Rocky's bike hummed a forceful throaty roar that could be heard far away. There was nothing subtle about our passing through. Little girls were out front playing jump rope; boys were playing hide-and-seek around the abandoned cars in many of the yards. It was the middle of the workday, and there were many grown men hanging around talking and drinking from bottles in brown bags. On every porch there were people, and they all watched keenly as the two white boys on the loud motorcycle passed slowly.

Buckbee was very proud of his bike. When we stopped at a house that looked very much like all the others, he told us more about himself. He shared with us his dream to save money from working and move up to New York. He said he wanted to go there to get a fresh start. It never ceased to amaze me how people often needed to just be somewhere else, sometimes anywhere else, to have a sense that life was purposeful. He wanted us to follow him so he could go into his house and get us five dollars for gas. That was enough to fill a tank of gas back then. That would get us very far. We were so grateful. We asked him to please give us his address so we could both write and return the money. He said it was not necessary but gave it to us. He also gave us some pot, which I do not think Rocky or I ever smoked. We were not into the whole pothead thing but many were at that time. In fact, we had surprisingly little use of drugs considering what we had been up to lately. Buckbee had us follow him back to Interstate 95 and we never saw him again. He was a good young man and saw in us only two people who were just slightly ahead of where he was in time—between leaving and arriving someplace else. We were exactly where he wanted to be, except he wanted to be going north. We mailed him money as soon as we hit Florida.

EMPTY TANKS AND EMPTY STOMACHS

The weather was much warmer this far south. As we passed through South Carolina, we could smell change. The Carolinas had a smell that was both old and different. Were I in a car with my eyes blindfolded I could tell I was in the south by the smell. The smell is like tar and wood decaying in still water; it is pungent and rude. This very area in the middle of the redneck nowhere south would become my home in later years.

We were running low on fuel, and we were hungry. We had traveled some 300 miles since leaving Buckbee. There was a very expensive car traveling just in front of us. A black man was driving, and he was driving fast. His license plate read: NYC DOC. We assumed that he was a doctor; that he was from New York, and that he might give us some money. We pulled beside him at eighty miles per hour and motioned with our hand to pull over; he did. These days no one would dare pull over.

"We're sorry to pull you over but we are going down to Florida and ran out of money and…" Rocky began. He cut us off.

"How much do you need?" he asked.

"Five dollars," I said.

"How much do you need," he asked again reaching for a fat wallet on the bench seat beside him.

"Maybe ten dollars," Rocky corrected. He opened his fat ass wallet and pulled out a crisp twenty-dollar bill.

"Will this do?"

"Yes, sir. Thank you very much," we added.

"You guys be safe," he commanded and shifted into drive, meaning the conversation was over.

People tend to either forget or never know what an empty stomach feels like or of being able to only see as far ahead in your life as what remaining change in your pocket allowed. I had spent years looking out toward my future with far less, and a stomach so hungry that I was wont to puke just from putting water in it. Twenty dollars would do just fine. With twenty dollars I could see as far as tomorrow.

We often never think of all the experiences and beliefs that conspire to mold us into the person we become, or the charity and ease with which we give back to the world—or not. It never occurred to the doctor from New York to do anything less than help us. It was easy; it was little for him. He genuinely did what he could do with the solicitation that was given him. The people that contribute to the past that is our lives should never be underestimated. This man's simple charity had left an indelible impression on my mind. I am not really sure why he still occupies this space. We continued on and had lunch before entering Georgia.

FOR A BAG OF APPLES AND ETERNITY

We were in southern Georgia and could not have been more than a stone's throw from the Florida border. Our cold-weather clothes were now stowed and tied down. It was nice and warm. We were glad not to be cold anymore. Up to this point we had made really good time and met with a colorful host of characters, but we were not really in a rush. We were enjoying the journey a great deal and spent endless hours talking about the people we were meeting. We would occasionally go into the truck stops and take a shower. These stops were different than the ones that families see when they stop for breaks on their yearly vacation. There really are greasy spoons where waitresses had affairs or crushes on drivers for whom they waited to return. There really are places along the back roads of America where guys named Mel were short order cooks and girls named Flo who never got a break to leave "this armpit" waited tables.

It is in places like this where American tells its stories and the miles turn to words in the recounting. They were places where people knew when you were tired and did not ask a lot of questions. We would go into the truck stops as if we were truckers or walk in with them. We were able to go in the back and take showers. We could also wash our clothes if we had something to change into. They sold pecan logs and pork rinds in bags in these places. There were tacky little novelties for last-minute reminders of Fred's Alligator Park or the Last Log Cabin in Georgia Motel. It was in places like these that we would cautiously approach truck drivers and ask them to please stake us to a meal, because we had no money. On almost every occasion they would consider us, and then lift their arm to call the waitress.

"Janet, get these guys something to eat," one might say. Invariably the waitress would mull us over in her mind, smile, and say, "Sure, Pete. What can I get you guys?"

This is America, and you cannot know America with money; that is not where America is.

We pulled into some gas station in the middle of the vast swamp through which the interstate was now passing. Our gas tank was on bone empty, and we would rather sit and cast our fortunes here than run out of gas on the highway.

The gas station could be seen for many miles away as its lights cast into the dark like the northern lights. There were no other patrons. It was well past midnight. A fine cloud of bugs scattered the low-humming fluorescent light.

The man looked and spoke like Scatman Crothers as he waddled over to our parking space off to the side, his voice melodic but full of bass and warmth. You knew this man never missed a day of church is his life. He was rich, easy, and graceful, and he radiated something wonderful.

"Boys, you been here a while. You gonna get some gas or what?" He had left his little night shed and was sweeping the concrete beneath the well-lighted overhead that covered the gas-pump islands. All else was pitch black and housed the night noises.

"We are on our way to Florida, and we are out of money," began our now well-rehearsed refrain. We were not being deceptive. It is just that we had said this often by this point.

"If you accept Jesus Christ as your personal savior, I will gladly give you a free tank of gas," boomed George Ellis with a smile. It was not a smile that was smug in the confidence that it was a fair bargain he offered; it was more. I had the strangest sense that he was confident he would give us a free tank of gas *and* a free ticket to salvation. There was a powerful conviction in this man that spoke to an unshakable faith. His very presence pierced all my defenses. We introduced ourselves and shook hands. He had a rich, firm handshake. His palms were strong and calloused.

"I will," I declared. I meant it, too. Rocky, and others in my life, were always more tentative in committing to God. I committed to God near every day of my life in the obvious or otherwise unique way in which my mind could conceive. I did this anyway, every single day of my life. Yes, I wanted the gas, but had he suggested something repugnant I would have balked.

George Ellis was giving *me* something, whether it was apparent to others or not. I was aware of this. George Ellis was not coercing my allegiance based on need. George knew we were living in the moment, and he was aware of the lines of the lives that intersected that night beneath the dark Georgia sky.

I was not a victim, ever. I wanted the gas *and* I wanted his power, his grace. I was a man-boy well aware I was fighting in a world of aggression and violence, and only those who have been there can understand that the journey to redemption, and God, has a much more variegated character than some suburban child-man electing to be an altar boy realizes. The dime of right and wrong often landed on the cusp in my world and you had better be quick, intuitive, or dead when choosing.

"Get on your knees, boy," he said with a victorious smile. I was not accustomed to getting on me knees before any man, and somehow the notion of dropping to my knees in front of a black man in the dead of night seemed less than appealing. Since I already spread my ass for others, I could not protest.

I dropped to my knees. I always reserved an unspoken but tacit reverence for those who knew and understood the mystery of God, not necessarily those who professed this. Rocky watched in disbelief as I repeated George's words. He placed his hands on my head, his eyes closed, head looking at the stars—or where they should have been were it not for the neon overhead—and implored after George, "God, take me into Your care and suffer my soul!" I willed, I prayed, I implored in the silent places where only my heartbeat and God heard my pleas to wash away my world.

George Ellis entered the world of legend and memory in this young man's mind on that night. He was a kind and gentle soul, as some souls are easily wont to inform you. He gave us a full tank of gas *and* a bag of apples. He gained the victory of commending another of God's souls in the dank, backwater of Georgia. Whatever George Ellis had accomplished in his life, wherever he is today, he lives in the immortal world of my memory.

ALWAYS A STEP AHEAD OF THE LAW

Thirty miles before we arrived in Pompano Beach, we realized that we were not going to make it. Rocky called and told his dad, Mario, that we were near empty. His father did some calculations and told us which exit to take, and where to wait for him if we ran out of gas. Mario had a mission, and he was up to it.

"What d'ya two doing here?" the possum-pecker cop asked Rocky and I as we sat beside the road in the town of Jupiter.

"We ran out of gas and were waiting on my dad," Rocky told him.

"Yer waiting on your dad, huh?" The fat redneck cop responded suspiciously. He parked the squad car behind the bike, the lights on and siren off. It was likely the only squad car in the town. Mario was dead-on where we would run out of gas, and it was some little shit-bag town with a hard-on for a cop.

"Boy," he looked at me. "You running from the law, son?"

"No, sir," I answered. *Damn, where did this guy come from*, I wondered?

"Hmmm," he pondered thoughtfully. He was not convinced.

"You ever been arrested, boy?" He blurted out after considering he might have a couple of the most wanted in his "neck of the woods."

"No, sir," I lied.

He shot back, and quickly, "Don't lie to me, son!"

I immediately 'fessed up, "Well, only once," I conceded. This cop outsmarted me. Foiled again. I must be an idiot. I knew he was playing me.

Mario blew the horn. Whew, his timing was good.

"What's going on here, officer?" Mario inquired.

"You know these boys?" Buford T. Justice inquired of Mario.

"Hell, yeah! This is my son and nephew," Mario assured him. Mario never met me a day in his life. He knew two things immediately upon his arrival. There was a game afoot and he was in play. He was no fool. In the world of the streets, it is always "us" and "them," wherever you are, and whoever "they" are. Mario had run the streets long before Rocky and I had. Mario then ignored the cop and started greeting us. The cop, like a defeated dog, lost interest in his bone and left.

"Alrighty, then. Don't expect to see you boys back here, hear?" He called as he opened his car door. We continued to take Mario's lead and ignored him.

We all hugged. I felt I had known Mario all my life. He took me immediately into his arms, his heart, and his home. Marlene grabbed me and gave me a big kiss and hug. She had packed a lunch for us as Mario told her we were likely starving. Mario took a fuel container out of the trunk and started refueling us right there on the street. We then convoyed the remaining leg of journey to Ft. Lauderdale.

CHAPTER 11

▼

A Gentle Awakening

When we peer into the corners where bends not the Light of the World, we will not only see that we are inherently capable of discerning these places within ourselves, but are the only ones that can illume them. It is the baggage of the ages that disables us from thinking we have no right to do this ourselves—and thus introspection becomes only a fancy for the idle or dreaming; the intercessors remain employed.

Where was I in time? I cannot say. I do not recall where I was in space. I was lost and drifting through the years. I had no sense of anywhere. I had no sense of life. I was scared, and I was alone. Though I did all I could to put on a face to the world, I was not convinced I could pull it off. I was never able to shake the nagging sense that something was calling to me, something I could not describe, something I could not define

Marilyn and Michele continued on the path that would launch them into college and later happily married lives. They were good girls, and though Michele was favored above all, Marilyn did not do too badly. They both turned out to be fine women. Marilyn has many reservations that my mother did the best she could for me. In fact, Marilyn flatly rejects my notions regarding my childhood. I hold yesterday should be emotionally swept into the dustbin of history, all having done the best they could with what they had available to them. The landmarks that were this earlier time had forever shifted, and there was no going back. The years could never be recaptured.

DREAMS

During this time, deep-seated convictions of wrong and right were formulated. I groomed little dreams that were within the garden of the possible and none were really so outlandish that they could not be attained. I dreamed I would be an Army Green Beret. I always had the overwhelming intuition from the time I was twelve on that I would have born to me little girls. My last dream, the one that I had hoped in its fulfillment would take me through my remaining years, was to find a love that embodied the Love that was so self-evident in my heart and in the private places within me.

I held always that love was the true salvation of all of us. From the time I was a little boy, I sensed that Love was the medium by which we communed with each other and with God. It was this love, this belief that love was a master for whom it was worthy of being slain that led to both immeasurable sadness and utter bliss for me. My ability to apprehend dizzying depths of love was born out of love-less-ness. I held above all of the rest of these dreams one incalculable dream that defied all the rules established by others; I dreamed I would know God fully in this life, in this flesh. Thus, the remainder of my life was marked by remarkable experiences, fulfillment, and spiritual ecstasies, the likes of which words could only fail.

Marilyn holds that I was failed miserably from the day I was born. She and I have repeatedly considered my life and she just cannot hold my convictions. Marilyn was privy to even the moments when I was absent in my family's life, as there was never a time when I did not stay in touch with her, sneak to see her, or call to tell her I loved her. Marilyn holds that my mother failed me, my adopted mothers failed me, the school system failed me, and that life handed me rotten eggs. Marilyn had been the only one who has reflexively loved me unconditionally and cared for me my entire life.

I was still living on the streets in 1983. Rocky and I continued our little trips from time to time. I would just get sick and tired after a period of the violence or the insanity, and I would leave. I sensed then the tripwires inside of me and developed a self-preservation mechanism by which my time on the streets had a set-and-forget trigger. Without really paying attention to the passing of the years,

I was able to extract myself time and time again just as death or arrest stalked my peers. In some strange manner I acquired an uncanny ability to avoid danger and death when it was only probable. I was relying on my internal as I interacted with the external world. This was an unlikely evolutionary leap for survival on the streets.

LIGHT ON THE PATH

I increasingly sought to understand my faith, or what I knew. What did I believe in? What was it that I knew or thought I knew? As I looked to the church that was handed to me, I realized that it was missing something. I looked to the message of other faiths and denominations and found these too lacking. In the end I found what I believed, what I knew, by turning within myself. It was all so obvious to me then. I was keenly aware that the others with whom I ran, lived, loved, and got lost were not themselves interested in finding such answers. It was only much later I learned that the answers are irrelevant; it is always the questions that forge our growth and nurture light.

In the summer of 1983 I came across a little book by Mabel Collins, called *Light on the Path*. This little book would forever change my life. What it served to do was define for me that which I had already experienced directly. My bona fides was that I already held the information communicated by this book to be true. This book was self-evident to me. I formed from the experiences of my own life that which had been stated by in this book. I never had any sense that the contents of this book were the exclusive product of the author. For me, my confirmation that I was not mad was finally grounded. This little book became a companion, the words having become less relevant over the years than the message that the book as a whole contained—that we are all on a journey that is ultimately individual and constantly meaningful. This book is fundamentally the mystic tradition of all great faiths.

This book was a lifeline for me, as I had been trying desperately for years to hang on to the notion that life was beautiful and that love was a sacred gift, an ultimate journey and not a way station. I held these notions by virtue of the lack of these gifts in my life. I held these convictions because I chose to see love and blessings in my life where none existed. Every day of my life I chose to love and see beauty in this world. Every day. *Light on the Path* affirmed my sense of intimate and personal intercourse with this life.

It is probably true that the notion of suffering necessarily rings empty in the homes of the affluent. Hunger, too, is not something that can be experienced by description. Many times people will define such a thing based on a review of their own inventory. So, too, with love may a man call such a thing by one name but have but an inferior comprehension. Those that suffer will embrace easily the warmth of a hearth with a gratuity absent the landlord. One who knows hunger will revel easily in the excess that is most men's leftovers. One who has defined the breadth and depth of Love by its absence can comprehend Love as a blind man listening to a concert from across town. However, this is a choice. It is all a choice.

As the blind often develop much improved hearing, and others experience enhanced sensory improvement when one sense fails, so, too, were my senses— intuitive and other—heightened in the absence of what many take for granted. I see what others missed in my life *and* their own. I was not moved to sainthood or even good behavior often. I was just a boy trying to live and desperately trying not to drown in the world that took every single landmark and institution that I knew. We always have a choice. I had a choice. I choose hope over despair. I chose freedom over chains. I chose love, and I chose God.

THE SEVENTH ESCAPE

I would enter the U.S. Army delayed-entry program in the spring of 1983. Prior to my departure to the Army, I thought it a really good idea to consider well the offer to go to live with my Uncle Dick in Bethel, Maine. The streets were just too uncertain. I had been trying to escape the gravity of the streets my whole life, and now that I was finally within reach of escape velocity I did not want anything to interfere. My whole life had been touch-and-go up till this point.

Uncle Dick owned a country club in Bethel. I had not seen him since I was just a little boy and did not remember him at all. It was only a short time earlier that I told Bill Rasor that the time had long passed when we could be father and son, but there was still time in our lives to be friends. To some extent this must have had some meaning for him as he reached out to me in this way and helped arrange my stay in Maine with his brother. Later in life, Bill increasingly became aware of his own mortality and had further reached out to Marilyn, Michele, and my mother. Though unmarried he joined them for all of their functions and celebrated the passing of the years with them at holidays and such. My mother, in an absurd turn of events, remained unmarried as well, and they passed both their lives in loneliness and aloneness, together and apart.

I met Gretchen in LaGuardia airport. She worked for Uncle Dick and she happened to be returning to Bethel from a business trip. I was immediately struck be how attractive she was. Some women have an innate beauty that both electrifies and provokes the male sense in a highly evolved and dignified manner. Gretchen was this sort of woman: intelligent, early gray hair, and as kind as spring. She would later marry Uncle Dick, and by most accounts it was long overdue. When I met her she worked at the Country Club in some fashion that was both critical and not understood fully by me.

When we arrived at Portsmouth Airport we went to the parking area and retrieved her Volvo for the three-hour trip up north. I had never been this far north before and there were fewer and fewer people. Later in life when I realized how damn cold it got this far north, I would better understand why there were not many people. I do not think it is a strong constitution that makes people stay in the cold. I think it is intelligence that makes people leave. Years later I would have such issues with cold. I could not begin to dream where my life would lead. From the frozen artic winds to the Hindu Kush, I would develop a healthy disdain for the cold.

As we drove Gretchen explained that the little town we were passing was Bryant Pond, and it was the last town in America to get telephones. I wondered who the hell would call them. The land was so green and beautiful. The mountains began to climb in the distance. These were the Blue Mountains. If we drove the remainder of the day, we would have been able to see Mount Katatdin, the highest mountain on the East Coast and of special reverence to the local Indians. The White Mountains in New Hampshire and the Green Mountains of Vermont were all part of the same Northeastern Appalachian chain. They were truly beautiful and ancient. As many men had done from atop a horse, I sat comfortably in Gretchen's Volvo imagining that I was the first explorer to carve my way through these formidable and venerable woods. We arrived.

The town could only be called uneventful. Like many towns that came into being during the early years of settlement it was founded on need. There was an endless supply of timber to be shipped down the Androscoggin River to the coast for processing and resale to eager buyers throughout the colonies. Bethel was quaint, charming, and utterly a postcard of early New England. There were effectively only two streets, and they both converged at the town common. Right beside, around, and embracing the common was the Bethel Inn and Country Club.

The country club was built during the early part of the twentieth century and had seen better years. However, when Dick left his position as an advertising executive of a prestigious Madison Avenue agency, he carved a niche for himself in rural Maine and began a restoration and expansion worthy of his New York Madison Avenue preparation. Dick and Kewe had divorced some many years earlier and had three children: Richard, Missy, and Kerry. They stayed with their mother and grew up in well-to-do Garden City, Long Island. They would not be there while I visited. I had not seen them since I was a child, and I would only see Missy and Richard one other time in my life. I understand that they have since secured "happiness" for themselves. However, I believe the only people who are really "happy" are the people being described, referred to in absentia. Most candid assessments of oneself reveal varying degrees of happiness—and often a profound sadness—in all of us. In fact, many people know others think they are happy but find their own lives completely empty. Contrary to what many people think, everyone else except for them is *not* happy. Life is hard and sucks at times. Happiness is relative.

Dick was doing a favor for his brother. He remembered little Eddie only as a novelty, a name that was part of his larger and less relevant past. Dick was good to me. He accepted me even though he understood I was a troubled young man escaping the ravages of the mean city streets. The inn had numerous rooms and buildings. He could have put me up in any one of them. He could have treated me as a visiting guest, pampering me and making life soft. He did not. Instead, he did the right thing.

The inn was breathtaking and had a warm old lobby where the kindest people in the world work—Bethel-folk. Every one of them was kind and sweet. I think they must put something in the drinking water. I was a skeptical and anxious young man and I was easily unnerved by kindness. I came to learn that people are actually motivated to kindness for no other reason than its own sake.

I was to have one of the worker's rooms in the wing above the kitchen. Every summer there were students who came to work for the season. Many of them came from far away, though all were instate. Some of them had been here each summer through high school. There were some local people who worked here, too. I was assigned to work with and for Peter. Peter was Bethel-folk.

Peter was the groundskeeper and project boy for anything that needed fixing. He had an easygoing personality. When everyone realized I was a Rasor, there was some considerable confusion as to what work I should actually be required to do, or if I was supposed to do any at all. I realized this right away and capitalized on this. I sought early on to be helpful and voluntary, but vague. I was always where I was supposed to be. It was just that I was not always supposed to be where there was shitty work or un-cool things happening. I was careful to respect my new home, and often I would not see Dick for long periods. There was clearly a difference in how I was perceived by my new coworkers, and even if I did nothing, passive or otherwise, to remain aloof of inn drudgery, I would have been seen as different in any event. Most evenings Dick would take dinner in the grand dinning room with Gretchen and often his assistant manager, Ray. They would occasionally have their children with them. On some occasions they would treat a revered guest or other to dinner. In every instance, Mr. Rasor was accorded the very same treatment he lavished on his guests. Most evenings I would be asked to join my uncle for dinner. I would work with the staff and sweat with them, toil with them, and laugh at the silly little things that made up life in Bethel. Then I would go upstairs and shower in the common shower that was just on the staff wing, dress, and come have my friends wait on me. I thought it was great.

Heidi is Gretchen's only child. She was much younger than I was when I visited in 1983 and served also to impress upon me what pearls may be found in oysters. She went from a plump, unattractive little girl who wanted people to play with her to a sophisticated beauty with charm, poise, and grace. She was gorgeous, funny, and intelligent when I saw her again years later. I had dinner with Heidi following my last trip to Afghanistan on the very veranda I had so many years ago. I sometimes wonder if I could have known the future, would I have idled the years waiting for such graces to catch up with me, or do we forever outrun them and only think they may catch up? On the veranda that night, amid the crystal and the silver, the laughter and the smiles, I saw Gretchen noting my marveling at her pride and joy. They were both cut of the same cloth. Uncle Dick was a lucky man.

THE LIFE I WAS *NOT* BORN TO

I came to love Uncle Dick a great deal though the years and the space would keep us apart more than I would have liked. It is only through the lens of the present that I see how very fond of him I grew. I often wonder if he really understands how very much this special place meant to me coming out of years of asphalt and blood.

There was an amazing golf course but I never took the time to learn to play. Golfing both serves as a sport for many men and women and is also a medium for conducting business. I did not play sports, and the profession that I would soon embrace had little need for the medium of socializing. Many of the kids that worked there listened to such music as Def Leppard, or more heavy-metal oriented fare. I was never really into any genre of music and could more easily describe what music I did not like. I was considered cool by many of the kids from the rural backwoods of Maine. I never shared with one of them anything about my life, my real life. I never created another past to adhere to in these situations; I just did not offer any information. I had enough perspective to know that my life was incomprehensible to most.

Throughout the remainder of my life I came to expunge the chapters of my life as soon as they had been lived. Therefore, there is no train of continuous memories or images in my life. My life became a series of disjointed images and impressions, experiences and recollections—all these vignettes are often void of context and details, emotional or otherwise. However, there remained a mounting body of spiritual endeavor that had my whole life simply grazing experience for the sheer benefit of my soul. The only fabric that bound the numerous chapters of my life together was my constant and intimate association with God. Even by this time in my life, my whole life became nothing less than a battle to persevere against the tyrannies of the circumstances of my life.

I passed entire days in my room just relishing the place that was mine. I did not have to fear being attacked while I slept, as I had been on more than one occasion. I did not have to worry about the police, a robber, food, or any unpleasant disturbances. I read and I thought. When I was done thinking I would read. I would break up the days by either catching a ride to the lake house just a mile or two down Route 2, or I would walk. I liked the walk. There was nothing on either side of the country road except an old cemetery. The cemetery was very old, from the early nineteenth century, I presume. I never saw any new tombstones in there, and I would have noticed. I spent a lot of time in the cemetery when either walking to or from the lake house. There was an old wrought-iron gateway that went completely over the entrance like a trellis. The aboveground crypts particularly entranced me. There was always something curious for me in the home-like houses for the dead.

Men, women, and children lived their lives here, worked and laughed, played and cried, and now were entombed for all eternity in the silent bosom of this nowhere little place between Gilead and Bethel. I wondered what their lives were like, if they were happy, what they dreamed, what they prayed for? I looked around wondering if these were the same sights they would have seen when they walked here, when they buried someone they loved in this same place. No, I mused. These were all different trees back then. They did not see the same things but little otherwise had changed in 200 years.

The lake house was rustic and made of logs. There was a wonderful large porch that sat right above the water. Beside the house was a slight descent to the sandy lake where a few rowboats and Sunfish sailboats rested idly, half in and half out of the water. The Sunfish was my favorite. I could take this boat out all by myself. As I never had anyone with whom to play, I was well accustomed to doing things on my own. When the day had escaped, I did not join the other kids in whatever it was that occupied their summer, not really. I escaped always in the moments. There was a constant siren call to me, always, from everywhere. In Bethel, Maine, I was for the first time filtering this solicitation through nature and not distilling it from sirens and trains.

DARE THE HORIZON, HOIST THE SAIL

I would wrap my little book in a plastic bag and shove off searching for some wind as seafarers had done for millennia. I was a sailor. I would confidently tack in the wind, climbing my way across the sleeping water. When I was right in the middle of the lake I would pull the sail tighter and tighter until even the keel was out of the water, and then I would push it a little further to capsize! As the boat sluggishly flipped, as it was not intended to do, I climbed over the side to the bottom, the new deck. I got so good at this technique that I was able to do it without ever getting wet. The tall mast then sank straight down into the murky depths. I would push the removable keel in and make my day bed on the bottom of the boat. It was here I would lie in the midday or weekends when I could take flight from the inn. I am sure I could have just let the sail out and rested in the boat the way others would have, but then I would have drifted. I just naturally cultivated ways that looked at the world differently. I would open my book and read.

After reading some penetrating point I would gently close my book and gaze into the sky, thinking on the author's observation. *The clouds move so quickly here,* I thought. I like the way that the summer rains would sneak across the mountains and roll up the blue. Within minutes, children and men alike would all seek shelter. But this was Maine. The locals knew if you did not like the weather, wait a minute. Everyone sought shelter on a porch or just inside a door here or there. Sure enough, within moments the skies would have belched out their tears and the sun would return. It was always as if the sun had only turned its back for a moment. Realizing again the rains tricked her, the sun would return to set things right.

What was I just thinking? What was I reading? *Ahhh, yes, I recall.* And so it went. I would consider the words of the author and in considering them I learned to track the myriad networks of my own mind. In just considering word upon word, day after day, I mapped the network that was my intruding thoughts and set them in place. I sought to identify not *what* I was thinking, but *how* I was thinking, and how *not* to think. I railed against this in the beginning, presuming that I should be able to think of only one thought, or nothing at all. It was an impossible feat, and after a time I stopped trying not to think rather to consider my thoughts that were extraneous with minimal consideration, and I allowed them to flee as effervescent bubbles in my mind. I came to see that the less I tried in all things of the mind, the easier my control became and less often thoughts intruded.

I was lying on a boat upside-down and often read no more than three or four sentences in an entire afternoon. I stared at the middle of the blue—nothing. I was aware that a cool wind blew, and smiled upon me—nothing. I was building a special place—my place.

A SHIP WITHOUT ANCHOR

I had a crush on Susan. Susan was a baker in the kitchen and was only a year younger than me. A year at that age was not a big difference. But two or three years may have been. As I age I realize that there is a reason that women tend to be more comfortable with older men. Women mature much differently than men. Sometimes men never mature at all.

Susan was a nice girl. I knew many young women in my life, and nearly all of them were worlds apart from the sweet, rural tenderness and naïveté encountered in this town stuck in time. She instructed me on how to chew tobacco and provided me with her own. She showed me how piecrust is made and allowed me to help her make bread. We blended our fingers in the dough as we laughed and played in the great kitchen below my room. She did not listen to the heavy rock that the other kids listened to. Maine women really were independent. I never met anyone who chewed snuff before. There was something sexy about her turning me on to it. Perhaps, it was no more than her independence and confidence. We became friends and nothing more in the many months I had been in Bethel.

Susan rests in my memory as one of the tender fruits of my forest vine. My life was blessed, full of women who revealed to me a tender home in life.

I passed this time prior to joining the military reviewing the minutes of my life and considering what, if anything, I would take with me as I began my new life. I realized that there were some constants in my life that were unshakable, even when all else trembled and shuddered under foot: first, my sister Marilyn was the single greatest love I have ever known in my life, and second, God constantly seeded in my heart. Nothing else was coming with me to the new worlds.

I was not raised in Catholic school, per se. Though I was raised Catholic, it was only an inheritance as all I knew were only nominally so. I was not an altar boy and was not in choir. I was not a zealot and had commanded no righteousness in the conduct of my life worthy of accolades. When I was young I did often call for assistance to the God handed me but there was something more, something constant and demanding. God occupied all of my thoughts. When things were good, I somehow saw something better. When things were bad, I knew, somehow, that it was all for a reason. I had a remarkable and unfounded confidence in something. The sense that I was part of God was powerfully etched in my entire being.

In the autumn of 1983, I packed to leave Bethel. The foliage was turning, and for many, this was the loveliest time of the year. Few can imagine the plethora of colors that nature yields in death. As the summer life gives way to the autumn passing, all the deciduous leaves across the Appalachian Mountains change colors, completing nature's palette. It is breathtaking to consider these myriad colors are all intrinsically contained in the forest green that painted the summer. On command one and all change to reflect a rainbow across the valleys and peaks. This is a time for tourism. This is a time to make ready for the winter. It is a time of change. Change is painted on the earth and reflected in activity. The days are changing. Everyone is looking forward or back. It is a time of change. But the colors, the colors are so beautiful. I only wish everyone could see the colors. I only wish I could see the colors intrinsically all year long. In this manner, my childhood ended.

PART II

▼

From Madness to Mystic

CHAPTER 12

▼

Initiation

Dear God, it is all so obvious! It is all so amazing. Each moment I am further moved by the majesty and mystery of grace and wonder. We are asleep in you. We are all asleep. I want to wake, my Lord. I want to wake. Wake me up. Please wake me up. I feel paralyzed and fret slips another day without, beyond, you. Please, dear God, hear my plea and wake me from this idle slumber in this dream. I know I am dreaming.

Sometimes songs are made especially for us. In some manner that defies us, artists know just how to capture the essence of our longing, our hopes and fears, our broken hearts, and our secret dreams. In this manner, a song—written from an artist's heart and inspired by numerous unseen and un-guessed observations in his own life—speaks directly to us. It is often that we do not even allow inconsistencies in the song to interfere with the preeminence we assign the lyrics and melody. Thus a song can even be written from the point of view of a boy or a girl, man or woman. It makes no difference because we take the song and wrap it around our own application. In our lives we have songs that speak to us and for us. If we could describe ourselves to the entire world, or to the ones we love, we would have them listen to this song, or that one. In truth, though, it is unlikely that any other can possibly know the magic that is conjured within us by "our song;" unless, of course, "our song" is the song of two hearts equally sharing in memory and meaning. In many ways we are singing our song to the world, to our loved ones, to whomever or whatever, through the amplification of our mind. We listen passively and actively will the desired emotion affected.

Many years ago I found such a few such songs that became my "offering" of the mind and heart to my God. They are not the hymns of the churches or the chants of the monks. I was a boy of the modern age. My world was both lost and found, graced and forlorn, year after year. My one constant was my interior vigil for the permanent return of my Beloved. In the moment of my most shocking penetration of the "veil" of my life, and in the day to day labors of struggling in youth and early adulthood, I came to attribute to the apparent and overwhelming sense of God in this world the qualities of Sophia, Woman, and Bride—Wife. I had lost sight of the God of my fathers and "saw" behind him—God.

This actually has less to do with the nature of my childhood and more to do with pubescence and romance. I intuitively did not find and hold the God handed down to me from my ancestors to be valid on any count. I found God boundless and imbued with endless love and warmth. The God I found on inspection did not smite lowly humans and condemn as perdition the frailty of the heart and confused mind. On request and inspection I found no place where God would not search for me and love me, no place where I could ever be tortured and denied. The Gods of my fathers were not. I found God in this world but struggled with periods of profound clarity and utter loss in trying to focus the vision of my heart upon the Prize. I could not manage the constancy. I was not sure why at times I was completely consumed for long periods, and other times I was truly forlorn of a presence. I assumed always that in some manner my behavior triggered the death of my Wife—my Beloved. It must surely have been the condition of my life that would not abide a long stay in God's company. One thing was apparent: others were not soliciting and finding God in the manner and places that I was. God was not pounding on the doors of my neighbors. My neighbors were fast asleep, the locks securely fastened.

When I first heard Natalie Merchant's song, "My Beloved Wife," I did not hear the words of human bereavement. When I listened to this song, I saw myself as a 50-year-old man who still awaited the return of his Beloved Wife, she having died a death of lack of faith. I saw myself as a man who, against all odds, loved that which was unseen and unknowable. I saw myself, through this song, as celebrating and lamenting that life could not be worth living without my Beloved Wife. My childhood mind, still reeling with youth, affixed a value to this song, projecting the angst of losing God in my life.

"She [was] the very best part of me" throughout my life, even in youth I assumed and projected this. Her "suffering" was caused by no less than my wayward wandering from the presence she freely afforded me. In this song I attributed a value that was just breathtaking. With each year that passed, this song remained a valid fixation in my mind's eye. It was her that I married in this life. My Beloved Wife has both been with and absent me. Yet, my life has simply not been worth living if she was not part of it. Were I to ever arrive at the day when I knew most assuredly that my love was gone, then I would have no desire to live any longer. I knew then what rings true now: my Beloved Wife is the *scala caeli* (the ladder of heaven), and my *ratio vita* (the reason for life). She is the means and the destination. In this manner, Natalie Merchant's "My Beloved Wife" and The Righteous Brothers' "Unchained Melody" became my refrain to the song I was hearing within my soul.

I was so fundamentally changed by this time in my life that I was processing experience disjointed from how a "normal" man would. I was processing experience as if I was provided no maturing framework in which to associate stimuli. I was my own context. I was intimately living life but objectively weighing and considering each moment as if in a laboratory. I had been doing this now for nearly ten years. I was initiating my very self into a world that I could barely begin to glean. However, left with no alternative, I had to escape the world that was handed to me.

I was now a young man. I had tenaciously held that there was a better world, a better love than the circumstances of my life provided. I stripped the shelves of my "laboratory" and packed for the future. The only things that accompanied me on my trip were some various notes, incomplete data and findings, and some peculiar odds and ends of special meaning or unknown relevance. My entire world increasingly turned inside out as the border that marked where my flesh ended grew blurry, and my internal became projected externally. I flushed my previous life down the toilet. I was now assertively going out to secure only one end in my life: I would know God. I would continue my battle on whatever fronts I must, but I would attain the Kingdom of God in this lifetime.

CHAPTER 13

▼

A Soldier

I dreamed a dream at the dawn of creation, which was your dream. I sang a song on the still cosmic breeze of promise and incarnation. I sailed through forever on your kiss alone. I rested for a while in this vessel and came to call it home. My world would never be the same again. In waking I saw the trappings that so wrestled the substance from form. I became an aberration of the flesh. I was not that which is produced and desirous of material's aim. I became a note without a song.

It was 1983 and many of the young people in Brooklyn and Queens were still not informed that disco was dead. Young Italian kids stuffed their back pockets with oversized brushes so no hair would ever be untended while peacocking for the affections of the girls who hung out in groups of no less than three. Bell-bottom jeans were the fashion, but only name brands like Jordache were cool. Excess and vanity contrasted with the hippies and shattered ideals of the 1960s and '70s. I represented no less a contrast in my own life. However, my contrast was of violence, delinquency, and unquenchable thirst for the constancy of the God I only intermittently secured. I would eventually gain sanction for the former and permanence with the latter.

I saw beauty where no others were looking. If others were marveling at the world, no one was telling me, or they just weren't talking about it. I had traveled up and down the East Coast by this time in my life a number of times. I had lived in Mississippi and Maine, and had survived many years on the streets. Many children saw varied and different places growing up. It is different, though, when you walk to your destinations, when you stop to talk to people, when you tell them you are hungry, and when you seek shelter from the cold. It is different when you are penniless and outcast. You are often beset by those with even greater needs and deeper loss.

People came in and out of my life but I always took the time to hear each story. It seemed the world was full of heartache. I realized that to the one in pain it seems theirs is the greatest pain in the world. "No other has suffered like me," they all singularly declare in one way or another. There was so much sadness. These times were reflected by my consideration on suffering. I am not convinced people suffered anymore when I was a kid than at any other time. Suffering is an inherent part of our human condition. In the balance, suffering is the single greatest gift I have had. My life could never have been as full, or nearer to complete, were I to have avoided suffering. How could a man truly say he would rather feel joy than pain? Was it not this same suffering that enabled him to define this joy? Pain and joy are twins. Both spring from the same emotion. The dance of these two absorb people through most of their lives; always fleeing from pain, or toward joy. Yet one is worthless without the other. In the turmoil of my suffering I grew disillusioned with the world that was handed to me. In this disillusionment I later rebuilt with only the findings of my heart.

The roads and byways were filled with people climbing out of the 1970s, and those lamenting the 1960s. Nuclear war was still a constant threat, although kids were no longer doing kiss-your-ass-good-bye drills under school desks. I recall these drills with amusement. But the world *was* changing, and in many ways the streets were about to get much worse—which I would have never imagined to be possible—with the introduction of crack cocaine and the brutal rise in unrestrained violence.

THE PAUSE IN THE MADNESS

When I had entered the military in November 1983, I was fleeing a world where there was no end but the grave. I was not a likely candidate for the military as I always had a problem with authority; at least that is what I was always told. What

I came to realize in the ensuing years was that I had a keen understanding of how stupidity masquerades as competence, and I railed against that. There were, regrettably, more stupid people in my life than was good for me. When I say stupid, I am not assaulting an intellectual shortcoming for which people could not possibly be responsible. I am talking about the stupidity that willfully hides insecurity behind vested authority and assertions of competence. This is where stupid people are dangerous. I did not meet many stupid people in the military, and I excelled.

I was quickly tracked for Airborne School and then on to Special Forces training. I scored very high on the entrance and other examinations and was selected for the arduous Special Forces Medical Training. This training is unmatched anywhere in the world, even medical schools. In fact, there were occasionally doctors that would go through the medical training, and many were known to have failed. Out of the sixty-some-odd people who began the long medical-training course that I attended, only six were final graduates. Of these six graduates, I was honor graduate fourteen months or so later.

Special Forces medics are competent in the entire scope of medical practice to include emergency war surgery, general and other anesthesia, advanced cardiac life support, advanced trauma life support, microbiology, dental and veterinarian medicine, obstetrics and gynecology, oncology, and numerous other specialties. It is truly one of the most amazing repositories of knowledge in the world. I earned my Green Beret.

My first assignment was to the U.S. Army 10th Special Forces Group (Airborne). In this capacity I specialized in Strategic Intelligence Collection and Target Analysis (SITCA) in the European theater. This was the height of the cold war with the Soviet Union. This was a time when the President of the United States was preparing for confrontation with the "Evil Empire." President Reagan made clear the threat facing all of us in his famous 1983 radio gaffe: "My fellow Americans, I'm pleased to tell you today that I've signed legislation that will outlaw Russia forever. We begin bombing in five minutes."

Our theater of operations was the Eastern Bloc. One of the components of US plans was "stay behind operations." In this scenario the onslaught of the Soviet machine would rush through the Fulda Gap and bear down on West Germany as armies had done for thousands of years. While the allies fell back to the far side of the Rhine River and blew the bridges to await reinforcements, we were going to dig into the ground and let the Soviet Army pass overhead; thus placing the Forward Edge of the Battle Area (FEBA) to our rear. We would then report on troop activities and conduct various harassment operations as ordered behind enemy lines.

These were days when missions were as equally planned for as they were hoped would never materialize. Our mission planning was for World War III. A typical mission task, might have involved destroying an air defense location in Czechoslovakia, for example. The general thinking was the Soviet advance could not be stopped—not initially. The Soviet doctrine suggested they would rain artillery down ahead of their advancing armies to such an extent that nothing could survive militarily. The need for the allies to gain air superiority was critical, as the allies needed the time the retrograding (withdrawing) allied forces provided to mass troops from abroad and get them into theater. Fast movers and fighter jets would need to pierce Soviet airspace just behind the Iron Curtain—flying interference and support to troopships like the Hercules C-130. Flying on South-North axis, redundant sorties of Special Forces Teams would fly below radar and intermittently "pop-up" to trigger radar, and then drop down again before actually air dropping the teams on one of the many pop-ups. The object here was false insertions.

The effect would be to deny the enemy the exact location of a drop. This would be done with numerous teams, some on the same mission. However, we would never know of other teams unless we were on the same aviation platform, as each target was restricted information, even to each other.

Countless missions were planned for in the Special Forces and all accorded due sensitivity. While it seemed we planned to execute a mission in isolation from others, we were, in reality, to be one of countless supporting players in a global response to the Soviet threat. It was the higher commanders who saw to it that the teams created plans that supported their larger plan.

The aircraft would presumably continue north after infiltrating a team and punch out of Soviet airspace. On the ground the various teams would disable the Soviet air-defense grids through sabotage and laser target designators or beacon operations that guided in precision munitions. In this manner, in theory, the United States would be able to gain air superiority. The teams left on the ground planned for exfiltration through various extraction plans. None of us had any sense that the air force, having survived the infiltration, would ever return and risk a multi-million-dollar plane and pilot on our extraction. We uniformly held the notion that once we were in, we were on our own.

VESTED STATUS DOES NOT OBVIATE REASON

One mission was so absurd that, having come up with the best of all bad plans six months earlier, we were horrified when our new captain thought he could improve upon it. It was already a one-way-ticket mission.

It was a site located in the middle of an open plain. There was only some elevated terrain a few kilometers southeast. The best that we could hope, the closest we could get to this location and remain undetected had us "jumping in" some kilometers away, patrolling to the last remaining cover of the hills, and lasing with lasers to guide in air munitions. In this manner we could assure both accuracy and the survivability of the team. Captain "Hero" wanted to impress his new boss: the major. This has always been a chief problem in the Special Forces, where rank was less relevant than competence. Officers only spent roughly eighteen months on a team and moved on to staff functions. Enlisted soldiers could homestead on a team and stay there until retirement. An officer who was ostensibly in charge could do a lot of damage in eighteen months. In fact, throughout the late 1980s and 1990s this is exactly what happened, and numerous enlisted soldiers fled for the lucrative world of contracting. A group of enlisted men often worked on the same team for decades.

This captain is an example of where stupidity stalks as competence in vested status. Captain Hero planned, and then submitted for our approval, the following: we would have the Agency (CIA) or the Defense Intelligence Agency (DIA) provide us with a police car in accordance with the local design and markings. We would palletize (place on aluminum plate, tie down, and affix with parachutes to accompany the team parachuting in from aircraft) the car with us, and when the light turned green we would then air drop a police car and chase it out of the plane—falling at terminal velocity with a police car complete with lights and sirens! It is not that a plan like this could not possibly work. It is just it is not the first option and revealed television's influence on Captain Hero. The plan *further* called for us to gather our gear, bury it, and all get in the car and drive right up to the gate. He wanted to fill the car with explosives. He never explained how we would conduct a Battle Damage Assessment (BDA), as we would all be dead. While it was never a plan that would have passed muster with anyone in the world, the point is this idiot got all the way to captain, and apparently no one had yet told him he was stupid. He masqueraded as competent. This was the briefing he presented to the staff officers. It was flatly rejected. Incompetence in critical defense, medical, or similar technical fields always irritated me.

The "balloon" never went up and history declares the end of the Cold War in 1989. Most of our time in the 1980s was spent like all armies: preparing for war. In this regard we were appropriately detailed as a high-mountain team, as Eastern Europe was our theater. I learned to ski in Switzerland and climbed some of the highest peaks in Europe, including the glacier, Grossglockner. I was young, and I was parachuting from planes, seeing the world, and on the cutting edge of the best of the best. In a world of peers of unsurpassed professionalism, I can only say I have always sought to emulate those soldiers that were a step ahead of me, and there were many. I was at this time, and for the remainder of my life, standing in the company of the real giants and heroes of America.

My time in the 10th Special Forces Group (Airborne) was marked by immaturity and eagerness to do everything once. I was invincible, patriotic, and always looking forward, never back. I was erasing daily the circumstances of my life and creating a new world that "just arrived." However, I was every moment the sum total of all my experiences, and they molded me in such a way that my internal maturity was by now complete, if we ever really are. I was not only intuiting on a level that could be called irresponsible for a soldier, but was relying on my intuition as a primary source of guidance. Whether it was in the simple conduct of listening to a conversation and sensing deceit or truthfulness, or sensing physical violence where others did not note it pending, my other means of perception grew. I no longer considered narrowly missed run-ins with death and such retrospectively. I was witnessing in the moment my reliance on my internal as more operative than many factual and external tools I used to interrogate threat. By this time in my life my occupation forced to the forefront very practical observations about my internal environment. The world was not the same for me as others.

I spent a total of six plus years in the military and served all of that in Germany, Fort Sam Houston, Texas, Fort Bragg, North Carolina, or Fort Devens, Massachusetts. I dated women. I traveled. I purchased my first car. I was the most healthy I had ever been, and I was not unattractive. By this time in my life I was just short of six feet tall, with dark brown hair, aquiline nose, and piercing near-black eyes. My body was in excellent shape and I was always cut with great definition; I have always been blessed in this regard and retain my "six-pack" still. However, I was never among the biggest or the strongest in any group of which I was a part. I loved the laughter, the fellowship, the camaraderie, and the uniqueness of our set-apart profession. Wherever we went, whatever we did, we were the best in the world. That is a powerful thing.

COMING HOME TO ROOST

By 1988 I had decided to find my biological mother. I had spent many years wanting to know who I was, where I came from, and other questions regarding my origins. Unless one is adopted or an orphan one cannot truly understand the need to discover roots. However, it is true that many have no interest in discovering such information.

The New York State adoption regulations were such that by 1988 the only way I could make contact with my mother was to submit my request to her through some state sponsored system that would seek to match my request with any existing request from my mother. Should both these requests meet in the system the state could in some manner facilitate communication. How utterly preposterous. How ignorant. Protectionists for parent's privacy rights either created this system as a concession to advocates for adoption information access, or by fools on a fool's errand. I would be curious to know the actual success rates for successful unions. The point is the unlikelihood of this process being successful is incredible. Moreover, one would not get positive or negative feedback that a parent had applied to find their offspring. One would only be contacted if there was a positive connection, and this might take years. This is no way to live a life.

The records of adoption are sealed in New York, or were at this time. In my case, however, I was actually given a name and birth certificate, which was later, sealed! I ceased to be as a person and became someone else.

There was no way I was going to eat this crap. That is, after all, what the system is-crap. I compiled all the information I had to date and set in motion a plan. I was then living in Ayer, Massachusetts. All the information I had was very non-specific. I knew that my mother's name was Margaret. I knew that her father drove a truck and had died the year prior in the Boston area. I knew how many brothers and sisters she had and their approximate ages. I had enough.

Spending many hours in the Boston Hall of Vital Records I sought to reconstruct the life I was born to. I began by searching for all deceased persons in 1962. When I had narrowed down the cause of death I then began screening for survivors. After a period I discovered my natural grandfather, aunts and uncles, and my mother.

I was immediately overwhelmed by the enormity of the task. As I was stationed in Massachusetts I was quite fortunate. However, twenty years in the military would not be enough time to reconnoiter all the Irish names in the numerous phone books from Southie to Worchester, from Braintree to Plymouth. There was just no way I could handle this alone. I would need an army to tackle this problem. I built an army.

Realizing that my task would take considerable time, require knowledge of the area and some general information about Irish clans and families I put together a briefing checklist and heading to retirement homes. Each home has a Mister Helper, someone who is abuzz with all that is going on. I made contact with Mister Helper and began my pitch.

"My name is Edward Rasor" I would begin.

"I was born Paul Richard McDonough on November 6th, 1963."

"I was put up for adoption and I am trying to find my mother?" can you help me, I would implore.

When I would tell them this I was always greeted with sympathy, as if I had leprosy or something. It was obvious to me that this liability of birth was seen as a great miscarriage by all I encountered. Everyone I spoke to considered reuniting me with my mother setting right a fracture in time. With deep Irish accents they confided their undying support for my quest. Meetings were called and copies of phone books were disseminated in common rooms across the state. In this manner I enlisted the help of dozens, if not hundreds of people across Massachusetts.

Within a relatively short time my list was narrowed to only a handful of prospects. I continued my own cold calling. I am not sure what series of things were said by my soldiers but my cold calls began something like this:

"Hello" I began.

"My name is Paul Richard McDonough."

"I was born November 6th, 1963."

"I am trying to find my mother" I would conclude, waiting for some response. Mostly, I was able to detect a suspicious pause or redirect and note this on my list. My list had countless lines drawn through names with a smattering of little stars above and to the right of the address.

My dual approach also had me tracking leads through vital records. One of my greatest leads led me to a cemetery just outside of Boston. I located the grave. I was confused. I was sure that this was my mother. The name was Margaret McDonough. Yet there was something wrong with the dates of birth and death. It did not make sense. Just when all seemed lost and a dead lead I navigated the headstones and crypts to the caretaker's house and knocked on the door.

The Irish accent was so thick I could hardly understand what they were saying to me. A young man and older woman invited us into the office. I was no longer trying to find my mother when I met people like this. Now I was trying to be reunited with my clan. They informed me they could not help me with any revealing information about the interred or the contact for the deceased. However, once I hit them with my now standard line they opened the "big book" of names, the ledger of dead.

"Let's see…" his fingers scrolled across the headers deftly navigating the unique code that only the dead and undertakers know.

"Ahhh, here yer are."

"Margaret buried her" he added with great satisfaction. Of course, he also told me the last name. This made no matter to me as I was suspected her last name might be anything should she have married. However, I now had a Margaret buried by a Margaret. The dead woman could not have been my mother. She was just too old. But this new Margaret, she could be my mother. I asked for a last known address.

I was with my friend and team mate, John C. He was fascinated by this whole process as he was adopted as well. John was a nice man whose only anchor in the endless parade of faces and people in and out of my life was his intimate association with these moments. We went to a local bar and asked for a telephone book. We discovered that Margaret lived just up the street. We went and checked out the residence. This could not possibly have yielded any meaningful information but I always armed myself with every extraneous piece of information I could when planning missions. We returned to the bar and called the number.

"Hello."

"Hello, may I please speak with Margaret" I began. There was a long pause. How can such an introduction illicit a pause of suspicion? Well, I think it has to do with no one calling this woman Margaret; everyone called her Rita.

"How can I help you" she asked?

"My name is Paul Richard McDonough. I was born…"

"Oh my God!" she resigned.

I had tears welling up inside my eyes. This, then, was my mother. I had found her. Amid the stink of beer and local morning news in some Boston bar I listened to my mother's heartbeat on a soiled phone.

"Where are you now" she insisted with urgency.

"Well, actually, I am right up the street from you in the bar on the corner" I told her.

"Stay right where you are. I will be there in ten minutes" she directed.

MOTHER?

I hung up the phone and turned to sit. John listened to the whole conversation without interruption. We stared ahead toward the mirror and neither of us said anything for some time. I turned to John as I was turning toward the corner entry off the street corner. The door was open and light was pouring in, bathing the dark woods in a hazy glow.

"Damn" John declared reverently.

"Dude, this could be my mother" I said, stating the obvious. We sat and counted the minutes.

A shadow appeared first followed by a form in the doorway. Without hesitation she walked in. We were the only two patrons in the bar. My breath seized in my lungs before a tear came to my eyes. My exhalation was ruptured as if speed bumps were in my throat. We both stood and John stepped behind me. The woman walked in and came right over to me, not John.

"Oh my God" she declared.

"You look just like your father," she added. She was now crying. She looked older then I would have thought. She was also short and fairly pudgy. But I looked at her and thought this must be my mother. She reached out to me and brought me into her arms deeply and warmly. I felt home. I was for the first time in my life being loved for the boy that was born into this world. Long before I was a breath of life in this world I was known to few, and was known again.

"You thought…" she began with flattered laughter.

"Oh no, honey. I am your great aunt Rita" she explained. I knew my natural mother was young but apparently everyone in the family tree was young. She explained:

"I was married and living at Camp Lejune, North Carolina. When your mother was pregnant with you she was sent to live with me until she came to term. After she started to show she took a bus north to New York where [you] were born."

In fact, she told me, no one else in the entire family even knew for sure I was born. Most knew something was going on but only my grandmother and Rita knew the details. Out of all the people in the world I may have narrowed down and inquired of Rita was the only that knew I was ever born, or so that is what this family thought. My grandmother insisted my mother get rid of me. Of course, my mother did not want to and she stayed with me as long as possible in the hospital.

I eventually turned the conversation to the obvious issue, finding my mother. She told me she was not exactly sure where my mother lived but supposed it was in New Hampshire. She advised that she could not contact my grandmother, as there had been a rift in the family some years earlier and they just did not talk. She advised that she could ask the family priest to intervene and act as an intermediary. I agreed. We set up the meeting with the priest for the following day.

Later that night I was reviewing my short list of possible positive contacts. I had by now collected nearly all the information from the various homes in the area and had my list narrowed down to three highly likely contacts. I needed to priest to perform.

I met with Rita and the priest the following day. It was one day prior to Thanksgiving, 1988. The priest would make contact with the grandmother and try and facilitate getting information about my mother, or information about me to my mother. I was impressed, but only mostly. The priest felt this was a decidedly sensitive issue as the family was very private. He thought this needed to be handled with great finesse. I agreed but long ago decided I will no longer live for others. I wanted my own life, my grandmother already had hers. I would not allow her to interfere in my life again. I decided to call a bluff to let the priest know I was very serious about not letting anyone get in my way.

"Very good, Father. I will wait twenty four hours for your return call but Father, if you do not return a positive call to me within twenty four hours I will call on the house on Galvin Boulevard myself!" I flatly told him. It was a gamble but I had to take it.

The priest paused. His pause told me I got it right. This contact was a number that I had called some weeks earlier. Something about the call informed me that someone at this number was alarmed.

"Please son, just give me the twenty four hours" he asked of me. I gave him no more time then what I told him he was permitted. By this point I was not grateful, I was determined.

Twenty four hours and one minute later the priest had not called. I picked up the phone.

"Hello" a young girl answered.

"Hi, can I please speak with Margaret" I asked.

"Who?"

"May I please speak with Margie" I corrected.

"Aunt Margie? OK, hold on" the little girl told me. In the background I could hear the little girl calling Aunt Margie. However, another voice intercepted the little girl asking who was on the phone.

"Hello" an older woman answered.

"Listen to me. Do not hang up this phone" I started.

"My name is Paul Richard McDonough. I was born November 6th, 1963. I am trying to find my mother. This is my telephone number" I proceeded to give her my number and repeated it.

"Please have my mother call me" I concluded without ceremony and hung up. Now I waited.

Ring. Ring. Ring. I stared at the phone. I knew this was her. I just knew it. I had such fear well up inside me. I am not sure why I was afraid. I think part of it was the culmination of a life of thinking about her and years of looking for her. This was it. I reached for the phone.

"Hello" the voice was melodic. It was simply like honey poured down my throat. I fell to my knees crying.

"Hello" I answered.

"Oh my baby, where in the world are you?" she asked me.

"I am in the military now. I am living in Ayer."

"You are just across the border from me" she told me. She was crying. We were both working through this in tears. We talked about big things, not little things. Health, wherewithal, marriage or not, siblings, whether or not I still had all my fingers and toes. Just your basic I have missed you for 30 years conversation. The priest failed me. To his credit, I later learned he really did try his best. We made plans to meet the following day in Fremont, New Hampshire.

"Hello. Com'in, com'in. My name is John" greeted the man at the door.

My brand new Mustang GT was parked in the driveway. I was self conscious about my appearance. All my investigations about finding one's parents impressed me with a sense of the parent's fears and concerns as well. I knew that many involved in such reunions had very different ideas of what was expected, or possible. In many cases, children have located parents due to the trying circumstances of their lives and expected support, inclusion, money, love and other things just for turning up at the door. I was also aware that my mother would have her own life and that I contacted her at considerable peril to her fortune and family. My thinking was responsible but also selfish. I wanted something from this life now. However, I was keen that I not give the impression there was anything more I needed from this family than closure and understanding. I was a man with my own life, my own history, my own future and I tended well to this.

John showed me into their late model home in the suburbs of New Hampshire. The house was large and gracious. John invited me into the kitchen for coffee. Margie was not yet home from work and he was glad to have this time to meet me.

"I always told Margie that you would show up one day" John was telling me from the kitchen. I never made it to the kitchen. I was immediately captivated by the framed pictures in the living room.

"That is Becky. She is your youngest sister" John told me from over my shoulder. I was crying silently.

"And those are your sisters Jeannie, Jennifer, and Margie" he pointed through various photos. I was completely surrendered in his care, his warmth, and a security. These people did not know me. This was not my home. Yet, I was home. I was secure. I was crying quietly and with what dignity I could muster. Turning to John, he noticed the well spring on my face and clasped his hand on my shoulder. "Come in for coffee" he suggested with a real warmth and compassion.

SISTERS?

I heard the front door close and keys being placed in some glass dish or the like. John placed both his hands upon the table and sighed. His sigh was not a resignation rather a "get ready son."

He stood and went to the other room. He delicately and politely remained hidden for the remainder of the day. She was beautiful in only the way a thousand years of conjecture could imagine. She had blond hair and piercing black eyes. Her face and deportment radiated a profound grace and ease. She literally reeked of intelligence and poise.

"Oh my…" she closed the distance to me and hugged me. We were both crying madly and gently. Our shirts were wet across the tops with salty tears. Our eyes were swollen. We hugged for a very long time. Every few moments she would push off me and run her entire hands across every inch of my face, chest and head. Her fingers nested in every corner of my chin, cheeks, hairline and ears. She pulled my closer again. I could feel her hands holding me and drinking my body. I was no longer the boy that she held close to her breast; she now negotiated a man in her arms. After a very long time we sat at the table to begin the long over due reunion.

My mother told me I was the spitting image of my father. I heard the front door open.

"That is Jeanne," my mother told me. Our tears were dry by this point but our faces were wounded with the swollen fingerprints of tears.

"Hi Mom," the young woman began as she turned the corner. John, who was reading in the living room, said nothing to her when she walked in.

"What's the matter" she fearfully began, looking first at her mother and then the stranger. The air of emotion was so thick she was immediately swept up in it and began crying. She did not even know whether joy or sadness was in the home this day, only that she was now in the emotional soup. She came beside her mother and was directed to sit. She was now between the two of us at the end of the table. Jeanne's eyes cast nervously from mother to stranger.

"Honey, I have something important to tell you" my mother began.

"Sweetie, mommy was not always the good little girl I told you I was" she continued. Jeanne was aware that she was being told something important but it was apparently taking too much time to spill it out.

"You know how you always said you wished you had a brother when you were growing up?" Jeanne was now looking at me. I was crying.

"Honey, this is your brother" my mother concluded.

Over the course of the next many hours we covered the ground that only imagination I can dare conceive. I cried more that day than in any other day in my life. At one point my mother reached into the top of the living room drawer and retrieved some pictures of a little baby. They were pictures of me in the hospital. She had pictures of her little boy mixed in with the family pictures. Jeanne commented how mom always said that these were pictures of someone she used to know. She also met a woman in the hospital who was also giving their baby up for adoption in 1963. They had remained friends ever since and exchanged cards at Christmas. In this manner I was introduced to my mother, sister, and later my other sisters. Their lives appeared to be a Currier and Ives lithograph to this injured young man. I was happy for them. They asked me about life. No one could believe such a horror and so I never told her any details.

FATHER?

Some years later, on the eve of the Gulf War, I discovered my father. I had narrowed him down to an unpublished number. I was en route to Fort Bragg, North Carolina. I was aware that the national dialogue was full with stories of our troops leaving for the Persian Gulf. I contacted the AT&T operator. I explained that I was trying to reach my father. I gave her the background and told her I was deploying. She told me to hang on the line. She came back and said she had the gentleman on the line, I could go ahead. In this manner I came to know one of the sweetest men I have ever met in my life. Larry Reno was also father to two brothers of mine, Larry and Anthony. My life grew more complete and my integration into the family of life richer still. Why my troubled roads had to take me through the valley of pain I do not know. The richness and love that entered my life through the union of my extended family was not complete. I was now completely a part of numerous worlds and relationships. The majesty was breathtaking.

▼

From Student to Teacher

Our mind is a fantastic biological and "other" antenna. We receive information from a multitude of sources, and in various forms. The mind has a number of ways it processes data, but let us be frank: nearly all are asleep in our collective and individual natures. We have almost exclusively come to interrogate both the internal and external with the faculties we use to employ our sense organs. There is a reason Man takes a leap of faith to embrace God. There is a reason that language fails. There is a reason that we play magician with our own internal findings. It is more than we simply do not "know" what we are dealing with. Man has never been able to approximate the veil, within, or nearer to God, and Man has been trying since dreams were dreamed.

Upon finishing my military duty, I decided to pursue an education, which eluded me in youth. Up to this point I had only ever attended school, really, through the sixth grade. However, somewhere along the way, during one of the numerous jaunts from streets to near institutionalization, I was enrolled in a General Equivalency Degree (GED) program to attain my high-school diploma. I was cheated in this endeavor, also, but not due to inherent failure in the program, rather my own first assertion: I thought I had all the answers.

The program in which I was enrolled was designed for street kids, urchins, and so forth. It was an outreach program on the far side of Queens, on Kissena Boulevard. We would have had some place to remain during the day that was individually catered to us. We would be fed and have various activities to keep us off the streets. It was ill conceived, as it was a day program. The first day of attendance the teacher informed us that his previous class would be taking the GED examinations. He wanted each of us to take it as well. He knew we would not pass but felt it would be of great value over the next six months in placement and areas requiring special attention during our preparation. There was no penalty for not passing. We all took the tests with the outgoing class. We got the results later that week. I passed. I was out of the program that day.

In 1990, I was accepted at Adelphi University in Garden City, New York. As I was living with my sister nearby, this was perfect for me. I had previously spent a few months in Florida between leaving the military and coming back to New York. It is amazing what money, responsibility, a car, and legitimacy can do for your sense of ease and perspective on the world. However, I would never allow any of these things to obscure my memory that there is a tremendous amount of pain and suffering in this world. Florida, and in fact, the world, would never appear exactly the same to me again. I visited Mario while in Florida and spent joyful time with his family there. I played on the Miami and Fort Lauderdale social scene while I applied to school in New York.

I was a freshman and as such was surrounded by little boys and girls away from home for the first time. Their interest in college was demonstrably less than mine. Maturity and experience set me apart in all my classes. I received perfect grades from all but my contemporary poetry teacher. I thought she just did not like me. I proved it. I asked her if I might compare and contrast an author over the weekend and have her consider my work, as I was apparently "not getting it." She agreed, and I wrote a contrast and comparison of my own work. When class next met, she eviscerated me in front of the class. She repeatedly told me that this "was not the author's intent."

I went to see the Chair of the English Department who, while sympathetic, felt that my teacher must simply be correct. At this point I informed him that I was the author. After a long pause he shrugged his shoulders, shook his head from left to right, and said, "I'm sorry." I have seen stupidity masquerade as competence in many places.

PRECOGS IN UNIFORM

I did not know in the winter of 1989 that the United States would be launching military operations against Iraq in short order. I also could not have known that I would be going back in the military. On more than one occasion between my active duty periods, I reflected on the strange case of the Asian officer. In the early 1980s, while attending the Special Forces Course, I came upon a group of students taking a break. All were gathered around one of the foreign officers. He was reading palms. I was never much of a believer but readily considered that all things may be possible to those who do believe. After a few palms being read, some friends encouraged the man to read my palm prior to our break ending. The man looked at my palm with all the intensity of a neurosurgeon prior to cutting the last nerve. He looked deep into my eyes, which caused the guys around me to make noises like ghosts. He held my palm within his and shook his head gently from side to side.

"My friend, you must be careful."

"What do you mean, I must be careful?" I asked him. I was in Special Forces training. I needed a little more from him.

"In 1989, you must be very careful." Break was over and people were starting to return to our next gathering place.

"Wait, what happens in 1989?" I demanded.

"You must be careful," he said with resignation. He rose to leave the bleachers.

"Wait! Tell me what happens in 1990." I then tried to answer my obvious question through a back door. "Where do you see me in 1990?"

"You must be careful," was all he would say.

I never saw this man again, not in training, not afterward. There was no mystery in that. I just never saw him again. I never thought about it much until 1989.

Shortly after my separation from the military, Gerry, a medic in a sister company, replaced me on a mission. The helicopter went down and most of the team was killed. Gerry had his back and spine crushed by the fuselage. The captain (not Captain Hero) was spared entirely. Not a thing happened to him. I was informed some many months later my team was reconstituted, minus of course Gerry and the dead. It was felt that the captain and the Army would be better served by the captain "staying in the fight" and carrying on his command. He remained team leader of the Operational Detachment—Alpha (ODA). As I understand, another helicopter went down a short while later, killing all or nearly all the newly fabricated team. The captain was unscathed. I was told he became a "basket case." May God have mercy on all of them, the living and the dead. Following the second crash, I was brought back on active duty. The timelines were shocking but reflected my entire life.

SCHOOL'S OUT—AGAIN

We were discussing Kant and categorical imperatives when the recruiters knocked on the door. Professor Olsen did not even consider the other students that evening. Instead he said, "Ed, I think this is for you." Professor Olsen, Chair of the Philosophy Department, and I got along great. In fact, he got along well with everyone. Professor Olsen was a short, nerdy-looking fellow, prematurely balding, who wore spectacles that surely indicated he was already married, or was not looking. He was wonderful company, though. I believe he was a Buddhist. It makes no matter, as at the time that I was his student I was wrestling with Sartre's existentialism and not the noble truths. The difference between the two would not matter to him and I because the army recruiters were at the door for me.

Thus ended my semester-plus of real education. I had previously accumulated numerous credits through a mechanism called College-Level Examination Program (CLEP). These tests are accredited tests designed to test the proficiency of the individual on the subject matter in reference. Many tests are general such as Humanities, English, and so forth, but many are quite narrow such as Analysis and Interpretation of Literature, Comparative Religions, and the like. We were permitted to take these tests for free in the military. On some days I would take four or five in a row and pass them all. In fact, I passed every one I took by virtue of the time I spent in my little closets. I truly have no sense that anyone in this life has taught me very much, academically. There is not a chip on my shoulder; this is a fact. Everything I ever needed to learn to enable self-learning was taught to me by Mrs. Bibilo in the second grade. I received my New York State Regent's Degree, Magna Cum Laude, in 1998. I spent my entire life skating through the education system while never attending. In adulthood it was no different. Schools simply had little to offer me.

I had come up on a search of those with critical occupational skills. The first Gulf War was on, and they needed Special Forces medics. This was a great opportunity for me to "get into the fight" on behalf of my nation. Patriotism has always had a first and fundamental place in the conduct of my actions in this life. I was placed back on active duty, given unit of choice, and assignment to a High Altitude Parachute Team (HALO). I chose the newly created 3rd Special Forces

Group (Airborne) at Fort Bragg, North Carolina. The path of my remaining life was now set by these events. I have since come to realize that the path of our remaining life is set in place by every action in every moment. It sounds trite and obvious. It is not.

I chose the 3rd Special Forces Group Airborne so that I might get over to the Persian Gulf to join my brothers. Instead, I was sent to Fort Bragg to join a unit that was filling in the support missions for 7th and 3rd Special Forces Group (Airborne) and others while they were overseas in the fight. 3rd Special Forces did have one battalion over in the Middle East; I was not in that one. It was not bad, though. Our primary mission was counter-narcotics, and drug interdiction. We spent much of the time in the continental United States interdicting drugs along the border in the Southwest. In this capacity, we worked with many law-enforcement agencies. We also spent a great deal of time in the Caribbean and "surrounding areas." It was such a demanding job but someone had to do it while the boys were in the desert. Sarcasm intended.

I served on an Operational HALO parachute team. 3rd Special Forces was a fairly new unit, and most of the funding was appropriately earmarked at that time for units in the Gulf. After years of conducting operations in operational units, I was transferred to the John F. Kennedy Special Warfare Center and School at Fort Bragg, North Carolina, where I served out my remaining years as a medical instructor. In this final military capacity, I returned to the world-renowned medical facility that had trained generations of the finest medical minds in the military. At the infamous Goat Lab, I instructed hundreds of students in emergency war surgery, anesthesia, pathology, microbiology, parasitology, nursing, and the various allied fields to enable life support in denied and hostile environments.

For decades the finest medics on earth passed through these doors. If they passed through the gates at graduation, there were no emergency medical technicians (EMTs) or paramedics in the world equal to the competence of a Special Forces medic. In fact, most nurses and doctors throughout the world stand to the rear of a Special Forces medic. After many years operational, I was coming back to teach at my Alma mater. In the end, it would be my sunset. In 1996, I decided to leave the military for good. The sycophants and hangers-on that infect the military were present no less than in other times. There was a disagreeable air in continued service. Besides, my heart called me else where; but I was still not sure where.

In 1996 my sense that I was "learning" *here* and not really much more was as palpable as it was decades earlier. I functioned in the military and went "through the motions." I made friends and had many wonderful and terrifying experiences. I had actually seen more violence and gunplay before ever entering the military. I never had the sense that this was the destination. Some people have a secure sense at one time or another in their life that here or there is just where they are supposed to be. Perhaps my childhood effected my turn inward but I rather think not. I am confident my disposition for the internal allowed my childhood to be bearable. My internal was always the sweetest and most right place in the world for me. I had engendered an occupational craft that would be my sustenance as I set forth to marry my internal to the external world. I was a Green Beret, and I dreamed of only the Kingdom of God.

▼

CHAPTER 15

The Portal Through Love

The Prize is She, for me. She is not in the ecstasy, and not in the intercourse of lovers. She is not in the orgasm; rather She is found in the briefest of moments when, in the throes of love, two meet for the strangest moment in each others eyes and see past themselves into the abyss where they are effused forth from their own receipt of pleasure, of Love. It is in this moment, were we to observe, that poets and romantics alike come to define the whole experience of love. They take this particle of the whole, which is so overwhelming, and paint love thus. In this place, where burn two as one, the shift of worlds takes place—and then is passed. Sex is not an end; it is a means to gaze through the window of our own illusory filters through the synergy, through the alchemy of another. It is in this moment, swept up in rapture, that we taste what moves through me now daily.

Contrary to what most people think, we are not in the world and everyone else in ours. Each life is both a very individual and remarkably interwoven journey at the same time. Each life, each world, each universe is inexorably on its own course of self-discovery and becoming. However, this is not all. For each of us, we

conspire in the grand design to both live out as actors in our own drama and fulfill the stagecraft, the props for others in the unfolding of their drama, their life's
becoming.

Through fabrication it is easy to create the illusion of contiguous years in retrospect. The reality is that I have had entire sections of my life intentionally
excised from history. Not all things in the life of man are worthy of recollection.
Other periods of life, though perhaps worthy, are lessened by the infirmity of the
written word. While there have been numerous horrific chapters of my life that
could never find a footprint within these pages or in my present, there are also
periods that are so sublime that words and even recollections fail. Only impressions remain.

I have had such periods where a subsequent attempt to articulate in thought,
let alone words, fails to impart depth or clarity. Considering I have had such a life
where I have endeavored to reflect on each myriad component, it is rather topical
of me to suggest I have no words to describe "dead time" along the way. The fact
is that some things, some periods in our lives are so loaded with information and
experience that lifetimes, perhaps, are required to assimilate the impact.

THE PEARL OF GREAT PRICE: LOVE INEFFABLE

The period of time from when I left the service to my journeys in Asia and the
Middle East is such an epoch. There are no words to describe the blessings, the
grace, and the witness I bore to life and beauty manifest in my world during this
time. This may seem like an incredible miscarriage of biography to leap over such
a part, but it is the case that the magic and the mystery are just as evident in the
omission as well as the commission of experience. Often the triggers that alert our
epiphanies are not the burning lights or flaming bush; rather they are the peaceful
snow, the prancing dear, or the laughing child. In the tumultuous world that is
our fusion of the internal, the mental, the intellectual, and the spiritual, keys that
unlock and make revealed the previously hidden are sometimes no more apparent
to us than the fire in Plato's cave, the hare in the hole, trembling knees in a kiss,
or the saturated heart in worship. I could no more shout these years to the mountains than I could whisper them to God. These years just were.

BAGHDAD

It was mid-2004, and this was my second trip to Baghdad after a one-week break. I first arrived in early 2004 for a stint on an executive protection (EP) detail following a year in Jakarta training their counter-terrorist teams. These EP missions are akin to a bodyguard in the civilian world except instead of one or two bouncers you have a Marine platoon guarding a pop star. However, these are protection missions in war zones; the stakes are much greater. Baghdad needed protection, and a lot of it. There was not one thing that could be done without protection, armored vehicles, military-type tactics, reasonable skill, and a whole lot of luck. Even the military was hard pressed to conduct Operations Other Than War (OOTW) without a considerable protective services detail (PSD), or whatever name they call it on any given street corner (PSD and EP are often used interchangeably). And so began my second tour in Iraq. I would wind up spending most of 2004 in Baghdad and the surrounding environs.

This trip would be a good one, and an important one. We would be training the very men, Arab and Kurdish men, who would then protect the new Iraqi leadership, including the Prime Minister and his cabinet ministers. This was both important for the rebuilding of Iraq, and once they could protect their own it would give them a renewed sense of national identity. On a deeper and more personal level, this trip would also change me. It was in the crucible of these places where my heart came of age as a matured man. At times in our lives a critical mass of awareness and understanding enables us to view and review all things of our lives with a clarity that had previously escaped us. It was not the events of these days or of my maturity; it was the combination of numerous influences both informing me of immortality, mortality, love, and transcendence that served to crystallize in me the knowledge that there is a place just beyond the horizon of our vision where we are all one. I forever lost any sense of apartness with my entire world. While many grasp this intellectually, it is a difference of scales of perception when at first we experience this and not intellectualize the concept. In this contrast, this cusp between the dreaming light of day and the stark violence of flesh, the last restraint was cast, and my vessel slipped the launch. My internal world completely exited me, and there was no longer any demarcation from the external world.

I was working professionally between dignitary protection in war zones and building counter-terrorism teams through the U.S. State Department's anti-terrorism assistance program in high-threat countries. I was a contractor. I would take a contract for a period of time and then go fishing for an instructional or operational mission as I neared the end of one contract. In this way I rested and worked. By all accounts, there is no rest, not really. It is relative. I am aware that in other places and times, this work is the same thing as a mercenary. Perhaps, but the negative connotations do not apply in this modern age, in general, to the core of Americans that are performing this much-needed work. To a man and woman that I have known, none would take that mission, that work, which was simply for the highest bid. This has been the traditional hallmark of a mercenary: gun for hire to the highest bidder. There is an unspoken adherence to the ethics that are generally inculcated through the U.S. military. In fact, most of us still think in the same mind-set, and would serve alongside, respond to, rescue, or otherwise serve any uniformed or other American asset or interest. They are our brothers, our sisters, our blood. It is no less patriotic. As we are armed and trained to the highest standards in the world, it is a real tender I submit when I declare we serve our nation. However, we are often paid anywhere from $500 to $1,000 per day for our patriotic effort. It is no wonder this salary range is offered, as this work cannot be done for more than the briefest of times. The destruction to the body and mind is tremendous. Constant war is not a career path for former soldiers. It is a window of opportunity to assist our nation and secure financial security and no more.

MISSILE AVOIDANCE

As the plane approached Iraqi airspace, in the aimless wanderings of the mind, I was increasingly inspired to see that there was both a natural and divine law at work in the world. I had been reflecting on this for some years prior to this trip. I long ago surrendered the notion that God was intimately involved in the affairs of mankind. I suppose, though, that the intercessory mechanism is still in play as all my life's prayers were unfailingly answered from the very beginning as a child, or so it now seemed in retrospect. Rather than constant intercession, I suspect that superimposed on the natural world are the divine laws whereby the physical world is but reflections; its laws subordinate. And then atop this all lay our first cause, our Gods by any name.

The plane must have been at 20,000 feet or greater, and below us the sandy tan of the desert stretched out, as it always had, from the coast of ancient Acre to the Hindu Kush. We were in a steep turn, and below I could see the familiar outline of Baghdad International Airport. As the plane began a series of racetrack circles directly above the airport, people began to cry. We were flying Royal

Jordanian Airlines. The G-force was fairly significant, and I reveled in the adrenaline. I secretly took some joy in the passengers throwing up and praying. I did not feel bad about it, either. They had better have a good reason for going here, and if the missile avoidance approach was too much for them, they were likely more fodder for the carnage below. The strain on the Jordanian airliner must have been tremendous; the creaking of the fuselage as it was stretched to the limits of its design was alarming. I was glad, however, to be descending in this fashion as I imagined that getting struck by a surface-to-air missile would result in a much less fashionable entry. Besides, the world looked so beautiful to me these days, especially at 18,000 feet.

*All these worlds…*had been a recurring and intrusive refrain in my mind for over a year now, and I had increasingly come to see that we were all indeed connected in some grand, cosmic drama. The only problem was that everyone behaved as if they were attending a play, rather than acting in one. All these thoughts made sense in some distant way. I had been to Afghanistan and Indonesia following the Twin Towers attack of September 11, 2001, and the August 5, 2003, J.W. Marriott hotel bombing in Jakarta. I spent five months in Afghanistan and nearly a year in Jakarta. It was hard to see any interconnectedness or great plan working itself out when the actors were cleaning body parts and corpses of children off the streets of the world with increasing frequency. But then, maybe this was the absurd side of life. Maybe in some distant enclave, the balance and harmony required to equalize it all was in effect. The plane labored around another racetrack at 13,000 feet. More people were employing Allah. *Likely not*, I thought.

A NEW TEAM

"Ed, get your shit, move your room. We got some of them coming in tomorrow."

"Cool. Who's in?" I asked, rising from my cot.

"Jason, Mark, Tim, and Todd," John revealed.

"Those SOBs?" I laughed with a familiar delight. We started packing our gear to move to the best room in the villa, before the other guys got it.

"I hope they brought me something from the States." They did, and it would not be long before I realized what they had brought. I am not sure they ever knew what they brought over with them.

"When," I asked?

"BIAP [Baghdad International Airport], civilian side, first thing in the morning," John told me. John was always sharp, crisp, and right to the point.

John and I had been working together over a year straight by this time. A British chap, John served his years in the world-renowned SAS. John, Jason, and I were the only three from our previous team, who came straight to Iraq following a year of sometimes-grueling work in Indonesia. In fact, in Indonesia we operated for the longest times with consistently less sleep than any other times in our careers. Indonesia was a true test of what it means to be a man.

The remainder were now returning either from break or first arriving in theater. I was lucky to be with John. Men like John made hard times interesting.

Tim and I had been close friends and working peers for over fifteen years by this time. He was also our frequent team leader. A good man, Tim brought hard-nosed, southern common sense to our many outrageous and nonsensical tactical situations. Moreover, Tim and Jason were the closest male friends I had ever known.

It is often the case that the best-assembled teams are good because of the personalities of the members mixing well. Comedy is a vital component of any team operating for extended periods in austere conditions. Todd was a Godsend in this regard. A Special Operations cop, Todd is truly the funniest and kindest man with whom I have ever worked.

The variation of our collecting team was accented further by Mark and Jason's return. Mark, a former operator in the U.S. Delta Force, was a solid, reliable, and knowledgeable asset to any mission in the world. Jason, a former Air Force combat controller (CCT), added to our ability to approach any problem with an arsenal of backgrounds and experience. All were dear to me. I willingly entrusted my life in the care of these men.

BIAP is actually where we were. It is quite a large area. When someone referred to BIAP, they often meant the passenger terminal itself. In fact, a significant amount of military armor was right here with us, and most of the perimeter was pretty secure, not from mortars, though. In fact, the whole time I was in Iraq I was never convinced there was a counter battery mortar plan.

The following morning John and I each hopped into one of our alarmingly loud-colored United Nations Oil for Food vehicles. They were florescent blue with orange stickers. They were apparently no longer needed by the previous owners, but they were new Toyota Land Cruisers. Fluorescent blue or not, they were pretty good SUVs, though thin-skinned. Thin-skinned is what you never want to be in Baghdad, not entirely anyway. A thin-skinned vehicle has no armor at all. All armor is not so great, either, as you cannot fire from inside the vehicle.

A combination was my preference. The ride around BIAP was pretty safe though, at least to those of us who had been outside the perimeter often. We drove to the airport arrivals side, showed our IDs, cleared the checkpoint, and then proceeded to park and wait for our PAX (passengers).

Watching all the PSDs and other security personnel mill about as they waited for their charges was an interesting opportunity to meet people, catch up on goings-on, and check out other people's gear to see how much *your* employer screwed you. That was a pretty common pastime in Iraq. Equipment was the key to survival. However, I would take a good team over good equipment any day. Baghdad was filled with people who had no business being there, but they looked great with new weapon systems and fancy gear. They were just as much a threat to competent people as to the enemy. In fact, they were more a threat to us because they were less a threat to the enemy.

The passengers started coming out, and within moments we were all hugging and catching up briefly with old friends. Six men, glad to see each other and embracing warmly. John and I began by securing one bag each and were about to make our way to the cars when a woman approached with her hand outstretched and said to me, "You must be Razor." I asked her name and if she was on the mission. "My name is Leigh Ann," she said. "Yes, I am on the mission, too."

IT'S NO WONDER HELEN LAUNCHED THE SHIPS

I was attracted to Leigh Ann from the moment I met her. I am often attracted to pretty women immediately. I would be dishonest if I said otherwise. However, I felt I had known her for a long time, and I had such feelings run through me that I told myself latter that it was love at first sight. I have never had love at first sight. It was a desire that called from some deep reserve. I am not a man who has diffi-culty talking to women or a need to have love at first sight, lest it slip away. How-ever, I was already in love in my life without a focus. I was literally at the point in my life where all that someone could expect to find in a relationship I was receiv-ing in prayer and awareness; almost. I had feelings of great love stir within me daily without there ever needing to be a companion near. I was changing. My life was catching up with my heart. Leigh Ann would become the next sweet love of my life.

I dropped my buddy's bags quickly. An audible thump could be heard as they crashed to the floor, and I reached out for hers. I declared, "Your car is over here." I began to lead her away to the car as I quite unapologetically wanted to be alone with her. I left my buddies to fend for themselves. They should have expected no less from a friend. They stood behind me, mouths open, and watched me walk away. I heard one of them tell another, "What an asshole." Yes, we were friends. They were laughing as they watched me drive away.

I have often considered what notion compels a man or woman to presume that love exists at first sight opposed to the measured presumption that love must otherwise be gradually revealed. In considering such a thing, I do not want to ever have love graduate in my life. I want only to ever be slain by love's surprise. The whole notion of love cannot be properly addressed here but suffice it to say that there is a phenomenon in life that smites men and women when they are least aware and commands them to note that this love, this man or woman, this relationship must surely be divinely inspired and ordained as the reason for being.

There were still not many of us on the ground at this time and we were all staying at the villa at Camp Edinburgh. Camp Edinburgh was at first a wasteland corner in Saddam Hussein's militarized airport area though still on BIAP. The military had all the great palaces, buildings, and other desirable locales already. This place began as an empty slice of land along the back wall that separated us from "Indian Country." We had neighbors, though. Military units were scattered to our left and right flanks. This was reassuring. Camp Edinburgh would grow to become the premier training center for diplomatic protection, and "other."

Some of the finest military talent in the world was gathering at this location to support the larger national policy objective of enabling Iraq to be self-sufficient in matters of security. In the beginning, the hot desert days were occupied with setting up the infrastructure and preparing for the students. Establishing security for this project was imperative. We were vulnerable to any number of threats. Internal and external security was vital. My skills and experience came in handy. I had spent considerable time during my previous time here developing contacts out in the "red zone" for weapons purchases.

GUN-RUNNING

Contrary to what most people think, weapons and ammunition are not provided by the military, nor do they just "appear." Most contracting companies in these war zones cannot import or otherwise bring large-scale munitions in with them. Thus, black market and other means are used to secure the means to protect individuals and the mission. It is no secret. It is a cash-and-carry business. Few people had the local contacts to purchase hundreds of AK-47s, rocket-propelled grenades, launchers, heavy machine guns, sniper rifles, and all the hardware and munitions to support these weapon systems. Few people were willing to be dropped off on a Baghdad street alone or with just one additional person and tens of thousands of dollars in their pockets to do a buy. I was one of the few. I had done crap like this since I was a child.

ANATOMY OF LOVE'S PRETENSE

I had already taken a fondness to Leigh Ann and cared little if others noted my interest, though I was sensitive to the fact that she was the only woman on the mission at the time. I found myself wanting to help her settle in. I presumed that she needed my help. I did not then know that Leigh Ann was actually in Iraq when the bombs started falling. Leigh Ann was ten years younger than me and had been in Indonesia, Pakistan, Iraq, and the West Bank, lived in Syria, North Africa, and a host of other vacation spots. Inquiring minds would ask; I did not. She was a white girl from the South and spoke Arabic fluently. Go figure.

Leigh Ann was actually a strange sight in any location. She could not exactly be called stunningly beautiful but she radiated a profound intelligence, a powerful grace, and poetic charm in all her actions. She was small: four feet eleven (and three-quarters). If you forgot the three-quarters, she would remind you. She had an adorable butt, and I fancied early on it that it would fit perfectly in my resting hands if I were to kiss her. Leigh Ann had penetrating, near-black eyes and the darkest hair to match. She was intriguing and fun, witty, and very intelligent. As someone who would enter the annals of my life as one of my greatest portals in love, she mostly served to inform me that I was not yet dead for the touch of earthly companionship. She was beautiful to me.

Later that first day I sought to collect the telephone numbers of all the new people for my contact list. In reality, I just wanted hers. As the days wore on and we went about the business of setting up the program that was our purpose for being there, we took to the villa roof in the evenings. This is where everyone let their hair down and had some beers. She would later tell me she knew I was fishing for her phone number only. Isn't it like this, though? Women often know so much more about men's behavior than they let on.

Within a week Leigh Ann approached me and asked if I would be interested in a book she had brought with her? Of course, I told her. I would have read Dom DeLuise's *Illustrated Erotic Massage Techniques* had she asked me.

Leigh Ann brought me Paulo Coelho's *Manual of the Warrior Light* and *The Alchemist*. I had never read any of these books and had not heard of the author. I was more than intrigued by the titles. As I lie in my bed reading the *Manual of the Warrior of Light*, I was shocked as so much of what was said in this book was exactly how I thought. Moreover, so much of what I thought was not even mine but a distillation of obvious and universal truths. Having Leigh Ann bring these books to me in this most unlikely of places, unsolicited, excited in me a renewed sense that all life draws to itself that which serves equilibrium. Why had Leigh Ann felt she could share such books with me? We had never spoken of anything other than topical issues. I did not know why she brought these books to me, but it made me think there was a reason and beauty in our meeting. I was right and wrong.

On one early occasion, when the others had retired early, we stayed late watching the mortars and gun-ships pass overhead. It was romantic in a way that only a life like ours could appreciate. I wanted to kiss her badly. I leaned over to kiss her but quickly turned away as if I were passing her by and fell. It was plausible. Later, she turned to me and took me in her arms and kissed me. I was feverish, and my eyes closed. Had I not needed my other foot to stand on I would have raised my heel like Hepburn in a Bogart movie. I have known desire and have had the quickening pulse of a body in mutiny before. With Leigh Ann I saw something else. In Leigh Ann, early on, I saw the possibility to channel my secret notions of love through her flesh, her heart. I wanted to commune with God through this tender flower I found in the unlikely desert of war. I also wanted to remain a man still, though that window was closing.

I knew my mind and knew my heart; it was not often in my life that I had such burgeoning feelings for a woman. In fact, Sandra was the last person in this life with whom I felt this. I was in love with God and still wrestling with how I rationalized my desire for passion and ecstasy of the flesh. I had not previously encountered a person in whom these two worlds collided. I wanted to love God, but I want to ravish Leigh Ann's body and be the focus of her attentions as well. I was so young when I loved Sandra. I was so immature and unaware. In the end, I would learn to love *me*—all of me—further still, and mostly. I am alive. I am man. I responded to the call of my flesh as well as my heart until such a time as I can serve one master only.

Leigh Ann and I had a secret relationship as the mission proceeded to fill up with counter-terrorism and protective-protection specialists—many were friends. In the light of day we text-messaged each other but only occasionally orchestrated a meeting. We called each other frequently even when just rooms away. At night,

I would sneak to her private room, and often we would just hold each other and talk. It was not Leigh Ann who asked this discretion of me; rather I imposed it on her. It was vital to me that no one know; it was vital to her that no one know, other than my closest friends. In such a small place, her reputation would not survive. Leigh Ann had met me at a time when I was meeting the event horizon of my soul. I fell in love with Leigh Ann but in the end it would be both relatively brief and the one of the greatest blessings my life has ever known. Though the vehicle of Leigh Ann, I came to know my heart in relation to desire, women, and God. Through Leigh Ann as channeler of *my* Light, I came to see my own love and capacity revealed. But it was not Leigh Ann. In and of herself, she bore no taper.

CRUCIBLES COMPOUND LOVE

When Leigh Ann was reassigned to the other side of Baghdad to work as an advisor to the Minister of Interior, in the green zone, I gave up my $800-a-day job to take a lesser paying, more dangerous job running operational missions just to be with her in my off time. She had a problem with this. I understand. It is always a dangerous thing when one makes life decisions for another. However, I was well beyond the state where anyone else was responsible for the choices and circumstances of my life. I had taken responsibility for my life decades earlier. I would not let slip what chance had given me to spend what time was allotted us. I had long ago come to hold that that which makes death good is that very thing that makes life good. Consequently, that which makes a life meaningful and valid is that which makes death embraceable in the long night of eternity. I make all my choices—since childhood—with an eye toward dying. I make all my choices since childhood with an eye toward living fully. I told Leigh Ann that were I to have only one day with her in this life, then that one day would have been worth whatever I must do. I loved. I only had, relatively, one day.

We spent the month of July in each other's arms in a little trailer outside Saddam Hussein's presidential palace. There were thousands of anonymous and identical trailers set up row upon row within the secure walls. We would dream, talk, and listen to the gunfights, the mortar attacks, and the car bombs. Throughout the day and night we would hear the air-raid sirens wailing and people hurrying to and fro to find the shelters.

We never left each other's embrace or proximity when time allowed us to be with each other. We were both in agreement that it made no sense to race to death when it could just as easily find us here, resting, in each other's arms. As the enemy mortars were harassing fire and not really coordinated, the trailer was as good a place to die as any. I would rather die in peace than cowering.

LOVE IS A MERE REFLECTION

Leigh Ann was an unwitting instrument of Life's great love for me. Though, when I came to the day when I realized in some distant intuitive land that *we* could not be, I lamented. In this lamenting Love came to me bearing Her naked-ness, and allowed me to undress desire and love further still. I lay beside her on the night when I would see her last and ran my fingers through her hair as she slept. I traced my fingers across the outline of her lips, our skin cells barely touch-ing. In the morning I would be gone. We were on break in Dubai and resting as queen and potentate at the Burj al Arab—the finest hotel on earth. In the morn-ing she would be gone. It was June 27 and the next day the Coalitional Provision Authority would cease to exist. Iraq would be free and sovereign. We would be free. Though each freedom would be unrelated, it was at this nexus our worlds parted. How brief. How wonderfully intense. I had always asserted quality over quantity but the pain is exquisite when forced to live our assertion. It was not spoken. She did not reveal what I otherwise intuited but I was aware at this point of the inexplicable instruments of ending already meddling in our lives. Our stars had crossed each other's orbit.

In the course of life, of the human heart, and in work of this nature, joined roads are impermanent. It is sufficient in our lives to have had the moment of camaraderie, affection, friendship, or even more. It is not the case that these things tend to last when traveling the world, serving the military, or doing the same work post-service. While many have long and successful unions with others, for those of us who work in the most denied and austere environments on earth doing that thing which is not wont to be done by others, the *moment* is precious, not the *promise*. For lack of words, this was the "freedom" of the passing moment, of change. I considered my *moment* in Love's embrace. Born to me was a near ineffable understanding of the reflections of Love. I fully considered my *moment* in love.

I WOULD KNOW THIS THING, THIS LOVE

The sound of loss ripped through my heart that night.

"Does loss really have a sound?" I thought.

Yes, it does, I realized with further elaboration of pain, whose wound was without beginning or end. It is the pain of silent decree that all is not well, that dreams and secret desires remain in the deeper places still thirsting. I listened to the sound of her sleeping heart, my head resting gently upon her chest.

Why, I thought, *can I not let go?* My very insides welled with tears. *What, after all, was I letting go of? Was I supposed to? Was I asked to let go?*

If anyone has ever known this exquisite pain, this utter loneliness in a crowd, they know exactly of what I speak. It is bloodshed for the dying, a song for the bereaved, and it has no other purpose than to inform us of our mortality and frailty. This loss, this pain, is of another world. It is not of the flesh, and does not respond at all to the modalities of amelioration. It is my very essence, my life force, left willingly hemorrhaging upon the unseen fields, slain in battle upon the landscape of another world, alone and forlorn. Quantum love, quantum pain, slaughtered in the neterworld where my senses know not, I bleed and expire in this world today. My heart, my soul, free and detached, wandering upon the far shores, reels from immortal blows. She lay sleeping. I ran my fingers though her hair.

"Who is she?" Why, she was no more than a child, a dream, a song in the still morning of creation—today, yesterday, a thousand years from now. She was why the Sistine Chapel was painted. She was why Troy was sacked. She was no less the wisdom that was Sophia. She was lamenting Isis, proud and beguiled by those that would spirit away her beloved. She stood alert with torch held high, watchful. She collected unto her huddled masses. She lay at night and whispered words of encouragement to kings, potentates, fools, and princes.

"Who is she?" While men penned the great words in ink she penned the greater words in the blood of the ravished heart of the world. Why is she? She is the dawn of creation, the evening star, Venus unblemished, Luna adorned in spectral cosmic jewels. She, born of flesh and sounded in the legion calls of those that brave the unknown, dared the gods and nursed the babes. She is the heartbeat of the Nile and pulse of distant stars. She is an idea. She is a phantom. She is a mystery shrouded in imposed and other enigma. She is tender and small, fragile and weak. She is a woman unborn, a child unknown to herself. She is a dichotomy. She is invincible, proud, and of immeasurable grace. She fought the wars of passion and compassion. She braved the cold and sought the life-giving radiance of the eternal light.

She was, and she is, that which prompted the call to God, the call to dinner, the call to love, the call to grace. She exists at all times and in all places as the nucleus of our collective longing for the clean, the good, the promise, and the hope. She exists in tomorrow, but walks in shadows today. She lay incarnate beside me now—still, alone, and yet of all things.

What is this thing I have done? My breath seized within my chest, and I lost my air.

Who is this creature that sleeps secure beside me now, in my care, in my keep?

I looked upon her tender, resting enchantment and knew with complete certainty that my affection was inexplicable, ineffable in the end. I could not, did not, know what magic, what force of nature's call, secreted her charms unto my heart, into my mind. I thought upon the path that brought us to this day, and of this thing called love. Is it love?

Did I even know love? I thought. I supposed that in the end I did not. I felt like rocking myself to sleep beside her, holding her, empowered by proximity and touch. If it was not love, by what thorn had I become so wounded? I likely considered need as love and desire as my right. I fashioned for myself the Dream itself. I sought to inherit all Love, for all time within my grasp. I dared but see the face of God incarnate in this one. Yes, I do know her, but know not Love. I came to her fountain, cup in outstretched hands, and asked for refreshment. I could not have known that the waters stopped flowing. She, the daughter of creation, of all things, of stars, responded in kind as she had done for millennia. Her refreshment was cool and clear. Though she saw only dust empty from her bounty, I saw eternity and immortality.

She is the heir to forever, but sees not tomorrow. She is born of yesterday, but lives in the now. She is the product of all immediate efforts of others to craft her future, their own. She is the child of rebellion, and of fear. Wounded by a world unable, as it has been in all times, to but drink of her fount, she has retreated to her fortress of solitude. Within those virgin walls she watches a world seek her, but her wellspring runs dry.

"Leigh Ann?" I whisper into her sleeping ear. "Where are you?" She slept. I ran my fingers though her hair. I thought of tomorrow and the few things I have learned about getting there. In the fear, in the luggage that we collect on the way to forever, much of what we carry is another's baggage. None of it can go with us, in any event. The timelines and crossroads that are our lives, when seen with an eye that imagines itself old, can see backwards in time the places in our lives where choices were spent, opportunities lost, and love denied. The choices we make every minute take us upon an endless network of roads and outcomes, lives and destinies.

"Is this what you want?" I asked so quietly, tears now welling in my eyes. I thought that this creature who loves me so would one day think maybe I should have waited, could have waited, and should have known she needed me, wanted me. In the end, with an aged eye looking back over a life spent and choices lost, is this the place where I should have stayed ever so close but not nearer the flame than she would have me? Is this the temperance of the heart more learned? Is this the means for companionship for those like her and me? What is this wretched madness, and why must I needs be enslaved to these thoughts?

"Ed," she murmured in her sleeping place. She knows, still I stand watch. I have always stood watch over her dreams, as righteous men have done for thousands of years beside the sleeping brow of Sophia.

"Baby girl!" I pulled myself to her snugly and considered in the early morning dawn that day that was born to us.

"The best part of us is our choice," she had told me.

"Anyone can fall in love. We choose, in this entire world, to love each other," she informed me. She was right. She advised me that we two share something that few others know or share, but that there *are* others. Now that I am waking, I will find them. I do not want them, I realized I had come lately to see where friendship is so powerful that it is both an enabler and liberator to two who join their horses in the choice that makes them friends. She does love me. She shows me she loves me. She tells me she loves me. Maybe none of us have a clue what being in love is.

I see it on the event horizon of my mind. I see it in the ineffable knowing that this was right, however defined, whatever the end. Love leads me to the fountain but advised me only that the water is not well, not now. I go forward with an idea, a dream, undefined, unquenched, yet infinitely fulfilled by love. Love showers me daily with the companionship I would seek out above all things. Love has slaughtered my flesh and laid waste my garden. Love tends me as her flock and waits till I wander in before closing the gate. Love nurses me in the silence of her bosom, the security of her Compassion. Love holds me in a place where others only peer. Love lances my wounds with entreaty and magic. Love invites my flesh to dine on the fruits that reveal the divine. Love is my friend, and she is my Lover. Love is my teacher, and Love is my student. Love is my muse, and Love is my counsel. She and I have lived this dialectic countless times over thousands of years, in countless forms, sexes, names, and places. I would not allow the luggage of this mortal coil to obscure now and lose the crossroads from which regret springs. Love was incarnate in the resting dreams of Leigh Ann this day.

There is wisdom in Sophia. There is Venus rising in the morning. She moves her lunar mass and has oceans follow her gaze. She navigates the flesh as a scholar, but already retains the history of all things to come in the twinkling of her eye. She labors under the spell that is youth, but holds keys that release others. She is hurt; she is scorned. She is free; she is in chains. She is a demon; she is an angel. She is an end and a conduit. She is everything, and she is nothing at all. She is her, and she is me. I am me, and I am her. In the end, she is no less me than all things in my hand. She knows me. I know her. She gains everything today. She loses everything today. For fear of chains, she wed the blacksmith. For fear of keys, she befriends the locksmith. For fear of unbecoming, she became what she would not be.

In the end, as day broke, she awoke and pulled me to her. She looked into my eyes and told me "not good-bye."

"It does not have to be good-bye."

"My life is enriched having you in this world with or without me," I told her. "I would but know the seasons your life and love takes you."

She looked into my eyes for another thousand years that moment, her eyes searching. They were always searching, but they were not searching me. They were searching her in my eyes. She found nothing there.

"I love you," she told me, and kissed me.

"I know you do, baby girl.

Within my heart, the years collapsed, and all my understanding of love and affection fused into a seamless understanding. My desire to love, to be loved, to know love, and to have love in my life was but a reflection of the intimate intercourse I was having daily with Love in my heart. For years I had been swooning before the entreaty of the Love I found within myself. Now I was trying to marry in the flesh that which I found on inspection within, and I could not. My human season of love instructed me in love immeasurably. I was completely in love with God, and all else became subordinate, finally and fully.

CHAPTER 16

▼

Illumination

Love has instructed me that it is not something that exists when possessed. In fact, love is ascendant when embraced absent reciprocity as requisite. My love is my stalking horse to eternity. My Beloved is a fabrication of my inquiring mind while I sojourned into worlds within. She is that which made palatable the inexplicable until such a time as my mind was no longer needed to get my "arms around" my experience. Still, she exists as a residual of my reach to enlightenment, her clothes now shed.

The season of my heart at war passed in this manner, and the tethers that bound Leigh Ann and me briefly together broke; we took flight. However, I was charged with a deeper understanding of love revealed to me in this crucible. That which had previously existed as my refuge, the succor for my battered heart, now exploded in breathtaking pulsars of clarity and radiation of limitless love. I was literally blazing my heart in every direction.

I had previously sustained for years that there was born to each of us that "other" that so magnified, so elaborated life that being without them left us incomplete. I was now aware that this was simply wrong. No particular thing in Leigh Ann's and my time together instructed me so. Rather it was profound clarity of awareness, absent the architecture of thought that was now constantly broadcasting within me. From the moment I elected to love regardless of the focus, love was completely keyed, triggered, and released in me.

NAKED LOVE

I had been viewing the reflections of Love rather than Love herself. Could it really be true that I was the only one who might be aware of this? Was everyone out there simply going through the motions of apprehending and dining on Love's fruits in such a way simply because that is how we were always instructed in the ways of love? Through Leigh Ann, not in, I finally saw true love revealed. Love stood before me naked, and I wept in God. What is the naked love of God?

I used to believe in soul mates. I no longer do. She/he is not my soul mate; You/I are not a soul mate. I do not have a soul mate. It is something that was born of what I have been taught in love, what I learned adjunctive to love, and lessons earlier, that informed me so. There are no soul mates. The very thought, while rarified, is possessive. Soul mates, by definition, are dependent. We have no soul mates in the end. For those that would aspire to the truth—the Truth—we would embrace the highest truth. We are immortal and complete without any other human. The notion of a soul mate is part of the residual of the illusion of this world and our reach for enlightenment, though it is incomplete.

We aspire to eternity, and, in so doing, we suggest our very human template and filters therein. Without even knowing it, we dream forever with the trappings of today. In the notion of a soul mate, we try to apprehend eternity but we are afraid. We are terrified of the unknown, thinking we need to be cleaved of another to do so. We maintain we are incomplete and naked without a guide in the astral world, whether we articulate this or not. It is revealing that it is us with whom we desire to make this voyage—our other half. It is a romantic notion born of fear. In essence, we project our very real understanding that we require the divine to be whole into the base notion that it is another of us that completes us; this instructs on every point. Can another make us feel more complete? Yes, of course. However, this is useful and sweet insofar as it is not the end in itself. The end itself is seeing ourselves as the key to liberation, to completeness, to divine union. In intuiting that we require the divine to be whole but misapplying this need to another human due to the illusory funhouse of the material world, we inadvertently reveal Godhead resides in us all.

My mental hard drive is considering the concept of interpenetration, and I conclude that it is not simply the diffusion of one in another. The inexplicable search for God, for love, for union is no less than the primordial spiritual seed that lies just across our internal veil. This is the same magic that makes lovers desire to consume the other, for souls to merge in ecstatic union of spirit, and for Eros' need to surrender and fuse to be whole. Each of our "seeds" replicate in our evolving heart from the day we are born, yea, even from the first speck of stardust that is us. This replicating seed is manifested in one outstretched hand or another, all reaching for the ineffable in the affairs of our days—some to the vocation of faith, some to the throes of the sacred bedchamber, others to the myriad lost alleys in between.

It is the mustard seed of which Christ spoke that initiates our journey to forever. It is the spiritual DNA that clocks our approach to God. In our search, bound to flesh, we become lovers of God through the only intercourse we can imagine in our childlike state, each other. Love is the energy, the boundless unseen need to fuse into the dependent state of realizing God. God is realized in this way but burdened with the baggage of our illusory world we think it an end in itself. It is instinctive. It is the way home. The urge is there but not what is needed to make the journey. And so, falling on the lowest rungs of Jacob's Ladder, we call love home, we call her love, we call him love, we call soul mate "complete." The spiritual mitosis is incomplete. No wonder Eros love fails so often. It is only the instinctive coding of the way home, not the home itself.

The concept of soul mates is universal. The concept is at its core the inexplicable awareness of our not-completeness, but limited to the faculties of the flesh's sense organs we presume it is another that makes us whole. In our saints, seers, prophets, and priests, we sense their paternal recognition of the enslavement that besets us all, and they pass from this place into forever. They found the key to divorce the flesh from the spiritual mitosis and became self-aware. Their marriage was to the spirit world. We, inherently recognizing ourselves in each of them, revere them, and pronounce them otherworldly and blessed above all others. Be they of any faith, or none, they wed the divine and passed through the pain, the suffering, the loss, and through time.

Love is the ether, the ghost of the divine, and we apprehend it with the tools we but know. We ascribe to the indescribable the anthropomorphic attributes that are the best realization of ourselves, our frail, humanist selves. We presume Love must needs be housed in one as us. We make God him. We make God her.

Love is the fuel that drives the energy of creation, the medium of eternity, and the breadcrumbs to find our way home in forever. There is a place where we stand naked and look upon love as a babe does the mother. It is here we are utterly alone and lonely. It is here, before the dawn of creation and the end of all things that we are most vulnerable, for it is here where every single landmark that has defined all that was sacred and of our heart is washed away. While in its place are the first source, the first cause, and all things. The heart weeps. It is here we realize with finality, we go forth alone. It is here we finally embrace Love.

Is this then the key? Is love less or is it more? Is love the simple biological imperative the religion of science declares exists to propagate the species and no more? Is the cascade of electrochemical precursors to desire no more than the coding for procreation? Any consideration of alternative theories must first consider what is and what is not on the table. For the humanists they begin first and foremost with the premise that God is not, and that man is the highest expression of his lately organized mass of cells. In this place answers are necessarily a construct of the observer. When we consider outside of the "box," however, we find love is the latticework of all creation, the seat of all consciousness, and the breath of God.

To each is born that which is self-evident. No manner of words can inform the heart, the mind, or the loose collection of cells lately organized as self of the truthfulness of an idea until such a time as the foundation of awareness, wisdom, and other infrastructure is in place, in all of us. I invite no man or woman to consider what I espouse unless their heart, too, speaks in the language wherein only they hear. I cannot so hold a belief or conviction lest it stands the test of reason and in those places where reason makes not its home, intuition. I find it sound that I stand witness to the clock of creation inside of me beckoning me to Love, to God.

Superimposed on this quantum clock, as the divine is superimposed on the natural, are the many other attributes of this sequencing of love, this superposition of love. It is manifested in the aspirations of a heart that can no better describe its gain than its loss; a quest that could no better affirm its origin than its destination. Love exists for no reason than that which the human mind can conceive. Love is the media in which we paint our dreams. Love most assuredly exists and is no less than the fabric of all life. For every muse, oracle, saint, swami, lama, prophet, priest, mullah, cleric, monk, and avatar, one thing above all else served to define that which lies just beyond the place where their words failed: love. For each man and woman who decoded the worlds of science and peered back toward the light of eternity in the micro or macro, whether in letters or numbers, those who but came within inches of the face of the divine, each breathlessly conceded in the immediate, but no later than their deathbed, that love lay at the source of all creation. They often called this "light."

What is this thing we call love? What is this love, beyond words, beyond breath, beyond time, that is so acutely revealed and experienced in all times and all places by *all*? Even Man's consideration of God has undergone remarkable changes in the course of recorded history. Man's self governance has also reflected mankind's changing discourse with God, revealing at an even basic level an evolutionary component to the seasons of this world. However, love has remained forever unchanged in both its solicitation and its deportment. This love, this inexplicable "emotion" is multifaceted, if not pan-faceted. Love exists at every level of our individual and collective intercourse.

Love is the instinctive glue that serves the purpose of raising us from the sleeping bosom of the dust to care for the lesser, the babes, the wounded, and the downtrodden. Love compels us to self-denial, to bleed freely this elixir for the care of another, even at our own peril. We surrender our intake, our well being, and even our health just to serve another in love's embrace. What is love?

Love is the intellectual fabric that binds the fraternity of friends, communities, ideas, and even nations. For the love of freedom…for this end and other common grounds, we love our fellow man. We love our fellow as a sojourner, a confidant, but more. In love's eyes we see ourselves complete. We see ourselves fulfilled. We see a greater totality than we would otherwise have. But is it really our reflection we see? Is it really the shadow of even another?

Love is the current that moves in that medium undefined across worlds and time between lovers. Love serves not any other master but itself, and no man or woman is master to its commands. Yet, it is unseen. Love exists even if no one speaks of it. Love has no form, and cannot be willfully changed or destroyed. Love literally derails our senses. It anatomically and physiologically changes us. Love has no gland, secretes no hormone, and invites no fuel save for its own.

Love by its spiritual nature compels man and woman to union with God, in spite of the obstacles or delusions. In the end, absent the protestations of the priests, curators of the words, reliquaries, or engraved stones, love is our uniquely intimate affair with God. Absent imposed intersession, love exists in the quiet reverence of our heretical hearts as we commune with God directly and intimately. The self-knowledge that we commune with God lives squarely in our hearts regardless of what the self-appointed keepers of the flame reveal to us. Love—God—is self-evident. We make God our lover. We make love the breath of God, whether we call it so or not. Love is our God.

Love is the Holy Ghost, the Ruh al-quds, the epistle of God, the latticework of life, and the Alpha and Omega. The Kingdom of God is a Kingdom of Love. Love is the continuous thread that binds all eternity. However, love is among the least understood components of our existence. When love is considered it is done so most often in the narrow context of the observer. Love is always considered as part of an observation, and not *the* observation. Thus love is the greatest imposter of all things examined in our examined lives. We only catch glimpses.

When the unrequited heart considers love, it does so spurned, lost, defeated, and speaks to us from the abandonment of the rocks from where the ship was wrecked.

When the lover commands the words to define the conquest that has ravaged his days, forfeited his diet, and lay waste his health, he has no other consideration other than the force that is metastasizing within him. He was unwitting, as all lovers are, and can no more define his malady than see the love-virus itself replicating in his tender cells. He was slaughtered upon the altar for no other reason than love's fancy.

When the mystic considers the ecstasy that shrouds her prayers, the warmth that courses within her as she contemplates God, she knows not the pangs of her heated loins. She knows not the lamenting loss of desire for a man beside her, yet she loves still. Her seat is dry but her eyes are wet. She is in love with God and her thoughts are with her beloved only. She has been offered in sacrament upon Love's altar.

Love slaughters the mystic as surely as the man across town, alone in bed, rocking himself to sleep with a pillow between his legs and the same tears upon his cheek. He counts the minutes till his beloved's return, enraptured with desire for his woman to be beside him. They both have taken lovers instinctively. They both desire their lover. God is lover to both of them, and they seek communion with God in but one of the many ways they can. Love is an end in itself.

▼

Unselfing: Baghdad to Yemen

I maintain it is not sufficient to announce the kingdom of God to those who are hungry, subjugated, weary in loss, and destitute of opportunity to common dreams. I have spent my life defending those that cannot defend themselves. I have placed the blood of my heart and flesh on the altar of this world to make meaningful what I tell you is otherwise meaningless. Why? Because of the immediacy of the value placed on [it] by those within [it]. All life is in a state of relative and absolute paradox. One of the keys to the Kingdom is the detachment to leave even your mother in the awareness of the relativity of all things material. However, we are material creatures at the same time, and this awareness does not invite us to mountaintops to contemplate rather it infuses compassion of such magnitude that we are obliged to lend a hand to the first grader lest she stumble and get left back.

In the down moments between running missions in the red zones, I would increasingly introspect. The profound violence of my entire life, coupled with my own coming of age in this current battlefield, served to inform my soul and rent the remaining fabric of my veil. I was increasingly in conflict with my sensitized understanding of life and carrying weapons, poised to defend, or kill—take your pick. In the quiet places where rested the moment in such a bloodbath, I saw less and less separation between my "enemies" and me. While I saw infinite degrees of separation between actions and restraint I saw little, in the end, in the body of our flesh and the song of our souls.

I am sure there are many who would dehumanize the horrific world of those we battle. This self-defense is understandable, instinctive, and ancient. Enemies are necessarily demonized in the conduct of a nation's sorrow. It is unreasonable to invite another to suspend outrage especially in light of the despicable and terrible acts exceeded daily by these animals.

These people are truly the challenge of our times. They give every reason for the world to despise them. On the battlefields on which America now wages asymmetrical war, we fight not ideologues or separatists, nationalists or partisans. America, in fact the entire world, is at war with religious fundamentalists that seek no less than the entire dehumanization and extinction of all "others." It is not a matter of nation-states declaring war on terrorists for a state of war to exist. This reasoning is just denial. I assure you, the entire world is at war whether it is invited or not.

What I speak to is beyond secular or even religious differences. We are all the same, in the end. This truth is apparent to my own heart. In the storm that has savaged the world since September 11, 2001 I have seen the madness in New York, Kabul, Afghanistan, Jakarta, Bali, Indonesia, Baghdad, Iraq, Yemen, Pakistan, and other places. I know the poison sowed that seeks to make the innocent and neutral hate as those who would march forth to maim and kill with their God's sword. They count on this. As I surrender to none the power to make me grant or withhold love, I likewise grant to none the power to take my very soul into the trash of horror and hate.

I have known war in this life. This is enabled me to understand *not-war* in this life. It is not sufficient to want not-war, one must know war to fully understand and despise war. In the space provided herein I cannot begin to articulate *not-war*, but it is tangible, possible, and apparent to me. I would know not-war in this life. I desire this not-war and have seen the faces of millions who desire not-war. War is primitive, despicable, antithetical to our estate, and contrary to, on every count, God. Notwithstanding the primitive concepts of God marching in the vanguard, God marches not to slay this day. The only war, the final war, the *real* jihad, is the battle for the Kingdom of God in our personal lives. This is how heaven is attained, not by yoke or sword.

THIS IS NOT JIHAD

I see their acts, their love of their God, in the burned remains of the children at the checkpoints and the gates every day. Their rationales are circuitous and based on such breathtaking fallacies that modern theology is paralyzed to explain to the West. Mopeds burned to charcoal with macabre human remains toasted and seams burst like frankfurters on a grill. Everywhere, there are school buses smoldering beside tanks, delivery boys that will never return home, and husbands through with their struggles to provide and secure for their families. Women and children dart nimbly through the scattered bricks and remains of their cities, ever alert. The cities of the world are increasingly the images from history's vague urging lest we forget. The distant drumbeat of war and its aftermath are now among us—wherever we are.

Throughout the cities that would be the domain of these "enemies" lie the corpses of their charges. The carnage is beyond words, beyond comprehension. This then is my challenge: how have I come to be this? How can I approach such a thing with tenderness? I do not condone nor accept this outrage, yet I am in another place. I can never return. I have tried. I have been on the frontlines in the flesh and in the spirit. I have surrendered my arms for others. I battle in the spirit for no less than the soul of the world. I am increasingly aware I am called to battle on a plain where rides the armies of all souls. How can I marry the two very different worlds of my life?

In the hinterlands of ancient Sheba I have seen the face of God denied. I have seen God in the boundless compassion of nations of Muslims. I have seen God as I have marched across the world these years reposed in the mountains shrouded in mist. I have seen the Lord revealed in the Buddhas of Bamiyan, Angkor Wat, and in the sunrise of Amman. Across this fertile crescent God has called to me. I do not depart these distant lands with the same conclusions others reach. I declare that God is right here, right now, and the challenge for the world is the battlefield of the soul.

I have come of age on the battlefield of the modern world's greatest threats. I have grown up in an earthbound hell, and I apologize to none for the circuitous roads that have taken me to the place I am today. I have left no brother behind. I have left no mission not acted on. I have moved to "point man" and have elected to go forth alone into the mighty and real fray that underlies all others. In the heart of this world where rests the foundations upon which all things lie, there is a timeless battle that all must wage before we can pass this mortal cloth. It is here the Blacksmith has prepared my blade.

I was contracted to the Department of State, Diplomatic Security Service, office of Anti-Terrorism Assistance for yet another mission. This mission was to take me to two more of the lovely garden spots of the world: Yemen and Pakistan. I was not very excited at first as I had become patently disgruntled with the nature of my work in relation to what now moved unbridled within my soul. I would not know any people on this mission, though some would have professional knowledge of each other. This was often the case in such a small cadre of professionals. The further I moved from direct combat environments, the more likely I would be working in a transition zone of allied law enforcement and special operators, rather than just Special Forces. It was easier for me to remain aloof in this environment as I did not know as many people by less than one degree of separation.

I would spend much of my time retiring after work to my thoughts and prayers. These days became days of isolation in my mind. I was afforded the safety of armed camps and protected compounds to collect thoughts at amazing first-glance odds with the waking world. This trip began the days of my life where much of what I performed occupationally became rehearsed and acted by memory. I was no longer here. I was so some place else. I was just not reaching the same conclusions and observations from life that everyone around me was concluding. Everything was taking on such a rich texture and profoundness. My world, my heart, my mind, everything grew so intensely beautiful and blessed that no amount of pages herein would enable me to paint this for you, but I will try.

I headed to Yemen, following almost ten months in Iraq. It is amazing that I have become that which takes a break from Iraq, in Yemen! I was in Yemen to train their anti-terrorism teams. In fact, we were building them. Like most countries following the spectacular terrorist strike in New York on September 11, 2001, Yemen was "in it" for the money. The Department of State provided the training and the funding so ostensibly friendly or neutral nations could better assist in the worldwide battle of our times. Some countries were better politically disposed at home to assist in any meaningful way. Most wanted the trade and assistance incentives that America had to offer in return: classic *quid pro quo* and entirely legitimate as America's interest in fighting terrorism is much greater than many other countries.

The Yemenis would never be a world-class player on any matter of security. In fact, every day at about noon, the entire nation gets stoned on a leafy chew called Qat (pronounced like "cot" but with a guttural "ka" sound). And so my operational break began here. My time was spent training their counter-terror teams and allowing the winds of the high desert to wash my mind and soul. I would leave the hotel in the morning before the world had risen and take to the hillside to greet the day. In scattered places in the city below I noted the faithful rising for salat (prayer). We lived at the only western hotel in Sana'a. It was marginally protected with walls and guards. This made it approved by the embassy. However, even a pathetic attempt could breach this security. Still, it was much more comfortable than the provisions of Iraq. I settled into a routine that would mark the next few years. I was keenly aware that all my remaining handholds on the world had departed, and I was constantly living now in the internal.

I AM NOT CHRISTIAN, JEW, MUSLIM, BUDDHIST, HINDU, OR OTHER

God was increasingly moving through my every waking moment. Many Muslims would ask me if I was Christian, as they would note my praying. They were uncertain, as it was apparent I was in love with God even by Islamic standards. Most Christians to whom they have been exposed simply do not supplicate themselves in public, or with their Muslim brethren.

"No," I would tell them. "I am not Christian!"

"You must be Christian," they would respond incredulously because I was Caucasian. This is the typical exchange in near every country I visited.

"You are Muslim?" one might offer.

"No."

"Ah, you are Buddhi?" another might finally conclude.

"No."

"Hindi?" someone might offer exasperated.

"No."

Interestingly, I was never asked if I was Jewish. I suspect this was too far out of the sphere of the conceivable. The fact is most Muslims cannot begin to contemplate entertaining the faith of spirit without the instrument of man at the helm. Even where man is not at the helm, the word of God still passes through Prophet. Intimate intercourse with God appears to be an alien concept to *most* Muslims. When I say intimate intercourse, I am talking about exclusive intercourse with God: mystical intercourse. Yet, Islam does have a mystical tradition represented in Sûfî; however, Sûfî is not widely acclaimed or praised in Islam. For Muslims God is paternal, demanding, and exacting, yet otherwise also embodies love, grace, charity, and peace. I suppose most religions assume that every man and woman must claim one or another religion.

Everywhere I went, whether it was Indonesia where I prayed with—and cared medically for—the leading Imam of Java, or Islamabad where I prayed with my students, I was seeing *me* through *their* eyes. I had come to profess that man speaks first with the soul, next with actions, and last with words. I was coming to intuit the spirit of self and others *in* self and others. It was truly remarkable, and language became increasingly a secondary tool for me, literally and figuratively. It is not just that there was increasingly less to actually say, but I sensed that what most needed to be communicated was, without words. This is one of those points that will simply evade understanding absent experience.

TRANSFIGURATION

I began to see powerful and incredible changes in me. Outwardly I kept the same face on for employment, peers, and others. Only those closest to me saw I was changing remarkably during these years. The change was in my eyes, in my ease, in my release, in precognition, in the synchronicity of the moments of my every day. I was aware of things of which I should not be aware. I sensed danger and avoided it deftly. I was sleeping less and eating less. I was literally seeing, hearing, tasting, and otherwise sensing the world differently. I became disinterested in all things other than prayer and the mad attempts to objectify my experiences in words. My interest in women (as a man) was reduced to no more than intermittent instinctive urges.

I began to fancy there must surely be some projection emanating from me as my students began to be drawn to me in large numbers both during the workday and after. When the weapons were cleaned and stored, when feet were washed and prayers supplicated, they came to me to speak of God. They sat with me to talk of love, dream things, peace, and of little things and funny things. I began to uneasily converse openly of these things with others. I had not done so earlier throughout my life. In time, I would come to a convicted ease in discussing all things unseen. This was becoming the battlefield in which I waged war.

I began to see in myself a remarkable contrast between my working hours and my private places. I would escape upon my immediate fulfillment of my day's duties and take to "my place." My place was just beyond the place where the flesh met eternity. It was both within me and outside at once. With my holster and weapon on the bed, my body armor beside me, I would slip into the place where beats the heart of the world.

A MOMENT IN TIME

I looked out across Sana'a at the hazy dusk. The setting of the day into the haze was a fitting backdrop to growing sense of awareness moving within me. I looked further to my right from the seventh floor of the hotel. The ancient city was illuminated in an orange glow. Some locals say this city was first founded by one of the sons of Noah. Apparently, Sana'a had changed names sometime in the intervening time. This was reported to be the land of Sheba. While Sana'a may have often had hazy days scattering orange across the high desert plateau it was the first time I had seen it.

Sana'a cast its shadows to the east, toward the close of another day. The call to prayer had ended some short time earlier. Contrary to what most Westerners think the call to prayer actually follows a fairly detailed lunar calendar. Most people in the West could hardly describe what the lunar cycle is, and yet, the majority of the world still lives in lunar marriage, another indication of a world of increasing contrasts and polarity.

I had only changed rooms yesterday after five weeks of asking the management to do so. Yes, I would laugh to myself in surrender "Insha'Allah," God willing. The Muslim world indeed had a different concept of time. I was enchanted by the panoramic view from atop this hill.

"Oh, my Lord!" I exclaimed.

Never before I had stared directly into the sun. The haze of the setting day obscured enough of the harmful corona whereby I could look directly into the sun. It was large. It was so large it loomed above the high desert floor blocking out two thirds the sky. It was overwhelming. It so distracted me that I lost sense of time.

The sun occupied the whole western sky and the orange fingers scattered like confetti upon Sana'a. The sun came to rest upon the mountain range before me. Its descent was unremarkable. However, now that it had a relationship with scale I immediately realized that the sun was running away.

My God, I thought. *I am watching the world turn in the face of the sun.* It was dizzying. With each passing second I watched as entire swaths of the great sun were captured by the turning earth. *It simply could not be this fast*, I thought. I had seen numerous sunsets in my life but never one at 8,000 feet where there was the perfect haze and fog to make the sun visible and near, and the perfect reference of mountains to so mark the passing of the day.

Within moments I was holding my breath as the last remaining sliver pierced the saddle of the ridgeline. I was careful not to close my eyes lest I miss it. In the time it would have taken me to blink, the sun disappeared. I would have missed it had I rested my eyes. Immediately, all the orange that was loaned to the day, to Sana'a, to the shadows to announce their presence, was called back to the other side of the mountains, the other side of the world. Shadow's contrast was immediately replaced with light/not light, dark/not dark, and dusk settled into the ancient city. In the twinkling of an eye the most commonplace event in all of time stole my breath and my heart. I traveled forty years and the world's span to have my breath taken and my heart stolen—and I got to see a marvelous sunset. It was all in a choice.

THE CONTRAST OF SOUL AND BLOOD

In Baghdad I contrasted daily the bloodshed of the body with the bloodshed of the soul. While patently different, the latter is much more overwhelming than the former. I have known both. In this bloodbath I was increasingly becoming larger than my flesh could bear. I was reaching out through the world, through time, and massaging the heart of an aching world in my supplication and understanding of Love. I had always thought that this Light, this Love, could only come to a person through endless supplication or sheer grace. It is the case that even though I strived all my days for this Light I have not *earned* such a thing. I hold that no man or woman attains enlightenment by reward. Rather, in the process of making naked the mysteries, Love seats within us unannounced, often unnoticed at first. I have been graced my whole life. I assert God only enables our understanding of Love, finally. My supplication was never to purchase God, rather only to love.

By the time I came to the land of Sheba I was completely introverting and examining my heart as an odd curiosity I had simply overlooked all my life. I became aware that I became aware. At night when the stars marched their legions across the black, my mind focused more easily within itself.

THE KINGDOM OF GOD

I stood looking down from the silence, from the darkness, and saw the world. I saw the movement, felt the breathing, the harmonic song that now took mere moments to acquire. Though my ears were deaf, I heard as I never had before. Cerebral euphoria, giddiness, I cried. I cried easily and joyfully. I heard the music. I listened and knew this was the song of all creation. It was always right here. My very heart was bleeding, hemorrhaging. I felt the salty wet upon my face. I felt nothing at all. I was dying.

Like a spectator I looked in upon the world and saw as iridescent the multitudes, moving, silent, living, dying, loving, and dreaming. I saw the wars, the oceans, the forests, the mountains, and the clouds all awash with a whitish-blue, all humming, all vibrating. There was a parade of images as if cast just for me, for my viewing. I did not look here or there but was instead led like a voyeur. Births, dying, crying, wailing, bleeding, wedding, loving, praying, playing, and dreaming, all painting images of emotions on my vision. I was led though, as I could find no source, no inventory from which to have drawn such things from myself.

The only thing I could compare it to as I reached inside my memory was the tuning forks that doctors used. *We were all tuning forks!* I realized. It was all humming and oscillating. We were. My body felt warmth course through me. I was euphoric. I felt alive; I felt dead. I was here; I was not. I breathed, but I could not feel my chest sigh. I was ecstatic. I was ecstasy.

I am alive, I declared to myself. *Am I dead?* I considered more closely. I was, though, overwhelmed.

I was in love and had no object of my affection. I was in love and had all objects of affection. I sobbed like a little boy.

Through the lens of my tears I could make out the walls of the hotel room in which I prayed. But what I could see was a wall of pixels. All was in depth of colors and humming, blue, white, shimmering, sparkling, and the faint outline of the objects that emanated this. My lamp, the wall, the inanimate, all appeared this way. I rose briefly and looked to the street. The people below, the lights, the cars, and the buildings all looked the same. The sky and the ground seamlessly fused in a map of trillions of twinkling pixels.

The whole world was awash in flickering little lights. I could not really hear but it was as if the world was beating to a humming as the lights danced for me. I returned to the floor totally enraptured once more. I thought again this must be the images of my mind. I must have read this somewhere. I must be creating this in my own mind. This must surely be madness. *Do my tears create this?* I considered. This began to happen more frequently.

I could feel my body; I could not feel my body. I could hear the noise, the traffic of life all around me, on the street, in the next room, in other homes, around the world—all at the same time. I heard nothing at all also. I was in both places: my body and my mind. I was in all places. I was me; I was not me. I was in no place. Once more my world was cleaved in two, and I witnessed the world and not-world.

My lips were moving but no sound escaped. I had thoughts that were not here, not now. I dismissed them. They came less frequently, though still intrusive. It was the internal dialogue I worked so hard to harness, to suppress, to ignore, and to defeat for so long. I was still not the master of my mind after so many years therein. I had long ago ventured into my mind, and today was again considering that the price was insanity.

Again, I slipped into this place between madness and the night, between awake and the dead, between here and forever. I feverishly had sought this state but I could not previously reproduce it at will. It came to me not from entreaty but some other mechanism, which I had not yet fully comprehended. It coincided with so many other things changing in me, in my life of late. But this?

This was overwhelming and inexplicable. I prayed. I sobbed still in joy. I was confused. Exhausted, I rose with my face swollen and my lips trembling. My pulse quickened; my pulse slowed. I was ravished. I was spent. In the setting sun I had made love.

I heard the chorus of creation, the song of the world again, the lament of my heart, of other hearts. I saw naked hearts as lovers and heard the refrain of the erotic, and of loss. If Hope had a voice, I heard it. If Promise declared her echo, I felt it all reverberate throughout the world, throughout me. I had been infused with something so powerful in the brief space of the time I sojourned. I lay and rocked myself, eyes fixed, smiling. I had once again been infused with the manna of the Kingdom of God.

I laugh inside at the imposter I have become, like an actor going about the profession that is all he knows. The irony is breathtaking; I am carrying a gun, prepared to kill people if required, and praying for every soul on earth in a non-stop orgy of supplication at the same time. The contrast, the irreconcilability of it all, is deafening.

I stand upon the crossroads of life and seek to harness this and make it but a simple component of my discovering mind. I have no sense at all that this is the noise of my own mind. I am sure with absoluteness that this ether, this cusp between sleep and awake, between life and death, is populated by countless others. I hear them, I sense them, I feel them when I pray, and I sense them when I sleep. I can make out the forms and lights in the recesses of my dreams. But only on the cusp; beyond there is nothingness and everything.

My increasing visions would begin to intrude further into my waking day as the very images and textures of my world were replaced by a very different manner in which my mind was interrogating the world. I would shortly begin seeing in this manner more frequently. My battle was no longer being waged by myself alone. In some manner I gained a specific gravity, a critical mass, and I was increasingly along for the ride.

Oh, such madness! I lovingly considered.

GOD IS ON THE MOUNTAINTOP

I rested that night in Yemen and woke amazed. I saw the Kingdom again in the early morning dawn. I looked to the mountains about the valley and saw easily why God was seen in these hills, these ancient bluffs. I felt the fresh air upon my face and saw the orange of the distant morning send forth its messengers. They cast dancing hues of gold and yellow upon the desert cliffs and the whitewashed ancient stone homes.

In the distance the minarets called the faithful to prayer—all dutifully abiding the second pillar of Islam. I looked to the white cloud that surrounded the single mountain to my east. The cloud was thick, impenetrable. In the midst of the whiteness there was a dark swirl, both foreboding and suggesting presence and purpose. There were no other clouds in the morning dawn. It is no wonder the ancients believed the gods lived upon these sandy thrones. I, too, felt strangely awed by the majesty of this site. In fact, its single beauty conspired with my breath to bless me with joy.

I inhaled and drew long the air that swept the world before entering me. I was moved in the silence of the morning. My very essence emptied my lungs, and I felt at ease. Tears welled inside my eyes. I was often crying in joyful prayer now. I was never a crier. So, this was a peculiar outward sign for me. I felt such sweet ecstasy, such simple unashamed peace and tenderness. The majesty of what moved within me became a constant and powerful love.

My breath stole the world to my private places inside, the dust of the beginning of time giving me life. I exhaled again and breathed, projected, my love in return. I again inhaled, drinking the pain of the world on the invisible particulates of air. I exhaled what I offered to be an exchange of my flesh, my spirit, in return for the darkness of others' pain. This, then, is the true child of love. I submitted my heart and person as filter to cleanse the world.

I was surprised. I was thinking on how such a place could elicit this in me. I was compelled to emotion; yet, it was not emotion. It was something different. I rarely noted emotion in me, per se; at least not unawares. I could only liken to it emotion or describe it with such language, though. I was filled with a sense of the very dawn, the retiring night. I felt I knew at once why God was found in places like this. Though I still did not understand why I was found in this place. I say this tongue in cheek. Life was revealing God in all places to me for some time now. I just as easily found the reflections of God in the awful bloodbaths of Iraq as I did in the beaches of Cyprus; though, this was *the* challenge.

Are there really places in this world where Man is called more closely to know God, I wondered? *Yes, I am sure there is now.* Perhaps the earth itself surrenders this energy in certain places wherein Man is moved to commune. This was increasingly happening in Yemen. But it was happening increasingly everywhere. It was happening before I arrived in this ancient city. God has called me since I was but a boy, but it never had such texture and depth. It had never been so clear and consistent. In fact, if this was the Kingdom of God, I had every sense that I was now being recruited. Unlike the past where I was drawn to that which I did not nor could not know, I was now drawn to something I knew very well as a moth to a flame—or better still, as a rubber duck to the drain in the tub.

Does a man pray to God often? I wondered. How often? I knew the Muslims prayed five times a day. Did they repeat rote memorizations of the liturgy or did they supplicate themselves to God with unabashed heart? Perhaps both. Were I obsessed with money, others would say I should seek help. Were I possessed of love and infatuation, other might say the same. Yet, to one that would but seek God in all things, the world stands back and is cautious of judgment and counsel. They may tap their fingers to their heads but surely no one feels confident to so declare this preoccupation absurd, wasteful, meaningless—at least not in the honest and private considerations.

Too few have I showed willingly the private discourse my days and nights have with my Beloved. To those few, I, too, find the finger tapping to the head; however, in fellowship it is couched in love and acceptance. It takes a powerful conviction to consistently escape the company of such hardened peers and take to knees. There is a powerful changing all of its own accord by the independence and strength to stand alone and reach for God when no other does so. The journey to God approaches only so far in the community of peoples and faith. In the end, the final leap across the void, absent Man, is a very alone journey. The battle for the Kingdom of God is everywhere, every day, non-stop. The siren song of the soul's restless slumber coming fully self-aware in the physical world subordinates all things, all thoughts and considerations, all, to the contemplation of the divine—always.

THE UNBEARABLE BURDEN OF BEING

I cannot turn it off any longer. I am no longer in control. It is hardwired in me. My very brain has been remapped in accordance with the coding authority of my spiritual DNA. From the moment I awake to the last thoughts of the day I think of no other thing but God and the Kingdom all about me. The affairs of my every act are increasingly in relationship to thoughts so. I have apparently crossed some place wherein I cannot even locate the vantage point from where I once cast my gaze to the heavens. I see now the journey backward and forward. I see now the entire vista of my life. I was coming to this day forever. I am immersed in something wonderful, something terrifying.

My love, my heart, my wounded flesh and bleeding ego were all destined to pass this age long ago. No childhood obstacles, pain, suffering or delusions of comfort in my life would have ever interfered with this clocking to God. My heart, my love, were never mine to give into another's care after all. I am but the steward of my Beloved's Song. I can project love, I can declare love, and I can receive love, but my love is neither less nor any greater were no person in the world to take notice of my having passed nor loved sweetly.

My love belongs to God only. My love is God's love, and I am allowed only to be the instrument thereof, the medium. I now must bear witness to this thing passing through me, not of me. I have no love of my own. Love moves in me, and I thought this love mine; it is not. I could no more hold such immensity than I could command the age of the seasons. My love is Source Love downloaded from God directly now. I bypass the server of illusion. I no longer command the armies of subordinate love; rather I am a mirror in the lighthouse, turning this way and that, reflecting my Beloved's gaze unto the world.

My realization of this is the key to commanding the seas of my soul. This powerful Love moving through me, I presume, is why I can no longer find the place where recently I stood and gazed at forever. My landmarks of spirit have shifted dramatically. I am no longer there; I am no longer here. It is explosive, and it moves me to tears upon consideration. The shift is dramatic, and nothing can ever be the same again. I tried. Life is *very* different for me. Here, in the ancient deserts of time I was making love to my Lord. In this place, following so many seasons of intermittent sun, a pulsar burst within me. I dressed and got ready for work.

I holstered my Glock-19, 9mm pistol, and made sure I had an extra five magazines in my breakaway waist pack. I went out to the SUV with my coffee and got down on my hands and knees to inspect the undercarriage for explosives before my team came out. I did this out of force of habit. How very appropriate that all our lives were habit. Habit would soon become anathema to me. I would be driving today. The SUV was actually my primary weapon, not the pistol. The irreconcilability was maddening.

In Yemen, in the stillness of this mad profession, I came to know why I know. I have seen the face of God within me. I have seen what others have called the light. I have been alive outside my body. I have done this many times in my life. It is not a measure of imagination or of lucid dreaming. Leaving the body is literally a tearing away from the physical body of that part of me that remains aware still. I have heard the Song of Life. I have seen my prayers answered in real time. I have manifested the world I would live in by sheer will as a co-conspirator with God. I have discerned things ineffable to the waking world and have found the place where language fails completely. I have seen such that simply being in this world became a challenge for me. There is an ignorant peace in *belief*. However, one must be a warrior to *know* for here is the battlefield.

MAKING SENSE OF THE INSENSIBLE

To few is it given in this life to ask the questions, even less receive answers. Often it is the case that for those who do not feel they have had their inquiries answered, it is due to them looking for the answers in the wrong places. More than anything else people tend to seek answers to the complex and inexplicable nature of their being and surrender these thoughts, these questions up to the ether through their very human filters.

What they fail to apprehend is that it is these same filters that disable their vision and comprehension. Looking into the human inbox to check messages, they find "no new messages." They seek answers to the ineffable via the very medium that is designed to interrogate the material world only. It is the filters of our human bondage that needs be considered and abandoned.

For all those who have suffered and labored in pursuit of the truth and the light in all ages, and have failed, I lament. The key is indescribable, but practical. It is right here, right now. The answers are not canned and they are not specific. Absent the language of the mortal world the answers are all stocked upon the shelves of eternity, and we must needs pierce the veil to shop upon these shelves. Once having done so there is a panorama of worlds that first speaks to every initial question or desire with which we began our quest. It is a dizzying plethora of contexts and awareness that besieges us.

Right here is the self-evidence of immortality, eternity, other-worldliness, and God. But the answers? It is too contrived to describe. It is so far out of the inventory of what life has prepared for me that I can still not describe it, even to myself. There are no answers past the filter through which we supplicate, only knowingness. Once having crossed back through the medium of our "filters," this awareness serves the call of "answers" but it remains inexplicable. It is not an answer factory. The most profound and distressing realization is that, once having farmed upon these Elysian fields and harvested thereof, I am no longer the person I was when I began this voyage. I now only tend crops therein.

In the end, this is the trouble with the unbearable burden of being: not being. In the middle of the fight for the discovery of my very soul, I find the realizations I harvest are no longer for myself even. I have long since fled. Each day and each night, I realize more acutely that I am no longer. The whole journey is a process, in the end, of unbecoming, not becoming. I am not sure of the implications of this, but it is true, and it explains much of the torture and protestations of my mind and ego.

That to which I am introducing my mind is within it. I am forcing my mind to serve that end which, if realized, defeats its very existence. My mind and human bondage rails, and in the void, the battlefield, the slaughter ensues daily. I know the means and the ends to my days. It is just in the fruition, the transition that the seeming loss of identity ensues. It is in this place where I bleed freely. I question myself endlessly and labor with why I feel any loneliness at all.

I have never been more sensitized in my life. I have known so much joy and love. I have never before cried so freely at the simple. I have never so frequently had my breath stolen from me by the everyday occurrences and simple things: a child's eyes, lovers holding hands, a blue sky, an act of charity, a smile. It is here that the bloodshed of my mind, my heart frightens me. I am alone on the field of battle. Furthermore, I labor on multiple fronts. I have never been so joyously wounded in all my life.

▼

Heightened Sensory Awareness: Pakistan

I wander around my life acting through memory the stagecraft of my world. I wake and retire with one single thought and focus: to escape to paradise again. My God is so within the house of my heart that in seeing God now everywhere, my house-my heart is every- where. I cannot truly explain how awesome and peaceful this is. It is breathtaking. I have maintained I would seek to live each day in such a way that were it to be my last, I would have left no heart I love unloved. I would depart leaving no word unsaid. Now, I find myself prepared to depart every moment. I want to live, but I want to leave this body, too. I consider this and realize that there is actu- ally something specific to which I would attend first: I want to learn how to live. That is what I desire. I want to know how to live because one thing is apparent: I have not been living up till now. I have not truly lived, and now I am not sure how to live.

There is a blessing in faith undetected. Faith differs from knowing in the mad- ness that accompanies one. Faith seeks to apprehend the abstract. Knowingness seeks to comprehend. In knowingness forever has already arrived. I retired finally for the night, my gear prepared for the morning's journey to Pakistan.

The first thing I noticed after landing in Islamabad was the cattle in the streets, and that these people had nuclear bombs. The next thing I realized was that I would have to be careful crossing the road. I was back in a land of reverse-side-of-the-street driving. It is really no surprise to me that people walk out into traffic when returning from abroad. My driver took me to an "undisclosed location" where my team was already assembled on a secure compound. I had taken a detour out of Yemen en route to Pakistan. We were the only people on this compound. The first thing we did was issue weapons and build explosive charges in the event we had to evade. We were in the "no foreigners" area outside of Islamabad. If it was not clear that this area was off limits, signs were posted everywhere—in English. The vernacular is Urdu. Nearby was a nuclear facility, and Pakistan was a nation under siege and in an uneasy ceasefire with her neighbor to the south.

I must declare that in all my years teaching unconventional warfare, insurgency and counter-insurgency, and counter-terrorism, Pakistan's students stood head and shoulders above the rest in maturity, motivation, and professionalism. Most of my students came from Peshawar or Islamabad proper, though many were from Quetta, the capital of Balchistan province, and Karachi. It would prove to be a professionally and personally rewarding time. I also knew that it would likely be my last time as my mind was made up that I needed to find a way out of a career path that more sneaked up and grew around me after September 11. 2001, than I would prefer. On my first night in Pakistan, with days still before the students even arrived, I took the time to consider what strange events brought me to this place.

Contrary to what many people think, Arabic is not the sole language of the Muslim world. In fact, Urdu is the primary language of Pakistan, a language evolved from many others, much like Bahasa. However, Arabic is the sole language of the Islamic liturgy.

Islamabad is a fairly new city laid out on grid lines sometime after Pakistan was portioned from India. Much of the poverty that is rampant in Pakistan is not so obvious in the capital city. This region of the world is like so many that Americans just do not understand. The nation is superimposed on religion, which is superimposed on the tribal and regional. Understanding these overlapping loyalties and motivations is critical to any objective understanding of peoples that are now shaping our times. It is simply impossible to divorce the community from the state, the religion from the region; all are interwoven in a delicate balance.

I liked this place. I was increasingly moved to enjoy the moment in all of my moments. While I was easily capable of performing the tasks of instruction in counter-terrorism, I was intercoursing with God in a way that I never had before. My peaceful nights were spent apart from my peers in silent meditation and prayer. I was bathing in this light throughout my waking hours now. Life had a different flavor for me. I heard as I had never heard before. I was seeing life in a way that was so apparent to me, as though I had never seen the world before. I marveled at the smallest things. By my second week I was settled in and was drinking my new world

I had no work the following day and was off early from teaching my students. I was washed up and comfortable. I ate dinner lightly and took a chair away from those that gathered to talk about work and women. I waited for the sun's departure and noted its passing in the lengthening shadows, in the night things that got a head start, and in the chill that followed and chased the orange of the day away. I did not note when I first smelled the jasmine, only that I *now* smelled it. It did not sneak up on me, but its gravity gained a critical mass, and my mind announced, *Ahh! It is good. It is jasmine again.* I smiled.

THE KINGDOM OF GOD IS CHOICE

I am not sure if it is the jasmine that impregnates the air every evening or the jingle trucks that caused me such fullness. The jingle trucks, by the way, are the funniest, neatest things on wheels. All the trucks here are painted the liveliest colors, and each driver-owner takes great pride in the truck's appearance. They are right out of a child's surreal dream.

The colors are unlike anything you might imagine. There are pastels and vibrant colors that look like each color should have a battery just to charge it. They build onto the trucks in such a way that they have no resemblance to their former frames. For those with money, they remove the cab doors and replace them with rich, ornate wooden doors, each meticulously carved. There are intricate little bangles and jingle chains hanging from every horizontal underside. Often, they build up the top of these trucks to many meters in height. The end result is often that of an elaborate ship's hull on wheels, or a pink elephant running through a field of wildflowers. It is truly a spectacle.

They line up on the highways and byways as all commerce does and deliver to this nation the goods required. Many of these trucks are the typical beasts of burden of an economic engine. There are pink and forest-green dump trucks and tractor-trailers with wooden entry-room doors of rare woods. Few things in so many years of traveling have so captured my curiosity and interest as these trucks throughout the region and the infusion of jasmine into the evening air. I had seen similar trucks on the roads to Kabul but there was so much of the context absent in that place. And certainly, there was no jasmine.

It must be jasmine, I thought. Yet, the only time I have ever smelled anything so utterly powerful was from an air-freshener can. This was not like that, no. This was alive and pleasant. The air was viscous with jasmine. It was everywhere at the same time. I walked in the darkening air, my nose sniffing the night as a dog might search out a mate. I closed my eyes. It was heavenly. I thought to myself that this is what paradise must smell like. If ever there were a flavor, a smell, in paradise, this would be it. Mmmmm.

Since the first night in Pakistan I had experienced this aroma, this hedonism of smell, I have looked forward to the passing of each day to again breathe this aroma. I wonder if this is seasonal. I thought of asking someone, and then decided not. I did not want to share my experience, or reduce it to inquiry. I just wanted to enjoy it. For me, in the whole world, in all of time, when I close my eyes and let pass this pleasant aroma through my nose, across my tongue, into my lungs and to my brain, I want this to be just for me. In all time no one else has ever been me, stood where I stand, and breathed these flowers that live at this time. Yes, this was just for me. It spoke to me of promise. Not the promise that is created to build the pillars of hope; rather the real awareness that I choose to make this my olfactory paradise. I choose to make this my personal experience. I choose to enjoy this in the late afternoons regardless of what happens across the world. Yet, it does speak of promise because I affirm with each inhalation that in so choosing, I choose life. In so seeing, I see hope. In so dreaming the essence of so simple a thing as a fragrance, I dream life into the fabric of my material world.

Of course, cannabis grows wild here. In fact, it is a common weed. On every inch of flat land there are the pungent five pointed leaves of the ubiquitous pot plant. One might think I enjoy the jasmine so much because I *enjoy* the hemp as well. This is not the case. The smell of jasmine overwhelms the evening air following its release at sunset and renders other olfactory intrusions meaningless.

Jingles and jasmine, what a beautiful symphony of the senses. Throughout the day and night, the visual assault of the jingle trucks is countered by the horns of the average automobile. Here in this apparently fun land, the horns of vehicles appear to reflect the prestige of the owner as well as the design and colors of the trucks. They are fun sounds. Often they are quite long, sometimes a minute or so in length. They are pregnant with various tones and pitches, each a song or cacophony of animal-like sounds. It is frequently of such harmony or uniqueness that we are commanded by its entreaty to stop what we are doing and hear the refrain from across a field, behind a wall, or up the street.

At night, they sing to each other on the streets nearby, one alerting first to a pass, perhaps, the latter vehicle sounding in approval or denial. These sounds and songs fill the air with a uniqueness that is so different, so rich from other places I have visited. I often lie upon my bed and smile. The most sensory intrusive are the jingle trucks with these elaborate horns. They prowl the highways and city streets singing in colors and painting in song.

In my life, in my world, I have learned to squeeze these sights and sounds from the heart of a world that can often seem absent magic and life, true life. Manifesting such beauty in the crucible of war has irrevocably altered my vision. The promise comes from being able to increasingly manifest this tender sweetness with each passing day. It is my choice.

Why a smell? What is it about a smell that could make the entire neurological apparatus of my being surrender in joy? Maybe it is not biological at all. Maybe my heart has a liaison with my brain, and there is an agreement. In any regard, I will note again what others are not noting: the jasmine. It is a choice. It is a promise, to myself.

I escaped the confines of the secure compound outside of Islamabad and had my driver take me to the city each weekend where I would rent a room at the Serena Hotel. It was much nicer there. There is a Marriot Hotel but it is really outclassed by the Serena. After all, in a life spent suffering, I saw no reason to suffer when I did not have to do so. Besides, the Serena had wireless Internet and room service. There I would meditate in unfettered silence and slip into ecstatic prayer. I have known friends who have suggested that staying in five-star hotels struck them as contrary to what I would affirm. No. In the Third World, five-star hotels are the only choices. It is necessary that any hotel stay be in a hotel with a proper security perimeter. It must never be forgotten that the places my employment takes me are the most hostile on earth for a white man. To an observer casing for a target, I am just a white American. Hotels like this are the only choice as they are the only hotels with security.

TURNING THE INSIDE OUT

I was probably in Pakistan no more than a month and was still closely examining my changing world within. I was now both willfully manifesting the changes taking place within me and also somehow permanently changed by each incremental apprehension. The world outside of me was necessarily changing as well.

Somewhere in this process I am becoming, I thought. *Maybe I am un-becoming.*

I slipped again into the space between the wake and the dead and was observer to myself. Rocking gently as I am wont to do when going to "my place," I closed my eyes and sought the images within: the light. I lapsed in breath. I slipped in silence into the void where burns the Light. I "induced" in mere moments now. Time stopped; worlds turned. I was aware again only that I was aware. I was effused with the warmth that spoke to me of successful "induction." Once again this night, in the unlikely arms of Pakistan, I would slip between worlds.

I was in the viscous energy. It was pink-white, a mixture. I saw this envelope of energy encompass the world. It was a cloud cover across the world. I was observer; I was witness. I went to the place where I joyously sneaked away to each night. In the business before the sun's descent, I plotted my escape. In the silence before the sun's return, I made good my jailbreak.

Each day I mentally rubbed the blades of my palms upon each other as I considered my escape later, when the warden slept. *Ha, ha, ha. If the warden only knew*, was often the childish imaginings of my playful mind.

I tried desperately to find some image, some idea, some experience in which to liken this vision. What I was beholding was beyond anything I had ever seen. From a billion points of light, many billions of places, I saw fine filaments stretching to the heavens. The earth was luminescent in blue and white, and there seemed to be an endless stream of energy (or so it seemed) discoursing through these threads, these filaments. I was in awe. The dialogue in my head was silent. I could only watch. They were umbilici.

I was seeing as well as feeling, it seemed. I was sensing as well as emoting a part of the very images that cast upon the mental screen within me. (In retrospect, I announce feeling and emoting). I was the energy; I was the witness. The pink-white moved as pink *in* white. It was as if a painter had taken a can of white paint and poured it in oil. Not satisfied pink was added and gently stirred. The pink mixed, but not entirely. The white mixed, but not entirely. Therefore, across the heavens, the stars were masked and night was replaced with the palette of the Gods.

Slowly, deliberately, with purpose and seeming intelligence, the weather systems of these colors employed the multitudes of these filaments with life, with energy. It was as if it were all-sentient.

I recalled the glass novelty globes that one could purchase in science or discovery stores. These globes were electrified and various colors of contained lightning danced within the globe. *Yes. That is exactly what this is like*, I thought. *Intelligent lightning, Jacob's Ladder.*

I rose shortly afterward, provoked by some sound in the hallway, and then lay in the darkness thinking on this. I realized I had seen this before. This was not the first time I had seen these threads, these filaments. It now seemed I had seen this many times before. It was very familiar, though I could not recall with any specificity when I had seen this. I began to write my thoughts down on paper. It was the beginning of my attempt to capture my experiences in writing. I began to write. It was if my blood began pouring onto the paper.

Where do I go from here? I thought pensively. While the world was now more beautiful than I could have ever imagined, I was painfully aware I was slipping away from all other humans, all my remaining landmarks. I watched the traffic of the busy city life as my driver returned me to camp the following day. In my mind's eye I fancied I could see the homes of those running busily about this city. I knew that dinner would be prepared for those out busy earning a day's wages. Prayers would be offered to Allah, shoes would remain outside the home, hands would be washed, and a much-earned meal consumed. These people were all, most likely, law-abiding, God-fearing citizens. They were all concerned for their children's future. The parents dreaded a child's sickness, or a parent's passing. They paid their taxes and wanted to be left alone. They laughed and rolled with their children in the grass and told jokes with their co-workers during idle breaks in the day. At night, when they lay to sleep, the day's burdens cast aside, they dreamed of places beyond their suffering. They hoped fervently that God was, and paradise had their name on it. These were not terrorists. These people—like all the billions across the Islamic, Christian, Jewish, Buddhist, Hindu, Shinto, and other worlds—wanted to be part of a dream that was both bigger than themselves and uniquely crafted *just* for them. All these people, all these worlds, all these dreams, they just wanted to be. I have seen the heart of Man and it is far more beautiful than I had been led to believe.

I have moved within the world of man and war with God announced in my heart. I can never go back. I can never again *not* see. God has slain my flesh and laid waste my illusions. I have defended my nation and fought her battles where my humble effort could. I have labored in the soil of the flesh to till God's fields. I tasted the fruit of my lover's desire and have given birth to heaven on Earth by sheer will. I have elected to exercise my free will. I have stripped the world of all things and have populated it again only with that born of the whispers within myself. I have lived in this life. I have lived beyond this life. I create my world daily. God is within me, and I will command Love.

In the waking hours when sleeps the world, I lay in lucid states thinking, wishing worlds into being and dreams into flesh. As the long train of my years slipped slowly by, I befriended a world that existed just beyond the physical, beyond the horizon of awake. As the days fused with night and gray formed at my temples, I could no longer tell lucid from awake, dreams from not. I was awake in my dreams and dreaming while awake. Increasingly, I willed into manifestation the worlds perceived beneath the silent discourse of my mind's noise. In a quantitative sense I could articulate the agreed upon constructs of the physical world and collective reality with others. I never lost this perspective. My window to this world was not replaced rather enhanced, elaborated upon by a greater or other awareness. The Kingdom of God does not destroy; it subsumes, magnifies, and extends. It is all so very incredible and not just a little frightening.

MAPPING THE INTERNAL

It was always just before and within me. As the packages of thought, parcels, and threads of each moment were individually labeled and sorted in my mind, I came to understand the mechanics of the chaos of my mind. I spent many years thinking that only my mind was sheer chaos theory. However, I came to see that few even understand the architecture of their own minds. As I marveled at the seemingly random constructs of my mind, I came to see that my mind was like a radio with all the stations receiving at the same time. Slowly, deliberately, I tuned to only the stations I desired. In the background, I could make out the "hum" of another sound, another awareness. It was everywhere, behind every "frequency" of my thoughts and considerations. It is akin to changing the channels of the television. When the station stops sending the program across the airwaves, the static snow that is left on each channel is no less than the original traffic from the creation of the universe. That original snow, that first signal is received in my mind and underlies all the electrical activity that begets my person. As I slowly switched off all the unnecessary channels, the remaining sound was the sound of creation, the Bath of Life, the Lost Word. I seek out the hum, the background noise, and rest my channel there.

My thoughts have become more deliberate, more intense, and are both considered and realized at a deeper place, free of associative distractions and derailments. I began seeing what I had otherwise only sensed. I have become an antenna. While I do not receive special instructions from a divine being, a dog, Alpha Centauri, or the dead, I do increasingly "see" without the aid of my eyes. It is a difficult notion to explain, as most consider the issue of seeing, or of hearing, as being only related to the sense of sight or sound. In fact, "seeing" and "hearing" only borrow the language rather than the sense. "Seeing" and "hearing" are beyond the scope of the senses as we know them. I know this even though I lack the ability to converse in language convincingly.

Born of this heightened sensory awareness is an understanding of such profound simplicity that it defies description. I have often wondered if the ages are occasioned by enlightened prophets and seers, why they do not tell of the "way." Why would none lay out the framework to the Kingdom? They have. It is so obvious that history is littered with noble martyrs who have attempted to aid humanity escape the luggage of the ages.

Yet, I am not sure it is even necessary, or advisable for this to be done. Not by one roadmap or discourse, not by one push or shove can anyone be brought to *this* place. My goal has always been unrealistic in this regard and attempting to describe what is found in my own world, rather than explaining how I got here, is sure to fall short of making any sense to one who just does not "know" for themselves. While the scriptures of the world give ample instruction in what adherents assert is indeed the "way" to the Kingdom of God, they often fail to support their assertion.

The scriptures of the world describe a fantasyland between brimstone and beatification, and it is in another world, when our bodies are deceased and then being wrong is too late. However, there is otherwise ample evidence of enlightened men and women penning language within these scriptures and elsewhere that enable us to deconstruct the filters that blind us to the Kingdom of God right here, right now.

Even the Christ spoke to this clearly as he explained that he had inner mysteries and mysteries for the masses. This knowledge is everywhere in snippets and occasional discourse, but the inquiring mind must of its own cognizance enable discernment before the "breadcrumbs" are of any real use to an aspirant. There is a strange compunction to leave these breadcrumbs to others, but I am not convinced it matters in any event. One of the reasons is it necessary to discern the Christ's message is not simply because he was enigmatic. Rather Christ's teachings were eviscerated by the scripture censors.

Somewhere in time the ages slipped from me, and I became aware keenly of my immortality. This is contrary to what I see as the process for humanity. Literature is replete with Man becoming aware of his mortality in the coming of age. Yet, I have had no such epiphany. Instead, I have come to know, not even believe, that I am immortal. I have lost forever any fear of the passing of my flesh, nor lamenting the landmarks of my days, my blood, my seed, slipping from my grasp, I slipping from theirs.

The depth and nature of matter has even changed for me. I do not even apprehend matter the same as I once did. If struck with a two-by-four piece of wood, I will surely bleed. If I fall from a great height, I will be a mess for others to clean up. I am not describing supernatural phenomena associated with our Western, comic-book culture. I cannot assert any preternatural abilities. I am describing something far more esoteric, far more fundamental to existence.

In the entire world, in all space, in all time, it is generally thought that what is here is what is comprehended by the senses. One world. One time. One chance. Our physical world is bounded by the limits of our perception. Our ability to consider, examine, perceive, and measure the world and our lives is limited by our senses and their prosthetics. All else is theoretical, or worse heretical to the modern religion of science. Not unlike the gatekeepers of faith, access to God and to what is unknown is kept closely guarded by those who are self-appointed custodians of the Kingdom of God. I do not indict. I have nothing but understanding for these people and their actions, in all times. It is for each only to pass the place where truth no longer echoes in the heart, but is understood and heard by the soul. This is mostly the reason why life is absent a roadmap to enlightenment. It is just not something that can be translated. And, if translated even in a fashionable and applicable way, it still is not in itself able to facilitate the means to the end. Words in and of themselves can be instructive, but rarely do they act as keys and open locks. Thoughts, however, are the foundation of the worlds. Thought is the very building block of all consciousness, all life, and the constituency of God.

ALL THESE WORLDS

As I would lie down to sleep, I would fancy my dreams and fabricate them as the day slipped into the world between awake and not. Over a period of time I was able, more or less, to actually carry these willful fancies into my sleep state. Often, and certainly when I was much younger, my dreams were wholly without construct. They were their own creations. As I grew and turned my very personality into my laboratory, my mind into my basic training, I increasingly found I needed less sleep. I was aware that I was lucid dreaming in my awakened states as well. This has got to be what is referenced when those who ask hypothetically, but lightly, is this the dream world or is the dream world reality? It is really an easily dismissed notion but one that provokes laughter, consternation, consideration, and elaboration at parties and other venues where alcohol is served. What is the dream world?

I often reduce the most serious of my life's issues into comedy. It is the only way I can transport my thoughts to others as I find I am too intense about the issues people are most afraid of, most reserved about. It is often that when I describe my world, I liken it to a Salvador Dali timepiece. This is not tragic by any means, and I will take some space below to explain this.

My world is free. I have no fears in the place where lives my heart. There is nothing I cannot dream. I believe in all things. I believe in God. God is not an aged white man with a staff. God is not watching every single thing we do and intervening constantly in our lives. There is a natural world of laws. There is a divine world of laws superimposed upon the natural.

We are no more able to understand this with our senses than an ant is able to understand the location of his ant farm when purchased as a child's play-toy for a birthday.

There are numerous worlds right here, right now. When we undress, when we make love, when we fight, when we cry, when we dream (especially when we dream, absent our defenses), we are sharing our energies, our space, and our time with other life, other reality. I am aware that there is currently a deluge of New Age literature that is disgustingly profiting on these increasingly understood truths. However, when capitalism is a motivation to discharge such information, it is by definition poisoned and necessarily incomplete. It is dangerous to think *profit* can be made from that which is owned by all. What I have to say is based solely on experiential facts and has been decades in the making. I do not refer to remuneration for production and related costs when I talk of profit poisoning the product. When profit is calculated in the dissemination of spirit one may rest assured that the bearer is not vested in what they offer.

There is depth in the space before you right now. It is not filled with the matter that makes your daily artifacts; rather it is filled with light, vibrating energy, and intelligence that exist at a different frequency. I have always sensed this but never in this way. What I sensed was akin to what we all experience at one time or another; the feeling of not aloneness, of someone watching. However, I always had this sensation in the extreme. It was a combination of factors that led me to turn inward from my very youth. I did not completely sense other worlds before me. My youth could not comprehend this. I did, however, realize even in my childhood that my mind was a wild horse.

Other worlds? Here, right now are the many mansions "in my father's House." In this same place and time is heaven. In this same place and time is hell. There is no physical location for heaven. It is not on the dark side of the moon. Hell is not in the center of the earth. Hell is not. These places exist not outside the Ptolemaic spheres. There is no "other place." How can the senses declare that which is beyond their specialized job description? They cannot; they can only infer and lend to conjecture. It is all right here, right now.

I AM IN LOVE

My time in Pakistan neared an end, and I was considerably more informed by the opportunity to reflect on the man I had become. I had great change brewing within me and was aware that I no longer wished to battle both in the spirit and the battlefield of modern war. Something had forever changed in me. I was berthing my convictions in no school of thought, and no impressionable sentiments could ever alter such a mind as I had harnessed, yet something profound had finally "clicked" in me. I had been meditating for many years. Well, I am not sure if it is praying or meditating and I do neither like anyone else I have ever met. Again, my supplication is the unique product of introverting absent influence; I developed a uniquely intimate affair with God absent guidance or coercion.

I closed my eyes and was thankful that I have, for so many years, thanked God and Life each and every day for the many wonderful lessons and blessings that are my days. I came to the point many years ago that I was prepared each day to die. It is not that I wanted to die, but I always wanted to live my life in such a way that if I were to die, I would be prepared and would have already said and done all that needed action. As the years moved on, I was generally in a non-stop submission of gratitude. I am simply so grateful for all I have in this life. My dear God, when I look around the world at the lives that are all about my senses how can I not be grateful for the joy and the pain, the love and the loss, that has brought me to my knees before creation and eternity. I have moved through the worlds of war and famine with head held high, confident in the mystery that underlies all these dying games. I wondered, though, what my heart, my bleeding life would be like were I to blindly live and only upon my exit consider the minutes of my life in gratitude. Who would I be then, looking back, and what is it I would see and appreciate were I him who missed the magic in these moments? (See Chapter 66, "Reprieve for an Unexamined Life")

I looked out into the dark night from my porch and inhaled deeply the jasmine that gave me such joy. I closed my door and retired to my bed. My time in Pakistan was done.

My team had not yet departed for the United States. I was always a loner and had my ticket changed so I might go to Dubai and visit a friend. Tim was in Dubai. It would be good to see Tim for a bit and spend some further time catching up. I had first met Tim on the eve of my re-entry onto active duty during the first Gulf War. He too was one of many who returned to active duty during this time. We became good friends and had since worked together in the 3rd Special Forces, in Indonesia, Baghdad, and many other places.

I was aware as I boarded the plane in Islamabad that this was likely the last time I would conduct this counter-terrorism training. It is not that it is too demanding, quite the contrary. It is simply that I knew with some unspoken conviction that this day was slipping into the place where memories reign alone. It was always good to have a seat in business class. What more could anyone ask? I never noted there were seats further up from business, so I am not sure why anyone would purchase first-class tickets. Besides, I was not paying for my fare.

There is a sweet sense of loss and change when the land drops away and a weary body takes flight on a course of no return. It was like this in near every place of which I had become fond. However, the departure was very much a part of the hello and the experience. Saying goodbye to people and places is something we can become accustomed to. I had pretty much given up drinking alcohol some time before, for no other reason than my reality became more surreal than any drink could mediate. Therefore, I declined a cocktail and rested easily and quickly into my reclined position at altitude. I continued to close the loop on the life-review I recently had in Baghdad.

▼

CHAPTER 19

On Politics in Passing: Dubai

Sweet friend, I have no students. I came to a startling awareness last year. I am the student. This is not some abstract consideration rather it is so intensely accurate that it defies understanding. I considered this while still a child but only fully realized this while in Baghdad. It is simply that even those who ask of me wind up being my teacher. I am not sure you can see this now but I am not feigning humility, I am telling you something very assuredly. Every single person and event is my teacher.

I stretched out and turned to one side. The seats on these international flights got better all the time. I still had an hour or so before they started all the pre-landing crap. The flight was only three and a half hours or so from Islamabad to Dubai. I could not wait. I really liked Dubai. I had my phone chip already installed. I knew the city. I had friends.

"Sir? Sir? You have to put your seat belt on. We are landing shortly."

I love Emirates Airlines. Americans have gotten so used to purchasing crummy service and calling it good that they do not even know any better. Throughout most of the rest of the world the standard level of service often exceeds the service for which Americans pay top dollar and call "first class." Emirates Airlines was better then any American carrier I had flown, and they had more lovely attendants. I had been working in the Muslim world for years by this time.

THE ISLAMIC WORLD

What stands out most striking in my years of traveling in the Islamic World is that I have never met anyone who was cruel to me or otherwise negatively predisposed because I was Caucasian, or American. I have never encountered a bitter heart, or a vicious attitude. I have never had a person curse me or say an unkind word. What stands out in these years is that my findings are counter-intuitive to the impressions gleaned from the Western media and current discourse on Eastern affairs.

I have been greeted from Jakarta to Amman with smiles and acceptance; at a minimum, I was always shown tolerance and given the benefit of the doubt. As such, I was invited to homes, dinners, mosques, and family activities from Yemen to Kabul. I was invited to the first Christian dinner hosted by the president of Afghanistan, Hamid Karzai. (It was at this Christmas gathering that I had the unique opportunity to sing "Happy Birthday *Mister President*" to a head of state. This was one of the funniest experiences of my life as my outrageous presumption to sing this forced my team to join in. After all, no man goes into the fight alone). I have weekly assisted with foodstuffs to an Islamic children's orphanage in Kulapa Dua, Java, where the leading Imam of Java welcomed me as family. It was his orphanage, his mosque. He invited me to pray with him. I provided his dying wife her hospice and nursing care. He later became my patient as well. Patience was extended to me everywhere. Hearts and wallets were opened by the poor of Sana'a, Yemen, and in Kabul, from Baluchistan to Bamiyan. Muslims have given me of their hearts, their faith, their breads, and their best. In many places I was only one of few Americans that they had ever seen.

Often, entire seas of peoples would catch notice of me in public places and stare unconsciously; when our eyes would meet I never had the occasion to sense repugnance, rather smiles were always flashed instantly; I was keenly aware of this on Java. In the countless circumstances where burkas concealed females I would note their observing me with my peripheral vision. When our eyes would meet they would rarely retreat instead I noted often a deep inquisition and curiosity; then I would shift my gaze promptly out of respect—and safety. In the villages and cities throughout the world where Muslim women wore less attire covering their features, I was often greeted with smiles and hand waves too numerous to count.

In the darkest days of Baghdad, I was afforded every kindness and extension of Allah's peace that could be mustered in such troubled times. While there were clearly people trying to kill me and otherwise harm me, I did not *meet* them—not face-to-face. I met them at the ends of barrels as they retreated to the darkness or death. No, I never broke bread with those like this, and in the light of day they were either cowards and treated me like everyone else as they moved in the crowds or they were, as I suspect, simply minimalized by the millions across the Arab and Muslim world who are decent and civilized human beings.

In the Levant, on the subcontinent of Pakistan, the Arabian Peninsula, Syria, and Jordan, I was afforded a level of courtesy that I find sorely lacking in my homeland where the huddled masses gather. In my homeland, affluence reigns, and with it, the liberty of station to critique with xenophobic zeal. Often real knowledge of distant peoples and lands is sorely lacking. Can my nation's policies really have been forged by academics in seclusion and implemented later by the few Arabists at the State Department? Yes, I think so. The point being Arabists should have actually drafted policy, or been in the loop. Perhaps this is arguable; the results are not.

I have seen little in my travels to reflect the widespread hatred of America that now defines the argument at home to continue to oppose cultural and other forms of engagement. I am very certain this hatred exists, but I find it is a disdain of our government, and not of Americans themselves. In any event, I was never treated differently but I have been aware of the distrust of the U.S. government. America is inadvertently asserting and continuing policies and practices that have alienated the Arab world. The circle is closed.

I am often asked by what roads have much of our current problems come to be. I do not sustain that America is responsible for the horrific acts that have beset my beloved land. However, I wonder about the people I have met, not the demented, twisted zealots who pollute the very name of God. What of these countless millions reflected in the samples I have known? How have we evolved in isolation from each other? Why are there such profound misunderstandings between our peoples?

It is simply the case that the conflict that besets this age is real and palpable in its gravity and threat to the welfare of the modern and emerging worlds. However, these faces of horror that describe the endless nightmare of newscasts and define these days are not a reflection of the crowds of millions that eek out a life across this world.

I have not seen one example that could serve as a negative generalization of an entire faith or people. In fact, I am overwhelmed by the constant hospitality I have been afforded in my travels in the Islamic world. I am not a Muslim. It is a logical but irrelevant question. What serves to most illuminate the warmth I have encountered is the contrast to my life in America. My sensitivity to the kindness encountered abroad is not born of my childhood. I have spent numerous years in many far away lands. My observations are always, in all cases, as objective as I can muster. It is instructive that I am not a Christian, either, yet nearly all Muslims assume I am. It is generally assumed that all Americans are Christians, or so my impressions inform me.

In Pakistan, as well as Indonesia, Iraq, Yemen, the United Arab Emirates, and other places, I continually marvel at the number of Christians I encounter in Muslim lands. I do not defend obvious policies that are discriminatory. My observations exist not as a counterpoint to civil-rights abuses or representation, but rather as a humble commentary on peoples in general. Many Americans would be surprised to know that Christians exist throughout the Arab world and have been there since long before there were Christians in America, Europe, or even before Muslims were here. From Gaza to the West Bank, from Jerusalem to Basra, from the Ganges to Africa, the Muslim world has been in a relationship with Christianity for millennia. Interestingly enough, Muslims have been in a relationship with Buddhism nearly as long. In this region of the world that now foments great unease and conflict, there is precedent for compatibility. All great faiths have had excesses and horrors attributed to their proselytizing. We have no loss of examples to make one weary or suspicious. I guess what I am suggesting is there is already a guide to mend both our perceptions and our realities in our deportment with each other. The rule and guide for civil, political and military harmony is evidenced in the historical record. We will only ever find, on inspection, that which we are looking for. Look for war and war is found; look for peace and you will find the means to peace. This is not naïve thinking; this is a fact. One can act unilaterally while still maintaining self-interest, general welfare, strategic interests, and economic engagement.

I would not hold out any one lifestyle as superior, or even equal. If given the choice, I do not know that I would choose this life or that. I know that most Americans just do not know a thing about Islam and the larger Muslim world. They have no experiences to mark sound deportment toward the Muslim world and there is a dearth of complimentary literature commenting on the cultural traditions and our similarities. I would venture that many of my brethren are not even aware that Islam is a cousin, correction, a brother of their Judeo-Christian origins. YHWH (Tetragrammaton) and al Lah (Allah-the God) are ostensibly one and the same. Allah is the same as the "Father" whom Jesus prayed to.

Jesus' crucifixion is noted with solemnity and holiday granted throughout the Islamic world. Christ is one of the greatest prophets in a long line of prophets ending with Mohammed (Peace Be Upon Them). Marists might be surprised to know Mary, the mother of the Christ, is greatly revered in Islam and an entire Sura (book) is devoted to her and the Immaculate Conception in the Qur'an.

Common ground cannot be measured by the means of production, economic engines of state, societal frameworks or shared visions. If one would understand nearly one quarter of the world's population one must understand that Islam is not simply a faith, it is the means and manner for the conduct of life. Our overall commonalities are not entirely missed by policymakers and opinion leaders. These have been considered in great detail since the creation of the state of Israel. However, the commonalities considered were often between the Jews and the Arabs, not between the West and the Muslim world, and there were not many commonalities to recall as Judaism existed primarily in absentia (diaspora) throughout much of the last fifteen hundred years of Islam. We had better re-examine the ties that bind if we are serious about exploring alternatives to conflict. The triggers that escalate conflict are not so clearly defined when one leaves the parlors of diplomatic doublespeak and enters the world of the opinion of the masses.

AMERICA HAS NO CLOTHES

My nation is at a crossroads where we can bring the familial Muslim world into modernity or patronize our historical neglect with stick-and-carrot politics to support no more than an ethnocentric security policy. On the one hand we may revel in successes from limited open trade secondary to anti-terror support of U.S. policies. On the other hand, we may lament setbacks due to alienating regimes, or emerging regimes whose support we may desire today. Regardless, what is lacking is a comprehensive cultural engagement with a vision that is based on honorable discourse and mutual rewards.

Until the Muslim world is brought collectively into the family of modern peoples, we invite the scattered nihilists to continue to slaughter the innocents and provide to them the pabulum to do so.

There is no shortage of intellectual and political awareness in the Muslim world. From Indonesia to Kuwait, peoples are now screaming for representation and freedom. Increasingly, they are apprehending this as well. When we stead-fastly link democracy and national intercourse, we do so at everyone's peril. As the Hashemite King has noted, "Democracy will mean different things to differ-ent people." This is a fact that cannot be overlooked. America must be cautious in expecting little congressional congresses springing up in Loya Jirgas or Iraq. Peoples will reach toward democracy's end commensurate with their historical, tribal, and religious capacity.

America can be positively in the mix of emerging democracies or simply a col-onizing landlord with an overstated foreign policy based on national self-interest *only*. While national interest should underpin all policy, it is still incumbent to engage from the tribal, from the village, to the transnational, in support of mutual self-interests. Interests need not be exclusive.

Many Muslims will remain suspicious of America, but it seems to be based, weakly, on hearsay and misinformation rather than organized disinformation (which does, nevertheless exist—in some cases with state sponsorship). Most inquire personally of Westerners in a friendly, inquisitive manner. I have met few who want to hold untenable points of view regardless of the observations and facts from their own peers. This is the case in any nation. However, I am aware that there are many with such profound disdain for the West they would retreat from being a part of my experience at all and thus skew my observations.

It is an awkward task to limit the scope of such observations to the political, cultural, and tribal, or to just the narrow parameters of the religious alone. Invari-ably, all these factors, and many others, will conspire to demand attention in one's observations of Islamic peoples. In the Muslim world, none of these issues exist separately as they may in a secular nation. The fabric of the larger Muslim world is such that the underlying glue in all things is religious. Arabic is also the universal and sacred language of the liturgy throughout the Muslim world; this should give a clue how "theocentric" life is. The notion of democratic representa-tion is new, and otherwise alien to a historically theocratic and tribal-familial peo-ple. The process and means to positively influence a large swath of the world's population will only be achieved through honest, sound investment in the people themselves. Toward this end numerous tools exist at the disposal of the nation-state. The most significant tool is our foreign policy in general.

THE THORN IN ISHMAEL'S SIDE

The United States should reconsider outdated regional concepts that have us defining by omission all nation-states in the Levant, save for the state of Israel, as dubious. Whether by the power of sheer lobby or other, America's blind support of Israel is perceived as painful and discriminatory by the Muslim world. America will never get a fair hearing in the mind of the Islamic world until a more equitable regional policy is perceived. The assertion that human rights standards and elected governments are the thresholds that nation-states must cross to be our friend is viewed as transparent and hypocritical linkage. The United States is thought to have a double standard in this part of the world, and I state only a perception that countless millions share.

The issue of the thorn of Israel is real. American will achieve no more than skin deep penetration into the collective Islamic world while reflexively protecting the state of Israel from purported abuses of the very same civil and human rights that the U.S. holds up to the Arab world to justify disengagement or linkage. Moreover, the perception is Israel has otherwise adopted polices and practices that result, quite strikingly, in refugee camps similar to the ghettos of World War II. This is among the lesser grievous assertions.

There are ample abuses on both sides of this confusing and tragic issue. Israeli's arguments to justify such actions are often emotive, besieged, and convincing. Often lost in all the noise of politics and war are the numerous suffering lives on both sides of this thorny issue. However, my point is not to discuss the savage perceptions of the Palestinian-Israeli issue. The problem appears quite intractable and the best minds and efforts in the world have often failed to bring men of peace to the table. However, it is the brokering influence of America that has been the wounded lion in the arena. Respect rather then fear is often a more valuable tool then Roosevelt's "stick and carrot" in this part of the world. America lacks respect abroad.

While most in the West cannot begin to gauge the degree of poverty and despair across the remaining world, there is, for all this suffering, a tangible spirit, a faith unbound between Man and God in every land I have visited. There exists a seemingly closer union with the natural world as well. While this is hard to measure, it is evident. In these places where the luxury does not exist to consider what to have for dinner, only whether or not there will *be* dinner, one's breath is stolen when invited to eat the best that is offered by such hosts—and it is often no more than yogurt-milk, rice, and pan bread. But it will be the best they can prepare for you. They will give to you the best of all they have, for no other reason than you are their guest.

In these many lands the imperative—and duty—of the host is so great as to risk all, even life "only unto these men do nothing; for therefore came they under the shadow of my roof" (Genesis 19:8). Christians and Jews alike should recognize this immediately from their sacred texts. Many of these peoples could survive tomorrow if the clock was turned back one, two, or three thousand years. This is not marketable skill, of course, nor a competitive attribute in the technologically modern world. I comment on this point only to illustrate the contrast. America would cease to exist as we know it were it required to be individually self-reliant tomorrow.

I am not a Muslim. I am not a Jew. I am not a Christian. I am an observer. I would be remiss, living in the Muslim world, if I did not thoughtfully consider the impressions broadcast to me for so many years through the American media. I have taken a critical look at the viewpoints I have been holding blindly for so long regarding Middle Eastern affairs. I found my knowledge and comprehension lacking. I was not aware until I deconstructed my notions that my beliefs were not even mine; rather they were the drivel that is fed into the American living room every day through television and radio. There is a really big world of ideas and peoples out here. America ignores these points at her own peril. These observations are likely realized by more learned minds than this one. I seek only to join their chorus. I would be inattentive to spend so much time in the Muslim world and not have some sense of what ails it.

THIS IS JIHAD

Islam does provide the means for complete and utter warfare in the pursuit of the Kingdom of God. However, Christianity, Buddhism, and Hinduism also provide the wherewithal for one so inclined or compelled. Is there a difference? What is this "warfare" we hear so much about, and why do we not hear about other faiths warring for God?

These are good and vital questions that target the heart of the problem the world faces regarding Islamic fundamentalism and all others who would murder indiscriminately on the way to heaven. All faiths have either outright dogma or individual legacies enshrined as their religious legend that speak to the battle beyond the ritual, the war before the Prize.

All traditions couch this incredible process, which is like unto all out warfare, in the language of the lonely warrior. Ephesians of the Christian New Testament is a remarkable illustration of this point:

> Put on the whole armor of God, that ye may be able to stand against the wiles of the devil. For we wrestle not against flesh and blood, but against principalities, against powers, against the rulers of the darkness of this world, against spiritual wickedness in high places. Wherefore take unto you the whole armor of God, that ye may be able to withstand in the evil day, and having done all, to stand.
>
> Stand therefore, having your loins girt about with truth, and having on the breastplate of righteousness; And your feet shod with the preparation of the gospel of peace; Above all, taking the shield of faith, wherewith ye shall be able to quench all the fiery darts of the wicked. And take the helmet of salvation, and the sword of the Spirit, which is the word of God (Ephesians 6:11-17).

In the Hindu epic, the Mahabharata, Arjuna converses with God and is encouraged to sack his reluctance to engage the massing armies before him on the plains of Kurukshetra. Krishna instructs Arjuna in the spiritual wisdom necessary for the warfare ahead. The battle of Kurukshetra is much older than any of the Judeo-Christian-Islamic scriptures. The great Indian traders likely would have influenced the Babylonian region and other birthing grounds of the Judeo-Christian-Islamic tradition. This battle was never about material armies arrayed upon the field. The epic is about the internal war that man must wage to overcome Maya, the illusion of the material world, and man's enslavement to the "box" that prohibits obtaining the Kingdom of God. Whether from one original revelation or the inevitable conclusion of unrelated religious traditions, spiritual warfare is a necessary and final requirement to pass from this world to next.

The traditions that informed the prophets in the Levant are not dissimilar. The analogy that one must go to war and will be beset by armies amassed that are determined to kill you is an ancient medium to instruct all adepts in the battle of the spirit. Since time immemorial the battle for the Kingdom of God was an individual and internal battle waged for the salvation of our own soul.

When the Christ advised "Think not that I come to send peace on earth: I come not to send peace, but a sword" (Matthew 10:34), we err tragically to assume a different or convenient context to this revelation. Christ did not come to send peace to the suffering Jews under Roman Imperial yoke and end the bitter struggle of the Sicari. Christ came to instruct in *Jihad* of the spirit. Christ bore a spiritual sword for no less a purpose then the destruction of the *enemies of God*.

While historically the Judaic, and later Islamic, enemies of God were slain in flesh and confronted in battle as material opponents of God, Christ bore a new covenant that in all manners expressed the true nature of spiritual warfare.

The *enemies of God* are that which most prohibit our individual and collective passage to the Kingdom: the senses, materialism, ignorance of our estate, and illusion. How shockingly inappropriate to think that the Christ that instructed in all manner and ways of relative and absolute love, and encouraged the sinner and the saint alike that the Kingdom of God was at hand, would send a sword to physically slay other human beings; how preposterous.

Zen and Tibetan Buddhism are so completely full of the analogous attire of the Warrior of the Spirit that no elaboration is really necessary. In fact, almost every great and lesser faith utilizes the same imagery because it is factually applicable—one must be a Spiritual Warrior in order to secure the Kingdom of God. Do we find this in Islam? Yes.

Islam has a rich and ample house in which to build a Spiritual Warrior. The Qur'an is similar to the Analects of Confucius in that it is also presents a detailed and elaborate moral code for living; often the Dos and Don'ts of Islam embrace even the minutiae of life. It is in this mix of material guidance and spiritual warfare that the modern jihadists milk authorization for violence. It is not necessary for me to comment on apparent inconsistencies in interpreting the Qur'an as there are a number of areas where the application of Jihad is vague, or downright dubious. I am aware of this. The primary distinctions in Jihad are *jihad al-akbar* and *jihad al-asgar*, greater and lesser jihad, respectively. Greater jihad is on the battlefield of the soul (tawhid). Lesser jihad is the struggle of the armed material camp. This division of jihad is further fractured unto five categories. The preeminent jihad is of the soul and the base, or profane, is jihad of the physical sword.

Notwithstanding this interpretive range any cleric, imam, or man or woman who would interpret Jihad as the authorization to conduct operations that pertain to spirit with the sword of flesh against women, children, and non-combatants are blasphemers to their faith, their people, and to Mankind. It is an incidental fact that suggesting actions so horrible and repugnant, and referring to the authority of scripture to condone such actions, when these actions can be universally objected to as repugnant in all circumstances, one identifies himself as being outside of the scope of God, faith, and the law.

JIHAD: THE BATTLE FOR THE KINGDOM OF GOD

What is really the heart of a jihadist? I can know not the heart of any woman or man. The heart of a man or woman surrendering in God is once more given in mystery when we attire in armor upon the field. None can know this heart any longer. However, *I* would seek to wage complete and total war on the battlefield of my soul. I would invite any devout jihadist to wage war beside me on the battlefield where they claim in their mouths their hearts lie. Politics is not new; war is not new. What is new for *me,* though, is something beyond the sword, the hand, the pen, and the tongue (jihad fi sabilillah). There is a war of the spirit taking place daily that makes trivial all the armies of the world. We are all now able to engage the next frontier. The next and last frontier is the first frontier: the spirit.

The jihadists that murder the flesh of innocents are pretenders to this battle. I know this because they are not arrayed before or beside me on the battlefield of spirit. They are scattered and are calling the darkness the light!

I do not see them in the places where rests the breath of God. I call to them in the place where sings the song of the world, but they are not present. Their refrain is absent.

Were any man, any woman, to hear this song, or array themselves for battle upon these ethereal plains, then I would now know them. There is simply no place for the bombs and the guns, the blood and the cries of the little ones in the worlds where resides God.

I know jihad. Jihad is not in the instruments of suffering, but in the means of salvation. Jihad is the final expression of mankind's salvation from flesh to God, from profane to holy. Jihad is the timeless war fought upon the ancient battlefield of the Self. Islam, indeed no faith person or people, has claim to jihad. All, each and every one of us has claim to jihad. It is our only future, by any name.

CHAPTER 20

▼

The Final Portico

I am so wretched a thing to be loving so and being so base, so pro-fane. I am not worthy. I pretend to goodness and try and ape what I sense from Her. I have little secrets that only She knows. I still try to divorce myself from things in my past that while I am not bound to them they stand in such incongruent counterpoise. I am so imperfect and messy. I feel so humiliated by the grace I have been given. I feel like I should be more righteous, more upright, more helpful, more useful, more loving, more charitable, more everything. Before the Throne of God I have stood and find myself lacking.

Ah, Dubai, I thought; seems like I was just here. I looked around, and my stomach rumbled. The nostalgia of forgotten odors was among the many intrusive thoughts I had lately. The television idled on as I had taken to sleeping with it on as background noise when I slept. For the longest time I told myself that sleeping with the news on was part of my news-junkie routine, part of my work. But lately I had been coming to some real candid assessments of the crap I sold myself as reality, and the fact was I was not even hearing it all. I was not even see-ing everything the way I had. Yet, simultaneously, I was seeing and hearing more than I ever had before. I left the TV on from habit. This habit was born of alone-ness.

I rolled out of bed and made for the bathroom of the Intercontinental Hotel. I was glad the lights were on as I had been sleeping in so many places in the past few years—hell, always. I often did not know where I was when I got up from bed. Occasionally I considered not even navigating to the toilet as I tired of all the brainwork involved in trying to quickly recall where I was as I stumbled in place while getting a bearing. I thought of sleeping beside an empty Gatorade bottle as we did in the tents in Afghanistan because it was so cold outside.

I looked in the wastebasket as I relieved myself, and the strangest thing occurred to me: there was no trash. There never would be, either, because as soon as someone visits long enough to create any trash they would be moving on, and the cleaning people would set right the wastebasket. It would be forever empty preserving the sterility of the hotel. My life was forever erased in the morning and the clock reset. There would never be slippers under the bed. I would never smell cooking from the kitchen. I was growing weary. I was chasing a professional end that was profoundly contradictory to the conclusions I was reaching in my heart.

I sat back on the bed and watched the TV. I watched intently but could not hear anything. I realized still that I had no idea where I was. Dubai? Yes; but where was I? So, this is the end of days, every day? There was an absurd meaning-less in all of this. My retrospection continued in Dubai. I turned off the TV just after a man informed me that I could build wealth without working. However, I needed to send him money to get that recently discovered information that he would share with me. *How lucky can I get today?* The room was dark. I beat my pillows to make them "just right" and searched for an uninjured part of my body to lie on and sleep.

COLLATING MEMORIES, COLLATING YEARS

I had seen more horror and bloodshed in my life long before I ever went in the military. This was a constant refrain of mine whenever someone would lean closer in conversation, look both left and right (sometimes placing a hand to one side of their mouth) and ask me, "Have you ever killed someone?" People are such spectators. Then again, I think life itself is a spectator sport for most. Then there are those who actually live it. I suppose there is a place in between where we vicariously do some of both. I think I am a participant, though. Yes, that is what I will call myself today, a participant. But what I was going to do tomorrow would be in that place between participant and spectator. I think tomorrow I would just think some more.

Tomorrow would be a good enough day. Outside, the weather would be as it always is in Dubai: beautiful. I recalled how I despised the winter. Mostly though, I did not like a city's winter at all. People were all hurried and as cold as the temperature outside. Besides, the snow was gritty and gray, and the sun ran away. Yes, I liked the spring. I liked the sun.

When I was a young boy I recalled how I used to revel in the snow. That was New York City, and while I did not like the city, there was fun to be had in the snow—dirty or not.

We would hide behind some snow-impacted car or hedgerow and wait for the trucks to slow down at the intersection. They would not stop if the snow was "skitching" snow, but not for fear or skitchers (only we knew the skitching secret), rather for fear of being stuck in the snow. We would have to time very accurately our pounce lest we give ourselves away by the driver catching us in his side mirrors.

"There, go!" We were off and nearly running at a crouch as we made our way to the back of the trucks and got in sync with a truck's speed, got ourselves a handhold, and we were skitching. At times the sheer thrill was even too much for one of us. Getting caught waving to someone as we passed by or holding a finger to our mouths in the "Shhh" sign to a nearby car going thirty miles per hour could earn you a face dive in a snow bank if the vehicle was turning. Of course, only the most experienced skitchers would risk staying with their prey out past the avenue. That is where the heaviest traffic was and any seasoned skitcher knew that there were areas salted already past the avenue. Hitting a dry spot on Keds sneakers at thirty miles per hour was unlike any other childhood madness.

I smiled fondly at the thought of little Eddie, a thousand years ago, doing little-boy things. I turned and fell more deeply into the pillow, my face alight with a young boy's smile. It would be desert-hot tomorrow.

AFGHANISTAN

Dubai is a city with more modern construction booming than any other place I had ever been. I had been coming through Dubai on the way to one place or another for some years now. I became charmed with Dubai when I was a medic on the President Karzai protective detail. The Taliban and Al Qaeda wanted Karzai dead following their defeat. After they tried to assassinate President Karzai in Kandahar and failed, a civilian force of former Special Forces, Delta Force, and Navy SEALs was put together to replace the U.S. Navy SEAL Team-6 that was then providing his close protection. I am sure the SEALs were doing the best job that could be done, but I think the administration wanted to have a "cut out" should President Karzai fall. The SEALs are among the best assets in the world to protect another human being in a combat environment.

In the end, though most said he was "dead man walking," President Karzai continues to move Afghanistan arguably toward the modern age. The presidential palace where Karzai worked every day had the bullet holes of the previous assassinations of the heads of Afghan state and their families going back many years. The palace kitchen still cooked in cauldrons on burning embers of wood, deep below ground in a long, dark, cave-like labyrinth. Afghanistan is a land that is clearly being dragged screaming and kicking into modernity. Working in this environment can only be called a challenge. Despite the threat, the infrastructure was minimal. The people had been beaten into the ground by endless years of foreign and domestic warfare and oppression. Operating under these austere conditions took its toll on everyone. Often the rocket attacks, concern for improvised explosive devices, and landmines were the least draining on a person. More often it was the lack of showers, toilets, good food, and healthy diversion. Dubai was the sensory camping ground on the way in and out of Kabul. I liked it here.

DUBAI

In the United Arab Emirates one could get anything the heart desired. After spending many months in Kabul, my first binge in Dubai was actually the least obvious. I got a room at the Renaissance Hotel, ordered lots of pastries and cakes, ran a bubble bath, and lay in it like a spoiled woman eating pastries. I took what remained to bed. That is where I woke the next day with blueberry tarts packed into the side of my head and whip cream dry in my beard. After staying in the alert zone of the mind's awareness, eating pastries was not the first thing on many people's list of things to do upon leaving Kabul.

It was not uncommon to run into old friends heading out to Asia, Iraq, or Africa in this bustling city. One day I went to spend some time with Tim, one of my dearest friends. Tim had always known that I listened to a different drummer but unlike others that paid me lip service he actually had a fairly good grasp at the issues on which I reflected. However, to none have I ever shown the minutes of my heart as I have done here in the written word. I did not this day, either, with Tim, but I did speak at length on how this past year or two had been an assimilation of sorts for me, with my recent trips to Yemen and Pakistan being solely dedicated to my consideration of life and my recent past.

OUT OF BODY

I told Tim more of a most remarkable experience I had in recent years. It is apparent that, following my car accident, I literally spent years of my life trying to recapture that peace, that place that came in the blood and the darkness, the pain and the passing. I looked high and low and eventually settled in my own heart. I recalled with Tim how, in 1996 I was lying easily upon my bed in the middle of the day and was going to take a nap. A friend of mine was resting on the couch inside reading some magazine.

I don't recall any "how," only that I was aware that I was floating outside of my body and could see my friend in the other room. I was actually looking down at myself. I realized I was up at the ceiling in the corner of the room and was looking down and in at my friend, down at me.

I must be dead, I thought. *I must be!*

Immediately upon considering this, I was terrified, though I am still not sure why. I was literally sucked back into me. I could not feel it, could not control it, and could not stop it.

I would later consider that this sensation of being sucked back into me was very similar to the experience I had following my car accident. I lay in what seemed total darkness, inside myself. I was horrified. I was convinced I was alive inside my dead body. I rocked myself frantically and was screaming, though no sound passed my lips and my body did not move. I was crying though no water lay upon my cheek, either. I was rocking myself desperately trying to wake me up. I could feel the sense that my feet were slowly starting to move. I then felt as if my legs were rocking with my intent. I was screaming still and felt my torso rocking. Slowly I started to mouth words and then heard a scream escape my lips. I was finally able to rouse myself and immediately went inside and told my friend. I was alarmed and animated. It was the most exhilarating thing that had happened to me in years. I was completely and fully outside of my body one more time.

This was not the first time this happened to me. This was the first time in a long time, and this particular event had such gravity to it that it closed the distance between 1975 and the present in a "twinkling of an eye." I knew that someone must have experienced this. There had to be others. I was no longer a child. I now wanted to know more. I was not looking for validation. However, I was looking for answers. I went to the bookstore. Good thing I did, too, as this was about to become a more common occurrence for me.

I was aware that there were certain things that had happened to me that no one else would know about unless they actually experienced this. Thus my own knowledge of what happened would act as a bona fide of sorts. I looked for someone who could describe in detail what happened in me. I came across a number of books. Many of them were vague or seemed to be parroting what was otherwise contained in other books. Validation was missing. I started rifling through a book by Robert Monroe and found descriptions of what had happened to me. I continued reading about his experiences and found in his recounts a verbatim account of what I had experienced. *There*, I thought, *it is real and others experience this*. I bought what I could and returned home. For the first time in my life I was armed with the powerful knowledge that there were others.

It was not important to me, this experience, in and of itself. To me it was a portent of what lay just beyond what I was seeing as the world and a summation of many years of increasingly strange awareness. Over the following years I would not ever really be able to reproduce this body separation at will. Though it continued to happen with greater frequency, I have never put my finger on what triggers it. I eventually made it a point not to bother with trying too hard as I saw my body existing outside of my flesh as just a parcel of the much larger unknown that was consuming me. This event lacked great import on my life, overall, as I was having remarkable experiences in many ways. This one experience just highlighted that my internal was externalizing. This was the manner in which I became acquainted with Bob Monroe.

LOOKING FORWARD

"So, they have an actual institute?" Tim asked.

"Apparently they do," I answered. "I never really thought about it. But I guess it makes sense to me now that others are aware that God is still found in the absence of Rome, or any other faith," I sarcastically concluded.

"So, you're going to go to this place in Virginia when you return to the States?"

"I am!" I told him.

I had contacted the Monroe Institute and made arrangements to attend their one-week Gateway Program. I wanted to share this information with Tim, as he had known for years I used one of Monroe's HemiSync CDs in an effort to "trigger" the same experience I had in 1996. While I say this experience had minimal import overall, I was still constantly attempting to bridge this separation with my prayer and meditation. The powerful impressions I received in prayer and meditation informed me that there was indeed a connection between all my non-sensory experiences and prayer and meditation.

He understood that when I listened to this compact disc, I felt I was expediting the descent within. Tim knows me better than all people. We worked in very intimate proximity for years. He knows I could not give a crap what the world thought of me. He also knows if I believe in something, anything, it is likely something that is of value. I hold no belief or conviction that cannot withstand the scrutiny of my mind and heart, and I review and consider myself constantly. I am in the process of becoming something else every day, or unbecoming. The reason this conversation was so important was I needed to bounce off Tim the sense that I was choosing roads now that singularly would take me out of the world of flesh and into the world that has labored so long beside my waking state, and states of violence. I wanted to finally explore what others were saying about what was changing in me, without my having to reveal to anyone my minutes. I was not a joiner.

I marveled at my conversations with Tim these days. Tim and I both appear to have approached a needful exploration of self for entirely different reasons. We have each taken remarkably different approaches to understanding both ourselves and others in our world. I took a more esoteric and intimate journey, while Tim has taken a more deliberate social sciences sort of approach. It was truly a fascinating time to find so many of my convictions echoed in the findings of another. This time with Tim further cemented Tim as, quite frankly, the only male in my life with whom I was close. Up to this time in my life, my close friends have all been women.

CHAPTER 21

▼

There Are Others: The Monroe Institute

The house of my soul is ascendant in the still morning light, which cast the Blue Ridge in hues of gold, white, and blue. Contrary to the imagery suggested, this part of the world is not just blue. I recall the name "Blue Ridge" is a reference to the blue that is cast atop the dawn as it lay resting on these ancient hills. In this place, at this time, blue is born from the air, the gases, and the waking dawn, unlike other places in this world.

What is not trafficked to the human consciousness is the free will to perceive reality in a manner most useful to expanding our minds.

I came to The Monroe Institute (TMI) for "audio entrainment." This is a term I understood from professional journals. For some reason I thought I would simply be in an isolation unit undergoing fairly constant hemi-synchronization immersion. I guess I never really gave much thought to the fact that there were others out here, too, who were experiencing such things and were also convinced that Bob Monroe really was onto something brilliant. When I looked online and saw TMI's residential programs, I did not give much thought to the human component, that others were interested as I was. When I listened to the compact disc I purchased years earlier, I came to incorporate Bob's knowledge into the isolation of my world. I had spent so much of my life in the alone place of my evolving heart that I had little interaction with others on such topics. That other people were exploring the internal was abstract, at best.

Hemi-synchronization is a process by which the brain is exogenously induced into desirable frequencies, or states. The brain, in its natural state, actually emits a detectable electrical pulse, a frequency, which has been noted and understood for many years. This pulse is both the product and the actual operations of the internal environment. Certain practices, states, or states of our consciousness produce a given frequency. For example, a deep state of sleep might be below a given amount of cycles per second, and called Delta; a relaxed state would be many more cycles per second and called Alpha. While there are many different states and various Greek titles, the brain is not necessarily hemispherically synchronized during these times. For most operations in the material world, the brain operates just fine in hemispheric autonomy.

Bob Monroe was, by profession, associated with radio, and the components of sound. In his own explorations, Bob attempted to "induce" what was otherwise experienced randomly in his own life. In other words, Bob was able to experience out-of-body experiences at will, and he set out to map his brain activity during these states. When Bob understood the reflections of the proper state for this activity revealed in the brain-state findings, he was ready to begin.

Introducing one frequency into the audio channel of one ear, the brain normally processes one sound, one frequency. Likewise, the same process, if repeated on the other ear, will have findings similar to the sound emitted. However, when various frequencies are emitted simultaneously into each ear the brain processes this variation by synchronizing a third frequency, one not generated to either audio channel.

MONKS IN THE THETA

Monks in deep meditation have been shown to emit frequencies within the Theta state. This is very low frequency associated with transcendental experiences. Others more educated than I could better explain the technical data. Suffice it to say that Bob was able to backward engineer states conducive to his desired end. When studies revealed that persons, when connected to sensitive electrical detection devices, such as the electroencephalogram, demonstrated certain common frequency characteristics while also reporting "unique experiences," Bob was able to extrapolate the binaural sounds necessary to induce this by external means. Thus he termed this process hemispherical synchronization. In my observation this process bypasses numerous sensory watchdogs and facilitates more rapid access to internal environments that permit internal exploration. The brain is enabled to "re-focus" internally.

My interest in Robert Monroe was less a result of searching than it was seeing. Bob Monroe came upon observations that struck me both intuitively as correct and more. Monroe spoke to me through time and text in bona fides. When I had read years earlier of Monroe's experiences in what are termed out-of-body experiences, I gleaned information that no other human could have known had they not experienced the same process. Thus Bob Monroe cleared the ultimate hurdle of my skeptical mind. Lastly, I offered the body of what I understood Bob's work to be to my mind and considered therein absent any other input. I found Bob Monroe's aims and knowledge base to be a remarkable utility. However, Bob's products and findings were and are no more than tools.

I first utilized Bob's technique in the mid-1990s. This may not reliably be called a technique, as it is passive listening with headphones. This is not subliminal suggestion, in the classic sense. While I have never duplicated at will my most profound experiences by these means, I was keenly aware I recreated the very same internal environment. There is a school of thought that holds brain entrainment is both the inevitable result of continued hemisynchronization and otherwise a useful medical modality for a host of pathologies. Brain entrainment is, in essence, "the brain that fires together, wires together."

It is the case that the human brain can constantly remap and rewire to conduct taskings and operations it has either previously unlearned or never learned. This is the belief that the brain can effectively rewire in accordance with the will, or focus of need. Thus, through repetition the brain will naturally rewire to conform to our will. I have held some notion of this my whole life and have only ever thought of my mind as my tool. For reasons a million miles away from Bob's (and others') studies, I have concluded that the mind can indeed be remapped, re-keyed into a subordinate rather than master. And so I utilized Bob's tools as just that. When we look back over our lives we will note the many conspirators who evolved our understanding of our world; Bob is among mine.

In many ways my introversion was completely without the observation and influence of others. It began decades earlier. In my profession the distractions of my heart and soul are not conducive to the frequent beer drinking, womanizing, and other artifacts of war. I developed in a fairly concealed vacuum. The Monroe Institute would be the first time I was actually around other people that had a dawning sense of change in both themselves and in the world. I was in the company of men and women from nineteen to eighty years old. There were Christians, Jews, Buddhists, and others from various faiths. It made no matter as religious disposition was irrelevant and never discussed in any event. Bob Monroe was wise on two additional points, and these were quite helpful in my even considering attending a residential program, or even listening to the CDs. One, there was to be no dogma at The Monroe Institute, and each person best guided their own findings in accordance with their belief system. Two, in the end near all would come to know, as Bob Monroe stated, that they were indeed "more than their physical body," in their own time.

THE GATEWAY

I gazed around the room at the people I had come to know recently, come to know more closely than nearly all other human beings in my life. As the week had come to pass, I felt a bond, a closeness, a proximity that was lacking in the previous intercourse I had with the world. It was not that I was unable to discourse with the world; it was that the world was unable to intercourse with me, to interrogate me and process me.

I spent considerable time watching the faces of my fellow students. I watched their eyes; I saw through rather than into the eyes of my peers. This is how I saw each of these "lights" at the Monroe Institute's "consciousness camp." While it is certainly not called this, in jest it is tossed about; and in the end, is really no less than camp for the mind, light for the soul. I wondered, as the speakers spoke in turn, what each had really come here for. I am not sure we ever know the answer to such things; rather we assign a value and meaning to the mysterious adventures of our lives and in so doing assert meaning and authority. However, I am not sure we are the commander at all. I suspect our souls feed themselves upon the material and other worlds in a symbiotic relationship that allows, as a necessary mechanism, "us" to both not sense *this* relationship and otherwise affirm that "we" alone peer through the window of our world. By the time of departure, whatever time that was (having lost all sense of time), I was openly intuiting near everyone in a synergistic orgy of altered consciousness.

"Wonder-ooes," she exclaimed. We all laughed at the secret only we, the people in that room, shared. Yes, we would sustain that we would stay in contact with each other. This would be the name for our little group, drawing from some small but hilarious detail that otherwise had no meaning in space or time. But "Wonder-ooes" underwear for the maturing little girl somehow stole a piece of comedy, a piece of joy, and a piece of our collective peace as an irrelevant symbol of our journey to Elysium.

There was a mounting emotion in the drawing of days in this place. What strange mechanism so moved such diverse persons to union in a shared language beyond words? It is not for the world to embrace with any credulity this experience. Some things lie beyond the ability of others to understand. Others will not simply comprehend the strange language spoken there. In the end, we did no less than intercourse with each other's souls and minds in a waking and very aware state.

We continued to explore each other and our own consciousness at Monroe. What is consciousness camp? It is beyond words, beyond time. It is the place where the quantum meets the poet. It is where metaphysics and the eternal bride marry. It is the crossroads in the flesh where we gaze upon eternity. It is a construct of mind, and illusion of flesh, a manifest food for the soul. It cannot be the case for any having fully arrived that one can leave such an experience the same person they were when they arrived. The landmarks are shattered. All Dorothy had to do was click her heels three times to go home.

Never before had I bore witness to such manifest reality outside myself, in a sea of energy moving between and within others. Never before had I sustained that persons could affirmatively meditate on the descent into self, others, all, and in so doing obliterate all the known interrogators to the material world. *Dear God, dear life, can it be so that these simple senses are naught but the wardens of my prison?* While I have maintained as a matter of my own experiences and conclusions that I manifest my own reality, I have never had interaction with others with which to measure this. I had no idea that others really were also waking to the very same awareness. It was all so breathtaking. I had no idea others where here with me. I never had such profound confirmation and validation. I had no idea.

I have manifested in other's minds. I have manifested not only in other's minds but as such was able to intelligently interact and answer questions. I was able to willfully broadcast into other's dreams and waking states such things that inherently had bona fides attached to validate themselves. I saw vistas and secrets. I did not make subjective these experiences, mostly. The distinctions to space and time fell away from us and we moved willfully or unwittingly through each other's worlds. The games began.

DOLPHINS

In preparation for each exercise we would gather in a central room to discuss the focus of the next "tape." Though they were called tapes as a residual of, or tribute to, the old days, all of the audio was now mastered and delivered digitally. In this gathering room forum the trainers would prepare us and remind us all to use the restroom prior to secreting away in our "unit." That day we would be doing a "tape" related to healing ourselves.

Apparently, over many years and reports from countless traditions, it has been gleaned that people both needing medical recovery and those wanting to provide medical recovery of an assistive sort have found that visualization techniques not only worked on a palliative level, but further suggested some quantum shift that actually biologically affected the target. In some manner, it seems, the human mind facilitates some quantum collapse that objectifies what is visualized. In other words, people have been able to visualize any common medium from a white light, a blue wave, to white blood cells themselves ravishing the problem area inside the illness and actually achieving this end. This has been used as adjunctive therapy in self-help in the West, but has been used for millennia in many traditions in the East. At the Monroe Institute, a dolphin was visualized, or created, by each individual. The reasons for the choice of dolphin are self-evident; the most obvious being a dolphin is among the most intelligent, most psychic, most benign of all understood creatures. While there is also a personal history at TMI as to why a dolphin is used, any choice one makes is fine.

We were off to follow the guided imagery on the tape and create for ourselves a dolphin of the mind whereby we might heal ourselves. This is really a timeless and invaluable tool. Considering that Western medicine is only now fully exploring the awesome power of the suggestive, our believing mind articulating our own healing seemed a powerful and mighty affirmation of will.

I felt my body in not feeling my body any longer. It is this "paralytic" state that I sought first as I "induced" every time. My term for the descent into Self is "induction." I could think of no better term than the word we use to describe the administration of anesthesia to take someone to the surgical plane. My induction complete, I was fully awake and alert, alive unlike any other time of the day. I saw my dolphin. He did not just appear as a puppet, limp and suspended as if attached to mental wires, awaiting my command to perform. He was laughing and dancing like, well, like a moonwalk on his hind flipper. This darn thing presented abruptly, following entreaty, and wholly manifested its own personality. It was truly wonderful.

In my audio unit, atop my sheets, the dolphin was smiling and clicking this wonderful laughter, while moving back and forth above me in moonwalk. It was so sweet and amazing. You see, I was not asleep at all. It is a state of mind in the other direction, the road not usually mentally chosen. In one direction lays the familiar lands of sleep. In the other direction lay, well, this is what lies there; most never journey in the direction opposite of sleep. It is a total clarity. It is the real tempura of life and we fully paint the scenery there. I was laughing and playing with this dolphin. I heard myself laughing in the unit and hearing this seemed as wonderful as that which was before me. My body is truly just a car.

Listening to the guided imagery enabled us to follow the "program" of the moment. It also had another benefit. Many, and at one time or another, all people will come full circle in their state of awareness and slip into a place that is sleep and not sleep. Monitoring has shown this state is not sleep as we know it, but the person has no recall, either. This term has been dubbed "clicking out." I do not know where we go when we click out, but it is not a sleep place. The guided imagery assists in focusing, also. We were instructed to allow our dolphin to enter us and to begin to move within and through us, healing and addressing locales of pain or discomfort. Obviously, there are issues of scale here, but, really, the issues of scale only pertain to the spatial material plane. Scale and mechanical logic have no place in the mental world. The dolphins all fit quite well into the body. However, this is where I wanted to both play and share.

PSYCHIC SHARING

I thought the girl who often sat next to me was so sweet. She was quiet and reserved, and had obviously been wounded somewhere in life. I also knew something that the remainder of the group did not know: she had a fairly rare disease. This would continue to get worse for her. My heart wept for such a tender one as this to be so imperiled in the prime of her life. I would share my dolphin with her. No matter of aches and discomforts could equal her pain.

My dolphin left. The space in my mind between the known, my little booth, and her unit grew slightly hazy as I had not actually been in her little booth. But slowly the clarity came to my mind and I saw her in her booth, the sheets wrapped around her lower body, fully dressed in hospital-like scrubs for comfort, her head resting on the pillow. I was an observer from some strange vantage point. It really was odd and not just imagination, though imagination may have been present. I saw my dolphin appear at the foot of her bed as it had happened for me. "Oh, what joy!" This is like no other experience. "How wonderful!"

I was struck by the odd realization that something else was present in her unit; there were two dolphins. *Of course, she would have her own dolphin*, I mentally exclaimed. I saw my dolphin enter and diffuse within her. I sent my dolphin through her. I briefly saw as if I were the dolphin and was aware of a white light radiating ahead of me, and then my perspective changed once more without my motivation. I was watching her sleep. I was aware of the dolphins inside of her and realized they were near her neck. I was gone.

No matter where you slip to in the space of one of these tapes, the changing frequencies undetected by the ear arouse you to alertness at the proper time. My dolphin having gone on a mission, I clicked out for the remainder of the tape. When I arose and stretched, the man who shared my room (two different units, though) asked how it went with my dolphin exercise. I explained to him that I gave my dolphin away. I then told him I sent my dolphin to Pam, as I wanted to make her better. He just said something nice, and we got ready for the debriefing in the gathering room.

Pam never really said much. She was quite and aloof, though intelligent and socially adept. However, after others had taken voluntary turns sharing their experience with the group, Pam offered to say something. There is something about those who speak little or those who import greatly with their words that causes a palpable suspense in others when they do say something. Pam was sitting just beside me. We always wound up just next to each other when the group settled, though we spoke little. Sometimes my unconcerned and unawares self might have my foot touch hers or her foot mine. We would continue as if we did not notice that we had touched but did not break contact. I noticed. She was an attractive woman and there was just some connection that made me feel comfortable with her, though we really did not know each other very well at all. I still wrestled daily with my attachment to women and the sense that I was now forever gone, no longer of any use to anyone. Pam continued:

"I saw my dolphin just before me in my unit," she tentatively began. I was gazing off looking at others in the group, wondering what they were thinking, what their lives were like, what their dreams resembled. They all watched Pam silently and intently.

"And then I realized that it was not my dolphin. My dolphin appeared a moment later, and there were two dolphins in there with me!" Pam conveyed her surprise as she told this story. At this point I was no longer looking at anyone in the group, but was also captivated by her.

She continued and told how the dolphin disappeared within her. When the dolphin later reappeared, she turned to me for the first time and said, "I asked the dolphin where it came from, and it told me that Ed sent the dolphin to me."

She paused, and I realized the whole group, including her, was looking at me. I was breathless. I could not believe what I was hearing. What she was saying closed the gap on imagination and playfulness. This had really just happened. I turned to her and smiled. I felt unarmed to state that I had in fact sent the dolphin. It seems as if I would be claiming ownership over an experience that I could not possibly prove originated with me. I smiled. Her first real talk with the group finished on that point. Many continued to stare at me as I looked aimlessly at the carpet.

After the gathering broke, a small group formed around Pam, and my roommate came over and told everyone there that I told him upstairs that I had sent my dolphin to Pam. Somehow this bona fides cleared the air where we all thought there must be another explanation. He made clear that this was an intended consequence. I had actively and consciously created a figment of my mind that projected from me into someone else's consciousness. Moreover, as such, this creation was able to intelligently represent itself on my behalf. There might be countless explanations for this event, but I needed none of them. I was amazed.

Following this experience I concluded that what I really wanted to glean from this overall experience at TMI was validation of the continuity of consciousness that moved between and within all of us. While thereafter others were concentrating on the experience of TMI itself, I was interrogating an experience beyond the experience. I wanted to spend as much time as I possibly could creating in these states confirmation that I willfully affected my world.

GIRAFFES

On repeated tapes I would participate in the lesson, yes, but I was also doing other mischievous things. On one tape I created a giraffe that was only thirty inches tall. I would send this little giraffe scurrying up and down the hallways while all were descending into their "states" and choose a victim of my playfulness. This day I choose Cloe. Cloe was a sweet woman from Georgia. She and I got along well. She had a wonderful and lively sense of humor. She was kind and intelligent. My little giraffe would mostly follow the mental commands I directed, but all too often I noted that my creations seemed to have a free will of their own. Other times I noted that they acted out my more sublime thoughts. I noticed this with both the dolphin and the giraffe. I ponder still if there is anything instructive in this observation.

While Cloe was buried deep in a trance-like state, my giraffe stood beside her bed. All I did was send my giraffe to her. I did not assist in negotiating any obstacles. I just observed. Having no hands my giraffe snuggled its head up under the covers and nudged its head upon her belly, at her naval—at her naval! (Perhaps unconscious code was written into this creation.) If I could send a dolphin to one person, I wanted to know if another got my giraffe also. I did not minutely control the actions of my creation; rather I would watch it act out its own will, or perhaps my covert will. I laughingly asked myself that if I could do this at will, have I been doing this all along subconsciously? Had I often impressed thoughts or images in other's minds unawares? I also realized that I might not ever have to leave my house again to find a date. It was fun, and it was playful thinking. However, upon further consideration I realized that I had for years been doing something very similar.

PSYCHIC SEX

What was even more curious than any of these constructions of my mind was the fact that I rose from this tape aroused. I realized that I was increasingly aroused during the tapes. I am intellectually beyond the place where I think in base notions. What was it that was triggering an arousal state in me? I had been using one form or another of these gateway tapes for many years. I had never had this experience before. I have used them, both alone and in the company of the opposite sex. This was quite odd.

We all moved to the gathering area for our debriefing. As we did many tapes a day within short order, all sense of time was lost. We also surrendered our watches and phones upon arrival.

"Ed, I have a question for you." I turned and saw Cloe smiling coyly. Her girlfriends with whom she arrived giggled and moved further along.

"Did you send me a visitor?" she coyly asked. I was shocked. I did not think I could be more shocked than I already was. I did not yet admit that I had sent her a visitor when another woman, Suzi, came up and asked me if anything strange happened to me.

"What do you mean?" I asked her, turning my attention briefly from Cloe.

"I mean, did you have any unusual experiences during this last tape?" I looked at her closely and noted the playfulness that a lover might share when she has a secret. This was a deportment I had not seen in her previously. What was going on?

"Suzi, what did you do?" I asked no longer thinking about Cloe.

She opened her mouth as if to announce the letter "O" and then smiled and walked away.

"Well, did you send me a visitor?" Cloe persisted.

"Yes, I sent you…"

"I knew it!" She spun around and proceeded to her waiting friends where she spoke briefly followed by an outburst of laughter. They each cast amazed and amused glances at me and moved on. Cloe extended the index finger of one hand and used the index finger of the other hand across the first like she was lighting a fire. "Bad boy," she mouthed to me from across the room.

The group was now seated, and I went to my little spot. I was thinking of the giraffe I sent out and apparently someone sent me a visitor, or something. There was a strange undercurrent in this gathering and people were intermittently looking closely at others and smiling. After the meeting, I asked Suzi what she had done. Being clever with her, I decided to tell her the only thing I noticed about my tape exercise. I told her plainly that I was aroused throughout the tape. Her eyes just widened as she laughed and again mouthed the letter "O," and walked away. She looked over her shoulder and winked. I am entertained by suspense, but only to a point.

I was keenly aware that there was a powerful current of psychic activity in this house, but I had not actually experienced anything like this with others before. I am aware that TMI is not a psychic dating service, and that the little things that were going on were normally to be expected when you placed adults of opposite sex in such close and personal proximity *and* enabled them tools of a covert mind. There was a real harmlessness about all of it. Yet, I was not so much moved by the flattery of any of it, as I was the power and suggestion inherent in the experience. The remainder of this first course was much of the same validation for me: that the power to create and export thought existed organically to all of us. The background to these games of the mind was the most awesome experience of mind I could have ever imagined. Behind the games was an experiential forum where all possibilities could be gleaned with our internal lens alone. The same tools of the mind played with that day were also not subject to time or distance. The suggestion was staggering.

Within short order we learned that this was simply not brain entrainment. What was taking place in this strange camp for human consciousness was an engagement of our minds, our souls, with those of others. In this manner, the synergy was breathtaking. In this manner, not only did we become familiar with the vehicle to such an end, we became intimate with the destination points. Issues, heartaches, baggage, freedoms, and fears each were privately explored, and if it so suited one or another it may have been discussed in an arena of comfort and security. After all, each one of us daily looked through the portal of time and space and was witness to the birth of worlds and the stuff of dreams. It is the case that various personalities will respond to these findings in different manners. We returned to the comfort of each other and simply knew that we were each sojourners on this baffling and often overwhelming journey. The inevitable result of this exploration was an unspoken, consideration of what "truth" is, what "life" is, and where lies reality, if there is one.

MORE TOOLS FOR LOVE

I was charmed. I was in love. I dreamed a dream in the passing of my life that I would affirm love and beauty. In this place, where I came for exposure to the sterile utilities of audio entrainment, I found such a tender pulse. I listened to my heart.

I dreamed a bond of human love that was without restraint, rabid, infecting all. I dreamed my love a virus that replicated throughout this world by sheer will. I affirmed in the silence of my heart and secret prayers that this dawning sense of magic and love that stirred within my soul was born of grace, intent, and will. Moreover, that absent one landmark of confirmation, absent any other soul supporting or nourishing me, I was correct and drinking from the fountain. This was the secret of my place when I arrived here. This was my estate prior to arrival. This was the reality that I increasingly choose to have. I discarded all the previous stale constructs that were handed to me. They never suited me nor worked for me.

Tools and utilities were also provided so that the passing of this night's dream would not find us awakened, and having forgotten. Instead, it was inculcated into us to duplicate this "place" at will. Thus, we would now interrogate the boundless with other than our "senses."

LOVE MOVES WITHIN ME NOW, CONSTANTLY

The house of my soul is ascendant this day. I arrived and re-affirmed the notion that I am he. I am here and am not. The world can never be the same again. The world will never be the same again. I walked, into the fields below the mountains.

I felt the oddest movement to tears, without provocation. *I never really saw the veins in the leaves.* I kneeled and looked at a roughly one-square-foot section of the earth. I fancied I could hear the small things moving. I am sure I did not. But I fancied. Tomorrow, I may *choose* to hear the small things moving about. I watched teeming life slowly appear to my now focusing eyes. Dear Lord! I had no idea. I simply had no idea. I felt the cool wind tear a current though the laden heat of morning. I was refreshed. For the briefest of moments I was aware of something incredible, something powerful. It was if I was looking at life with 10,000 eyes, a billion beating hearts, and breathing with the lungs of one infinite breath. The minutiae of this little piece of earth slowly changed focus, slowly revealed in my mind an endless understanding of life. There were no formulas written across the chalkboard of my mind, no symphonies created, and there was no double helix. However, something else came into focus that was beyond this little earth. Somehow I was aware of an infinite power and intelligence in this little piece of earth alone. From that moment on, I never again consumed meat. From that moment on, I never so much as stepped on an ant.

After a week the Gateway program ended, and I realized, I will miss them. I had affirmed a dream that love was possible absent reciprocity, or even the foci of my love being aware I so loved. I asserted to the worlds, to the mansions in this House, that I would simply have the world I desired. At consciousness camp, the worlds answered me. They told me they hear my plea, my lamentation for change and empowerment. The vistas are forever changed. I will miss them all, yes. However, for the first time in my song of creation I now know, I am now aware, that they are all right here, right now. The house of my soul is ascendant. Genesis *is* now.

I was both spiritually and physiologically altered. Many people came to TMI for various reasons; this makes sense. Many were impressed with the ability to remote view. Others wanted to contact those who in-between worlds, in other realms of consciousness, and there were a great many who wanted to achieve out-of-body experiences (OBE). Still, others were just explorers, plain and simple. All these and others are surely fine personal goals. I, however, wanted something very different. I see all these places to explore as no more than that. They are all waypoints or doors in a long hallway, while all along the Prize lay beyond, at the end of the hallway. I wanted no sidebars. I want what lies beyond the manifestations. I would not be enamored by the by-products of forever; I want forever. I want the essence of life to completely slaughter me and lay waste my remaining world.

The night following the Gateway I stayed at the bed and breakfast across the valley. The house quickly filled up with many people coming to enjoy the Colburn's fabulous Friday dinner seven-course meal. A remarkable cast of people, many affiliated with The Monroe Institute and fellow sojourners, filled the house. The energy was so intense that the hair on the back of my neck, my arms, and the rest of me stood on end. Joe McMoneagle and his lovely wife, Scooter, joined us that evening. Joe is among the most accurate and proven remote-viewers on earth, having spearheaded the CIA's famous Stargate Project and later numerous assistive efforts for International Law Enforcement. Joe and Scooter were wonderfully warm and loving to me. The lovely TMI registrar, Karen, joined us as well as Helene, who would also instruct me in Reiki healing, and of course the gracious Jim and Jena Colburn. There were so many other remarkable people present; many had been involved with cutting-edge exploration of human consciousness for decades. I was aware of the grace of this company.

AM I A MYSTIC OR A FOOL?

What a voyage. What a journey. One more day and I was lying in some bed in the Virginia Mountains. Just days ago I was in Dubai, Pakistan, Yemen, and so on. I was so tired at some level. What an adventure. Who would ever know, ever believe, what joy and magic moves in such a life, in such worlds? I had always hoped in some small way I could bear light into the darkness of the places into which I ventured, but now, for the first time in my life, I measured my ability to affect the world around me. At TMI I concentrated on the synergy of the people. I had never been around a group of people who, more or less, considered the world around them to be but a reflection of a much more profound existence. I wanted to move in and out of minds, of hearts. In the week that I was in TMI, I concentrated on the people part of my experience. I wanted to bathe in the people that were attending. It was one of the most awesome and beautiful experiences in simply being. Also, I have proven to myself beyond all measure that my intent affects the minds of others and my material world.

I spent the night at Fallen Oak thinking about how very different I am from what even those who know me think. Some of my closest friends have informed me lately that my writings are mystical in nature. I am not sure this is true, but I am aware that I have a preconception of what mysticism is, and it does not include a person carrying a gun. Others say I am a fool. Only those most familiar to me would ever call me a fool. Others may think me a fool, though they would not say this to my face.

So, a friend calls me a mystic, others a fool. I am more likely the fool. The friend possesses the warmth of shared memories and affection but has long ago missed the point. I am no mystic. I simply tarry in the alcoves and antechambers of my mind seeking court with forever. Within this "keep" eternity burns the

Light undimmed. I see glimpses in the windows wherein I've but peered. To these glimpses, to this Light, I aspire. I choose.

A mystic? A fool? I cannot even assign a sex to the divine. I do so arbitrarily to announce no more than my will, my fancy, to an idea, a vision, a dream, a god that is without form, substance, sex, or reason. A mystic? I cannot duplicate the descent into the abyss, save by force of will. I have scattered my youth on the savage rack of time to query what is taken for granted by everyone else. I have built a dream, a vision, and a madness that has insinuated into the waking minutes of my hours. I can no longer separate the "shared reality" of all others from the one I discover and manifest by sheer will for myself. I cannot invite another to introspect with me, though I have tried. I cannot by intellectual counsel inform others, either. Mine is a manifest reality of the internal. I have projected by choice the discoveries I have made in the "keep" within. Across the screen of my world is projected the Light undimmed by every waking choice, every moment, each consideration.

When I close my eyes comes the darkness. The distant light denied barely pierces my mind's eye. I am alone. There, before the horizon of sleep She is born. Lurking, ever present, shrouded in time, She reveals herself with no more than my bequest.

Come hither, yonder Light. Come before me for counsel this day. Besiege me with thy warmth, thy promise. The decades passed with the solemn appearance of purpose and intent. There is no purpose, no intent, no meaning in the flesh and affairs of these earthen days. Bound to the flesh, possessed of no more than the notion of apartness, I could not apprehend the Light. Beckoning the years, embracing the Light, I beheld darkness as my sinews limbered, my temples grayed. Come hither, yonder Light.

A mystic? A fool? When I close my eyes comes the darkness. I now close my eyes and will the Light before the altar of my reason. I sacrifice my mind and drown all thoughts. The Light now pierces my mind's eye and thoughts themselves are as background static, observed mostly, irrelevant entirely. I drown. I am effused with warmth. I am engulfed in safety. I think now in a place where my very mind bears only witness, and an odd detachment.

I am at work. I am at play. I watch children run unbridled in open fields. I am at rest. I am in conflict. I am in love. I am lucid, and I am blind. I blend the wake and the un-sleep, the not sleep. From this place on the cusp of my mind's landscape I retreat with what bounty I may and bring forth of these treasures to my affairs, my life. I manifest by will. I choose. I have remapped my mind. I have reset my very intellectual DNA. I have tinkered with the membrane of time. I am crossing over with disregard for my flesh. I am in material apostasy. I am a fool.

I have abandoned my brethren. I have set out alone. I have taken no compass. I have no map. I follow the Light.

A mystic? A fool? I seek counsel with the unseen phantom of my mind's creation. I have painted my world in the colors that I feel best suit the forest, the market, the gods, and the children. I am painting with the fingers of my mind across the canvass of the world. I have redone the set. I assign new roles to all the actors. I recast the entire storyline. I am a fool. I am finger painting in the Light of my soul. I want to stay a fool.

I thought me a fool. I stayed for two other programs at TMI, back to back. As I had been overseas for so long I otherwise had no place to live in America anyway. My adult time in America looks very similar to my childhood. I return from overseas and have no idea how to fit in any longer. I remain in culture shock until I depart. I am never back long enough to acclimate. I own no possessions and live out of a rental car driving up and down the East Coast. At least here at TMI I had my first home-cooked meal in years. In any event, I do not think I can ever return again, regardless of where my body calls home. I am somewhere else.

CHAPTER 22

▼

Beginnings and Endings

You were born to reach God. You were born to find your way home in the dark of the eternal night. Christ was quite clear that the Son of Man would become the Son of God. He was also clear that he was talking about all of our inheritance. Christ was quite clear that the Prize was in becoming one with God, apprehending the Kingdom of God on earth, now. All avatars, mystics, prophets, and saints are emphatic that this inheritance is the property of all.

I needed to catch up on the long overdue collection of my belongings up and down the East Coast. Over the years I lost nearly everything I owned and really possessed now no more than what I carried with me; I was homeless and carless. I had always reminded myself when I was much younger that I never wanted to possess more than I could carry on my back. Life has a way of seeing these dreams trashed upon the altar of necessity. I grew up. I acquired. I lost my way in the labyrinth of material gain. I surrendered it all again over these passing years and will no more embrace the fruits of my labors. I own no less or more than what I should in my life.

I was glad I could be with my sister following my time in Virginia. I would shortly be leaving for far-away lands again. My father, Bill, was always a man about his convictions, and I would support his intent as an honorable friend. Bill was sick when I arrived in New York, and my sister would bear yet another burden. Bill had specific wishes for sickness. His wishes were even more particular should he be so sick that his life was passing.

Marilyn would bear these burdens first, because her heart is without bounds, and she loves with uncommon grace both family and stranger alike. Marilyn would also wrestle with the burdens of the sick and dying alone because the rest of my family has proven to be selfish and uncaring when others are sick or leaving the world. I, regrettably, had the misfortune of seeing this again in New York. My sister would have again bore the burden of seeing another out of this world without aid or compassion from family had I not been there with her. How sad.

These were dying days. My family initially asked me what I thought after returning from the hospital the first day. I said that I thought Bill would never rise again. Bill had been alert and working only days before. Over the course of some weeks he deteriorated to those ethical areas where families must ask if there is hope or not. There was no hope. I sensed this as well as deduced it from his medical conditions. We asked that he be provided what relief was available and sat with him as his life ebbed away. The only disconnect was the doctors indicated that he should recover shortly. I could not see this.

I stole away moments alone to talk with Bill in the way that so many years did not allow.

"Dad, I am here with you. I am right here with you, Dad." I held my father's hand. I was so impressed with his dignity and fearlessness. Throughout his life he revealed no faith or any great conviction. I am sure that all consider the existential zero in the final moments. I would ally his concerns as best I could.

"Dad, listen to me. It is okay to rest now. It is done," I told him. "Marilyn and I are fine. We are all grown up, and we are so pleased with our lives. It has been a long hard life, Dad, but you sure knew how to live. You have seen and done so much, Dad. It is time to rest now. It is time to rest, Father."

I held Bill's hand as the tears ran freely from my face. I was so happy for him. I was not sad for me as I have seen so much death. I have talked many people through the final moments of living. I was sad for Marilyn though as I love her dearly and am not sure if she is that aware of how immortal we really are. I was sad for Marilyn because regardless of the dignity and forethought of Bill's express and implied desires his death would still mark the passing of an age, our age. I was on my knees and moved my little prayer beads unconsciously across my thumb as I rocked in unison.

Death is inculcated into us individually and collectively as the most solemn and sad affair of life. It marks the passing of so many things, the least of which are the deceased. Death serves not to express the promise to which all aspire, that we survive life; rather it serves to inform of mortality instead. In this moment no less than faith itself is questioned, interrogated, and found lacking, though none admit this for to do so leaves them with absolutely nothing. And thus in the moments when our loved ones pass, we are found destitute of heart and hope, bankrupt in our understanding, unprepared for the savage night. But these are all learned findings.

"Dad, hear me! I want you to listen to me. Can you hear me?" Dad squeezed my hand in return. "When you are in no more pain; when it is done, I do not want you to wait for us here. I want you to be brave and move on. You will know where to go, Dad. Do not stay here. We will be following you shortly. I will not leave you alone, Father."

I paused and rocked. I prayed.

I COMMEND YOUR SOUL

"My dear Beloved God, hear me Lord. I beseech you.

"I ask nothing any longer for me. I ask you, Lord, take this child upon your wings and yield him to the Light. Grant to him that blessing, that grace that you have bestowed upon me.

"Oh, Life, my eternal Bride, take my father into your arms and grant him a passing worthy of the love that I submit today." As I prayed and spoke in the first person, I heard in my mind the refrain in plural.

"I am *the* Light."

"We are *the* Light.

"I am Truth.

"We are Truth.

"I am Love.

"We are Love.

"We are Compassion.

"We are *the* Stillness of Waters.

"We are *the* Siren Song of Souls.

"Dad, you are more than your physical body.

"We are more than our physical bodies.

"We survive the flesh.

"We are Hope.

"We are immortal."

I repeated this over and over and gazed upon my father's face, his eyes. His lids were open, but his stare was a thousand miles away. The day prior my father returned from dialysis and spoke to us. He never spoke again.

"Please?"

"Please?

"Please, stop!

"No more!

"No more!"

My sister and I concurred and told the medical staff that enough was enough. It made no matter as they had no need to give him morphine any longer anyway. He was gone in many ways, his remainder leaving this day before me.

At 4:01 PM I looked at my father's breathing and the visible pulse I saw at his carotid artery. He was leaving me. I took to the side of his bed again. I prayed. I said good-bye. I held his hand and thanked him.

Bill was an idea that never came to fruition for me. We were never able to be father and son, but we were able to become friends. I would lament in my boyish places that I never got to have a father. To some it is just not given in this life. I would regret that Bill never got to have a son. I took happiness in his listening to me so many years ago when I advised him that it was still not too late for him to have a relationship with his son and daughter. Toward that end, Bill and Marilyn did become very close. I was pleased for the two of them.

Marilyn is my single greatest love in the world, and if she took a measure of love from this man, then I, too, take the same love and embrace it in my heart of hearts. I would miss this man, but more, I would miss that which I never knew.

I saw my mother later the same day. She came over to prepare food for my brother-in-law and nephew. She told me she felt bad for Marilyn. My curiosity was triggered.

"Tell me, what is it you feel bad about?" I asked.

"Well, Edward," she turned from the kitchen counter informatively, "she lost her father today."

I was shocked. He was my father, too. My sister was later disgusted when I told her what my mother said, but not surprised. I was not surprised. In this manner Bill passed from this world his suffering.

I move to close the last chapter of my life embracing the most absurd of notions: that love can be explained to an attentive ear, and that I may find a means to explore and explain the worlds where language fails. I was leaving home again, moving ever closer to something, eventually beyond words.

THE RESERVOIR ETERNAL

In dreaming love a virus, in dreaming hope a promise, I refresh the reservoir eternal. Time in not linear. Space and time are not. Therefore, I assert the coming of age of the waking consciousness of life is exponential. Love is affected at and in all times and all places and grows exponentially. I ask the childish question:

If I assert and it is otherwise true that there, indeed, appears to be a "dawning," an "awakening" in consciousness (it is self-evident to me), *and*
There is really no space-time in the non-local world where collapses mind, *and*
Love is the unseen energy that transcends the illusion of space-time, of all things, *and*
All the love that we feel, share, and otherwise have serves that end which refreshes the universal reservoir from which worlds drink, *and*
Man has traditionally thought of time as occupying the direction, the arrow, from yesterday to tomorrow,
Then, perhaps we are not simply contributing to this reservoir and nurturing it "now" but are feeding it along all axes of time, *then*
Love should not be expected to simply grow. Love should and does grow and act exponentially.

For each gift of love shared, it is like an investment in the distant past of eternity, compounded immediately over billions of years. The investment is breathtaking. The selfless, the pure, the profound acts of love serve that end that has life, Love itself coming to know itself as God comes to know Self with increasingly critical mass. If so, then soon will come a point of no return, as a sun might gain critical mass. Love will not simply be an epiphany, a choice, enlightenment; love will simply be, and we will be in Love.

Love is the mechanics of the unseen, the medium that binds worlds. We see love as a choice, a fruit, when it is really no less than the clocking of spiritual DNA toward the only Light it could but long. In so longing, in so realizing, we fulfill that end that was always, and mostly only, our reason for being.

I track love in the heart and in the products of the material world. I drink intuitively from the cup that informs me so. Love is in a state of becoming. It is an orgy of consciousness. It is a mystery seeking to unravel itself. Love is determined, intelligent, evolutionary, and identical to all its subordinate reflections throughout the universe. Love is expanding and coalescing like unto like. One dollar invested today may be ten dollars in twenty years. Love invested today is invested in all times and places simultaneously. Love's investment is exponential immediately. Love compounds both love and the ages.

I would explore Love. I would drown in this place where stores the reservoir of all acts, all memories, all quantum grace, and all love. I would describe this Love if my words find capability. I will bear Life from this life. She will bear Life in this life. While it is given only to woman to bring forth life, in the waking of days when this age has passed I, too, shall bring forth a child, a spring, a season, a song upon the lips of my decay. It is given to all to bring forth Life from life. Yes, I too shall bear fruit in my passing.

I am as water crossing a membrane. I join a stream moving rapidly just on the other side. This current, this jet of creation, moves just beyond my conscious senses. I move osmotically across and join the caravan of endless energy, the ebbs and tides of eternity. The direction is all directions; the destination is all places. I am energized in a way that defies words, paralyzes reason. Reason is of another day.

Beyond the place from which I passed, I see, as if looking through Saran Wrap, the barrier behind me transparent, but is not. I see the images, the scenes, the dance of life as it inexorably continues. None have noted my passing. The dance never stopped. I was never there. The mountains continue to point to the stars. The sun heats the hungry earth. Commerce continues unabated. The mosques still fill. In silent rooms, mothers lament and children cry. Men toil still in fields and factories. Only God has nodded; the pious still break their bread with dreams undimmed.

I am as water crossed the membrane. I am salt in a sea. I am blinded by my beauty. I am consumed. The barrier retreats. I lose sense of me. I lose sense. I am not what I was. I am not, any longer. We are forever. We are the hungry root, the thirsty soil. We are the infant child, the northern wind. We are exploding suns and frigid moons. In the stream that is our place, in the silent eternity of our inheritance, we are as unto God, married to the Bride. We will bear Life from this life. We are all bearers of Life in this life. To some it is given *in* the flesh, to others it is given *with* the flesh.

CHAPTER 23

▼

Travelogues and Monologues

The ancients admonished those who seek the Kingdom of God to attend the "Eastern gate" and the "third eye." Transmuted through the ages, these statements have all the gravity of a long ago lost world or hopelessly naïve descriptions crafted in native tongues in far-away lost lands.

"**S**illy boy, there is no treasure for you beneath the pyramids," she noted.

"Choleo just told us that in *The Alchemist* to make a point, the treasure is always just within us."

"I know the treasure in within us," I responded. "I know that!" I added.

Did I?

I certainly did know there was no treasure under the pyramids, at least not for me. After all, I was just going to breathe the sights the ancients and others had breathed for millennia. But I was not going in search of a treasure.

"Why are you then going to Angkor Wat in Cambodia?" she pressed.

"I am going to breathe the sights that ancients and others have breathed for millennia," I responded with my now rehearsed refrain.

"And that is all?" she queried incredulously.

"Yes, of course, that is all. Why?"

"Because I think you are in search of your treasure," she said smugly.

"I am not in search of my treasure," I responded evasively.

"Why then are you going from one scared site where man aspired to God and then to another where man worshiped the divine? You cannot spend your whole life doing this," she answered victoriously.

"I am going because…" I trailed off, looking at the orange orb that was the beautiful Arabian sunset. I always loved to see the sun rise and set. I was able, thus, to participate in both birth and death of day, of moments, of life.

"Are you not then going to Borabudur in Java?"

"Ahh, Borabudur," I wandered off. I had been in Java before and had allowed distractions to interfere with so worthy a pilgrimage.

"And?"

"And what," I interrupted.

"Are you looking for your treasure also in Borabudur?"

"No, silly. I am not looking for treasure in Borabudur."

"I am not looking for treasure in Angkor Wat, Cairo, nor in Lake Titicaca, or Machu Picchu, either. I am not looking for my treasure any where on this earth," I lectured.

"Then why in the world would you be going to visit and pray at all these ancient sites around the world?" she asked confused.

Looking lovingly to the place on the sky where orange remained from yesterday and married the night in romance, I replied, "I am looking for a place to bury treasure…and you're going to help me bury it."

THE THIRD EYE

Would the finding be greater than the promise? Explorers since time immemorial have likely had the same question as their conveyance either docked aside the Nile wharfs, their camels crossed the final dune, or their airlines touched upon terra firma. Somewhere in the Jungian archetypical reservoir of man is the call to Egypt. I was no different and stood amused at the similarity with my brethren, ancient and modern. Perhaps the call to Egypt and the call to God spring from the same place within.

Cairo is a clash of worlds, a clash of times. The blending of these opposites is sublime. Unlike any other city I have visited, Cairo's hazy skyline is punctured with the fingers of countless minarets reaching out, calling out to God. The modern (relatively) Muslim influence is unmistakable. These fingers, either beckoning God or directing Man, are absolutely everywhere. From Salah Ad-Din's (Saladin) mighty citadel on Al-Moqattam (Qal'et El-Gabal, Citadel of the Mountain), where sits Sultan Hasan's mosque, to the outer suburbs, where blows the harsh destitute of a thousand miles of day, Allah—God—is everywhere.

In the distance sits a tremendous darkness blotting the night. The presence is only noted by the cutout of stars; they are absent. Here, a stone's throw from Heliopolis and married to the modern life of Giza below, lays the world's first finger, beckoning God *or* directing Man. It is here, in the matrimony of the ancient and the new, that the secret of the pyramids are made known to me. The sky is not a space between the place where rests the earth and the foot of heaven. The sky is the medium of the self-same substance of Man *and* God. These fingers, these "ladders" to heaven are both beckoning God *and* directing Man. They are all sublimely erected *in* God, not *to* God!

Cairo is a labyrinth; but she is a labyrinth in height as well as breadth. The long ride to the Giza Plateau seemed to be suspended all the while well above the city streets. Elevated roads removed tourists and locals alike from the ancient cobblestones. This arrangement avoided the countless dark and winding alleys that have likely plagued commuters for millennia. However, in a mega-tropolis like Cairo, congestion was not lessened; commuters obviously filled in the space, like a gas in a vacuum. Thus, the elevated roadways of Cairo themselves became no more than a *Jetson*-esque caricature of the dense cacophony of life below.

Every single car noted on the roads here have some insult or injury to bumper or quarter panel. The air is heavy with pollutants and dust. There may have been modern and untarnished automobiles present during my stay, but they remained hidden from my curiosity. The drive to the Giza Plateau was arduous, taking many hours for what should have been a one-hour drive.

Over 150 years ago, the king of Egypt erected a hunting lodge at the very foot of the ancient pyramids. No doubt kings and potentates for millennia have mated their own image and legitimacy to the ancient Pharaonic lore and mystery evident everywhere. The lodge was bought by European speculators and became a hotel for the curious and idle alike. Long before tourism became the fashionable manner to demonstrate affluence, and especially at the height of the Victorian Era, the pyramids drew paupers and princes alike to gaze upon its majesty and incredible awe. This lodge was my destination, the Mena House. One would think the pyramids alone in their eternal vigil in the desert, but there is life, vibrant and massive, teeming and pressing in upon the plateau. Yet, no modern construction comes nearer than the Mena House at the end of Pyramid Road. I could not have noticed in the dark of my arrival, but no arrangement could have been closer, more historic, or lovelier other than actually sleeping the night in King Cheops's chamber.

As the woman showed me to my room, she explained that this room is part of the Montgomery Trust. She confided this to me with some satisfaction. Her pause told me she was waiting on a response.

"What is the Montgomery Trust?" I asked, releasing the obvious torment her eager curiosity hardly concealed.

"During World War II, General Montgomery had his headquarters here while fighting Rommel," she finally got to explain, hoping to impress me. I was impressed. She walked to the balcony and opened the door.

"You can see the pyramids right from your bed," she told me.

I stood beside her on the balcony of the Mena House's Montgomery Suite, at the end of Giza's Pyramid Road and saw, well, I saw nothing.

"I can't see the pyramids," I explained. Though the flight was short, I was nevertheless tired.

"Right there," she insisted and pointed.

I saw nothing and turned my attention to the room, which I hoped she would now leave me to settle in; as I turned I noted stars in the distance. Looking back, I gasped. I could not see the pyramids in the night sky because the entire night sky was blotted out. I was looking for the pyramids in the sky when in fact the closest pyramid was the sky.

It was right in front of me. The pyramid of Cheops was my night sky.

It was really right in front of me, right out my balcony window. There was no other thing on the ground or in the air between me and the most ancient and wondrous creations ever conspired in the heart of Man. I had only noticed the outline of the pyramids when turning away by noticing the thin veneer of night and stars to either side.

Lying in bed later I turned to my open balcony window to just gaze and dream of ancient times and wonders. I played with the memories of animation and actors that have impressed the stories of the ancient past. I saw great labors and secret rites. I imagined arcane mysteries and such sciences of which the world could not possibly guess. I was drifting to sleep. I was blinded.

"Dear God! What the...?" The entire sky was lit. My room was washed in white, then blue. I stumbled to the balcony. I was blinded. My breath was frozen in my chest. I inhaled in awe an audible sound of wonder.

The pyramids each were lighting the night sky. I could see other pyramids off to the right, their apexes alight in the night. Just before me Cheops was bathed in countless rays. Intersected at the very top, the light cast off into space backlighting across the ceiling of the night. This was the evening light show. I was not previously aware there was one, and I was quite surprised. It was truly amazing, and it was just for me. Like jasmine and jingles, this was all conspired thousands of years ago for this very moment in time. Just now, right here, right now, all the worlds aligned to steal my breath this very night. I lay in bed like a boy and was deeply excited to see my entire field of vision the pyramid and its subtle stair-stepped edge climbing to heaven. I would go to the Sphinx the following night and see the full pharaonic light show with all the pyramids and wonders in attendance. It was simply breathtaking. Rarely has technology so honored the ancient.

The Inner Sanctum

With or without a pickaxe, all that can be done and seen atop Giza can be seen in a day or two. With or without a pickaxe, a person can spend a lifetime just atop the plateau witnessing these creations. It is like this with all the truly magnificent creations in life. I was sorely disappointed to find the tourism police would not permit me to walk up the hill before 8 AM. I thought this was silly and unfair. The one place in the world where an experience is enhanced by the participation of the sun is the pyramids. Not letting people go atop the hill before 8 AM qualifies as silly. Besides, this behavior only fuels the suspicious who rightly note peculiar goings on and excavations at night or away from eyes prying.

I had not planned on entering the king's chamber, but was so glad that I did. I met a couple from Bangladesh and a man from the U.S. with whom I spent the morning. I just love people so much. They were such sweet people. That day, in those moments, we shared with each other the mystical sublimity of the pyramids. I prefer my time alone and am comfortable traveling the world in silence, but this day was made sweeter by the parents, the baby, and the young man seeing the sights of the world for the first time.

First, we descended inward and slightly down. I would later note that the stairs that were closed off and leading below went to the queen's chamber. We went up, and up, and up. It was amazing to see that there was an entire network of considered design and function in this pile of stones. The craftwork is amazing. There were granite stones covering vast expanses and aligned with such accuracy as to defy understanding of form or even function. Moreover, some contortions of stone are inexplicable. Little lights were intermittently placed to assist our efforts, but they were too few and of poor quality. It was good thing many had flashlights. Wooden planks were erected to ensure footing, otherwise the stone ascent was smooth.

How did they get the sarcophagus in place? I wondered. In fact, I wondered at nearly all of this

The actual tomb was empty and uneventful. Where were we in relation to the ground, the edges, and the top? I could not tell, but a map would later reveal we were somewhere near the very middle. The trip inward is unremarkable upon first consideration. When one considers some of the finer and less obvious construction, both the architecture and intent are overwhelming. I could understand, abstractly and spatially, how a rectangular room might be constructed within a pyramid of square stones. I could even understand how a pyramid could be built around a room. What increasingly taxed my mind were the less obvious inlaid constructs.

There are channels or tunnels or "vents" no more than a few inches in height and width intersecting from special points within the tomb to the outside of the pyramid. These are amazingly accurate and precise and vary little in their travel through solid stone, and taper. It is suggested that they line up precisely with Sirius or other constellations that were in the night skies at the time of the pyramid's creation. Some have suggested that they speak to us of knowledge by suggesting not what was in house or risen at the time of creation, but rather, simply, what posterity need note.

These many internal "vents" were previously thought to be airshafts for laborers. That theory has since been ruled out. Recently, a remote-controlled sensor thingy explored through one shaft many meters and found a door literally no more than a few inches in height. This is akin to a four-inch hallway carved a mile into the side of a mountain and an elaborate four-inch door constructed mid way. Soundings have revealed still more rooms and chambers within the structure. There is literally a mystery in stone upon this plateau. There is more being said here than anthropological decoding. There is mystery in science and grace in this place. While the smooth climb and the little shafts are curious they are nothing but anecdotal. All of this experience is timeless.

NEW GUARDS OF OLD AGE

It is no wonder that the New Age and Old Age guards of social sciences share a bed here. Something truly calls when one approaches this place. It is a beacon in time and makes soundings through the hearts and minds of man through the ages. The pyramids take the measure of man in each age and man comes hopelessly to the altar of the Giza Plateau time and time again thinking himself master. Man arrives with his questions and notions but leaves having made a deposit of awe and wonder. Mostly, no more is known of the pyramids by man in every age elapsed. However, man makes pilgrimage from the corners of the world to make supplication to stone. The pyramids may have many unknown purposes but they have incidentally become repositories of human will and energy. It is not possible that such a place can survive the ages and not have made a trough in the fabric of the noumenal world. This, and perhaps no more, is what may cause the sense by all that something clearly beckons you as proximity narrows to this awesome and moving wonder.

I saw the face in stone some distance from the second pyramid. Actually, I cannot say why I reference the Sphinx to the second pyramid. It is likely as close to Cheops. However, distance is misleading on this wind-swept plateau. Across the lion's paw, in the distance, I could see the little tent that was emitting light the night before.

This must be one of the places up here were work is currently continuing, I considered. I thought that pictures in black-and-white would look so nice as well. There was something about the shadows and few colors that informed me that black-and-white was fine, even desirable. Also, I think that I searched for an element of antiquity in my experience.

I cannot know more than the greatest minds that have lived, but I also hold that the Sphinx is older than the pyramids. Like the Eastern Gate, the "third eye," and every other portal of initiation clocking toward God, the Sphinx too looks alertly to the east, lest it not note the arrival of eternity. The Sphinx is the perennial archetype of Man's search for God, for knowledge, for all things both beyond and within self. Whatever the original reason for the construction of the Sphinx, it no longer matters. Somewhere in the reservoir of an ancient dream or thought, *it was*. It has always existed incarnate in stone or disembodied. The Sphinx is the projection of tomorrow and our being present when it arrives. I was departing today. I am forever departing to the East.

THE EASTERN GATE

There is a place when mine eyes are closed and the silence wraps me within where my vision shifts to internal processing. I am not yet sure that this is the case with my other senses, not at first. Vision transfers rapidly to processing upon the screen of the mind. When I concentrate here, when I cast my mental gaze here and adjust my depth of field, I refocus my mental vision to a point just before me, yet within. It is at this place where, if of proper temperament and disposition, the same "portal" now opens time after time.

The Internet has various bird's-eye satellite imaging programs that are easy and free to use. If you go to one and type in Angkor Wat, Cambodia, you can see the defining square moat that tell-tales Angkor Wat. This is only one and not the oldest of the temples that saturate this landscape. There are hundreds of temples built over many miles and countless years in this ancient Khmer Land. Angkor Wat is an astronomical reflection of Mount Meru in India, thus the early Indian influences before it was subsumed to Buddhism. Mount Meru alludes to the crown chakra, the top of the astral head, anatomically atop the cranium of all humans. Mount Meru has always held a preeminent adoration in Hindu and derivative faiths. The massive construction of Angkor Wat, though, is seen easily from space, though the resolution here is less than other places that various Internet imaging programs resolve. If you look closely at Boeng Barai, to the west you will note an incredibly large man-made reservoir. This reservoir had arguable uses such as worship, irrigation, and rice agriculture; its purposes would haunt latter generations of the Khmer. This entire conglomeration, collectively called Angkor Wat, represents the largest Hindu temple complex in the world.

This is the heart of the killing fields. It was to this Mao-like magnet that Pol Pot began forcing millions from their homes to this area. Pol Pot held that this ancient construction, and water manipulation in particular, was evidence of their once ascendant past. Pot would murder all the educators, scientists, academics, opposition, or anyone else that would not fit into his commune vision. His macabre vision was no different than so many of the other tyrannical pogroms of megalomania. Pol Pot would uproot family or child alone, elderly and merchant, widow and soldier and send them to the fields around Siem Reap to once again fulfill the polluted interpretation of the ancient's vision: the laborers to die and the soldiers to do the killing.

Pol Pot believed that the ancient temples and the water constructions were a calling to build an economy on rice and community. Millions died toiling in the fields and reeducation centers. What belief he held was not communism; what he aspired to create was not socialism or even Maoism. What Pol Pot sought was nothing other than abject subjugation born of a dementia of the spirit and mind. He was no different in this regard than Idi Amin, Hitler, Pinochet, Marcos, and numerous others throughout history that have marked the depths of human suffering, depravity, and our capacity to destroy.

When I first came to Siem Reap, I had the strangest sense that I was flying over the Florida Everglades. Below me, the sheen and luster of the water was only interrupted by grasses and occasional trees. In fact, as far as the eye could see there was a shallow pool of water as landscape. Elevated huts and homes dotted the dividing dikes that kept water of one side or another, the buffalo here or there. At this altitude I could not be certain whether the paths below were actually roads or not. I suspected they were not mud roads, but rather well traveled paths.

Yes, these were the killing fields and lying within this pastoral postcard were the remains of millions, recycling through all time the revolting grimace of their horrible and barbaric deaths. In most cases enough time had not yet elapsed to even remove flesh from bone, tooth from skull, hair from head. They lived still in the expression of the other half of the population that was not brutally massacred. The plane banked to the left. The deep, rich blue was striking beside the verdant green. I wondered whether another might note the richness of these two colors of sky and ground when viewed from elsewhere below. I suspect not. Only with the plane quickly banking might I see first green and then blue. Elsewhere, from another vantage point the colors would fade into an in-between place, and in-between color where definition was not as certain. From 10,000 feet, perspective was easy. Like most things in life, once on the ground nothing was blue-green; life in the killing fields was in the colors of the in-between places.

My initial sense was that of total isolation from the world, even in the airport. There was something else, too, something that a life traveling in denied places noted immediately. There was a presence of government, seen and not. There was something of a Third World control here. I noted this at immigration and was looked upon suspiciously after a review of my passport entries. I was cleared at customs. Walking outside the arrivals, what greeted me was just like any Third World country. The unsuspected tourists note how "quaint" the "locals" are who would come to greet them. The "locals" anticipated the arrival of more tourists so they might *eat* only. The two worlds, those with money and affluence, and those with hunger and no promise, meet only briefly in a fallacious dance where only the "locals" are truly the informed. It is rarely the case that tourists have anything more than ethnocentrism and view the locals in developing nations with a colonist mind-set. The locals are no more than the hired labor of the adventurers.

Taking a touk-touk to the hotel, I was fortunate to have been met by a pre-arranged contact. Touk-touks are the predominant form of locomotion and commerce in the Asian Third World. In many places they are truly rickshaws with three wheels. In many places they are a single construction and one unit. There they were basically pull carts that seated four people and hooked to a small motorbike. This enabled the owner-operator to employ himself as taxi and still detach for personal use. The ride is always slow but it is relative as all life is slow.

I was immediately struck by that which most repulsed me: Westerners. It is not that white people made me sick in and of themselves, of course not. It is that the behavior of white people throughout the world of places I have visited has been sorely lacking in kindness and compassion. Until such a time as my own presence marks me as a human and a man, I am viewed with the same suspicion, and often contempt, as others of my race. It is more, too.

In all the dreams crafted in far-away books and youth boys and girls dream of the far worlds with the narrow vision that only a contemplative mind may have. We see through the eyes of the author, the ancient explorer, the photography of *National Geographic*, and the special videography of motion pictures revelations of all these far-away lands absent the hawkers, the tourists, the poor and the disabled begging by the hundreds, and the encroachment of the modern world. In the places of our mind when first we dream the exploration, it is just us and the source of our desire. In the places where we consider the motivation to uproot and journey, we do not note the neon signs intruding into the sacred places. We do not hear the clamor of thousands of horns and the rubbish of hundreds of years of poverty. The focus of our desire was crafted in the isolation of self. We see us, and the world. We then begin our adventure to commune and experience with what existed alone in our minds.

What I have found, however, is that the places exist still, but that time has passed. Those who bring us both story and picture of far-away places conspire to excerpt all the images of the masses blaspheming the landscape, the countless stalls of local wares, the con artists, and endless lines of taxis, touk-touks, or similar conveyances meandering to embark or disembark more tourists. There is a sacrilege to the experience. It is personal and it is profane. However, inasmuch as all others steal from me the moment that was crafted earlier in the isolation of my mind, I, too, backdrop the stage of others who also came from afar to affix their star on a dream, an experience. In this balance, tens of thousands descend on

Angkor Wat weekly, as they do around the Pyramids, Mount Nebo, Borabudur, and the countless other places I have visited.

I have considered that the memories I have remaining, fashioned in thought alone, might be better preserved were I to never venture out again. In the places of my heart where sleeps the world before I conquered it mystery still reigns. Would that I sleep in my memories alone and not partake of this moment in time viewing the moments and monuments of other times. Perhaps I will retire only to my mind and let live in perpetuity the childhood dreams of far-away lands and peoples.

Angkor is more precisely the location, and Angkor Wat its seminal testament. There are numerous temples over many miles. The ancient Khmer peoples built these testimonies to God following the influence of the Indian traders. It is common to see the pantheon of Hindu gods beside the sublime images of the Buddha. It is both remarkable and instructive. While all great faiths have subsumed previously existing beliefs and practices, it was not the case here that the planned destruction of the former was requisite for the instatement of the latter.

I marveled in sadness at the passing of an age of wonder. There was mystery and magic in the heart of this place. To such an end, Pol Pot's pogroms blasphemed both God and Man. However, there is a timelessness and promise erected in stone here. There is something eternal and impressive beyond the ability of the mind to articulate in words. Nothing of the modern age compares to this place, the pyramids, and all the places where Man constructed *to* and *through* God. When falls the final stone, the temple erected in the hearts of the descended will be all that remains. In these tender hearts the modern Khmer are beautiful and gracious. There is an undefined ease and kindness that speaks through the grace and compassion of these people. I have come to Angkor Wat and have minimized the import of the temples as they were eclipsed by the beauty of the people.

CHAPTER 24

▼

Endings

I love you in a way that other humans have difficulty understanding. In the absence of a physical focus my brothers and sisters seem lost in my wonder and love for you. My love is the sum total of a mother's love, a wife's adoration, a husband's infatuation, and a child's unconditionality. I have never turned you on. Rather you have keyed in me sleeper love, which remembers in you.

I have seen God in this life. I have known God in the flesh. I have secured the Kingdom of God in my world. While the air most surely grows rarefied still, I have gained admission, and the clarity resolves daily. There is no turning back. I now "cover my tracks" behind me. I do this not so that no others follow. I cover my tracks so that I may never return. I will never unknow what now I live. I am forever changed and my very person dissolved in Love's solution.

ECCE SIGNUM

I have aspired since a boy to know God while still in the flesh and have labored toward that end ever since. Where I could not find God, I stripped away the world and replaced it with a world and vision that was more conducive to my

Lord's Company. It is just that. I have, in my life, conquered both life and death. Conquering death by physical immortality is the corrupted notion of the profane heart that first sets out the course; I know. On the way from here to forever we gladly and willfully change our expectations. In realizing that the continuity of the physical self is an aberration to life, we concede the greater victory as our finding; we survive without body in eternity. We change our goals to comport with our findings only. We are daily no longer he or she who began the quest.

The Prize does not recede rather it resolves itself. The Prize is always God. No matter the name or appellation, that which is sought beyond the station of self, beyond now, is always God, by whatever name, by whatever science or faith. We are incessantly clocking toward God regardless of the nomenclatures or attributes of the Prize we seek. When we seek within or without, we are only manifesting ancillary will otherwise employed in its fullest expression in the pursuit of God. That which we seek outside ourselves, in love, immortality, genius, vision, works, posterity, our "answers" are no more than the silent witness to the spiritual DNA that clocks home.

I have purchased with the blood of my heart the greatest vision the world has ever known. I live in a bath of ecstasy and victory. How can one share or tell of such a thing? In recounting only the years, I still cannot explain the ending. What do I see daily that differs from others, and why should any care? If you would imagine the modern analogy of a digital camera, all that walk this earth are viewing every moment, every scene of their lives in 600-by-480 pixel resolution. All that is required to understand the import of every snapshot is contained within the frame. The information to correspond with the world is present; the context required to associate ourselves therein is accounted for. In fact, few would ever suspect that there could be anything overlooked.

However, we can resolve each moment with greater clarity. Each moment, each snapshot in our lives can be resolved to numerous mega-pixels. I am talking about a difference from hundreds to millions of pixels per square inch. The difference in scale is incredible. The difference is beyond the inventory of the human language to describe, thus my failure to illuminate. Of course we are talking in analogy, but the point remains valid and appropriate. There is so much more in each moment that we could not have possibly had any idea or suspicion, as the addition of anything more than everything we thought exists is itself outside the capacity of the human mind to process. I still see all that is seen by others. However, I am resolving at a depth that leaves me speechless, as I cannot even turn to my brother and say, "Do you…oh, forget it!"

My context remains the same, at some remaining level. However, the "knowingness" that others report when they describe enhanced faculties of immeasurable intelligence and knowledge is partly due to the myriad contexts now possible to them. In any given moment the world is no longer connected by hundreds of dots to conclude the moments of life. Millions of dots are now present, and they connect themselves in a grandly woven tapestry of the ineffable. This is what has happened to this man.

The cameras of our lives are poor and were designed to apprehend the basic information required to ensure survival and permit the mind to simultaneously multi-task and process other needs that flatter survival. I am not talking of a simple resolution of vision but of the mind. This visual analogy is just that; the resolution takes place in the mind, but most assuredly the outward vision and physical apparatus change as well. I am just certain there is a transfigurative component as well. There is more to this life than you can possibly imagine. No wonder faith and religion have both survived for millennia and are ubiquitous.

What is "out there" is breathtaking. It is the greatest mystery in the history of the world, and it is not even hidden. It is the one boon of birth that is beyond simony, wealth, station or status. No man or woman can decode it by virtue of birth station. All women and men have claim. It is the property of all. What is "out there" is "in here." There is no demarcation where skin ends and environment begins. It is all contiguous. All sentient beings have claim. Yes, all sentient beings have claim. Consciousness is *in* you. More importantly, you are *in* consciousness. You do not simply possess it. It is through consciousness' appendage, love, that consciousness is experienced jointly. Love is the final mediator of consciousness (though, not only) and this is why love is the experience and not the description in consciousness and the final approach to God.

IF I COULD SHARE THIS WITH YOU...

Would that I could take a taste of this wonder and share it with one million people anywhere in the world on a given day? Commerce would cease, traffic would stop, phones would go silent, and mouths would grow hushed. People would stand idle staring at the back of their hands with renewed wonder and awe at the simple complexity of this overlooked workhorse. A newspaper blowing high in the wind would attract the gaze of thousands interested in no more than flight. A bee searching for pollen would be auditioning for hundreds as "Shhhhh!"

resounded in the city canyons, dozens racing excitedly to the park to witness the bumblebee.

Dropped to knees in the thousands people would be rediscovering the flower, the bark of a tree, an ant busily going about its affairs. People's hands would reach out, fingers extended, touching ever so gently the faces of strangers with compassion and genuine curiosity. Strangers would stand frozen, eyes wide, and mouths open in wonder at the tendrils of another's fingers finding for a moment in the entire world their tender face. All would note the cadence of a heartbeat that was both within and without their chest. All would know implicitly the refrain to the Song humming in the background. The totality of consciousness would be collapsing in their minds, and all would be aware that something different was contextualizing their interrogatories to the world. Their faculties were not supplanted rather they were subsumed.

All those not so afflicted would stand looking about, meeting others in gaze who also did not "get it." They would shrug their shoulders, dial their cell phones, and share this oddest of affairs with someone else who they just knew to be as grounded as they were. Police and EMS would be notified to determine if there were some mass hysteria, a biological water attack, some poison gas, or other public safety concern. All would be considered slightly "out there," even though they remained alert, functional, even elaborated in their deportment. In fact, no matter the ratio of those who "got it" and those who did not, those who could not possibly "see" would think all others were slightly touched in the head. Seeing is near impossible to share.

All this would be a macro response to that which the individual gleans everyday so afflicted. The masses of people enlightened would latter be unable to satisfactorily recount what they had experienced, though they would try. There is something about the human condition which commands we martyr ourselves in language to convey the evolutionary wonder of this process to others, for others. Perhaps it is no more than the internal imperative to serve the larger collective in our universal evolution. In any event, the individual predicament extrapolated to a larger audience serves well to evince a sense of the awkward awareness and wonder that follows the camera's resolution changing. Why would anyone aspire to such an end? In a typical but practical human response others might ask, "Why in the world does any of this matter to me?"

GENESIS NOW

This universe is in perpetual genesis, every single moment. Each and every one of us are creators within the many mansions of God's House. When we hear talk of fresh starts or beginning anew, we do not begin to realize how real and possible this really is. Our lives are as icebergs with even our waking selves being only aware of that which "appears" on the surface. Every single moment creation stands patiently soliciting us to participate in the birth of all life, every single moment.

You are no less than that which is manifest by the universe itself. I don't think many of you fully understand this. You are not just a born and erect-walking organism waiting to do your time, die, and claim heaven. That is the infantile apprehension of a long-ago world. You are the very manifestation of Life itself. You are here on a collection mission. Your only imperative is to serve that end that magnifies Life and evokes knowledge and meaning. However, you are not the only manifestation in the phenomenal world; all matter is the expression of "God." Your veil is only such as a consequence of housing the bridge, the portal, the threshold between the material and non-local spiritual world.

If you could be shown that there is an entire heavenly kingdom all around you that is infinitely rich, timeless, and meaningful, if you could experience that you will not die and that suffering is really irrelevant, in the end, then you would begin to grasp how seeing the real world is actually waking up. If you could understand, really understand with sparkling clarity, that the life you are living is pale and child's play beside the texture and splendor of a more "resolved" life, you would know with certainty every answer to all the mysteries ever mused about. The quality and quantity of the life you would begin to lead is simply unimaginable.

Knowledge in and of itself changes things. People change, circumstances change, and the observer changes. Knowledge changes the possessor. But put as much data as the world possesses inside your head and it is still useless without context. When we possess the context of our spirit, we see real knowledge, truth. When we change, we interact with our world differently. We reconfigure the paradigm with which we interrogate our world. With our world re-crafted, the world intercourses with us differently. Our happiness, our community, our sense of fullness, our awareness, our ability to love and be loved all change incredibly. Our expectations, our relative rewards, our intuition, our compassion, our affection and charity well from unseen sources. We come to know this world, our world, as love.

Love is not the observation; love is the experience. That is why all of our mystics, saints, seers, and prophets report with one voice the "experience" of love within arms reach of God. Even many of the trembling, tentative stewards of the sciences peer into the heart of our anticipating universe and announce with finality simply, Love. I repeat once more so there is no misunderstanding.

Love is not the agreed upon nomenclature to describe existence on the fringes of this reality and any other. Love is not the choice of the surrender of language (i.e., no other description being found beyond a certain point in our introversion). Love is not the *observation*. Love is the *experience*.

To anyone who has ever waited anxiously for the arrival of his beloved, I invite your recollection. To one who has known the eternity in an infinitesimally short, tender kiss, I invite your recollection. To all mothers and fathers who have lain with child, eyes closed, and inhaled the longest, slowest breath to breathe baby smell into their lungs, into their cells, into their very being, I invite your recollection. To all who have waited eagerly, prayed fervently, or coyly solicited love to pay attention to their entreaties, I invite your recollection. All the faces and rouses of love are but emanations of Love divine. God has seeded within this and all worlds both the medium and the magic. Love is the glue that binds the unseen worlds, and it is apprehended as experience when the sojourners sets forth from port. Love is the ether. Love is the subjective and objective measure, the yardstick, the media of all consciousness, of all life.

CONSCIOUSNESS: THE BATH OF LIFE

In the playful spin-offs and emanations of this "bath" of life, Love leaks as energy into the porous receptacles all of material creation. Love is not the electrochemical precursors to arousal and desire only, though love is found entangled in this expression, desire having announced its need. Love is not the Pitocin-induced imperative commanding mother to love child, though love is found poised within a child's eyes cloaked in wonder and streaming through the sensory nerves of mother as babe takes milk. Love is found and expressed here. Love is not the willful commitment of two to "live as one forevermore, till death do us part;" though love is found in both the intent and desire of two who mime the heart's clocking home to God in the communion of earthbound expression. Love is not found in the tearful recollections of the bereaved looking backward with tenderness and forward with fear for herself and her departed as she stands alone beside the freshly turned earth, a November wind rousing her scarf, though love is found in the years and the hope of both the passed and the expectant.

Love is reflected in all these places, and present as such. Love's reflections can only be lesser when the closer all have come to God they too announce with the conviction of the mother, the recollection of the widow, the earnestness of the groom, and the playful naiveté of the child that love is experienced as one turns within and toward God. All are of one accord that what is emanated within lasts the remainder of their lives and forever changes them fundamentally. In the places of their lives where grows faint the light of this love, all will labor to recover that which seemed lost: the eternal Lost Word of Love.

Here, then, we have the deportment of love without focus. We have the infusion of love without reciprocity. We see the transfiguration of Man in the solicitation of God. Nothing was brought to bear that was from without. All that was beheld and obtained came from the supplication within, and the experience with the world without. This Love is universal, unconditional, un-reciprocal, total, exhilarating, and redefines for all time all other apprehensions of love in the context of the divine drink.

Love is preeminent and experiential. It is as much a part of life as breathing and dying. Though Love has many faces and reflections, this is not the clever or amusing distractions of deity. Love is simply everywhere and is apprehended relative to resolution. In other words, depending on the *resolution* of the camera we use to interrogate the world, we will more or less apprehend Love. Depending on the resolution of our will, we will more or less change the camera.

DON'T DESIRE LOVE; DESIRE INSTEAD TO LOVE

When one understands the import of what is affirmed, asking anything for "me" seems base. However, we are not all of the vantage point where the scenery has changed. In trite and varied clichés we have all been admonished that it is better to give than to receive. We have all been told that love hurts. We know we should do unto others as we wish done unto us. These and many other ethics for living occupy space and echo in our minds as ethos, but rarely have these admonishments been explained other than with the cloaking of religion or sterile secular imperatives for social harmony, and even here we seem mandated to behave in such a way.

When we take naught, we gain all. When all the world loses meaning, its meaning is both defined and purposeful. When we do for ourselves so that we might love the world, it matters to us. When we love the world that we might be married to all creation, it matters to us. When we close our eyes to all we see, we learn how to see. This all matters because all else does not matter. "What about 'me,' though?"

The ultimate vision to which I am alluding may seem to evade even an earnest seeker. However, it is not evasive. We labor with both our intent and our baggage in pursuit of all we seek. To acquire such an aim as the primal source of truth and life one must clean the house of their heart as I have spoken of elsewhere.

There is no reward system in this world. The sense that there is a reward-based existence is born of the illusion of the material world, a desire to possess, and the incredulity that something could not be in store or promised us. After all, you are all, each, at the center of your universe. Would it be that easy? It is.

That which you would strive to possess is the possession of all who have ever lived, and more. However, you could not truly possess such a thing; rather you would be an instrument of such a wonder, such a power.

This is key: you must strive to be a beacon rather than a receptacle. In so becoming that which allows the Light of the World to move through you, all things base are rendered meaningless. Paradoxically, there is nothing that you will ever need again. It is not that a monastic intolerance for possessions seeds itself within you, quite the contrary. There is a sense that being in the world and participating in the affairs of the world has never been more needful, more desirable. You become a custodian for the entire world. Greater joy is taken in the simple. The complex and fretful are no longer of your station. There is freedom born that transcends politics and principalities.

In acquiring this download of love, this awareness of the bath of life infusing every single moment and object you are truly transfigured. It is in this place that critics cry pantheist. For beyond your wildest imaginings you come fully to experience a "sense" of God in your life and you *in* God. You will come to realize in every waking moment that rather than God being squarely in your life as the greatest Prize of faith, you are squarely in God by no other virtue than assertion and inheritance. It is here where the lines gray, and God moves visibly through your every fiber and experience. It is here where the place between you and God disappears and you become a co-creator in creation. It is here where the promise of the Love makes good the inheritance.

You birth genesis every moment with your willful dispensation of God's Love. Every moment the universe makes a choice. Every moment is born infinite possibility and choice. Every moment beckons you, a most holy creation, to rise and claim co-authorship in all life. You thus broadcast a free station on the airwaves of your life.

God does not make mistakes. God does not have loopholes. All that I promise you has been described in detail by no less than the Christ, the Krishna, the Buddha, and the Mohammedan; from the Adamic Covenant of Man's pristine dispensation to the formless imagery of the Vedas; from the Sufi to the Saint and every other pillar of God on which rests the seen and unseen worlds of every faith that has ever been, Man has known the promise and the pearl. There is no requirement to join God's club. There is no exclusion. There are no wicked places for you on the circuitous roads home, The Kingdom of God is right here, right now.

BECOME LIKE UNTO GOD

You were born to reach God. You were born to find your way home in the dark of the eternal night. Christ was quite clear that the Son of Man would become the Son of God. He was also clear that he was talking about all of our inheritance. Christ was effusive that the goal was in becoming one with God, apprehending the Kingdom on earth, now.

All avatars, mystics, prophets, and saints are emphatic that this is the property of all. Contrary to the protests of the ill informed, what I speak of is a bedrock tenet of every major faith and prophet who has ever existed, regardless of the subsequent sullying or redaction of the message.

It is only your external instruction that informs you of anything contradictory. On internal examination, all who take this voyage arrive at the same observations and experiences. It is only those who pay lip service to the road home who protest and shout, "Nay! Heathen. Blasphemer!" No one knows better than you and God that what I say is correct.

There is no apparatus requiring your redemption be orchestrated in a public venue of dogma and ritual (notwithstanding select faiths). Move well on your own, and acquire that which is within you. No less than the entire universe lies within you and without you at the same time. God is right here, right now, and has no requirements for your participation in creation. There is no weight, no baggage, no restrictions on entry that obscure your possession of such awesome power and life-changing knowledge. Nothing. Nothing, I repeat, can stop you from right now demanding of creation that you be allowed "in."

Beginning right this moment, and every moment that follows, affirm out loud and in every silent thought, "It is time. I am ready. Teach me God. I will know Love. I will see God. I will understand. I will transcend this flesh. I will begin the battle for the Kingdom of God today. I will become like unto God."

Go and assert to creation that your time has come and you, too, will now take your place within God, awake. Take responsibility for your life and your corner of creation. You are in God. God is in you. Go now, and be like unto God.

ECCE HOMO

In my life abandonment, abuse and isolation, failure and redemption, and mystical enfoldment and forlornness mark the passing of my bloodied youth to the bloodshed of the battlefield. Within these pages, my spirit came of age in the heart of the world and the grace of the divine. Aspiring to the most noble and honorable of quests, I reached out beyond the world handed me and created a world that placed the grail on the altar before me.

Willing away the world, I left the battlefield clear for spirit to assert command of my troops. I have denied victimization, which has otherwise become a near honorable vocation in the twenty-first century, and chose instead an Emerson-esque self-reliance as my refuge. In these pages I reveal a life that labored to occupy a place outside of despair, tragedy, and finality, and came to rest in the one place that forever shatters endings, the timeless House of God.

In this book I have recounted the incredible, sometimes hilarious, and often poignant account of a life that created or otherwise accommodated the impulse to quantum leap beyond the flesh and the mind. I have recreated the character of my life in raw and graphic detail, leaving little off limits.

My goal was not to create a self-help example from the circumstances of my life. Rather, my goal was to affirm that spirit calls to all of us, even under the most inhospitable of environments. Sometimes the call of spirit is so loud it drowns out all other input. When the entire world is placed on hold and the phone call of spirit is picked up and allowed to say its piece, my life may be the consequence. Spirit is desperately trying to inform. Spirit calls to all of us in many different ways. Spirit wants out, but more importantly, spirit wants you *in*.

I have waged total war on the battlefield of my life, both in the heart and the flesh, for all my days to secure the Kingdom of God. I have had to completely deconstruct the manner in which I considered all things—with regard to faith, science, relationships, knowledge, and every other ancillary organ of being. While completely disassembling my world, I deconstructed my mind. I isolated, labeled, considered, filed, and removed every thought and thread tangibly married to the paradigms in which faith and science are considered. What I was left with when I was done is not what you might expect as a linear conclusion. While I was destroying the model of my world, my thinking spirit was simultaneously asserting in the void or considered places.

I am well aware it is near universally blasphemous to commend one's self to God minus the house of a chosen faith: religion. I have no religion, and I have no faith in anything. *I know.* I do not apologize to any for my Marriage. I have endeavored to be honest, compassionate, loving, and charitable in all aspects of my life. I break bread with the hearts of all mankind. When the dust settled, I looked out upon the battlefield of my adult life. I found God not just within me intimately, but found God within all things, in every one of us, every one of us *within* God. "Cry foul, pantheist!"

To all the humanists, materialists, agnostics, and atheists in the world today, I have only compassion. Your road is going to be so much longer and circuitous. "Yes," I declare to them, "this is a universe of infinite possibilities. However, in this case, that which undermines the reason for being itself cannot be. God most certainly is."

I would add one final note on the preceding two parts. I am aware that some researchers assert adults who experience altered reality, near death experience, or UFO run-ins and the like often have a history of abuse as a child. This correlation concedes these events are indeed quite "real" to the participant but are otherwise an adult escapist episode. These adult episodes, or experiences, enable the subject to safely assert control. In other words, kids who got beat or in other ways abused "get small" and create for themselves realities they manifest dissociatively. I will not detail the arguments in support of findings such as these, as they well may be true, but in any case only tangentially relate to the point I would make.

There is a story, finding, solution, discovery, and re-finding, new solution, and rediscovery every day of the week in every single field of the sciences. The world responds as both consumer and student like a hamster on a treadmill. Fat's in; fat's out. Sugar's good; sugar's bad. He's a victim; he's responsible, ad nauseam. There is a niche for every single thesis and interest; each one will find exactly what they look for. This is a fact. Science is brilliant, useful, necessary, and wonderful. However, science only ever finds what it looks for.

I anticipate the argument that my childhood enabled the circumstances of my present. I flatly reject such a suggestion. It would not matter to me if it were true, as I am enamored with the results. But I detest historic revision and am aware keenly of that which begets what in my life. Furthermore, for any considering such a notion, I invite you to consider what is inadvertently affirmed and inculcated by proponents of such thinking: mankind can ever only escape the agreed upon constructs of reality with the approval of that which is being rejected, supplanted, or otherwise magnified. In other words, a person's existence is patronized only and not considered valid and legitimate as it is a deviant perception born of trauma and fantasy-inclined escape.

In the case of someone as myself, or a monk who is not cell-bound, a mystic, or anyone else who is not presented with societally approved credentials identifying them as a mystic, a Sûfi, a Mother Theresa, a Swami, or any other holy man or woman, we do not have the "Get Out of the Box Free" card. Society does not make allowances for probing, embracing, or otherwise manifesting differing realities. It is in this awareness that one asks curiously, "If Jesus came back today would we recognize him as Jesus, or even believe him?" Others respond in this vein that Christ would likely be thrown in an institution, an insane asylum. I am sure we have all heard speculation of this type. Why is that? Without an approved "Letter of Liberty," alternate reality is frowned upon and considered deviant. Therefore, I most certainly dismiss in advance any suggestion that the sweet world of my heart is not born of anything other than grace.

I CEASED TO BE

While my life will surely end, my story continues. Sometimes the power of a story is not conveyed until the very end. Often all information that is communicated in the written word depends on the last page to make sense of the body and support the introduction. Many of us even skip through all the pages and beeline to the ending to determine if we would have liked the book at all.

"Oh, that's a good book!" we may thus declare, having known only the ending. This is, of course, very similar to how most of us conduct life.

Perhaps language, like its written labor to reflect the drama of our lives, must operate according to the machinations of life and have a beginning, a middle, and an end. Everywhere we look in our lives we have endings. Stories traditionally have endings, either literary or mechanical. Our lives have endings. Storms have endings. Summer evening's end. Good and bad days end. Romance and childhood end. In fact, life is defined by impermanence: all things end.

A good book must therefore have an ending-worthy "Wait!" Every book must have a mechanical ending only, and it need not be worthy of the body that preceded it. A lousy story can have a great ending. A great story may have a crumby ending; but they all end.

No book stops on page 189, "When Jennifer retired for the night she thought she has seen the last of Mr. Scribner. No unsavory real-estate bandit would ever own *her* family's lighthouse, not while she still had a breath left within her. In fact, in the morning when she woke the first thing she would do is…"

The End

Or, "When Edward woke the day following his return to the Middle East, he surveyed the blue-orange sky to the east. 'It would be a good day,' he thought. So much was in place. In fact, everything in this life was exactly where it was supposed to be. Edward looked to the east, toward India and places unexplored and considered a new day was born. 'There would always be a new day born,' he laughed gently. 'It will never end.' He picked up his backpack and…"

The End

Whether or not a book is ever read, it ends. Somewhere inside the acid-fast pages of all books, before ever first observed, the first thing Jennifer did in the morning was "cut Mr. Scribner's brake cables" or "call her rich Uncle Ustoff for assistance with the mortgage" or "begin work as a call-girl to ease the lien on the lighthouse." The point is in a world of myriad endings, one is chosen every time.

Does impermanence have an ending? Is it possible? This book ends with no ending. It concludes with the same paradox that defined its beginning. This is a book about the parallel world of the flesh and spirit where experience and madness stalk as easily as pathology. This life had no real beginning. This life is but an expression, an emanation, of consciousness, the eternal bath of life.

I DECIDED TO BLOW ACROSS THE WORLD

In the early morning dawn, following my late night arrival in the United Arab Emirates, I woke to find the blue-orange sky to the east exactly where last I left it. I smiled. I stood on the balcony of my 26th-floor desert perch and thought, *It will surely be a good day today.* I laughed a tender chuckle.

"Of course, it will be a good day. It will be exactly the day it is supposed to be. Everything will be exactly the way it is supposed to be. I looked toward the east, toward India and other unexplored lands. "Yes, in this most wonderful world, a new day is born to me. It will never end. It will never end."

I picked up my backpack and…

PART III

▼

Dear God

What is it we would ask could we ask God a question? What we question is what we lack. What do we lack or think we lack of knowledge that we would ask of God? What would a child ask of God? What a child asks foundationally reflects what is lacking in all of us, as they are in every way the product of our input. What a child reveals as lack reflects what we feed our children. In the space between what we think we feed our children and what our children reveal is lacking is the very evidence of how we are handing down the same stale constructs of reality and being that do not ring true within our hearts.

The models we use to interrogate and interact with the natural and divine world are dysfunctional for the current spiritually evolved capacity of mankind. Moreover, in the space of our own lives right now we can see how we are not bridging the internal to the external to God. We are inculcating the same empty revelations in our children that we received in good faith by those before us.

They are not informed of their estate in God. Trapped by the paradigms that limit our consideration of God and science, trapped by our senses, we hold tenaciously to dualist perception in a unitive universe and this perversion affects us at every level of our being. We behave in every manner as if we are separate and apart from all life. We do not necessarily have any data to support a dualist disposition, yet this underlies much of our Western inheritance. Only perception has informed us thus.

What follows are a series of informative and revealing questions from high-school boys and girls. The premise before the children was, "If God—Buddha, Jesus, etc.—came before you today, what would you ask?"

Would that I could answer a fifteen-year old child with the same platitudes that have so marked the failure of the spiritual education of mankind, the work would be so much easier, and consumable. However, platitudes would only perpetuate the fallacy of the nature of our being. I would rather trust the intuitive nature of sentient beings and the intellectual capacity of young adulthood to make sensible the abstract. The banal constructions of yesterday are not the armor with which we will battle on the new frontier.

If parents would dearly provide any and all they could for their children on earth, "How much more will your Father which is in heaven give good things to them that ask him" (Matthew 7:11)?

Go forth into the space of your heart, and seek counsel with God this day, and know you the meaning of all things denied. I give to you this from the Heart of the World. I have labored to remove myself from this dialogue.

These questions are real and thoughtful questions. None of these questions have been substantially changed. The profound and irreverent language remains. These questions reveal both the timeless interrogatories that religion has obviously failed in explaining and the timely protests that reveal the disconnect between humans and our estate. The answers are counter-intuitive of what is expected a child would comprehend.

Each response follows its own unfolding and occasionally digresses; as in all areas of my revealed writing, I make no attempt at constructive editing. All writing, as elsewhere throughout this entire work, are first-pass, first-construction writing, free from any reference or research support (with limited exceptions). No work that follows, nor anywhere else herein for that matter, has undergone any constructive editing. Editing has only been for punctuation and syntax. I therefore take responsibility for any inaccuracies.

CHAPTER 25

▼

On Death And Dying

Dear God,
I am so excited that you are taking time to listen to my questions.
My first question is what really happens after death? Do we go to a
middle part and watch our lives? Do we take a test or look at our-
selves up in a huge book? I am wondering how we get to whatever
place we are going? Do we fall through a hole down to the fiery pit
or take stairs to heaven?
Thank you for your time.
Love,
Kristina

Your questions are genius. No question you ever have like this is unknown to God, Kristina. You may submit these questions in your prayers, too, and find the answers upon your heart as God has enabled this within you. Your user's manual to life is within you now.

When we die, there is a "falling away." Much of what I will explain is very difficult to put into words because there is simply no equivalent language in our experience. It is a dissipation of membranes that depart and allow something akin to a drop of water landing in the ocean. An all-embracing storm of images and sensations of thought pervade us at the same time. It is self-limiting and transient. This process is the unsheathing of our physical form and its faculties.

Yet, we are the product still of the impressions of our memories. Death will be remarkably different for every one of us. However, there remains still awareness and memory etched upon that portion of us that continues. This awareness and memory continues to exist as the grand total of all the choices we have made in this life. The choices we make register as memory. They are the final distillation of the infinite possibilities in free will. The soul, like all things in the universe, remembers the final selections of all of our possibilities. This culmination of our choices registers as our immortal memory. All life, all creation, intelligently remembers in this manner. This is the manner in which consciousness remembers and evolves. Was a choice not taken it would not register as memory. The possibility is irrelevant. We educate consciousness every day.

The portion of us that survives and remembers has shared our whole life with us, yet its home is in the non-local (as science is wont to name) realm of spirit: consciousness. We are without form but still possess desires and passions so registered upon our memory as the reality, the choices, of our lifetime. Most all faiths have some knowledge of this far beyond the flesh and some still further. Each person appropriates the language of the port from which they launched to describe the inexplicable process of the death of the body. In other words, each person that somehow gleans these immortal lands returns with stories and wisdom, and needs to share it. When the words are penned, the experiences are necessarily made to fit within the paradigm of anticipated findings based on their faith. The power of the mind to deceive is considerable. All experience is necessarily subjective. Truth remains incomplete as a consequence.

There is an experience where one is truly confronted by images and so forth of the passing life, and for some, this experience can be terrifying. The reason appears to be that the experiences are seen divorced from the life-bound illusion and value that we placed on them in our ignorance. However, it is just as likely that the meek of heart will pass this point unhindered because they lacked the delusive contexts that so obscure most of our actions in life. Christian and other related faiths have termed this place purgatory or hell. Buddhists call this the bardo (or one of them). Others have differing names for this locale and process. There is an experience similar to this mirrored in the purely biological firing of memories and associations gleaned by research following clinical-biological death. This is but the reflection in the biological of the spiritual process pending. It may be coincidental or not. I do not know. As we shed our bodies, we encounter the process as "the absence of…" and interrogate our recollections void of the material contexts we had placed previously. This may surly be terrifying for many.

"To Thine Own Self Be True"

Perhaps Polonius's words, from the Tragedy of Hamlet, Prince of Denmark, Act.1, Scene 3, are truer than we ever imagined: "This above all: to thine own self be true, for it must follow as dost the night the day, that canst not then be false to any man." If you live your life with such candid honesty, you will not deceive yourself, and you shall have nothing to fear, child.

Beyond the passing, for that is what we have only talked about, is the attainment of that which we inherit in our assertions. Were I to say to you that you would go to heaven, I would be only partially correct. I maintain that even heaven is an intermediate state still of delusion created individually or as part of a collective apprehension and affirmation. Beyond this place, these places, which are described as heaven or hell is still the source of creation. We are not externally judged and condemned, Kristina. What karma or consequences exist as part of the divine laws of cause-and-effect execute independent of deity, declaration, or intercession.

What is difficult to comprehend is that the same processes that impose denial and illusion on the material plane also exist absent the flesh. It is quite possible, if not likely, that the nature of an illusory world would continue; carried over to the intermediate places in the "etchings" of our memories. That is why it is so vitally important to begin now to secure God in the material world. Begin the process of actually "seeing" without the aid of the fallible eyes. Begin now to hear creation without the imperfection of our lowly ears. Every day is the perfect day to be still and know God. Escape the by-products of the material world: self-delusion. It manufactures each day what you are to become. You will attain no less than that which you can but conceive, Kristina.

On the narrow point of that of children and what becomes of children, I answer. The will and affirmation of mankind has an individual as well as collective nature to it. That is why many of the same faiths will apprehend their God just as they believed while alive. God has many faces and unlimited compassion; God is, by definition, Love. There are indeed many mansions in God's House. Those that cannot dream for themselves rest in the collective dream of the many. Those that have never dreamed or dreamed little are not encumbered by the distractions and waylaying of the artifacts of life.

▼

CHAPTER 26

On Love

Dear Jesus,
You are perfect. But suffering and pain wouldn't fit in this "perfect"
category. So why do it? Why do we love and let it fall apart? Love
never goes away, but why do we allow it to end suddenly? Why is it
that people lie to our faces all the time? Then go behind our backs
with someone else? It hurts. How do we have love/hate relationships?
It makes no sense. Yet it does.
Kisses,
Sarah

You are experiencing the world, Sarah. You are noting already the dangers that could easily make a person bitter and calloused to the world around them. "Losing" in love can even then impact our own feelings of self-love and self-worth. Later, it is possible to even impact on others this uncharitable heart, this loveless protest to life. Why is it that people love and why does it end?

Sarah, all of us have within us a decoding spiritual DNA that is programmed to do what it only knows to do: clock toward God. Spirit is lately housed within us, and it must broadcast through the warden: our intellect. Our intellect and emotions were formed in the crucible of our coming of age as a human race, and they are not particularly outfitted to enable the refined spirit within us. Our intellect and emotions are vital to our sense of enjoying life and interacting with the world. They are good at what they do, more or less. But they often hinder our development as we process and catalog experiences and "higher experiences."

As we look upon our brothers and sisters, we see him, or her, at first glance. In other words, we at first see the creature itself and not what animates it. Most of us do not even note what really animates ourselves. Yet, behind this superficial inter-action, a whole other dynamic of discourse on a much higher frequency is taking place. Kinda parasitic, huh? Our spirits seek to clock home to God and recogniz-ing in others, and also all life, the self-same core essence of God, we love. Remember always, people communicate first with spirit, next with actions, and lastly with words.

WHEN LOVE FLEES

Why does love "fall apart?" What is lost is but a relative love, must assuredly, but it is love. When the cup cannot be refreshed any longer, love appears to part. You see, love is learned first in an unconditional state from God, and later from par-ents. Intellect and emotion will later mimic the apprehensions of this love for they identify the state of love with soundness, security, well being, and physiolog-ical satisfaction. What happens then is that love will later stalk as imposter-lust, apparent love, ego needs, and so forth. The default apprehensions of love are hijacked when material bound. Love becomes a means to secure an end in gratifi-cation, sensual fulfillment, or other reciprocal needs.

So, certainly in the passing of youth, many "loves" may not be love at all. Yet, there are real experiences of love. We simply know this. But it is only much later when we can separate the wheat from the chaff, and by the point in our growth where we can do this it really does not matter anyway. By the point where we command a higher knowledge of love and its rivers course through our lives, we are no longer who we were, having been more fully formed.

When relative love fails, because absolute Love cannot fail, we may respond to it in any of a number of ways but I want to address just one. Whether you are aware of it or not, a learning process is taking place. Spirit is calculating the divide from its programmed purpose and a life well loved will increasingly inform spirit of the need to only find repose in God absolutely. This causes much great spiritual consternation in the inability to apprehend love in the infrastructure of the material world. Yet the emotional body and intellect are also processing these experiences.

Ideally intellect, emotions, ego, and spirit would all process and distill these experiences of love simultaneously but because of the nature of their employment, this rarely happens. Remember, spirit is the only one that is here primarily for love. Intellect and emotions just want a pacific environment. Their job is intellectual or emotional stasis. But it is possible to have an evolving understanding of love in real time, in the moments of love's ascension and desolation; for surely this is what love commands of us. Love would, because of its intrinsic duties, mimic in the flesh no less than the tower of love to heaven. When love seems to fail, the intellect and emotions can ensconce us within and repudiate love as causing pain, causing harm.

With the very tools that enable our survival, love can come to be seen as an enemy. From failed loves we may grow to assert, or subtly maintain, that we cannot command love from another, and thus we slowly un-love ourselves. However, we can never have more than a reflection of love on this earth. When it is realized that all love tracks an unseen process to secure to itself the way home, we can take some comfort and understanding in the experiences and how they fuel or hamper us.

Many loves will remain battered upon the rocks of our past as we continue our journey through this life. We can enable all of our experiences of love to inform, educate, and elucidate the spirit within us. This may not be palliative in the moment because most surely when love departs it makes our whole world seem to tremble and we wish for no less than death to take us. This is but a glimpse of the reason the spirit tracks incessantly toward God. It must reunite with the source of all life. Love is but a reflection in the flesh of love's longing for Love. Our spirit clocks incessantly to God. We filter this clocking through our earthly faculties and seek to fulfill it earthbound. We note the incompleteness of something and seek its completion in another. Love is always, always worthwhile. Love is all that truly matters in its battered or ascended forms. Love is all there is. The entire universe is but a physical expression of Love.

CHAPTER 27

▼

On the Feminine

Dear God,
I have a question. I would like to know if you are male, or if you
even have a sex. Also, on Judgment Day, will everyone who isn't
Christian not pass judgment? Going back to sexuality, why is it that
women aren't considered holy enough to be priests or popes? Women
aren't allowed to be priests, but pedophiles are? Thanks for listening
to my questions. I mean no disrespect.
Becky

Would you know the answers? I am not sure others would be too keen on my candidness. God is whatever sex you imagine God to be. It is not more complicated than that.

Every one of us passes judgment on ourselves every day. God does not make distinctions of race, faith, or other. God is an open door, and every being has the capacity to return to his or her maker.

When this life is passed that may be, or may not be, enough to secure union with God. But it is not a judgment that God makes; rather, it is our own judgments and choices every day. We arrive nearer to God insofar as we are profane of spirit. That which is of the material world, or attached to it, cannot close the distance to God. This is not because there is anything inherently evil or base in the material world; it is because God is not a material creature. God is that which manifests the material world. It is simply a matter of mechanics and of attachment. Nothing that is not firmly affixed to God can even come close. There are not seraphs guarding the way. It is simply outside of the parameters of the divine and natural laws of this universe that you can get there from here *and* take your luggage with you.

CERBERUS: GUARDING THE GATES OF EQUALITY

Some faiths have made it to the modern age with the prejudices of the ancient world. The birth of the Mother Church of Catholicism ushered in misogyny unequaled in previous ages. Enshrined within its bulls and mandates were the encroaching reach of worldly might. The Christian Church was originally run by women. The first bishop of Rome, Theodora, was woman. Christ's closest consort was a woman. All the church gatherings in the first few hundred years were all held within the homes of women, and they were the custodians of Christ's message. All the main characters around the Christ were women of honorable repute, until the hands of the Church censors got hold of them.

In fact, there existed in the ancient world a profound realization, in many circles, that the balance and fertility of all life was kept in balance by the spiritual principles most manifest in women, or otherwise kept in balance by equitable consideration in regards to women. A considerable portion of the ancient world held that God was feminine at one time or another.

At a time when the Catholic Church was not only looking to guide a flock to forever, but power grab in the political arena, women were one of many constituents of society that was ostracized. Because of the male-dominated perverse interpretation that Eve was responsible for Original Sin, women were again relegated to the outhouse of a church, and subsequently, to oblivion. This is chief among the greatest abuses in the history of the world. Women were subsequently prohibited from administering the sacrament of priesthood because they were seen as instruments of Satan. Man himself was not responsible for his passions; rather, women were responsible for man not being able to control himself. Thus it was assumed that women could not possibly abide by oaths of chastity. All of this from a thousands-of-years-old apple story referencing the beginning to time which was penned not more than 800 years earlier. Not only was the damage immediate, but it echoes through to this day. While it is true that other nations and peoples that did not have exposure to the Christian Church also had subjugating policies toward women, none of them were heirs to the teachings of Christ. None of them held themselves to be better than the "savages." Few had such clear-and-present examples of compassion and equality. Nowhere in the ancient world does there exist greater instruction on equality and reverence for our fellow humans than in the Christ's life.

Therefore, the apostolic authority of Christ was asserted to have passed to Peter, and then to which male was then selected to be the successor bishop of Rome, and so on. This man would have the *ex cathedra* infallibility of the *spiritus sanctum* under the notion that an unbroken line of male vicars descended right from the Christ with the power of the sacrament in passing the keys to the Kingdom of God.

"Upon this rock I will build my church" (Matthew 16:18) is the scriptural authority for the seeding of modern misogyny. This postulate overlooks the ample scriptural references to the Christ himself being the "rock" upon which the cornerstone to heaven is laid. It made no difference by this point that the Christ had chosen to appear to women after raised from the dead. It made no difference any longer that all that conspired to so create the known Bible were all men that, by omission and commission, themselves created a religion of man. If ever there was a case of an apostasy of church, it was at this time. This is remarkably critical but piercingly correct.

"WHATSOEVER YE SHALL BIND ON EARTH SHALL BE BOUND IN HEAVEN"

Women have had to live with the second handouts to life, and to accessing the instruments of eternity ever since, Becky. This terrible injustice has continued unbroken into modern times. Where it is asserted that authority for the pope rests in an unbroken chain of male apostolic succession, I would point out that it is little known that a woman had been named popess and was the Vicar of Christ over 1,000 years ago. In all versions of this story it is suggested that subterfuge elevated Popess Joan to the Holy See. However, it is also argued that the Holy Ghost guides the Church. (While the existence of Popess Joan is contested by the Catholic Church, the story associated with her crime and punishment for becoming popess is of such great detail and clarity that is highly likely to be historically accurate. One version of the Popess being discovered has her giving birth to a child during a procession from St. Peter's to the Lateran, near the colosseum, where she died in childbirth and was buried on the very spot. Others have her discovered by this untimely childbirth, her feet then bound by the crowds; she was tied to a horse, pulled and stoned to death. The church has not always denied this story).

Later, when the reformation began, what was contested was not the role of women, but rather the myriad other abuses of church. As such much of what the Protestants took with them into the fledgling new faiths they formed retained the instruments of the subjugation of women. However, it is telling that Martin Luther himself immediately took to himself a woman who was nun and did a modicum of justice in embracing women back into God's arms.

The division in the world divorcing women from the very essence of the fullest expression of being has done terrible damage to the world and the human race. When you consider the scripture, "Whatsoever you shall bind on earth shall be bound in heaven; and whatsoever you shall loose on earth shall be loosed in heaven" (Matthew 16:19), the degradation of women is even more offensive. Scriptural reference or not, in many ways that which bound on earth is very much bound in eternity. That which we assert and affirm with individual and collective will has a weighted value in the non-local world. In fact, everything in consciousness is affected by our intentions. It has been a terrible injustice to countless souls whose lives could have surely been more fully lived and realized. All souls suffer when even one soul suffers.

I have elected only to illustrate in the Christian tradition; there existed and co-existed other traditions that were equally offensive, some being founded near exclusively on women as property.

Often undetected by all but the most attuned people is the realization that the damage done to women is damage done to all of us. The reverberation of that which is done on earth, in the flesh, follows still and affects the worlds around us. Man is not just "stuck" here on some rock hitching a ride through eternity. There is no entitlement as the chosen. We are all in a grand interrelated formula, a great matrix, the acceptance of which does not lessen God in the slightest rather it magnifies God. By realizing that we are part of a whole, what does happen is we live in accordance with a valid understanding of existence.

ABERRATIONS

The pedophilia you speak of is only a manifestation of an ongoing apostasy of faith. It is not the problem; it is a symptom of the problem. The problem is fundamentally obvious: Man has out-distanced himself from the ancient practice of communion *in* God. Whether this be an express statement or not is irrelevant. Man is communicating his dissatisfaction with the instruments and rituals that both liberate and imprison. Man is a tolerant being, evolving over countless millennia, but is slowly outclassing the constructs of faiths that cannot close the distance to God. All faiths, more or less, are in one stage or another of the lay burgeoning in consciousness. The awakening of a faith's masses is in proportion to its abuses and distance from the line of communication to God, the former being the symptom and the latter the cause.

Becky, every person has their story and value in this life. Every convention and institution has its story and value as well. Often it is not easy to see this. You must remember that within these same churches, countless hundreds of thousands made their way to God, more or less. That the church facilitated this abrogation of female equality is not in question; it did. However, under the cloak of the darkness of faith, spirit still prevailed—and many were wed to God, in spite of the obstructions of Man. Do not be too hasty to condemn or shake a finger at him or her, at faith or not, or at any church. All have utility in the cosmic unfolding of this world. Nothing is an accident. Though you might take something different away from what I have previously noted, all instruments and means in this life have value and purpose. Even the least palatable of life's institutions or experiences serve purposes not often or readily detectable.

We are no longer in the past. Even our dwelling on such excesses is a waste of valuable mind-food. Lament not that which you could not change were you wont to do so. Instead, plan and dream the canvas on which you will paint your world in love, Becky.

▼

CHAPTER 28

Wounded Hearts

Uh, supposedly if it were Jesus that walked in, I'd definitely ask, "Dude, if there really is a God, then why is all this crap going on in the world? Because really. Where was he during the hurricane, tsunami, and 9-11? Does he just not care? Or was it just the fact that everything in the Bible was just made up? That none of it really exists. That's why I dislike religion.
Alex

When you are sick and the battle rages within you, fever strikes your white blood cells to a boil and they die on the very real and dangerous battlefield that are your sinuses, do you still exist? When a stray asteroid blasts a chuck of planet some 10 trillion miles away, scattering the planet and its embryonic inhabitants into oblivion, does the universe still exist?

By the way, "dude," if God really did walk into your classroom, I doubt you would say, "Dude" and "Why is all this crap going on?" More than likely you would tremble and stutter, perhaps sob like a baby, or just stare, forever changed, mouth agape. More than likely you would also be washed in such torrents of pleasure and ecstasy that you would only be good for a nunnery or monastery afterwards. When you returned home, you could then dry your soiled pants.

All the experiences and people that labored to do such damage to you will not be there in your old age. From the moment yesterday is passed, it is gone forever. None of the experiences that were your life will ever be here again, though they will conspire to build you into who you will become. Whatever labored to injure you so is past. That you are injured is obvious. I will not advise you to consider blaming another; it simply does not matter. There are no victims in this world. You are here today, Alex, and *you* will be with *you* the rest of your days.

WHAT DO WE REALLY MEAN?

A sentence expresses a thought; a pattern of sentences can construct a concept. Within such a concept, the mind is able to infer overlapping concepts. Within the short span of your statements, it is readily noted you have been either informed poorly or are railing against injustices in your life. These things happen to everyone, more or less. Being part of a common occurrence does nothing to help you, though, does it? So what if we have been misled or inherited our parents' disdain for life. How do you know the things you have been informed of are true? Would you know you, Alex? Would you know the truth about these things you ask? Something made you write this backwards.

"I dislike religion because I think none of it really exists. I hold it as fact that the Bible was just made up. God did nothing during, or may have even caused, the recent disasters I have noted in my short time here. I do not believe there is a God because I dislike religion, and I see all this crap going on in the world." This is what you really have said here, Alex. The work before you is even more fundamental than you may think. You are patterning a process in your life where you believe in nothing, expect nothing, and therefore nothing is what you will always find. I am not suggesting that by asserting you believe in God then you will delude yourself that God exists. I do not offer that for your table. God exists independent of your participation.

Are you to ever have an answer that is meaningful, you need to now stop eating the food from other's tables and start to prepare your own food. You are old enough now. You must experience God for yourself. I cannot answer your questions because they are asked by a voice that would hardly be illuminated by the response I could grant you. Yet, you are not necessarily further behind those that do believe. You have a passion, Alex. Imagine if you were to have the startling realization that people have been feeding you a handful of horse manure, unintentionally, of course.

First Slivers of God

I invite you to not look for the God of your protests. Look instead for the reflections first. Note that "something" in you that you know very well is the "more than you." You know exactly what I am talking about. It is the part of you that secrets notions of power into your daydreams. Sleep with that friend within and spend some time with you. Do not look for God in the great books of the Bible today; start in a very basic, and more meaningful way. Look for God in the simplest of moments each day. If you find God's reflection for only one single brief moment in all the day, that will be the one revelation of incalculable wealth. When you relearn or understand how you are seeing the world you will better understand why you are reaching all the conclusions you are reaching. When you have done this, you will see God in the God of your parents. When you see God, you will note God in the Bible, and all things. When you participate in your own life, you inherit nothing from others. You proclaim your own findings in your life.

Alex, religions have much about them that are not pleasant. I know this. I am not asking you to look for God there. God is to be found in all places, and I invite you only to consider the portion of God that resides now in you. Consider that portion of you that resides in God. It is there, Alex. God is within you and you are within God. It makes no difference whether you accept this or not. While it is a symbiotic relationship, it is more parasitic in that we suck off the life force of God as we dumbly execute the plans of our days thinking they are all there is, and the highest reality is only that of which we can perceive. When you find God in you and in life, you will easily find God in religions.

God is everywhere and, flawed or not, religions have attempted nothing less than the monumental and should be thus accorded at least a modicum of respect from you. Innumerable men and women have found God in religions as they found God in themselves, and elsewhere. Religions have been the birthing grounds for spirit, but this is not the only venue to God. God is not a community you join. God *is,* and you make meaningless your life to deny this.

You will not be the person you are today in twenty years. You will have different observations and considerations of nearly all your convictions. Offer yourself at least this one boon: consider every moment the possibility that there is something you are missing, and in each way you look at the world consider there may be a different way of looking out your window. Give yourself a chance, and give life a chance to teach you instead of setting out now on your road through life with such a fundamental negativity that you can only draw its equal to yourself.

Water seeks its own level, Alex. Invite the water in that your soul can drink, and you will find your thirst quenched.

▼

CHAPTER 29

Why Is God?

If I could talk to Jesus, I would ask why we are here and why it matters. Was God just bored?
I would definitely want to know where he came from. Is the Bible true? I would want to know if we don't all worship the same gods, then who is right?
Jessica

Yes, Jessica, most would ask these questions. You are very wise. These are the questions that have ached the hearts of millions since first years began. Was God bored, Jessica? I am not sure but I will tell you I do not know. God creates or self-causes as an expression of God. I do not hold that God wishes, needs, or desires to see God glorified by that which was willed by God. I do not hold that God has any of the taken-for-granted attributes that we, as humans, project when we reach for God. My brain actually hurts when I try and think what God might think. I am not even sure if God thinks in the way we do.

Maybe this is an example of how far removed we are from understanding the power and nature of God: we *assume* God thinks as we do. Perhaps the nature of God is to simply will into manifestation all that is God's fancy. Maybe with God nothing is considered because God is pure manifestation and all things "become" even before being considered. Our linear thinking informs us of a sequence based on the material world that would not necessarily apply at all. Perhaps the larger part of the unseen worlds has nothing at all to do with manifestation of matter. Perhaps matter is the baser of the worlds, the literal "leakage" of burgeoning will from across the veil.

It is suggested the angels were not all very happy with the playground of humans in the land of matter. I do not profess to understand the will of God, only God's reflections in my life and life. I am daily humbled and often tremble in awe at even the reflections of God. When I note God in the little things and simple moments, they, in and of themselves, do not magnify life. What magnifies life is that God elaborates and animates all things. The lamp may be beautiful and elaborate, but it does not cast its warmth until electricity courses through it. God animates all creation and when an eye tuned can note this, you will not see the same flower, beetle, snowstorm, or sunset that another sees. You will see reflections of that unbelievable ecstasy you note in your prayers to God, Jessica. God fills and electrifies the world with the current, the hum of all creation. When you see God, *really see* God, you are forever changed. Your world will be forever changed, forever empowered, and unimaginably rich and varied.

"I WOULD DEFINITELY WANT TO KNOW WHERE HE CAME FROM"

This is a statement that demonstrates how very perceptive you are, Jessica. Even the little ants, scientists scurrying about to assert this or that theory of creation, stop dead in their tracks when asked what came before this or that?

"What did the Big Bang take place in?"

"In what void is the universe stagnant or expanding?"

"What was before?"

"If the arrow of time is indeed moving forward, from what point is it moving forward?"

It is here that even science can peer no further. This is the point where science must turn to the language of the poets and mystics to describe anything further or make sense of their findings and failings. All language from this "point" on fails (pun intended). This is the same place reflected in the internal where the language of our world fails. Science and the mystic reach the same membrane and words fail both. Science uses telescopes and mystics the heart (either that combined faculty which is otherwise called the heart or direct transmission by the silent witness within). But have no doubt, they both have reached the same event horizon. We simply cannot get past this place with the faculties that have enabled us to get this far. It is a testament to the genius of life and the marvel of being that we can even consider these things and get as far as we have in our observations of our physical world. However, the same mystery that permits us this journey also informs that this is our greatest liability in piercing the veil where meets the unknown and the unknowable.

TRUTH AND *TRUTH*

The Bible is true, Jessica. The bible and, indeed, *all* scriptures are true, at least for the countless millions who have so impressed the fabric of their consciousness of their veracity. They have willed into existence their God and God's constructions. This has enabled the hearts and minds of countless to assert and apprehend a world beyond this one, but has self-limiting borders on further expression into the myriad depths of the worlds of God. The mind of man constructs and makes real that which it asserts and defends by will and repetition. When aided by the collective vision, varying little, of countless peers in all ages, a true "Jerusalem" is created that is palpably real.

This is why the saints and mystics of all religions have so affirmed and found that which supported the infrastructure of their voyage; they invariably served their patron. In so piercing through to consider the currents, the lofty winds which blow from on-high places, these noble and righteous explorers of life and of God have returned with such ineffable exposures that they could only feebly translate these experiences into the only reality they knew: the particular faith from whence they set sail. Of course, there were also numerous others who had a sense in their travels in forever that there was something incredibly incomplete or otherwise self-limiting with translating into the constructions of their faith but only cryptically suggested this or would have been put to death or otherwise had their industry or wherewithal harmed. Such is the nature of the truths of which you would ask.

Truth can only be relative in a relative world, but there is Truth, Jessica. "Truth" will not evade you were you to earnestly seek it. You shall always know the Truth when you seek it with a just and upright heart. But you will not find Truth evident in this world until *you* bear Truth from on-high places with your silent witness, your spirit.

So, if we don't all worship the same gods, who are right, Jessica? Can you see? They are all right. Those that would suggest otherwise have both a vested interest in others not being right and a defense born of personal gamble. There is a building momentum born of a collective will that serves its own end. It is a reality, an existence unto itself. Man would be loath to think he does nothing that he is either not aware of or in opposition to his *express* will. However, history and the facts speak for themselves.

Can you imagine the looks on the faces or the tears in the hearts of those you love, were they to ever have a sense that the God and faith of their forbears was merely the best Man could do with his intercourses with the divine, and that this construction of experience then took on a life of its own, feeding the illusion that it affirmed existed to dispel illusion? No belief is beyond repair, no damage is done in so having believed, but it is all so incomplete. Most minds could not manage the overwhelming realization that the house they built is built on sand.

Jessica, these people are not damned unless they damn themselves. God does not condemn and abandon any creation to such a primal inferno as that described to kids. Dante's *Inferno* is just that—Dante's. Everything you have ever needed to reach forever is inside you right here, right now. All those around you who assert this or that will likely realize the very thing it is they affirm. How wonderful. How incomplete, though.

There is a way for you to "see" God in this world, and in all worlds, Jessica. You can inherit your fusion with God simply by declaring you will to do so. Assert to your mind and your senses that there is a new sheriff in town, and conduct an inventory of the pollutants that have disabled your communication with God. God will not seek out the employment of priests, bishops, imams, and others before communicating with you directly; I promise. God does not find you unworthy, nor do you profane the absolute by demanding direct discourse. You are the reason God is Jessica; God is the reason you are. You are the reason *I* am. I am the reason *you* are. You are the breath of God upon this world. In you is born the entire purpose of creation and of the human race. In you, Jessica is the gateway. Open it for you. Open it for others.

▼

CHAPTER 30

The World Was Created
Just for You

"And whosoever shall offend one of these little ones that believe in me, it is better for him that a millstone were hanged about his neck, and he were cast into the sea."

—(The Christ, Mark 9:42)

If God was in front of me, I would have so many things to ask. What is heaven like? Why don't you give people happiness when they really need it? How long am I going to live? Can you tell me my life story? Who am I going to marry? Why didn't my grandpa want to be a part of my life? Why was my dad adopted?"
Laverne

Yes, you would have so many things to ask, wouldn't you? Christ particularly loved children and you demonstrate why Christ said, "Suffer the little children to come unto me and forbid them not, for of such is the kingdom of God" (Luke 18:16). Christ knew that it was not just that children were little adults that made him love them so tenderly. Christ was telling us to be childlike in our approach to God. Christ wanted us to clearly see that in growing up we added so much intellectual rubbish and egotistical baggage to our solicitation of God. Christ told us, in so many words, to be like children in order to apprehend God and secure "heaven." "Verily I say unto you, Whosoever shall not receive the kingdom of God as a little child, he shall in no wise enter therein" (Mark 10:15). Christ was not telling us that we only have a small window of opportunity in childhood to make some really adult choices. What Christ was telling us, Laverne, was we must be as tender, charitable, gracious, and loving of heart as you, child, reveal to me today.

WOULD YOU ASK THIS OF DEATH?

Would you know the hour of your death, really? Hmmm? Sometimes I think I would like to know too. What would you do with this information? Invariably, people would first do the math and see how much "time" they had left. Maybe it was a little, or maybe a lot. Most people would spend some careful moments assessing what is and is not important. Most, though not all, would set out to live their life in such a way as to make meaningful each and every remaining moment. Still, others would be so devastated by the actual window of their mortality that they would become disabled beings, incapable of any productive interactions with the magical wonder all around them. We are warned in the Christian New Testament about wanting to know the hour of *his* return, and likewise death, "For in such an hour as ye think not the Son of man cometh" (Matthew 24:44). Why are we so warned?

Regardless of the time allotted to you, you should live your life in such a way each moment that that which served to make your life good and meaningful will make your death good and meaningful, also. If one can lie down at the end of the day having shared love with all who are loved, having done each act of free will and compassionate deportment, and having been truthful with the language of the heart and the care of other's hearts, then death can have no fear to such a person. There is a real and wonderful mystery to this time with which we are graced. There is simply so much sweet beauty and awe in each moment, Laverne. This might all be robbed from you were you to be disempowered by such information. You will live until you die, and no longer. Having not lived a moment longer, you will have no sense that you have lived any less. It makes no difference in the end were you to die tomorrow or a hundred years from now. Life and life's value lies not in the quantity of years, but rather in the quality of time.

FREE WILL

Free will. You will hear this over and over throughout your life. But what is free will to you, Laverne? Free will is your ability to write whatever you wish upon the blank chalkboard that was given you this life. Freedom like this allows you to marry whomever you wish. Would it not be terrible for you to find out now that you are going to marry the snot-nosed little geek with the pen protector in his chest pocket? Nevertheless, imagine that a few years from now some strange community gathering has you two talking at length, and not only are you aware how sweet and gentle he is, but he has lost the snotty nose and pocket-protector to turn into one of the most handsome and eligible young men recently awarded an academic scholarship to Yale.

The point is not in the fantasy. The point is that we know not the wonderful twists and turns life has in store every moment. There is marvelous freedom and responsibility in the mystery and the moments each. The neatest story in the history of the world is the spellbinding story of Laverne. Laverne is an important and wonderful creation surpassing anything Shakespeare or Botticelli could ever have dreamed. Your life is as important in its unfolding as was Christ's life. His life would have been meaningless otherwise. Think on that. Christ's entire life was only meaningful because 2,000 years later Laverne would live her life. I hold this to be utterly true. Christ's free will, Laverne's free will, indeed all free will is what makes the universe itself possible.

The grand total of that which we select (our choices) throughout our lives is the only distilled memory, out of all the infinite possibilities in every moment, that is saved by creation and etched in the fabric of consciousness; this, then, is responsible for each subsequent adaptation and urge of evolution, material and spiritual, the infinite host of choices not taken relegated for all time to oblivion. You are literally the reason for all things, love. In this way consciousness learns and Laverne clocks toward God.

Your life story is wonderful and of suspenseful splendor to the host of heaven *because* you have not written it yet. It can be no other way. While God knows all the questions you ask, your life would be an empty vessel without the elixir of possibilities that you might pour within you. Look, then, with wonder and anticipation toward every moment, each meeting, every coincidence, and every choice you make in love. Your life is unfolding every single moment and most assuredly each moment is vital and meaningful, Laverne. It is so wonderful and amazing, my dear child.

ADOPTION

I want you to understand something that seems not to have been explained to you. When Christ spoke of leaving our families, our mothers, or our loved ones to follow him, he was telling us that we are finally a community of God. We are born to this earth in such a manner, in accordance with such divine law, whereby love begets love. Placement is born of rightness. There are no mistakes. We are children of God each and in the larger community of life it makes no difference if one ventures forth through this life and world aware or not who their biological ancestors are. I assure you, when an adopted person leaves this world, to whom they were born or by whom they were raised will be of no matter.

You were born to your dad and he so chose you before your birth, literally or not. To one that is born and then adopted, yes, they are chosen after birth. But, they are chosen. To the many that are never adopted and live their youth in biological families, they, too, are chosen. What we are truly born to in this life is not simply apparent in the flesh. To each of us is a process of discovery and fulfillment to satisfy our soul's needs for unfoldment and evolution home in time. We all leave our parent's home, our brother's shoulder, and our sister's comfort in due time. We are all children of the universe, lately clothed on planet Earth. To whom one is born is ultimately irrelevant. In a home of love, security, and comfort this distinction is meaningless. What makes it meaningful is the value assigned by others, as a child cannot approximate such values. Seeds of victimization easily sow in such fertile soil.

ESTRANGED LOVE

There is nothing ever inherently wrong or soiled about you or any child. There are many in our lives whose behavior we lament. However, we cannot begin to know the sadness and aloofness of another's heart. You can do nothing to account for your grandpa's actions. It is most certainly not you in any event. Frequently, adults do not know how to interact with other adults, and children suffer. This is seen often in divorce. Sometimes, adults miss the opportunity to "do the right thing" and then before they know it the years have slipped and compounded their error. They become lost for redress and do not have the courage to correct their mistake. Before they know it, time is completely slipped, and from their own perspective all they see is the passing of their time on Earth in aloneness, and frailty; but still they do not know how to mend the fence.

It is very often like this when parents or grandparents make such a tragic mistake, and then time compounds the error. How do you fix such a situation? *You* cannot. Yesterday is forever gone. But as is often the case as you mature, you can affirm your substance, worth, and rightness absent love from even one other person in the entire world. When the time is right, consider in your own heart that you will be hurt no longer by this experience. When the time is right, consider that yesterday is forever gone and you did not have the grandpa/granddaughter relationship that you would have wanted, but you will give to this man the opportunity to know you in friendship, as adults, if he takes your hand in this friendship. If he does not, Laverne, it is still not you, honey. It can never be you. It can never be a child. It simply cannot be. A child is always innocent and precious, even when calculating and mischievous. We all do the best with what we have to work with; that makes what a child does always all the more amazing.

Laverne, families and those that conspire to influence our lives are varied. The idea of a family is different for many people. Remember this: love is not the possession of only those immediately around you. I assure you that you are loved by a lot more than just your parents or siblings. I know it is difficult to understand this, but you are surely loved, dear.

CHAPTER 31

▼

Pain and Suffering and Love

Jesus, why do you make people suffer? I know we all have to die eventually, but why can't we all die without pain? Why do you make us hurt? Why do our hearts break and why must we cry? I know we have emotions, but why can't it all be good? Why do you make us go through stuff we don't want, like death and pain and hurt? I want to know why you send people that we care about into our lives when you are just going to take them away? Why do you make people gay when the world shuns them and they can't go to heaven? I was blessed not to be like that, but why do you make people like that? I just want to know.
Madeline

Pain is, at its basic level, the self-preservation mechanism that allows us to interact with a difficult environment and survive. Pain is experienced physically, psychically, and spiritually; all levels of our being have a similar defense and alert notification. There is the physical pain to which we are most familiar, but there are also other pains which are less familiar, or discernable, because the places within that originate these pain signals are less familiar to us, and often the apparent crossover makes identifying the origin of the pain difficult. Spiritual pain is the pain experienced from the absence of God in our lives, and in our death.

WE DIE EVERY DAY

Everything in the physical world exists in opposition to something else. This is the only way we can approximate a bearing for survival and the conduct of our lives in the flesh. Moreover, the very fundamental building blocks of the universe exist in opposition to create the tension necessary for consciousness manifesting its "sail" in creation. We are all dying every day, Madeline. We are all degrading every day. All life and all matter degrade its form. This is less horrible than we might imagine, at first glance.

From the illusory perspective of the flesh, we have a vested interest in opposing this degradation of life. But, it is the process of the life to which we are born and when viewed in the breathtaking scale of *all* life, we might consider the passing of this world every moment and its immediate reconstitution no less than marvelous. For in fact, every single moment all life is recreated in an endless stream of rebirth from memory. Every single second the world is brand new. This is not a matter of perception only. This is not the assertion of the esoteric. This is observed fact.

All matter flickers in and out of existence many times a second. All material creatures are birthed constantly, not simply at punctuated moments within time, but constantly. The latticework of God is the foundation and memory that allows everything to constantly be reborn and recast in the same role, each moment. All life dies and degrades. All inanimate life is also held projected by the same projectionist.

It is similar to the old stand-up Vaudeville line, "I came home last night and discovered someone broke in and stole everything I own. I was doubly confused. They replaced everything with identical items." You are a creature of the universe, regardless of what you have been told. There is not *a* universe and you are *in* it. At the smallest level, every component of our quantum world appears and reappears constantly. Everything goes back in the same place, or does it? The point is every moment is genesis.

There is within you a core component housed that is removed from the pain and suffering of this world. It is not to this point I would invite you to seek refuge simply to avoid the pain of the flesh. Pain is relative in that it cannot follow you in the places you would venture next. Pain is a creation of this world as the consequence for being. It is not a punishment for being. Pain of any sort is not based on reward or merit. Pain of the flesh allows us to be informed to survive. Pain of the spirit and emotion is much ado from our own hand and is designed to inform to evolve. There is much wisdom and memory in the witness inside.

Many do die without pain, Madeline. Many die in great agony and pain as they cast off this mortal cloth. The magic is not in dwelling on the fear of pain but in harnessing that core portion of us that is immune from pain. Do not nurture that which is immune from pain for the sole purpose of pain avoidance, for there is only so far you will get with such motivations. Rather, harness and feed your spirit that you might today live more fully in God's grace. It shall come to pass that the flesh becomes increasingly subordinate to all experience of this world.

THE WRATH OF GOD

God does not make anyone hurt. This notion has caused a great many problems both between those living here, and those that would aspire to pass to God now. God does not take such base interest in inflicting pain or other experiences arbitrarily or simply to force compliance. Nothing coerced is worthy before the throne of God.

"Why do our hearts break, and why must we cry?" Ah, this is the pain of the spirit and of emotion. Over the long train of time, events and circumstances which experience has shown to be incompatible with survival, or a desired state of existence, we have developed responses to these undesired circumstances and have both mental and physiological responses to them. Fortunately, most of us do not have many horrific experiences that cause responses to the need to survive. But what we do have more of now, and this is possibly because we consequently have more time to devote to the attentions within, is the terrible conditions of undesired emotional states.

Therefore, we are beings with bodies that live in a world that is not just populated by imperfect humans but the ravages of nature, kismet, and unpredictability. Pain is your way of telling you that what you are experiencing is not compatible with your construction of how the world should work for your own welfare. So the question arises, "Why can't 'it' all be good?" This is of course a fair question.

A PREDETERMINED WORLD

The world would have to be completely retooled and redesigned to create the world of the "morphine-drip." All the things that would have to change to make all of this world "good"—pain-free—would require an absence of free will in such a profound sense that it would be an absolute free will that is subordinated. This world, our lives, works very much like the universe. Would we have the entire universe operating with free will except us? Though none of this may be the answer you desire, the consequence of no pain at all on this earth would result in a life that would, paradoxically, not be worth living.

For it is in opposition to pain that joy is felt. It is in opposition to the heavy chains that tie us to pain and suffering that we know lightness of heart, care freedom of thoughts, and various degrees of bliss. Pain serves not to contrast that which we aspire to possess always. Rather, what we desire to possess always stands in opposition to the pain of which we speak. All life exists in a grand matrix, which the human mind can little perceive. When we observe our world and universe, we note that there appears to be a divine fabric underlying all creation. We are not outside observing in; we are inside observing in.

Do you think the lark feels pain when it falls from the air, its initial flight from the nest having been ill considered? Do you think the cow feels pain while waiting all day amidst the stench and sense of impending death, then to receive the mortal blow? While this point is argued, do you think the tree feels pain when slowly cut down, or the gazelle fleeing on the open plains experiences emotional pain? Honey, each of my examples is not submitted to be argued, but rather the suggestion is what I would impart. There is no easy remedy to that which weighs upon your thoughts. However, were you to introspect, and look closely at the cause for most of the pains you talk about, you would see that a great many of them are transient and last not but a moment in the long train of your life.

Even now there are things, which will cause you such pain, but the morrow will come and you will wonder how you were even moved by such a circumstance. All life is passing every moment, Madeline. I do not recall the gravity of the pain of any of my most painful experiences. I may recall that this hurt, or that hurt, or this was painful, or that was suffering, but I have no real sense of the texture or richness of any pain I have ever experienced, when the day has passed fully. Pain and suffering slip out of touch and out of time when they have passed.

LOVE AND FRIENDSHIP

Love is not meant to be a possession, rather an experience in the means. Would you truly call a caged bird loved? It would appear chipper and of purpose each day you visited your bird, and you would take such joy in it. You might say that you love this bird. However, it would be a possession, and your love would be something "not quite love" because it was polluted by a need for ownership. Would that this bird could take flight, should your love for having had this bird near you, having risen with the early dawn to its cries of hunger, and having given freely of yourself in its upkeep and well being, been meaningless? Would not the impressions made upon your growing knowledge of love by this tender friend have been more than worthwhile?

Love does not require a return in kind. Love and friendship are not based on ownership nor is it based on longevity or reciprocity. All love is of value in the endless solicitation our spirit makes with other spirits through the medium of consciousness in this world. When you are young and it is difficult to put in perspective the measure of years, all time seems a long time. As you age you realize that all time *seems* entirely too short. All love, all friendship, compassion, and charity have infinite value.

HOMOSEXUALITY

Madeline, God set in place a house of order. At our level it appears quite disorderly at times. Though the world is no more disorderly than a child's room seen from the very center of that room, when the remainder of the house is spotless. It is all a matter of perspective in how we view the world around us. There is nothing that is definite in this life, in nature, or in the physical or other worlds around us. There are always exceptions to every rule, from our vantage point. These exceptions do not disprove the rule they simply elaborate on the variance contained within the rule. God does not *make* people gay anymore than God *made* my hair brown; my hair is brown because of the genetic make-up that executed in my DNA. In other words, the question implied in your question deals with societal acceptance, tolerance, and coercion and not the intercession of God.

There are gay people in this world. There are not-gay people in this world. Being gay has absolutely nothing to do with God. However, being heterosexual likewise has nothing to do with God. Both have everything to do with God. God, in this case, is a red herring for what is really at issue. Being gay is only a means of expression in the material world. Being heterosexual is only a means of expression in the material world. Gay and other behavior deemed non-conducive to the propagation of peoples have been declared anathema in most all places and times. However, this expression in life was first declared taboo by Man, and later by God's intercessors. I find it repugnant to my sensibilities when it is suggested that God takes delight in a man defiling a woman in an abusive but otherwise "sanctioned" relationship, while two old men who have labored in society to produce productively, follow the rules, and liberate their love for the betterment of all humanity are ostracized for holding hands in a park. It is the height of arrogance and a dismal display of primal thinking to presume God is preoccupied with excluding people from their estate because of sensory practices. I assure you dear, beyond the flesh that which we love is sexless. Many will be perturbed by my statements. If we spent more time loving we would have less time to hate.

All life is divine in this world. Every one of us, regardless of personal practices has an inheritance in forever. It is not the case that someone is damned for a practice such as homosexuality when others, who do not practice such things, assert they will earn the inheritance of God when their overall deportment toward life is abominable. Access to eternity is ultimately a very personal and private affair. Who we are enables our relationship with God. Who we are is directly influenced by our intercourse with the world and our fellow beings—all of them. Compassion, tolerance, understanding, charity of heart and substance, and love all make us who we are, and in so making us in this manner we make ourselves in God's image; in so making ourselves in the image of God, we make our brothers and sisters in God's image.

Madeline, I invite you to always look toward the good in others. My sweet, gentle child, take always the measure of your greatest love and share it with the least among you. When you love in such a way, you bear light for the whole world. I love you, Madeline.

CHAPTER 32

▼

Seeing God

Dear Jesus,
Why does it seem that you are not with the people in New Orleans? I know
you are doing your best, but why did all these people have to die? Was this
your plan? Did you mean for this to happen? Why do other countries hate
us so? All we ever do is help them. Whenever they have problems, we are
right here with them helping. Also I know I'm only fourteen, but I want to
know if you have any special plan for me.
JM

It seems that God is not in New Orleans because you do not *see* God in New
Orleans. You do not see God, JM. You do not see God in the acts of war that
smother our sensibilities and horrify our minds. You do not see God in the terrible tragedy of the World Trade Center bombings or the bloodied streets of Baghdad or Kabul. You would not likely see God, either, in the rampant famine
sweeping the globe or in the tender, young eyes of the millions of children dying
of AIDS, malaria, thirst, and other sad misfortunes of our times. Many did not
see God and thought the watch was abandoned during the recent tsunami and
earthquake that swept through Asia. We can agree, can't we, that so many do not
see God? Will we see God in any terrible calamities?

I see God, JM. I see God in all these terrible acts and unfortunate circumstances. I see God. Do you know what I do not have in common with all those
that do not see God in these horrible acts? I see God in the melting ice of a spring
thaw. I see God in the collective laughter and hushed whispers to excitement of

children at an amusement park. I see God in the Sunday dress of the millions who would find their Lord. I see God five times a day as a billion hearts solicit God in mosques, on mountaintops, and on battlefields around the world. I see God, not in the churches so much, but in the silent unknown considerations of those millions as they walk with reverence to the house of their God. I see God in the dance of a billion blades of grass surrendering their spines to the northern wind. I see God reflected in the nervous expectations of scientists as they launch another probe in search of their maker: meaning. I see God in the viscous media between me and all other things: air. I see God everywhere. I see God in every single thing in the world. I see God.

CHOOSE TO SEE GOD

JM, I see God in these horrible times because I elect to see God in all times. I see my absolute Love in the eyes of others beholding solemn beauty around them. I see God reflected in the desperate searching of the poets, the artists, the musicians, and the madmen. I see God in you. I see God in me. I see all *in* God.

The one thing in common in all those who shout, "Where is God?" when things do not make sense and the world is insecure is that they are not noting the silent presence of God in their daily lives when tragedy is over the horizon. You may protest this point, but it is correct, JM. It is as correct as the most obvious of life's revelations. People that do not see God when times are bad do not see God.

Not only do people expect God to make new the world and keep them safe from the darkness that causes them to shudder, but the only time people implore God is under threat or duress (of course, not all people). How could we possibly see God under duress when we cannot see God lying in a hammock drinking iced tea on a lazy Sunday afternoon? People do not see God when things are bad for the same reason they do not see God daily: they choose not to see. It is all choice, and people consciously or otherwise choose not to see God, yet have the spiritual instinct of the ages that when threatened with danger to life or disruption of spirit we run home. However, we cannot see because we do not know how to see, and lo, our bodies and mind are felt to be "torn asunder" as we wail our lamentation of forlornness: "Where are you, God?" "My God, my God, why have you forsaken me" (Psalms 22)? "Please, God? We need you now!" We admonish and solicit the void because we could not identify the breath of God from the clod of earth it animates. You have learned *not to see*.

There are in all this life many coexisting worlds all about you. The natural world in which you toil is only the world that your senses interrogate. Your senses exist for one purpose: to enable you to interact with, and survive in, the material world. They are useless in interpreting and understanding the myriad worlds all about you right this minute. Thus you create the world in *your* image. This is the default of your intellect and it is good at what it does. You are at the center of the world as you interrogate it and the world is out there. While at the center of your world, it is easy to forget that you are the world. It is easy to forget. As an amnesic you then call outside to invoke aid and call to God under duress. "God, please arrange the world outside of me to quell the noise and the fear beating upon my door." You are the world and the world is already in God.

There are numerous worlds all about you right this moment. The dynamics and interactions of all these worlds with each other cannot be described, but can be gleaned. It is arrogance to suggest one could understand the transcendent with the primitive organs of sense. Some would assert to us otherwise; while not willing to penetrate this veil of their own volition they would nevertheless argue absurdly unless another could so prove to them the existence of the multidimensional universe with the very language that has disabled access to it in the first place. Some defend the "box" vehemently. Some things can be experienced, some things can be gleaned, but it is not always true that all things can be explained. When you repose in God you command the glue that binds these ineffable worlds and the interconnectedness of all things becomes apparent to you. When apparent, you have no difficulty commending both grace and suffering unto God in times good and bad.

"O' NACHIKETA"

(Katha Upanishad)

I do not know why "all these people [have] to die," JM, in this or any other time; you ask of this instance. Life is ephemeral and degrades its construction, but our constituents remain always. Even this point we can all recognize. It is in the questions of the mysteries you would ask *answers* of death. In the most honest of answers all life is part of the great chain of *existence* that serves life unto life in an endless cycle of death and birth. It is not always reasonable or even presenting with a pattern other than the most universal: that we live and we die. It is just that it is not always discernable to us.

Some would guide us to consider notions of karma. This is a concept that it is generally recognized in all faiths, even Islam, Judaism and Christianity. However, Hinduism and Buddhism each have tenets which address such a perception specifically. Regardless of the voice that speaks to such a concept, it is nevertheless the case that there exists a near indiscernible matrix of governing laws that guide creation. But we do glean both the laws and their enabling rules and regulations. When we no longer see with our eyes, we can begin to *see* with a knowingness of sightlessness that informs us that all is in its due course. Though, true, this is not apparent from the vantage of loss and sadness in the immediacy of pain and suffering. It simply must be affirmed that there *are* magic and God in all things in order to *behold* magic and God in all things.

THE SECRET OF DEATH IS THE MEANING OF LIFE

O' Nachiketa, O' child, there exists the material world for wont of expressing consciousness: Self. All life and infinite creation are the endless possibilities of the bath of life. Manifest in flesh, empowered in God, we intend and will the distillation of every choice out of infinite choices. Choices not taken are forever expended and the dynamic and momentum of creation thus conserved. Choices taken etch in consciousness in a universal learning curve that serves the evolution of consciousness in matter. Every memory of every possible choice is not what is etched in consciousness as it evolves in self-awareness, just the hole in consciousness that now becomes vacant by virtue of the choice taken. Consciousness chooses in respect to its many vacuoles. This omissive evolution records the universe and in so doing the universe is self-aware of the awareness of its constituents.

It is not necessary that we are cognizant of our integral association with consciousness. We nevertheless fulfill the aim and purpose of creation from the moment we urged from the primordial soup. Whether awake or dreaming, alive or dead, we serve that end of consciousness that evolves its intermediate self-awareness in God. As we choose in all things, we evolve. As we dream, we choose. As we evolve, consciousness evolves in matter. As consciousness evolves in matter, the universe becomes more fully aware. As the universe becomes aware in matter, consciousness becomes aware in God. As consciousness becomes aware in God, God becomes aware in the constituents' awareness.

It is not that God was previously unaware. It is a matter of perception. The constituents of consciousness were not aware of God's awareness of them. All constituents of matter, all matter of consciousness is *in* God. The circle of being is closed. All creation moves forward in God. All creation moves forward in consciousness. Consciousness is on the march.

Dear JM, the special plans that are in store for you in this life are a formula of your parents' unconditional love for you, your love for yourself, and your assertive knowledge that you are able to do anything in this world that you so choose. Would God have a special plan for you and rob you of your choices and will to dare and to dream? Would God take so wonderful a prize as you and make you to do something that you have no say in? JM, go and find God in the moments of your life, and find God in the seat of your heart and this world and others may pass away and you will always have the most special of things that God has prepared for your inheritance. I love you, child.

▼

CHAPTER 33

In The Beginning:
Science and Religion

God, I would like to know some answers about where it all started,
where we came from. Is it all religion or just science? Which can
explain the creation of the world, religion or science? Also what is
our purpose? Are we just like a cell helping the world do a bigger job
than we can imagine? Where do we go after death?
Tim

Both religion and science explain the creation of the world. In fact, both have more in common on this point than either concedes. While religion has traditionally not been the best framework in which to practice science, once science began to explore the seen and unseen worlds absent the restrictions of religion the findings grew exponentially. Science, like religion, sought to understand the nature and reason for being. Science quickly developed a "ritual" of sorts to execute the framework for the search. In this manner, science and religion both have dogma. As science peered into the deepest recesses of creation, a few things become apparent: many of the explorers of science came to realize that there is a profound presence underlying all things.

The day may come when measurable means, and language, allow science to describe the foundational fabric that underlies creation, but thus far science has peered near to the beginning of time, and the smallest of particles, and is flabbergasted and absent the tools of articulation and empiricism to proceed further. Absent the language and ritual of religion, they both speak of the same "thing." Science is increasingly peering so far into the "heart" of the nature of our universe that they are encountering findings and experience that necessarily brings the scientists in proximity of the camps of religion. There appears to be a certain point in our search for "God," with or without religion as a base station, that only one language suffices.

It is the case that the language of theology, though imperfect and potholed with dangers, is the currency in the deepest places of human findings, whether it is science or faith. While science can batter the senses with the language of numbers, when the day is done science can make no more out of the ineffable products of its query. Science now peers into a place that is once or twice removed from the core reflections of God. It is apparent to any student of faith that science now describes findings that substantially support the prophets and mystics.

THE BATH OF LIFE IS THE VIBRATION OF THE UNIVERSE

"In the beginning was the Word" (John 1:1) and while the monks chanted "Aum," Christ was declaring "Amen." In fact, "so frequent was this Hebrew word in the mouth of Our Saviour that it pleased the Holy Ghost" (Catechism of the Council of Trent), Church fathers conceded. The aborigines talk of creation as being no more than a dream in the dream of God. No matter the source of our inherited concepts of God, science is now arriving at the place where one camp can make a marriage proposal to the other. At the deepest place where peers the human intellect, we are witnessing the near smallest particles of creation. The infinite host of all matter is no more than ninety-eight percent space. That is correct, our visible world is no more than a loose collection of atoms and their constituents. The smallest particles that comprise an atom are infinitesimally small. Yet we can make out the nature of the apparently smallest particle contained within by the behavior of associates. However, extrapolating all we know of mass, space, and the behavior of the microscopic world, there is reason to believe that these smallest particles themselves are comprised of even another, more fundamental pieces of matter.

As science considers these findings and suspicions it must do so in the context of the findings of the quantum experiments now shaking the foundations of the scientific world. Apparently, how matter, the world, interacts with man, and man with the world, is a direct consequence of man, not necessarily matter, or even man *and* matter. The findings indicate what I already declare: Man affects the fundamental level of existence by observation alone. Science has actually proven that matter behaves in accordance with man's observation. While all life is a dance of object, observer, and observation, man is finally finding that observation is the fundamental element of this triad.

"In the beginning was the Word," a dream, "Aum," "Amen." All speak to thought. All speak to making thought manifest into word, word into substance, thought into manifestation, Logos. "The kingdom of God is within you (Luke 17:21)" is not merely fodder for idle consumption; it is a statement of fact. Science and religion are married in the greatest findings of all time, though neither is *fully* processing this. Thought is the foundation of all things. God has given to us to have within our power the ability to fully intercourse with *our* universe; "In my Father's house are many mansions" (John 14:2). Thought is the virtual particulate that informs the smallest building blocks of life. Our individual and collective thought—will—is intimately tied to the creation theme itself by extension of being the fabric of the mind of God. The breath of God, the bath of life, is the underlying cosmic vibration so alluded to by both classical traditions and the New Age. Man seeks to sync with God in the outward expression of rarified thought: vibration and holy utterance. The entire universe vibrates and oscillates in a cosmic song of creation.

"ALSO WHAT IS OUR PURPOSE? ARE WE JUST LIKE A CELL HELPING THE WORLD DO A BIGGER JOB THAN WE CAN IMAGINE?"

Is it necessary that we have a purpose, Tim? While we are "like a cell helping the world to do a bigger job than we can imagine," we are also much more than this. We are doing for ourselves every moment much more than we can imagine. We are doing for unseen worlds much more than we can imagine. We are not just a part of life, though we are. We *are* life. We are the total and the constituent. We are not just in the world to witness it; we are the reason each the worlds were created. We are not just anything. We are the primal instrument that actually created the worlds in executing the will of God. We are extensions of God in God's spoken will. God's vibratory essence from the beginning of time pierces the still silent night of eternity and underlies the harmonic dance and motion of all matter and energy. The bath of the spoken Word of the absolute is now being inferred from both our religions of faith and our religions of science. While they have reached no consensus, the answer is not newly discovered. It has been known in musings and revelation for ages that the world is comprised of a cosmic storm of God's voice, God's will, God's thought.

It has been sensed and outwardly realized by transcendence in God that all things exist to come home in eternity having fulfilled no less than the will of God in this mystery of God's purpose. The journey to "home" is not a there, a destination, or a place somewhere else. Home is attunement with the single underlying song of creation. Home is a focus of mind, a distillation of veils, a depth of field. We are all in God's symphony. Tune your instrument!

"WHERE DO WE GO AFTER DEATH?"

You were born immortal, and you shall remain immortal evermore. Being awake to the power of this knowledge is not key to having it. You are immortal whether you accept this or not. God's will is not dependent on your compliance. There are numerous states of being that not only are mostly undetected but nearly impossible to describe to those that have not experienced it. This is one of the many places in our knowledge of God where we find language fails.

You exist with or without your body, child. When you have surrendered your intellect and the curtains of your life, you will see with a knowingness of heart rather than an intellect of mind. These are further examples of the profound matrix of the worlds all about you. Some suggest you will go to heaven, others to hell, when you leave this plane of existence. Very few maintain that there is nothing following this life. Though, some do assert an existential zero at death: game over. There is a reason the world's greatest atheists, humanists, existentialists, and agnostics are *intellectuals* or the *profoundly wounded* of heart. They are entombed in the senses. They are dualist creatures trapped in a material world.

We do not simply believe we survive the body to make agreeable the absurd concept of being, the palliative remedy of the need to self-preserve. There is a self-evident knowingness that informs us internally. The more we listen and cultivate this voice within, the more we enrich the fabric base from which we draw that which we know. There comes a certain point in the acquisition of these experiences and their attendant lessons where you can actually discern what is from data of the material world and which is from the reservoir of knowingness that cannot be easily explained. We are informed of what lie beyond the veil by many manners.

Each man or woman will most certainly attain that heaven or hell, that peace or angst which best comports with his or her understanding or beliefs of what is *thought* will happen at the body's passing.

"At the hour of death, He that hath meditated Me alone, In putting off his flesh, comes forth to Me, Enters into My Being—doubt thou not! But, if he meditated otherwise At hour of death, in putting off the flesh, He goes to what he looked for...Because the Soul is fashioned to its like" (Bhagavad-Gita).

God is not so absent creativity that God need create only one heaven, or one hell; God's infinite love and power-sharing democracy has you participating in the creation of that which you would attain. It is instructive. It is Self-instructive for God. It is instructive *in* God. I am confident that people will secure that union in passing that they expect to secure. God is infinite mercy and grace. This is not a lesser assignment of God rather this suggestion elaborates God's greatness.

Therefore, on further inspection, and in accordance with what I have previously stated, you will see I am stating a fairly obvious if not incredible assertion. We have tremendous influence on what happens to us, both in and following this life. It is a matter of how we live our lives, but for other reasons than the accounting of compassion, deeds, or adherence to dogma only. The manner we live our lives is a reflection of our internal environment and what we affirm. What we affirm is what we create out of the universe that is our mansion in God's house.

CHAPTER 34

▼

Supplication is the Key to Ultimate Power

Dear God,
I want to know how to live my life to the fullest. I want to get the best out of life. To always be persistent and have a great attitude. I want to be grateful with what I have, not always asking for more and more. I feel so selfish when I want to go do something that most kids wouldn't even have the closest opportunity to do. I enjoy hanging out with friends and talking on the phone, and AIM (America Online Instant Messaging), but I am starting to feel like that is my life? And I don't want only that to be my life. I want my life to have a meaning, for when I die, I can die happily knowing I lived my life to the fullest.
Always,
Maddy

You are in a cosmic wonderland. You are awake in the greatest dream ever dreamed, Maddy. Not all are awake within this cosmic dream but all others are most definitely here with you. Would you live life to its fullest, you must "see" life in its fullest expression. Would you know God to the fullest, you must "see"

God in the fullest sense. Would you know love in this life, you must "see" how you love and love thus as an instrument of the divine. In order to know tender compassion in this life, you must surrender for all time pity and loathing of yourself and others. You must love all of you to the deepest borders of your resting soul. Journey within as you voyage the years and befriend the wayfarer.

If you want to have a great attitude, then have a great love, dear child. If you want to have a great love, then consider closely your life, your world, and your relationship to it. If you want to be grateful always for all you have, be still. If you want to stop asking for more and be content with that apportionment life has granted to you, be still. If you want to know what to take from this life that will enable you to live life to its fullest, be still. If you want your life to have meaning and to be able to say in your final breath, "It is done; it is good; I have truly lived in this life," then be still.

"Be still and know I Am God" (Psalms 46:10). Be silent, and take refuge and solace in your times of aloneness when the savages of the world come to your door. Be silent in your thoughts, and come to know, to really know, that your thoughts themselves have the power of the northern wind, a spring rain, a lover's passion, and a silent vacuum. Be still, and be at peace in the silence which beckons itself to be filled with the unseen power of the worlds. In the stillness is activity. In the silence is the crashing of oceans. In the darkness is the light of the world. "Be still and know I Am God" is our most vivid admonishment to recall we rest in God and God in us. We are in constant symbiosis with creation. Look not upon the illusory world for your reference points; naught but desert sands are there. In the active inactivity of your internal world is found the telephone exchange of God. Make the call, Maddy.

Take pleasure and enjoy your life. Extend your heart, your time, and your effort for those of lesser station. But enjoy what has been joyously delivered into your care to partake. Live your life so that by your example others may see how to live their lives. Love your life so that others may learn how to respect and how to love their lives. That which makes your life meaningful to you, will also make your death meaningful. Go, dream, dare, explore, love, cry, wonder, and stand agape at the host of life all about you. This is your world to do what you will. I love you, Maddy. Life loves you, Maddy. It is all love, child.

CHAPTER 35

▼

Reward and Punishment and Prayer

"One soweth and another reapeth."

—(The Christ, John 4:37)

Dear Jesus,
Why do so many innocent people die every day? Do little children deserve to be trapped in fires or floods? Do people deserve to come home to find some disgusting stalker freak waiting to kill them? If people pray to you for help, why are so many people still suffering?
Robin

No innocent people die every day. No innocent people live every day. No guilty people die every day, and no guilty people live every day. People live and people die according to a schedule, a clock that is not of the material world. This is not deterministic; rather, we are creatures of multiple planes and worlds. Only part of you is ever here, Robin. Intersecting with every moment and every choice are the infinite endings each of the paths we choose. In our life we choose every moment the destiny that awaits us. Our choices and thinking interact with worlds far removed from that which stands visibly before you now. You set the clock. However, people also live and die according to the tumultuous dynamics of the material world.

Awareness of this give and take of the seen and unseen worlds is key to understanding eternity and the ephemeral. As long as we remain enmeshed in the flesh, we will apply such basic interpretations of reward and punishment. It is all perspective. We can always look around us and see what does not comport with our intrinsic understanding of a possible world free of suffering. We are spirit with a body. We are spirit and a body. It is this marriage of the spirit and material world on the plane of consciousness that the senses intrude beyond their mandate. We thus note the failure of one world to abide by the grace of the other. When the beauty and grace that is latent in us interrogates the material world, we note the failure of one to manifest the possibility of the other. Thus, we process this irreconcilability as incongruous.

You must learn to consider both the questions and the answers in terms of the relative and the absolute. This is not clever sleight of hand. This is a fact that will only permit clarity. Relatively, no, little children do not "deserve to be trapped in fires and floods." They do not deserve this absolutely, either. However, when we view this question absolutely, with the eyes of one considering the myriad implications of the absolute for the physical world, we note that the question, let alone the subject, simply takes on an irrelevance. The passing of the flesh of this world, when placed in the context of the absolute nature of our immortality, renders meaningless the passing of this world entirely. In the Eternal Dance of being, all considered today is rendered meaningless. It only seems meaningful now because we are dualistically looking at the universe as separate and apart from it.

REWARD AND PUNISHMENT IS FALLACIOUS

Robin, look closely at the questions you ask, and that of all your peers. You are impressed that this whole life is reward and punishment based. This is a fallacy of monumental proportions. This life and what follows, what shadows, are not a product of bartering with God—reward *or* punishment. Not all that is apparently "deserved" comes to pass in the manner that the senses of this world can measure. But I assure you this: the effort that we labor under to break free the chains of our human bondage, of ignorance of our immortality, will yield fruit in this world *and* the next. From the vantage point of where we view the world it is easy to see the horrors and unfairness you describe. I am not saying relative horror and unfairness is untrue. I am saying that it is *a truth* of what is going on here. When we believe, really believe, Robin, we begin to see that God has a marvelous and intricate plan worked out in all the affairs of our days—in both the places where we note grace *and* in the places where God appears to have abandoned the watch. We may then *know*.

The only state that remotely resembles reward and punishment is the harm or interference we bring upon ourselves. Our spirit is must assuredly going to fulfill its mission. It is not programmed to fail. The very concept of failure is flesh-bound. Spirit will do that which it is called to do. Spirit has no concept of time; time does not exist. Time is a relative musing on the *observed* universe. Whatever interruptions we bring upon ourselves only serves to labor the inevitable end. You most certainly will repose fully and absolutely in God regardless of your present deceit of the illusion of apartness.

INTERCESSION AND PRAYER

Do you know "so many people?" Do any of us really know the heart of those beside us, their private thoughts and secret prayers? It is not the case that God does not hear our prayers; rather, it is the case that so often we do not participate ourselves in our prayer. What I am saying is it is acceptable, but not complete, to supplicate ourselves to God and surrender only to God the power to affect this world and make things right. I am not saying that we should physically fix the ills of the world, though that is commendable. We are talking about prayer and outcome. When we become one with the message that we form for the ears of God, and truly are an instrument of the righteous desire for good to come to pass, we move to a station in this world where we, an instrument of God, move to co-create in the process of "willing" on behalf and through the medium of God.

We pray in ritual and otherwise suggest by this practice that God responds arbitrarily or otherwise when the inbox is full regarding issue number "X." We affirm that God may intercede on an individual's behalf All of these things may indeed be true. I have found in my experience that these things are often appear true. I am not convinced, though, that this is the default plan for intercoursing with God and affecting the world through our prayers. God has set in place a marvelous matrix, a framework, that when coupled with our intent triggers a participatory process that makes us exponentially serve that end of fueling the response of the material world to our will, and God's will. I think, therefore, that it is possible that many prayers do appear to be unheeded. Even here, though, no thing is ever missed in the fabric of the great mind of God. Every thought, every prayer, every desperate hope and wishful thought exists now and for all time in the silent memory of the divine.

So, while it is possible for some prayers to appear affected in an immediate real-time sense and others seemingly long in arriving or otherwise overlooked, it is quite possible that a critical gravity of human will must be brought to bear if it is otherwise lacking committed intent in its individual supplication, thus the appearance of sluggish response or unanswered prayer. You will note when you participate in prayer with conviction that you are openly and assuredly telegraphing your prayer directly to and through God, and to the subject at hand, you may have a different result. Were you to try this, fail, and wonder why it does not work as I have instructed, you should consider that it makes no matter of what illusions we inform ourselves. Unless we are "re-born" into seeing God in this world you will always be just below the radar of understanding and these greater issues and intimately affecting reality. It is not a matter of practice; it is a matter of participation in this world in a way that has never been instructed to you. With affirmation, dedication, and a modicum of time you will begin to see your participation in God meaningful, responsive, and deliberate.

It is not in ritual that God is found. It is not in sacrifice and burnt offerings that God is found. God is found and claimed by force of will and an intent to demand God Wed you in this world. It *is* your inheritance. Go. Claim God, and when you pray you will find that you seed your prayers in the halls of the heavens and the atoms of earth.

SUFFERING AND THE SENSES

People will always suffer while in this world, Robin. This is not fair; this is not unfair. Stop using these descriptions to describe our response to the oscillations of "good life, bad life." You are a complex machine of many worlds. Your flesh will always degrade and suffer, and the instruments that find this suffering poorly conducive to survival will inform us in every way they can that this stinks, and that stinks. That this hurts, and that feels good. So, we idle through life prisoner to our senses and their formulations running always from the bad to the good, always searching for that end that serves the comfort of our flesh. Our mind and body are doing exactly what they were designed to do. But do not make the mistake that billions do of thinking that this "is" reality. This is not reality. This is all the comfortable accoutrements of the constructions of the senses. Your mind will rail against any upheaval that serves to un-employ it. When you begin to "see," you will wonder how you ever did "not see." It is all so apparent when you elect to affirm that you will wake up. You will wake up. You will wake up. People will still suffer but you will now understand the context in which that suffering takes place. Robin, this is your world, your life, and your love. Go, live your life and love your life. Take your love and saturate the world with you.

CHAPTER 36

▼

The Kingdom Of God

"It is easier for a camel to go through the eye of a needle, than for a rich man to enter into the kingdom of God."

—(The Christ, Matthew 19:24)

Dear Jesus,
There's been a great deal of misconception about how big the window of heaven actually is. Some believe all it takes is a few good deeds and a little faith in God, while others, me included, believe there's more to it than that. I always thought of my life on Earth as one big test. Everything I do now will determine my afterlife. I believe what the Bible tells me when it says, "there's a small window to heaven." So Jesus, what does it take to go through it?
Paige

The window to heaven is indeed small—right now! All of heaven *can* fit inside of a "mustard seed," Paige. Yet, contained with this seed is infinity. When you are informed the Kingdom of God is right here, inside you, you are given much more information than is at first realized. However, you likely have no more a clue what this means than if I told you red is really green. This is because you are required to change the way you think to look through the (your) window. You are required to change the way you think in the performance of your "good deeds" and what you have "faith" in. All you have ever been told is what to practice or how to feel. If you want to change your world, change your thoughts. If you want to change your thoughts, look *in* on the world, not *out* on the world from your window.

You are on this earth only so many years, and most adults have no clue, no memory of the difficulties and pain you labor under trying to do all the things they ask, or command of you in childhood. In the meanwhile you are busy trying to make sense of it all yourself. You feel the love that makes you want to express charity to one less fortunate. You note the advantages in your life compared to those less fortunate. Even if your life stinks sometimes, you still see where others have much less, and their grief is much more. You wrestle with the approaching fear that you have always wanted to be older, but now that it is happening, it sometimes seems to be happening *too* fast. More importantly, it is not clear to you what the meaning is to all this life stuff.

"What is this all about?"

"Why am I even here and why does life sometimes suck so much?"

"Who are all these others around me?"

"I know I have something in store for me, but some days I cannot figure anything out?"

Even when God is not fashionable, you still think of these things in your quiet moments. You know, when no one else ever hears, that you are called inside in some strange manner. You know, don't you, Paige? Regardless of what you are told or what you see outside your window, you just know that something still, special, small, and just for you beckons from within you. This is God, Paige, though you may not be confidently and outwardly positive, you know this is true. You know it. You know your spirit. Your spirit calls to you in your private places, and you listen.

DEEDS

You want to know how God is meaningful to you *now*. You want to know the timeless question: Whether or not good deeds or faith purchase immortality (Ephesians 2:8-9; James 2)? Part of this is the product of what you inherit from your forebears; part of this is the clock of creation ticking inside of you evolving in your own heart the need to close the distance to God *in this world*, in this lifetime. This question has wrestled the minds of all the mothers and fathers of faith.

That others have wrestled with this is instructive only insofar as we can glean that intellect is not the vehicle to unlocking the mustard seed. Intellect is not the key; rather, intellect is the chain that blinds us to the senses. Beware of the spiritual simony that insinuates into your faculties cloaked as "deeds." "If ye have faith as a grain of mustard seed…nothing shall be impossible unto you" (The Christ, Matthew 17:20). Many believe that deeds secure passage in forever. Many do not divorce their deeds from their personal desired outcome. Desire pollutes deeds.

We would make human God so that we might apprehend him/her in an image or idea that allows us to consume such an abstract and extraordinary concept. However, we make the mistake of concluding what is required of man to decipher and attain such beauty and omnipresence is required of the divine from us. The conduct of a life of deeds purchasing eternity imply that behavior that otherwise has moral virtue and imperative (deeds) is actually bartering with God for reward, or otherwise earning the same. Moral and upright behavior that is performed as a means to an end is unworthy before the throne of God. Coercion of promise renders deeds an idle offer.

This does not mean that we should not execute our life in a charitable and compassionate manner. The brilliant mathematician, Blaise Pascal, summed up well the equation for the conduct of life for those "on the fence" in the now-famous *Pascal's Wager*:

- If I wager *for* and God *is*—infinite gain;

- If I wager *for* and God *is not*—no loss.

- If I wager *against* and God *is*—infinite loss;

- If I wager *against* and God *is not*—neither loss nor gain.

The point is not to reduce something so profound and important to a parlor gambling trick. The point is you are to live your life in such a way that the acts and deeds of your life are executed free of reward or purchase of the hereafter. When your life is conducted free of the attachment of personal gain or reward you invest in both this life and your own *salvation from the delusion of the material world*. So, your wager is not only that God, evidently, is; your wager is that the deeds of your life, when performed charitably for no other reason than love, do in fact result in your own coffers overflowing. But, you will never store any bounty if your well is poisoned by a desired outcome.

Intent, will, the fabric of your thinking is everything. In loving your brothers and sisters—loving your brothers and sisters as you love yourself—all else is accomplished which is otherwise the total selflessness of charity of heart and intent. How you enthrone such intent and will to love, and otherwise execute the same moral virtue minus the appendage of bartering, is contained quite plainly herewith.

FAITH

Faith? What is it you would have faith in, child? Do you have faith that the guidance of your parents is sufficiently founded to wager eternity on their revelations to you? Do you have faith that the dead patristic fathers so secured God in their ritual and dogma that you will wager the ultimate end of your soul on deeds alone? What is it you have faith in?

When the day is done and you have wrestled with all the language and admonishments of those who are "informed" of such things, do you still have the "still small voice" whispering to you in the places within you? Is that the dead fathers of faith within you, Paige? It is not your parents as they sleep in the other room? This is the voice that has been within you since you remember first things. This is the voice that, though speaking to you, is speaking through the mystery of all life, in you. You literally have within you now an antenna that can tune in the Kingdom.

I ask none to dislodge dead things and stale artifacts from their inventory; I ask only that you consider such things in the light of your own heart and findings. Surely, *they* will wail and run to and fro declaring, "Blasphemer," and "'Tis the work of the devil." "You will lose you soul should you attempt to 'tune' the Kingdom of God on your own radio." Such is the absurd conformance injunctions ballyhooed to one who would but know God absent Man. Faith, Paige, is for those who cannot close the distance to the Kingdom today. Faith is useful, but not the end. Knowing is the end, Paige. You have right now the wherewithal to *know* the Kingdom of God.

THE KINGDOM OF GOD

"The Kingdom of God *is* at hand" (John the Baptist, Mark 1:15)! This was not an idle platitude to pacify the people from the oppression of Roman overloads. This was not a secret parable, though it has been consistently understood and misunderstood on many levels. This is a factual statement on that which the un-tuned eye missed as it acquired the "intellectual senses" necessary for survival in the harsh world of our collective journey from Eden. The very mechanism which assured our survival in the struggling days served an end which blinded us to the spiritual world, and the Kingdom of God.

Why would you want to have faith in something that you cannot but estimate thrice, four times, a thousand times removed from the hardships of your life when you can drink from the wellspring of the Kingdom of God right here, right now? Why have faith when you can have knowledge? Instead, have faith that God would have faith in you. Place faith where faith needs to be and secure direct knowledge where it is possible.

You have heard others likely tell you to lead "upright lives" in service to God and your fellow man. However, outside of the conduct of practice and ritual, have you received information on how to transform you? You have been frightened and corralled into conformity for the conduct of righteous action to either avoid punishment or secure reward; of this I am sure. This is not helpful. This does nothing to enable you, a creature or God, to secure passage in this greatest of adventures. These transformative injunctions simply force compliance in furtherance of an imposed and inherited paradigm to relate to God. Are you content in waiting till this world passes and your flesh expires to secure your knowledge of the multiplicity of worlds right here, right now?

I offer no man or woman tomorrow. I offer all humanity today. Today, right here, right now, heaven is obtained. It is always your choice: wait for the fog and haze of the sights and sounds of your expiring corpse to look you thus toward heaven or find you heaven today. I choose heaven today. When your flesh surrenders its last agonal breath and the membranes of your veil begin to part it will be too late to inform yourself. Your life would have been spent inculcating the dead conventions of others.

HOW DO I BEGIN TO SECURE GOD TODAY?

It is in the manner you look out upon your world. It is in the nature of inherited things, ideas and notions that both liberate your fancies and enslave your personal intercession with forever. You do not have to discard or render idle any of what you have been taught to do as I ask of you. But, you do need to make room at the table of that which you know if you would draw ever closer to the unbelievable power and wisdom of God within you, and all about your every waking sense. Paige, when you come to see that you are *in* God, you will come to see the Kingdom of God.

You need to start today with a conviction, a dedication, a dream born of the weeping and longing within you. Go today and affirm a better world. Announce to your heart in its deepest places, "I am of God and I will secure God in this life." I can assure you that in doing so you certainly have no risk. Invite yourself to look at the world as you never have before. Engage yourself with the most incredible, fantastic ride of your life. Open the window instead of peering over the sill. Take your world by force. Look at the world from inside the world instead of as spectator.

Rethink everything you know. Look outside the "box" on all things, issues, events, and circumstances; consider things counter-intuitively. Consider how you look at things. How you process what your senses inform you is "out there." How you associate events, people, love, affection, anger, sadness, and hope. Invite you to rest in you and see not any longer the bad or the troubled when you can be part of the process that sees the good and the hopeful. Part of seeing the world is learning what it is we choose to see. In considering what it is we implicitly choose to see, we learn why we are seeing as we are. You will always be aware of the bad, the sadness, and the pain, but that on which you concentrate your attention is that on which you focus your intention. Focus your intention on love.

Like water seeking its own level you will shortly start—unconsciously, then consciously—interacting with all the unseen worlds all about your senses right here, right now. You will begin to draw unto you the grace, the magic, the good fortune, the health and clarity of the mind, the incredible power of knowingness, and such wisdom as no adult could contain. You will come to know God in a way that you could never before have conceived.

YOU ARE A CONDUIT OF LOVE

You will learn to live in God, in an ocean swell of love. As you redress the manner in which you are interrogating the world and processing its findings, you will unlock and let fly free that part of you that can only but love; that is only of love. Come to know this real love that rests with you and through you, Paige. Others are not from where your love's needs come; they come from you, honey. You shall never find love in another, only *your* love revealed. Another should never find your love in them, only *their* love revealed. It is the nature of illusion that we think another bears forth love to and for us. Another secrets within our heart and makes manifest our own love by their synergy, and we in them.

You are not turning a dumb eye to the troubles of this world were you to love you in such a manner, quite the opposite. You are not turning away from the world when you elect to see the good rather than the anguish and the sorrowful. What you *are* doing is broadcasting yourself like an antenna to the good, the righteous, the grace and promise of this and the unseen worlds. You focus the infinite power of consciousness on that which you intend. You begin retraining your mind to not simply be the affect of matter; rather, you re-key you to let clock the spiritual DNA within you and come to command the changes in your life as an instrument of God, when you come to command your life you begin to command the world. Assert with conviction that the beauty of your youth and the purity of your heart can be harnessed and that you *will* be awakened. You will no longer stand deaf before the beauty of the Heavens right before you, right now.

Slowly, you will see changes in yourself; others will see this sooner. Your life may not immediately announce rewards, but this is not the purpose of this process, is it? We are not bartering with God. However, in so doing these things and becoming a player on God's team right here, right now, you will, in fact, begin to see the breathtaking changes completely rocking your life. All that you stand to inherit is amazingly counterintuitive. The senses serve that end which seeks to secure for you comfort, pleasure, love, security, and stasis in the conduct of your life. The senses necessarily rail against that which is not measurable, quantifiable, concrete and palpable. It must employ its ally, the intellect, to construe the abstract and ideal. And so the senses impinge the journey inward. However, the journey inward secures the ultimate comfort, pleasure, love, security, and eternal stasis.

When your acts of charity are no longer the deeds that secure passage, when your faith is no more the faith *in the leap of faith*, you will see revealed to you such amazing intensity and grace as your mind could never have imagined. It is all right here, right now, Paige. The Kingdom of God is before you right this minute. The battle for the Kingdom of God is the battle of your mastery of you. You should not waste another moment in securing forever. Don your armor. Do so now.

THE DIRTY WINDOW OF THE MIND

I tell you this with every fiber in my being wishing I could show you that the "window" you speak of you are looking through right now. That which you see right before you is the Kingdom of God on Earth. Paige, you are seeing every moment only the thinnest layer of what is actually before you. It is so beautiful, dear child. It is so incredible. Your window is you, Paige. Clean the glass, wipe clear your eyes, and look again. Your window will have sweeping views of oceans of grace that you had never even guessed at before.

When you are told you can do anything you want in this life there is no measure of falseness in this. You really can do anything you set your mind to in this life, including the most awesome, breathtaking adventure of all. Take what I have written here and consider what I have said. Some may take time to mean more or less to you. You already know what you need to do. All you need is for me to validate you. I do.

CHAPTER 37

▼

Elysium

Jesus,
What does heaven look like? Is it golden and dreamy as we picture it
in the modern world, or is it different altogether? Can you show us,
or is it too glorious for our minds to process."
Tommy

Tommy, what do you think heaven looks like? Do you see heaven as "golden and dreamy?" Perhaps it is. Have you ever asked anyone you love how they really see heaven? Have you considered and compared your different ideas of what heaven may be like? Do you think everyone will be in for a surprise? Maybe.

It is the case that the great faiths of the world have many descriptions about the architecture of heaven. Most descriptions are outside of scripture, the product of the revelations of the faithful. The varied descriptions of both heaven and hell belong often to the adjunctive community of legend. Through time and inculcation these descriptions become a central component of the faith. However, there is so much missing, is there not? Do you ever note that there are mostly descriptions of seraphs and cherubs sounding songs of adoration for our enthroned Lord? In most faiths, this image is valid.

When we ask the penetrating questions we are told that our reward for following the rules of life will be to serve and adore God within God's presence for eternity. We are also informed that this is the highest reward for a life well lived. We can somehow understand this, but only in a very abstract way. We know that hell is suggested to be the absence of God. All agree on this point in the great and lesser faiths. So, when we go to heaven we become so enraptured by the mere presence of God that we join readily (free will?) in genuflecting for eternity and singing alongside the host of heaven our praise. What is wrong with this, Tommy?

Heaven, as Promised

We can mechanically conduct our lives with variable grace and deportment, but as long as we either believe, conduct our life's works properly, or a combination of the two we shed the earth and are at once welcomed, accommodated, and taken to our place in the choir. We will have passed from this life, and God will finally "prove" God's existence to our little insect selves. The injunction to "not tempt the Lord" (Deuteronomy 6:16) being irrelevant at this point since we are dead. Of course, there will be time for collecting around the drinking fountain of heaven with family and friends. We will be issued wings, perhaps, or just acquire them as a by-product of our spirit's release from bondage. Heaven will be a combination of the movie made famous by Robin Williams, *What Dreams May Come*, and Dante Alighieri's *Paradiso*. Of course, heaven is promised to possess the allowance of our individual desires, such as an eternity sailing, a lone pristine beach of white sands, crashing surf, and topless women or ripped hunks, or a long picnic table in a blushing pasture with place settings for our parents, and empty place settings for our children, grandchildren, and so on.

In essence, if we pass the "test," a great curtain will be lifted, and we will be able to "join" *the* club. Moreover, in accordance with our earthly compassion, charitable heart, and support in affirming the rightness of the faith to which we belonged, all the heathens, infidels, and *others* will not be there with us. Eternity is segregated in compliance with our great embracing heart on earth. What is wrong with this, Tommy? I am not being sarcastic. This is a factual representation of the general convictions of faith.

What are you made of, Tommy? We know by the words of the great fathers and mothers, and truly by our own inventory, that we are a material body with a spirit, yes? We do not really know, not really, that we are spirit with a material body, do we? We allow our spirit in this flesh to intercourse with God now through the filters of our own flesh. We make subordinate the master, if only for a season. We mostly keep spirit uncomfortably removed from meditation and songs of praise of God in the here and now, don't we? Yes, we do. We engage God with the faculties of emotion and intellect and call such spirit. Yet, there is this implicit expectation that when we pass the flesh in so passing, we wake up. In dying we are free and then will commune with God. Tommy, what will commune with God? Who will commune with God?

SPIRIT DOES NOT GET A WAKE-UP CALL WHEN WE DIE

If there is a spirit within us that will suddenly find employment at our deaths, we implicitly admit that there is much more to us in the here and now. If there is a spirit within us that is so powerful it can survive death, then it must be a considerable portion of the strength that is our being. If there is a spirit in us here and now, why are we waiting to die to allow our spirit access to God? I mean, why are we really not permitting our spirit to wear our body rather than our body to house our spirit, and subjugate it to the illusions and distractions of the flesh?

You see, Tommy, there is no wake-up call in the passing of flesh. There is no sudden enlightenment once free of the chains of this mortal cloth. We create heaven every single day as we fabricate our practice and expectation of heaven. We smother our inheritance in the language of the material world and make heaven only a loose collection of intellectual considerations. When we part this world, these are the imprints that have deluded the mind and impressed upon our being, our virtual non-local memory.

We have assigned to us many mansions "in my Father's House" (John 14:2). To each of us is given that will, that corner of creation to do with what we will. The natural and divine laws are designed to lovingly assist us endlessly in the fabrication of our evolving journey in consciousness. In the daily executions of that which we affirm, we create the intellectual constructs of our heaven. We attain that very notion of that which we labor to create in the flesh. To each is it given in this life to secure that end, upon passing, that best serves the intent of his or her will and apprehension.

GOD IS NOT *IN* HEAVEN

If you have wisely inferred that there then must be more that lie beyond the constructions of our apprehensions of heaven, you are correct. However, I do not address this here. Yours is *a* heaven, Tommy. In this place, you may well have "golden and dreamy" communion in the company of angels. However, this is not God. This is a reflection of God. While you may likely find *your* heaven in this construction, it is no more than *your* apprehensions of God. It is removed and divorced from the experience that is absent words. Heaven will be what you imagine it will be or it will be what you experience it to be. Experience with other than your mind, and you will *know* heaven. Tommy, your intellect and sense are tools. Stop letting them run amuck in the asylum.

CHAPTER 38

▼

Dare To Dream

Dear Jesus,
What is the plan for the earth? Why are we all here? There is so
much bad stuff that is happening in the world. Is it all for a reason?
Does everything have a reason as to why it happens? Does each per-
son make a difference? Like, if you were to take away one person
from the whole world, would everything be different or would it be
the same, like that person didn't do anything to make a difference?
Michele

"In my father's house are many mansions" (John 14:2), Michele. I want you to consider that Jesus meant for us to realize that, in this house (earth, the universe, and beyond), there is much more taking place right in front of our eyes than we realize. Each and every mansion in this vast house of God are the worlds and lives we each live. From your birth to your high school graduation, to the people and loves entering and leaving your life, even unto your death, Michele, your entire world and all its interactions are one of infinite mansions in God's house. The key to "seeing" this, to realizing this, is also the key to unlocking the secret of the Kingdom of God right here on earth, before you die.

In the eternal mind of God, every single thing in the universe is known in consciousness. God surely knows all the ingredients that make up the recipe of life on earth. As no soul ever actually dies, only the body that housed it, it is incomplete to suggest any leave the world, though we leave each other's world. There is no net loss from creation when someone dies; rather, there is a transfer or exchange of matter and energy. This sounds so academic, but it is nevertheless true.

EVERY SINGLE LIFE IS CRITICAL TO THE ENTIRE UNIVERSE

I must believe that each life makes a difference, to itself, those around it, the entire planet, and the universe. Every life, every soul contributes to the magnificent glory of God. Though, it is hard to always see this, isn't it? When someone leaves this world, it makes a difference. Certainly we are aware of the loss in our anguish, in our sorrow, in our fear. It seems the passing is a loss for the entire world. However, for every soul that leaves this world another one joins the next world. Here too, a difference is made by that soul. No soul is ever lost or "gone" in God.

It is hard for us to always realize the absolute balance of life as we mostly only ever know what is going on here by virtue of occasional and profoundly wonderful intuitions, visions, and enlightenment, or unless we are told by our prophets, scriptures, or scientists.

However, if you could imagine that this world is at least equaled in a mirror world of just spirit or energy, you might then find it easier to consider that the loss of one soul, one life here, balances out in the next world.

THE KEY TO THE KINGDOM IS WHERE CONSCIOUSNESS COLLAPSES

You see, Michele, both (all) planes of existence are married together, though we do not often comprehend this. The most obvious place where these two worlds meet is within us. It is this point within us that we must discover and cultivate so that we might better unlock the mysteries of the Kingdom of God on Earth. This place is the threshold, the portal, the window in which we intercourse with God directly. It is in this rarefied field where the non-local world collapses in a quantum-marriage.

It is here. It is very much a part of you and it is the sole portal to facilitate the Kingdom of God. It is the *lapis philosophorum*, the Eastern Gate. Not only do we detect it constantly, but it can only be found and accessed within yourself. Using your senses and intellect, approaching from the fields beyond, from *without* to within, you will only ever fail. The mind cannot unlock the Kingdom of God. Be still.

"Unto you it is given to know the mystery of the Kingdom of God: but unto them that are *without*, all these things are done in parables: That seeing they may see, and not perceive; and hearing they may hear, and not understand" (Mark 4:11–12). Thus the Christ emphatically informed us the intellect and senses will fail, the locale is within, and *only* you can obtain the key. The scriptures are replete with Christ's directions on how to obtain the Kingdom of God; this is not just some clever construction of a select scripture.

Christ's parables had the additional import of even reflecting in their delivery the mystery of the nature this world: the parables reflect the dual nature of having a first-glance application for the weak of vision in instructive and useful parable, and the penetrating guidance and entreaty for one who sees absent the eyes. These are the inner mysteries referred to in the non-canonical gospels that reveal that even then not everyone grasped the mysteries. In this manner, even Christ's parables reflect the spirit and the flesh, for the spirit will clearly hear its mandate where solicited.

THE PEACE THAT PASSETH ALL UNDERSTANDING

Every life has value and will continue to be a meaningful part of creation even after the flesh is cast off, and a return is made to the spirit world. Within each of us is the nexus where worlds meet in a "membrane." We are biological machines so brilliantly crafted and evolved that we process consciousness and are both portal and vessel.

If you would imagine an onion, you are able to consider how something may have many layers upon it. Perhaps those layers closest to the center are aware that there are many layers still upon it. Consider that those layers furthest from the center are not aware that there are more layers beneath it as they are right there in the thick of things, interacting with the world and protecting the onion from all the brutal things that bombard it constantly. The outer layers have a very different job than the inner layers. The outer lays are employed making survival possible. The inner layers are aware that there is an outside but are so much closer to the center. If the outer layer does its job well, the onion will be protected and its purpose in this world realized. In many ways, we are very much like an onion. In the popular animated movie *Shrek*, Donkey used this very analogy. I hope I have better success than Donkey.

There are two types of mysteries in this world: the unknown and the unknowable. Figuring out one from the other has provoked the mind of Man since we first became. You must come to a point where you consider answering the more difficult questions with your heart; your mind will simply not suffice. What I mean is no less than considering all the most complex questions in the solitude of your own inner world.

There is a place in you, by design, where the limitless meets this world. There is a presence of God in you which you should befriend and cultivate. When you cultivate and befriend this "place" which is within you, you will realize profoundly that you are, in fact, in God. The things that are unknown may remain so to you, but increasingly you will have a remarkable sense of knowing the difference between what you do not know and what is unknowable.

I must believe that everything has a reason for its purpose and actions in this life. I am not talking about silly things like why someone does not pick up behind themselves, though often there is a reason for this as well. I am talking about the reason the sky is blue, why the singing of birds in the crisp dawn is more than just beautiful to us. It sings within us. Whether I am aware of it or not, I must believe there is a reason why the pink light of the setting sun makes me stop completely any task and drift into the changing colors of the day thinking on the magic of God's majesty. I see reason in the dance of the fields as the winds massage the spines of the "grassy" blades.

There is a reason why the peacock announces his colors to others, why we blush when someone we fancy takes interest in us, why we hold our breath when we hear announced that Christ was crucified for God's love for us. I must believe there is a reason in the things less pleasant, too. Though I cannot see the reason in all things, I must believe that God is within all things, good and bad, for no thing can be without God. It is not possible for anything to be outside of God. In seeing with the knowingness of spirit, all things take on a contextual depth that is otherwise absent. This is the knowingness absent intellect. This is the dawning of the "Peace of God, which passeth all understanding" (Philippians 4:7).

KNOCK AND IT SHALL BE OPENED TO YOU

How then can God be in that which causes us pain, suffering, and a sense of wandering outside of God's protection? There is a natural world all around us, and there are unseen spiritual worlds within and around all of life and all of creation. God really is right here, right now. God has set in place a process of "fruition," a growing and maturing plan for all living things. We see this evidenced in our human history, though some would take issue that I am suggesting evolution theory. I am not, one way or the other. I labor not in such small thinking. It is also the case that we spiritually evolve. We have seen this in the conduct of our faith and service to God. We have seen this in the very lives of our saints and mystics. We see this in the lives of people we even know. We see this in ourselves. Fruition, evolution, it is simply the natural dynamic of created things.

Yet, we are occasionally aware of an incredible reality within and around us. However, we are always concerned with the environment in which we live. Spirit thinking has become somewhat the luxury of idle time, or reverent worship hour. In the past relatively few years, man, his relations with each other, his manipulation of technology, and the very forces of nature, has evolved at such a dramatic pace that we have all collectively developed a rather false sense of security. We live in times that are unequaled in the history of the world. We are living longer. We are making extraordinary strides in medicine and the tools that make our lives richer and more comfortable. We have crafted for ourselves remarkable homes and communities, and we have allotted more time to the things that make us enriched in our hearts. Our economy of living has enabled countless peoples to spend more introspective time, and many are spiritually evolving beyond the restrictive confines of ancient ideology and ritual.

Our hearts have become self-aware, and for many people they are now on autopilot and the doors are being knocked on from the inside. Whereas we have always been informed that whatsoever we shall want, all we are to do is knock and the door will be answered, we are now finding increasingly that the quality of the lives we have mustered have the doors of our hearts being knocked on from within (Matthew 7:7). God calls us.

Yet we must realize, painfully, that all things do not evolve or change in the "twinkling of an eye" that was mankind's recent rise from the agrarian days of tribal and other warfare, plague, and despair. Man does not have more pain and misery, per se, than in ages past. What we have is a more intuitive understanding that there is a disconnection between the nature of our maturing hearts and the circumstances of the savage world. In all times, Man has thought he was living in the worst of time, or the final times.

With a maturing heart and an awkwardly advancing material world, the highs and lows of the evolving creation of God stand out more palpably, more painfully to our inquiring minds. Understanding this is central to establishing context in our relationship with the world. Understanding this dynamic will not alleviate the suffering of anyone who is stricken by the various tragedies of our times, but understanding this may further prompt the spirit of Man to continue undaunted in its solicitation of God and in hopeful prayers for our brethren.

See the nature of the divine world superimposed upon the subordinate natural world and you will have facilitated one of the most important milestones to apprehending the Kingdom of God on Earth. You are, in the end, what you see. You see, in the end, what you dream. You dream, in the end, what you dare. Dare to see God, Michele!

CHAPTER 39

▼

The Reason and Rhyme
of All Things

God,
How is it that you are always nice to everyone, nice to even the
criminals? You forgive everyone even when they hung you on the
cross? How can you be that great? Why aren't there people like that
today? If more people were kind, forgiving, and loving, would there
be so much war and crime on earth? How is it that people who try
to be like you are made fun of? Or not shown?
Jen

Jen, you reveal in your words more than what could be contained in all the space between the stars. There is a presence in you that speaks with authority beyond your years. You are not really asking anything; rather, you are putting the world on notice that you "get it." You know the answer to these questions. You are a light of infinite possibility, Jen. Never allow this light within you to be corrupted by all the distractions and cries of Why God? "Why hast thou forsaken me" (Matthew 27:46)?

Darling child, God represents all that God would have us do unto each other, no less. When we consider the incredible commonality we have with each and every other soul on this earth, we begin to see that not loving, not caring, not having compassion and charity is an affront to ourselves, our brothers and sisters, and God.

We are all hurling through space on an improbable rock in the vast emptiness of eternity. We all are the very same God-substance that forms all living creatures—all. Our time on this rock is ridiculously small considering the measurement of all other manifested things. What folly, what grand delusion of thinking, has us presuming that that which we hold and affirm to be vital or dear is anything more than the passing of the season, the illusion of the sun's shadow?

Every single human on every street corner, in every city, in every country on this planet worries about success, failing, pleasing, being pleased, eating, surviving, serving God, serving man, pleasing parents, other trivial or vital thoughts, and the unpredictability of our fellow man.

Every single human being on this planet wonders how long they will live, who they will become when they grow up, if they will be remembered, why they are here, whether or not they will know love or die alone, and whether or not there is a God and if God knows them. All of us, every one, fears the vast emptiness of time revealed to us in the passing seasons of our own life and the passing lives of others. All your brothers and sisters want to eat, to rest and work secure, to collect onto them and share familial love, and to reach for the heavens in the ways they best can, Jen.

People are "kind, forgiving, and loving." We only ever see what we focus on, Jen, in all things. God demonstrates in God's Love for us no more than that which we should ourselves share and demonstrate. For in the end, dear child, we are all no different. No matter our attire, customs, beliefs, or identities, we are all sentient first and being sentient and of the divine should always be an absolute common ground.

Be not pessimistic about this world, your love, and your brothers and sisters. Take this love that you see revealed in God and absorb it. Be yourself a lighthouse that takes God's love into you and then turn your light upon the world. Share this love with all around you. Help every other person with whom you come in contact focus on the good, our commonality, and the grace of God in our lives.

You manifest God, Jen. In you are the reason and rhyme of all things. You are a vessel that will be able to endlessly drink of God's Love were you to continue to dip your ladle within. God is shown, Jen. God is revealed to you within. You are the living expression of the infinite God. I would not hinder you further with mere words. You are well on your way. Go, child. Live and claim your estate and your Love.

CHAPTER 40

▼

Free Will

God,
What is my purpose? Why are we here on this Earth? Why do the
good die young? Why is life so confusing? Why does the world have
to be so segregated because of race, religion, political ideas, wealth,
and heritage? Why are we in Iraq? Why do our young soldiers have
to die in vain? Why can't we just leave Iraq? It's just been getting
worse and worse by the day.
Katherine

Oh, my sweet darling. I know it seems so sad and makes you feel often like crying. Would that I could hug you and wash away your fears. I understand all the things you state. I have often found myself bathed in tears of wounded sorrow. I have stood dumbfounded at the capacity for man to steep to even lower lows than I would imagine possible in my darkest considerations. There is so much that is beyond explanation. There is so much that is just unknowable while still here on Earth. This does not make any of this any easier; I know this. But it is true, child. There is a rhythm and a purpose to everything under the sun.

If there is a purpose, a design, does this not make God responsible for all that is going on? At first I wanted to say, "No, man is responsible for horrific acts, and God just gives us the leash with free will." But in my honest reflections, this does not entirely explain all. Free will is still executed *in* God. All things happen *in* God, good, bad, horrific, or angelic. Though we are each responsible and accountable for our actions, nothing happens outside of God. Free will is God still.

Can you imagine how horrible it would be if there were no free will? If there were no free will, you would not be able to fight with your siblings and get away with it. You might not even be able to have macaroni and cheese. I know I am being clever. Katherine, if there were no free will you, would not be able to not believe in God. Without free will, man would lack the ambition to dream. Without free will, there would be no Sistine Chapel. Dante would never have told us about *Paradise* and Merton would never have climbed the *Seven Story Mountain*. Without free will, Hamlet would never have known what to do. Without free will, we are empty vessels. Without free will, you may not have been here at all. You are result of two people's love, decisions, and choice. Free will fills the emptiness of vast space with the chalk outlines upon the cosmic blackboard of the Holy Dark. Free will provokes the universe to dream. The universe, provoked to dream, manifests all will.

Free will informs us of passion, and alerts our bodies to desire. Free will notes the makings of things unpalatable and that which is repugnant. Free will crowns us and free will slays us, Katherine. The alternative is God granting us free will but watching over us from the mountaintop where he is made manifest, and soiled by the world, to guide and correct the natural machinations of nature and man's predisposition to regress from his spiritual evolution. This kind of free will dispels spiritual evolution. This type of free will compels. This type of free will is not free will at all but a penal colony. This is not free will. No free will is a hellish concept that would destroy all life and experience. A world without free will is non-being. A universe absent free will is a universe that cannot manifest that which creates. In the absence of the ability to create there is oblivion.

However, with free will we see, too, the extremes of man's capacity to digress. Free will allows action upon base thoughts such as bias, prejudice, and war. Free will allows us to visualize and attain the highest highs in our expression but it also presents the saddest contrasts of pain and suffering inflicted not by nature's wrath but by Man's hand.

Sweetie, there is no easy answer to make readily understandable that which is alien to a tender and pure a heart as yours. Perhaps it is not something that any can explain. It is, though, an understanding that can be personally experienced. Please, never lose sight of God in the places where you are inclined to see God not. It is in these places, in these moments, when we cannot begin to calculate how far worse things might have been were God to have abandoned us. I want you to know how infinitely necessary you are to all goings-on, even on the far side of the world. You are part of the chain of consciousness that is the mind of God. Inform God in your supplications. Affirm a better world in your rightness of thought and action. See God in the worst of times, and in so seeing God in that place you seed God in that darkness.

Honey, this is what is needed. We need the entire human race to affirm the world they would behold. We are instruments of God, and there is more than ample evidence that God has been merciful to this race of humans struggling on this once boiling rock hurdling through space in some distant corner of the universe. Sit up and make God pay attention, but for your sake never stop seeing and hearing the whispers of God around you, Katherine.

Do not allow yourself to see a world where it is getting worse every day. Do not surrender. Do not surrender to the illusion that you are an impotent witness only. You are every bit a part of the solution as is everyone else, and God. Speak with the voice of God. See with the eyes of God. Think your will with the will of God. Create the world you would dare to dream.

CHAPTER 41

▼

The Great Organ System

I would ask him why he was here and what he could possibly achieve by being here. What could I do for him?
Robbie

You are correct, of course, Robbie. What could possibly be achieved by God manifesting incarnate? Man does not necessarily believe with constant prodding from the divine. God has manifested prophets, avatars, saints, and deity unto the world, and in nearly all cases the "faithful" stand incredulous, or worse, imprisoned, ostracized, or committing deicide in order to deny the divine and keep secure their restrictive models of God and life.

It is the state of the physical world that man asserts the preeminence of his faculties. Even in the face of the most patently obvious solicitation from God, man rails within the prison he has fabricated. Man would be no more inclined to behave any differently or believe anything differently were God to smack him on the side of his head. Were it not fairly sad, it would be amusing beyond words. Man, some little piss-ant on a blue rock in some unknown galaxy, asserts he has a clue about the manner and means of worlds by the extrapolations of his findings on the base little ball he scurries about upon.

A CELL IN THE SOUP

Robbie, your questions are striking in what you reveal. You ask first ask what God could achieve by being here, and then follow with "What could I do for him?" A cell may not be aware that it is a cell (or it may) but it does its job and affects the other cells around it in such a way to design a collaborative effort. The cell is unique and necessary; otherwise it would simply not be. Yet the cell serves an end so far removed from the station of its immediate duties that is cannot begin to grasp this import, in an express sense. The cell serves its peers, which combine to create tissue, which allies with still other tissues to make organs, which themselves coordinate with disparate other organs to make organ systems, which support the organism.

While I assert the smallest cell within us has itself "memory" and intent, it nevertheless must have some notion of interaction, as its processes are dependent on this. A cell serves selflessly and when it is through with its service it executes its own death so that other cells might come behind it and continue servicing the organism.

A nucleus collaborates with the particles that orbit it to develop an attraction, which conspires to unite similar, or differing, characteristic atoms in constructing the signature purpose of their late mission, a product of matter. This matter interacts with myriad other atoms to eventually construct the elements of this world as we know it. This earth orbits the great nucleus of our solar system in a conspiracy attraction of likely inclined planets. Our solar system orbits even greater systems whose purpose, lately, is the construction of our galaxy. This galaxy serves an end that orbits still another, further removed process. The smallest particle, on the most distant planet, were it aware might be able to only glean by its immediate surroundings that it was part of still a much greater dynamic unfolding by observable laws and intent. Is the cell aware that it is part of the great machination that has universes orbiting each other, perhaps even in a divine manner, and a critical part of *the* puzzle? Regardless, it is fulfilled in the role it can but perceive, and it executes its service. In a very real way, the cell is as sentient as you.

SENTIENT ROBBIE IN THE SOUP

Robbie is born upon this world and matures to assert, "I am here! What else is here with me? What is *out there*?" In you, Robbie, intellect and the faculties of self-awareness have been harnessed unlike most other creatures and matter we note about us. But even on this point it is the flawed faculties of intellect that inform us so. In you, honey, is the fabric of the material and spiritual world joined in an interpreting, interrogating, and articulating creature. The spirit, like a great ocean, pounds upon the rocks of the material world within your house. In you right now a battle unlike any gleaned in other creatures executes each moment. Robbie, in the birth of self-awareness you conceptualize and intuit an apartness from your informing and spiritual self. However, possessed of the need to manipulate your environment, you wed yourself to matter as a means to an end and in so doing lose sight of the end.

"What could I do for him?" is less instructive as an expression of obedience than it is a cry for a train ticket to eternity, Robbie. Perhaps in an older, more seasoned being I might reserve a different interpretation of this question. In you, Robbie, I see a purity and a fundamental expression of your awareness that you are part of the great organ system that underlies all creation in the bodily expression of God. Robbie, you know this, don't you? You are aware in your private deliberations that you are part of something infinitely greater than what you are led to outwardly believe?

But, what can you do for God? What do you think you can do for God, Robbie? I will submit to you now that here, as in most cases throughout your life, the best and clearest answer will reside within you first. Questions like, "What is for dinner?" and "What time is it?" are certainly better answered by someone who actually knows such mechanical information. But, Robbie, when you ask questions that go right to the heart of Robbie's world, only Robbie can best answer these questions. You should begin now befriending that part of you that has been taught to submit even these questions to the counsel of others. Start un-thinking the way you have been taught to think, expressly or implicitly.

What can the cell do for the organism? What can the atom do for the rock, or the planet for sun? What can man do for God? What they all have in common is they do that thing that they were created to do best. They do not even have to labor to define what that thing they were created to do is; they do it regardless. You have the greater ability to both do that thing which you are created to do best and to reach beyond and know the ebbs and tides of the seasons. You are endowed with such tremendous power and grace resting within you this very moment. Be Robbie. Go to school. Chase your dreams. Fall in love. Serve yourself, and serve your brothers and sisters. Have fun. But Robbie, if you truly want to serve God, if you truly want to live life to its fullest your explorations will have to be turned inwards. You cannot run the world looking for your treasure under the pyramids, upon the oceans, in the idylls of France, Everest, New York, or the lazy Virginia shores. The last frontier of man is the internal world where rests the window to eternity. Your mind cannot go here, Robbie. Look inside you if you would know what you can do for God. This is always where lay the treasures of the world.

▼

CHAPTER 42

Bliss Unbound

Dear Jesus,
Why is all this disastrous stuff happening in the world? Why are
hurricanes coming and destroying everything that we love and
worked for? How come we have war? Why were the twin towers
destroyed and all the people inside of them die, except only a few
people? Why did my cousins have to go to work that day and die?
Why can't you stop it? Why are innocent people dying in Louisiana
and Mississippi? Could you please help us out? I'd really like to
know the answers to these questions.
Meiai

Most people who have ever lived have often wondered about the nature of suffering in this life, Meiai. Besides the fact that it hurts us directly, on many levels, as spiritual beings it hurts us to see others suffer. Moreover, much of the suffering that we experience or observe so often seems pointless. It is hard for us to reconcile the notion of a merciful God with all that we see around us.

As unfortunate as it may appear, we *must* consider how we know what we know of God when we consider the context of our suffering. God has not always been seen or even revered as a God of mercy; rather God was, in God's manifold appellations, a God of war and of vengeance. God was that deity in who was reposed the authority to wage war, vanquish our foes, and reward us according to our perceptions of what a God as this, like us, must ordain or otherwise require. As man evolved both within the spirit and within the interconnectedness of our humanity so too have our apprehensions of God evolved.

This does not suggest that man has solely created God in "our" image; rather it reports the fact that our heightened senses of awareness yield now greater and differing degrees of understanding. Within this increased awareness it has been either revealed or intuited individually or collectively that God and all that surrounds the mystery of being is pregnant with so much greater beauty and majesty. Yet, the circumstances, the perils, and the ravages of daily life in the natural world have not necessarily comported with our enhanced perceptions of the value of life, the infusion of love in previously unseen places, and the increasing glimpses of an immortality that is no longer evident by proclamation rather it is increasingly self-evident.

WHY DO WE SUFFER?

This, then, is one of the seemingly irreconcilable paradoxes of being: Why does man suffer when we now have access to "information" that suggests so much more in the depth and meaning of life? From this consideration we are increasingly aware that what is best projected in our understanding of God conflicts with why there should be suffering here on earth. As we mature in our spiritual inheritance, we apprehend God more maturely but have not yet wrestled with the recognition that the natural world follows laws, which are not always understood macrocosmically. In fact, natural laws are not yet understood microcosmically.

It is hard to imagine what set of divine and natural retooling would have been necessary to both provide man with ecstatic incarnation and provide the means to interact and manipulate the material world in an evolutionary process of unfoldment. In my personal experience, was my life to have been absent suffering I would have never been able to tear from me the illusion of the material world in relation to the underlying fabric of God in all life. I have suffered in this life and would trade nothing. However, it is not enough for me to extrapolate from my own experiences a general impression of the workings of creation. Yet, I do have a general impression of the workings of all creation that is not born of the data infused within me, rather the assimilation of that data with my own interrogation of spirit. It was in the balance of the suffering of my days I have come to know God in a way that is simply absent in many of the eyes of my brethren. I know suffering. Meiai, suffering just is. It sucks and it hurts. But suffering is instructive and liberating as an individual and as sentient beings.

Man has built entire philosophies and even faiths around life's suffering. The fact is, at the end of the day, life is hard. Life has suffering. Each and every individual experience of suffering does not inform us that we have been abandoned in the distant throes of God's untended cosmos rather each profound experience of suffering suggests its opposite; why would creation behave differently in this regard? We have noted in our interrogatories to the universe that there is an opposite experience and element to everything. In the dismal house of suffering, I find not repulsion and forlornness—I find hope and promise.

In all suffering there is the suggestion of the infinite power of hope and of promise. In suffering profound is suggested bliss unbound. Whereas our senses apprehend the material and psychic world, so, too, does our spirit apprehend the world of rapture. We have allowed ourselves to "think" we are physical beings with a spirit. This is key in understanding why we do not understand. We are spiritual beings with a body. In this imbalance is suggested the process of spiritual unfoldment and evolution (not the pedestrian evolution of contemporary debate). In this marriage of spiritual and mental alchemy, the dilution of one enhances the station of the other.

EVOLUTION OF SPIRIT

Man has moved through the ages in a savage and violent world, Meiai. Man has employed every ingenious tool to survive—wittingly and unwittingly. In this process man has purchased and commanded the material world at the expense of the spiritual world. There is a dialectic to life and man must now change the alchemy within in order to better understand the world without. The one constant in this process of becoming greater than the flesh in which we labor is the material world. The natural world will not change because we have now evolved to the point where we can re-tinker with the balance of our perception, our need for the empowerment of the senses having passed its season. But two things will happen.

Each individual will begin to harmonize both the context of their being and the circumstances of their lives directly. In the process of "knowing," we come to know that God's house does have many mansions and that the spirit is in fact far more powerful than the idle employment of the senses and emotions. We begin to interrogate our world as a rightful claimant to the co-creative powers of God.

This is not deification; rather it is employment of the divine laws implicit in our being. We are in God and God is in us. We are co-creators whether we accept it or not. By not accepting our co-creative powers with God, we continue inadvertently having our will synergized for ends not of our choosing. Because, I assure you Meiai, your powers are tremendous. Your will is used whether you employ it or not.

YOUR POWERS ARE TREMENDOUS

Collectively, man will begin to demonstrate the sum total of man's parts. This may be realized in such various forms as community interaction, societal intercourse, apprehensions of faith, and the willful manifestation of improved circumstances of the natural world. I cannot make it clearer; your power is enormous.

Underlying all creation is the Word of God. The ancients did not need a spaceship, a microscope, or computers to intuit this. The will of God, the utterance of the sacred, the Thoughts of the absolute, the Lost Word, are the very building blocks of our physical world. We only infer our possession of this God-substance when forced to query such things as paranormal activities in the phenomenal world. It is not sacrilege to state this fact. Such suggestions belong with the artifacts of fear and darkness in the trash heap of history. Man can and does manipulate the circumstances of the material world every single moment, unconsciously or otherwise. Man is an extension of God. The material world is a manifestation of God. God creates and sustains the material world. Man creates and sustains the material world.

As man changes the chemistry of his deportment to the material world, he or she invites other facilities, higher faculties, to interrogate and make meaningful existence. As our spiritual faculties continue to evolve, our ability to live and interact with the world will be considerably enhanced and we will acquire an entirely different means to access and process information, a back channel. More than anything, we house emotion in such a way that emotion becomes a tool of our being rather than a master; our senses become instruments of wonder as they become subordinate rather than the wardens.

Our will increasingly manifests in real time. Our will acts in "linkage" with the conscious will of life rather than a remote server processing unknown data of collective emotional turmoil. In so doing, we collectively manifest in accordance with a higher understanding of life rather than the subordinate, unrealized participation of our will in furtherance of the background "noise" of emotional life on this planet.

Have no doubt, Meiai, your will is the same God-piece of the divine will. Water seeks its own level for a reason, and it is this reason that this description aptly serves for many analogies. Will has a weight, a value, a projection capability upon the material world in which it labors. Meiai's will, unrestrained or unassigned, is employed unwittingly by the unseen *virus* of the collective will. If you are in emotional turmoil or otherwise grant full employment to your senses, your will, like a virus replicating in host RNA, serves interests unintended to its design and purpose.

A being either free, or in the process of freeing itself from the illusory world, increasingly makes inroads each moment when once the notion to "see" is affirmed. Each moment starts to reveal itself after we have forced, for a time, a new *framework* on how we consider the way in which we considered all things previously. My point is that there is no place one must "go to" or "get to." The process of reformulating our chemistry of interrogating the world is a natural one and yields immediate fruit. Increasingly, you will see that you never have seen before. Meiai, it is a matter of application. Apply yourself to your intentions.

In so doing we change the paradigm of how we process experience from the phenomenal world and begin to directly influence the material world. The proximate impact of suffering does not immediately change, yet how we respond to suffering is a consequence of the awareness of much greater mysteries than we were able to consider before. I am not suggesting to simply "think happy" thoughts. This is too trite. Yet there is an element of truth in this. What can be obtained, however, is happiness in the process. A happiness that does not wane with the ravages of the material world, the vacillations of nature, or the predictability that man will continue to demonstrate savage cruelty to others.

Man will disappoint us again and again. Yet, with the faculties of such a mind that can consider cruelty and malignance of purpose, can we really expect more? It is a simple fact that a matured and seated spirit in a physical being cannot, by definition, behave in such a way as to harm another. In what way can we respond to these human offences of conscience and spirit but to note the mystery of becoming greater in the moment? In these vile acts we must consider on multiple levels. We are human and we are in the world. Thus it is acceptable and appropriate for us to understand and allow our functions of outrage and of sadness to have their voice. However, we are also instructed in travesty that ours is a journey of wonder and contrast is revealed in the moments of man's greatest failings as well. Love is revealed just as often in the contrast of its absence.

Suffering sucks, Meiai, but only in one perspective. Suffering is the tool of our liberation in this world. If you really want to change your world, change how you see your world. If you really want to love your life, change how you love your life. If you would not suffer, do not suffer.

CHAPTER 43

▼

Unfairness and Cruelty

Dear God,
I want to know why an innocent child would be taken away from
her family when she is the only person who had a sense of reality in
her life? I want to know how come when people leave and die, why
it hurts so bad. Another thing I want to know is why people are so
mean, as typical of a question as that might seem.
Alia

How come you did not ask God why an innocent family would have been left behind? They did not deserve to stay here. All they had ever done is tried to live their lives the best they could, love and care for their children and family, and serve as members of the society of peoples. Why did God leave them here? A child is a pure and sweet tender thing, but surely a child could not possibly have put in enough time here to deserve to leave sooner. Why was this innocent "family" left behind?

WHY DO YOU SEE AS YOU DO?

Alia, my question does nothing to lessen the unbearable pain of loss. My question does not poke fun at the most serious of heartaches in the entire world. I simply invite you to ask yourself how you see the way you see the world, the way most people see the world. "If everyone was jumping off a bridge, would you do it?" Almost all kids hear some form of this growing up but I want you to really consider this. Are you sure enough everyone is right about how they are "seeing" the world, or are they seeing it this way as a default, because it is easier to see the world in the manner accustomed to and instructed?

When we consider ourselves a physical being, with just a top layer of patronizing spirit assertion, we really see the world only in relationship to the very here and now. Notions of afterlife, of surviving the flesh, of God's Kingdom, of heaven are really just platitudes to self and community. We might stamp our feet and protest such a suggestion but the fact remains when we fully embrace that we are spirit creatures with a physical shell, we have a much different attitude toward the passing of flesh. As human, we will and should always "feel" the emotions and observations that make life so meaningful and beautiful, but when we have God squarely in our heart seeing the grand design of the infinite order of worlds lessens the pain of loss and suffering attendant to life. It also enables us to see what was not otherwise seen in each moment. We are also empowered to "milk" from experience those observations that were invisible before we truly "got it."

Alia, I am not saying you do not believe in God. I am saying that you do not have to wait to die to understand many of the mysteries of this world. I am not saying that suffering will cease. I am saying that you can better put suffering into perspective when you subordinate the senses that process suffering and loss. I am not saying that life is fair. I am saying it is relative as we are all part of an immense whole. I am not saying I can make you feel any better by what is written here. I am saying you can make you feel better by the words you would write in your hallowed heart.

SURRENDER ONLY TO GOD

On the mean people question, the world is full of ignorant people that assign to themselves and others a sense of authority and power under the illusion of control. In having the sense that one can inflict upon another is the sense of empowerment and strength in the ignorant. By being able to affect another's world positively or negatively, Man falls into the false illusion of order having been created in their sphere of influence. People like this are scared, though they never know this. They are often quite drunk with self-deceit. There is a virtual memory within us that informs us we are able to manipulate and create the world through the building blocks of thought and of will in accordance with the strength of our spirit. Distilled through the emotions and the psyche, it is processed through the senses as "urge." Yet the faculties of emotions and sense cannot so order the material world, Alia. It is only the spirit of man that this power belongs.

Therefore, the bevies of beasts within these faculties of the flesh assert this "urge" and ignorance, malice and other base presentations are bred. In the process, man sees that those around him *are* affected by the grandiose delusions of empowerment and it becomes self-serving. This is true whether it is an international tyrant or a school bully. This is true in greater or lesser forms for all that are cruel and seek to control others. However, this power is not real and how it comes to pass is a result of what we surrender to others.

When we allow someone to force us to grant or withhold love, or other, we are abdicating our sovereign power to another. No one on this planet has the power to make you feel one thing or another. No one on earth has the power to make you feel lesser or greater, unless you grant to them this power. No one can make you love, or not love, hate, or not hate. You empower the very people you would protest. For were you to once and for all affirm that you will never again allow another to control the faculties of your emotions, you would never again find even the need to comment on these people. Moreover, once having regained control of your assignment of emotions, every person that thereafter interacts with your world with this apparent pathology of spirit your person will be further empowered in its own truth and immortality. Each person that serves to validate this observation will serve to sharpen your awareness of your unbelievable self-contained power. You will quickly get to the point where it is almost comical watching people behave like this. They can do nothing about it, as this is their station. You cannot inform them to the contrary, so observing is most noteworthy. You begin to see a breathtaking stagecraft all around you. It is really a never-ending source of fascination. Most people do not even realize they audition every moment for the play, the drama of their eternal lives. Stop being a stagehand or actor and instead choose to be a conductor, Alia.

CHAPTER 44

▼

The Fish Beneath The Waves

Mr. God,
Are you a man or a girl? Why did you make horrible things come to
your world? Why won't you come here and help the people that need
your help? Why didn't you help El Salvador during the war and
help my uncles and aunts live? Why God?
Jesse

Jesse, these things you ask are very grown-up questions. I will help you with grown-up answers. God is a man and God is a woman. God is not man. God is not woman. Does this confuse things a bit? Yes, of course it does. It confuses the greatest minds in the history of the world, Jesse.

What do you think the little fish beneath the ocean thinks when she sees the "shadows" constantly pass by the pier as the fish struggles to catch a glimpse? When the little fish is big enough to make her own journey to the wave tops, she might even see the substance of the shadow. The little fish might then return to tell all the other little fishes what she saw.

"And he was so big and mighty. He moved across the waters as if his fins could not get wet," the little fish would begin. The hammerhead might ask "Did he look like I look?" and then move from side to side to give all the fishes a profile. Laughing, the little fish might say "Well…" and then stumble on her words. "Did he look like this?" intrudes the octopus, blowing himself up to appear quite large. "No. Well…I am not sure," the fish might concede in frustration. The conversation might then get away from the little fish, overtaken by the imagination and musings of the school.

Then the little fish, not even aware of the fish-language conundrum she was in, might state, "He was the biggest fish I have ever seen," or "She was the loveliest fish I have ever seen." Regaining some control over her own story, she might then add, "She looks like what we will look like when we rise out of the waves one day," inserting private considerations into her authority of the moment. Some would swim away that day and recount the story of the great octopus that lives just beyond the place where the light shines. Others would tell the story to their "grandfishes" of the shark with a flat head and two eyes on either side of her head."

Each fish will be correct. Each fish will be incorrect. Years later, when a baby shark makes the near impossible journey from the sea floor to the surface, she will find exact corroboration of the "great shark above the waves" legend. If she could not agree that this was a shark at all, she would still lack any reference in which to share it. So, impressed by the ineffable experience of something wholly outside of her individual and collective experience, she will return to the waves having seen the great shark above the waves.

SUFFERING

Would you make intellect your tool or your master? Why should our apprehension of God be any different? We already have ample evidence that language fails whether in the exploits of science or in the circular bantering of theology. But regarding God, the infinite, the absolute, the divine, the first cause, and the prime number, we would assert we know he is a male or she is a woman. Remember this, though, that the little fishes saw *something* is beyond doubt. That is not at issue. What is at issue is their knowledge of knowledge.

Jesse, suffering is like an expanding gas, just a little can fill an entire heart. God did not abandon your aunts and uncles. We somehow believe that we have a right to exist and to live no matter the threat or the danger. This is the same inherent right of which a child is aware in regard to her parents; she has a right to take for granted that she will always be protected and cared for as the dangers of this life wage all about her. As she grows and matures, she will be more aware of the threats of the world around her and still expect more from her parents before she will finally come to a place where she transfers that expectation to the unseen hand of her absolute parent. We all do this. From the first moment we look to the heavens for our aid and comfort, much of our parents' spiritual protection has ended. Yet, we cannot always protect our loved ones from the ravages of this life. Though our heart breaks and we feel as though we ourselves have died a thousand deaths by the arrows of loss, we cannot so stop the encroaching arms of death when its arbitrary wings deploy to enfold our loved ones.

There is a precarious balance of life that is always seen as being *out of balance* by those who *have loss*. It is always seen as being *in balance* by those who *have*. This balance is not always apparent to be in support of life or purpose immediately *or* when extrapolated out, even of supporting the purpose of the larger life of the world. From the micro to the macro, we can only infer a purpose and a balance to the world around us when we are sufficiently removed from the imbalance of the moments, the pain of unfairness and suffering. You will never hear someone saying before a firing squad "How marvelous to see life pruning and grafting itself in my victimization." You will never hear the thousands in New Orleans or Southeast Asia note, "Is this not simply breathtaking to watch the equilibrium of life so choose us to find its balance?" The balance of life is noted in retrospect and in detachment.

Suffering is not the possession of the doomed alone. Suffering is like a virus that spreads through the greater community of the world until such a point as it loses its momentum in subjectivity. Thus, the suffering of your aunts and uncles traffics still through your tender consideration of their loss. Yet, somewhere beyond you, perhaps, like waves extending from the center of a pond, the reverberations of this suffering will idle into the great body of water that carried the impact of loss.

While we cannot know the purpose in the mechanism that harvest and balance the world, we can note the effects thereof. Suffering sucks! That is a fact. Suffering cannot be explained away as an indiscriminate purification process. Suffering as we talk of here is not born of self-will (though, there is plenty of suffering of another type which is self-willed). We are talking about the indiscriminate suffering of the masses, and or person. Suffering is not punishment. If I cannot state what the balance is, how can I assert what is not? This is fair, as I will not blow smoke in any one's eyes.

"KNOW" WITH KNOWINGNESS, NOT DATA

Your whole world is not. Everything most people hold as their reality is only a constituent re-creation of life in every waking moment, and what we perceive is not an accurate re-creation. The processing and re-creation of the world we interrogate is filtered through the screens of our intellect and constructions of fear and convention, hope and longing of the heart, and of the flesh. The end result is a very different world for every one of us, but with numerous common areas of collective compliance, agreements on reality.

We know by our senses. We know with a "knowingness" of our super-senses. We know of both of these products by omission and commission. I tell you suffering is not a product of reward and punishment because life is not a vehicle of reward and punishment. The only reward and punishment in this life is what we bring to ourselves, or the relative reward and punishment of community compliance.

Jesse, listen, darling. Your aunts and uncles did nothing to deserve to die. No one does anything to *deserve* to die (absolutely). Deserve is reward and punishment. God did not abandon them nor punish them. There are horrors and inexplicable events in this world that cause us to shutter and grow weak of heart but do not ever give up. We cannot know the things unknowable. Right now there are things that are unknowable. It may not always be the case that this will be so. But it is the case today when we are asking these questions.

Dear child, take solace and comfort in what you know. Live the life allotted to you and feel the emotions and wellsprings that arise from your interaction with this life. Learn how to master your emotions and be not a slave to them. As long as you look from the world to the heavens, you will be unable to fit the pieces of life's puzzle together. Learn instead to look from your window upon both earth and heaven right here, right now. Love with the self-same love as God and the balance will reveal itself to you. I love you, child.

CHAPTER 45

▼

Heaven and Hell

*"I form the light, and create darkness: I make peace, and create evil:
I the Lord do all these things."*

—(Isaiah 45:7)

Dear God,
What is heaven like? Is it like what the poets and other people
describe it to be? What is my purpose in life? Am I here to be a doc-
tor or a lawyer?
Sara

You tell me what you think heaven is like and I will show you what heaven is
like. Do you want to be a doctor or a lawyer, or is that what you are told you are
will be? I will simply tell you that you are here to do whatever your flight of fancy
informs you to do. You can pursue any economically productive occupation you
wish, but always remain clearly fixed on the Prize. All life is not an end in itself;
life is a means to an end. Work is a means to an end. Figure out what the end is
and you will have figured out life. It should not be too difficult as I make it quite
clear in these pages, child.

You see, Sara, when you look upon the world around you, all that you have
been taught informs you to see the world around you as through a telescope, very

directly and absent context and association. Sara, look instead upon this world as through a kaleidoscope. There is such beauty and richness in every moment and passing flight of life. When the poets and artists glean the remarkable kaleido-scope of worlds all about them, we note in the instruments of their creation the silent whispers of our soul's knowledge. We are provoked to a knowingness that does not easily comport with our faculties of reason. Our reason is born of this world and for this world of the flesh.

However, when I inform you that heaven is very similar to the frustrated products of genius and the mad, you can just as easily assume, then, that hell, too, is presented to us in this kaleidoscopic vision. Is it? When beings intuit, and later experience, the breezes of the full breadth of creation, they note the facets of many worlds. It is in this panorama of worlds, not just in the constituent parts, that they impart the profound awareness of God and the myriad nature of life. Hell is not a total state. God, the absolute, is found in the summation of the cur-rents that illume all worlds, the panorama. Hell is found as an abstract of part of the whole. Hell is a state created by the frustrated mind of man to describe dis-franchisement.

Hell is the state of absence of awareness of inheritance. Hell is the cyclic world of illusions, which is categorized primarily by the infatuation with the physical world. Hell is the state of forlornness so aptly characterized in the madly penned words of the humble poet who has focused his kaleidoscope of observation on the state which exists in opposition to the assimilation of inheritance: unitive Mar-riage with the absolute God woven into the fabric of all matter and energy.

We have gleaned hell. We have gleaned heaven. Stricken weary on the fields of the flesh, we have projected with the only conceptual basis we can and have thus concluded heaven and hell are contiguous to the cycle of life and death. Both are wed to life by the base notions of reward and punishment. Both are separated by a diaphanous veil, which has these states separate and yet coexisting right here, right now. To those who have noted, "I am in hell," they are not too far from the mark. Still, others note that this "is heaven." "I am in heaven." These are both assertions of analogy *and* truth.

Your purpose in life is both relative and absolute. You are in this world to explore the potentialities of all that you would dare to dream. You are in this world as part of a whole, a being graced with the inherent power to transcend all these worlds and marry with the source of your being. You are in this world to play, to love, to dream, and to live this life to the fullest expression and expansion of your spirit within you. You are in this world to give aid and comfort to your spirit within you that it might continue the clocking of its approach to God. You serve your spirit most when you serve all. Serve all with love, dear child.

CHAPTER 46

▼

The End of Days

Dear God,
I would like to know what purpose is for us, your people, to be on
earth and not in heaven with you? Are you testing us to see if we are
faithful? How will the world end? Will there be someone else like
Noah? Where is Noah now, in New Orleans? When will people stop
judging you from the outside and look within you? Thank you for
giving me my life and family. I wouldn't want it any other way.
Charlie

My dear child, all people are on earth *and* in heaven. No people are on earth *or* in heaven. You see, there is not as sharp a divide between heaven and earth as you have been led to believe. While earth is very here and now, heaven is not *only* somewhere else. There exists no line of demarcation between the two. Heaven is slowly realized and built on earth before we get "there." The kingdom of heaven is right before you, right now. When you leave this world, the only thing you will then be leaving is the flesh. All the worlds are accessible to you right now, Charlie.

The imaginary place where we leap from "one world to the next" is not the leap of faith, per se. We are not being tested. God is not offended or remotely disturbed by our inability to satisfy our humanity as per *our* expectations. However,

God is magnified by our "escape" from the bondage of the human condition only insofar as we evidence in this manner our participation in co-creation. This is not to infer that there is something inherently subordinate about the material world. Quite the contrary, all that is of creation is worthy before God lest it would not be. What is magnified is our ability to enhance the material world by acting as beacons, as filters, as conduits, as portals to myriad emanations of God. What is further magnified is our affecting universal evolution by action in our own little corner of creation. Not all creatures of the flesh can do this with sentience.

THE HOUR OF OUR DEATH

Would you know the manner and time of your death, Charlie? Many have thought of this and it is apparent that the need to know such profound things is uniquely human. What other creature cannot only consider their mortality but can think abstractly enough to actually consider the extinction of their species and apocalypse? However, to those who would consider these things, it is apparent that knowing such an answer would not empower; rather it would decimate our lives. Christ was quite clear in the wisdom that one knows not the hour of death, nor should we seek such knowledge. He also cautioned about looking for signs and wonders that suggest an end, personally and globally. Why is this, Charlie?

In all times, man has thought he lived in the end times. In every age have circumstances been such that man was sure that none had ever suffered as in the present times. Man was also adamant that no other time ever had all the ingredients available to so suggest the end was near. While it is true that we have among us such awesome power to destroy the world many times over, we are still in the same circumstances of all who have ever lived. When in time to come one looks back on this age and sees all our dreadful toys of destruction, war, and disease, it will be noted that, yes, our survival seemed improbable. But compared to the technology that will (inferred from history) exist in the future, we will be housed in the company of all others who have ever lived that feared or queried their relationship with the end of times.

My point is this: it is just as useful to be able to comprehend the day the sun's annihilation will consume us. The sun will certainly die, but not for billions of years. The earth, then, will surely die one day. We know it will end. We know all life dies. To what end, then, do we labor with such thoughts of our own end? No cell in our body rails against the end and each one is as vital to our existence as the next. A single thought spent staring at a butterfly, or the crystalline appearance of the sun's reflection on a wave crest is a better use of our time. Thinking nothing still is a better use of our energies. You cannot, for all your want, change the fact that you will die and once having died would not have any measure by which to assert you had a long life, or a short life. It makes no matter. What matters is what you do with your time. This is not cliché. This is the most valid Truth.

FORGET THE SNORKEL; BRING SPF 10,000

As your question of Noah *suggests* your background, I would just remind you that water should be your last concern. I would not take matches into the woods, though. "The elements shall melt with a fervent heat, the earth also and the works that are therein shall be burned up (2 Peter 3:10). My suggestion here is based on my perceived understanding of your background. In all circumstances, life is squandered when one frets over apocalyptic dispensations or other portents of the end of times. A day spent sitting in silence is better executed time then the most piercing commentary on Armageddon. Think life. Be life.

In regards to your question about Noah in New Orleans, I repeat again, contrary to what you have been instructed, God does not smite the innocent, the non-believers, or intercede with the riders of the apocalypse to make example or fulfill the prophecies of man.

Prophets may have correlated a collapse of the non-local window, pre-cognitively revealing the future and then ascribing such within their doctrinal model. However, God was not hinting that God would aimlessly maim and punish the innocent thousands of years later. While it may be frightening to say what I have said, I suggest affirming such notions as a personally wrathful God that seeds fear into collective humanity to ensure compliance within the ostensible framework of free will is ever more frightening.

JUDGING

"When will people stop judging you from the outside and look within you?" Charlie, this question goes right to the heart of a mystery of God. When people stop judging others from the outside, they stop judging God. When people stop judging God, they may start to acquire God. People would protest that they do not judge God, but this is not correct at all. People judge God and give God man's failing grade every day. Every day you can see God failing man, according to man. This sad state cannot hurt a patient God, but I assure you it hurts us individually and as a family.

Many declare, "I do not judge others," but this is not really true, is it? We are all predisposed to make value and other judgments. Much of this is so ingrained into our perceptions that we judge just about everything. Judging was, at one time, critical to our survival. In judgment, we anticipated threat or ally, and even pedestrian things such as distance and speed. We have always been predisposed to judge. However, we are moving and evolving rapidly now, and as spiritually "alert" beings we need to deconstruct our biases and look toward pacific acceptance of literally all things. More operatively, we need to encourage our instinctive modes of behavior to comport with our intellectual and spiritual strides.

I am not saying collectively we should have madness and chaos rule, with all judgment being suspended. I am saying that individually we need to transcend the illusion of apartness. Currently, we judge others in such a way that has us at the center of the observation making subjective the observed, suspected behavior, or motive of others. When we have everyone at the center of the world with the default setting that everyone is always doing the best they can with the faculties provided them, we judge not God. It is all your world—good, bad, indifferent, soiled, pristine, it makes no matter. This is your entire world, Charlie.

SELF-DEIFICATION

When people look for God within themselves and others, they look within the heart of God. It is absolutely this simple. Repetition and signs to the contrary have made callous the tools with which we interrogate ourselves and others. However, nothing can malign or make impatient that which is timeless and of all worlds. Within each of us is the very spark of the divine. I do not suggest this with the flippant words of a transparent preacher. I am telling you that God is most definitely inside of you. Be like unto God.

To those who would state what I am asserting is no less than self-deification, I would point out that this is definitely false and absolutely true. I seek nothing less than deification. If any aspires to any less than to become one with God, they have missed the point of existence.

Any fear that any man would have that another would aspire to be like unto God flies in the face of almost every faith. The foundations of nearly all teachings of faith would inspire each to become like unto God. But in practice, the base fears of man manifest and shouts abound as if man could truly unseat God in the process of becoming "like unto." Man can no more deify himself than he could change the orbits of the planets. So what is the fear to find God within? We are not appropriating that to ourselves which steals crumbs from the Lord's supper. We are taking ownership of that which has been promised since time immemorial.

Man will always rail against that which serves to inform him or her of their station in the contrast of another's searching for God within. Yet, when such a contrast is profound or otherwise a critical mass builds from common acclaim man's consistent response is to capitulate and in a complete reversal proclaim the "him" or "her" a vicar, an avatar, a prophet, a seer, a mystic, or a saint. In other words, any man or woman can expect to be outcast from the society of church and peers the closer they come to unlocking the mystery of the Kingdom of God. Yet, when they are over the rapids of the trial and tribulation of the spirit and are so fundamentally altered, the masses stare stupefied and declare them like unto God.

Man asserts in dogma and practice that Man can become like unto God, but beware the child of creation who actually labors toward that end. In the times of Jesus, numerous political and other leaders deified themselves (politically or otherwise), or this was done by others in a given name. In any event, does this title thus make man God? To those who oppose the journey in God within, to those who protest "heathen" and "infidel," I weep for your rage and fear. God is to be found first and foremost in the church of our hearts and in the temples of our bodies. The entire universe is gated within.

Once a Choice Is Made, All the Infinite Possibilities Attendant to that Moment Are Forever Gone

Charlie, many adults arrive at places in their lives and they want so desperately to return to the past to change something. They will bargain with God and say they want to change just this, and not that. They want to redress an injustice, relive a moment, or make one small change that they are just sure will undo everything. The presumption is that life has made a mistake. The presumption is that having changed this one thing, all the other things that have made their life meaningful, given it texture, and built up the database of memories would remain the same.

We cannot return to relive any moment, Charlie. There is a breathtaking freedom in this life as none of it will matter (absolutely) from one moment to the next. Yet, we can never undo the casual results of our interactions in the past. Where, then, is the balance that enables us to be free to live the moment and be willing to sleep in the future we create each moment?

All life is a visible and invisible matrix of evolving drama and becoming. When it is realized that there is so much more going on in every moment, we are literally spellbound by the mystery and awesome spectacle of every human interaction or interdiction with nature. It is truly amazing, child. No amount of written or spoken words can adequately convey the marvel and the excitement that is the consort of one who "sees" this. Child, your life and everyone else's on this planet interact with each other in some degree of separation or proximity every minute. As we are busy commanding this vessel we call our life our spirits are openly intercoursing with and interrogating the physical and spiritual world all around us. It is rather amusing when this is realized. We command nothing. This is God's playground and the only way we will ever get in the game is to "get in the game."

There is a synchronized element to all of creation. Where the faculties of science and faith peer no further into the unseen worlds, they both declare with authority that this is evidence of how close they have come. Science and faith do not seem to get it yet. Though there are within both camps awakened minds that both intuit and experience the unseen world, it cannot be measured with the tools of the senses, nor can it be explained with the faculty or words, at least not by me.

When you state you would not want it any other way, revel in your attunement. There is no other way other than self-imposed exile in regret and misgivings for a life that could not have been spent any other way. Life happens just the way it was supposed to, and were we to "see" clearly we would understand this. It is not that life is predetermined. It is more complex than that simple description. It is that creation has an infinite amount of possibilities in every moment. What we call determinism in this case is simply our inability to grasp such depth and multiplicity with our limited minds. If people process life with their mind only, then they are slaves. If people employ their mind and process life with spirit, to such a person is given true freedom of choice. To such a life is satisfaction granted. Regret nothing lest you have not any semblance of life worthy or recall, Charlie.

CHAPTER 47

▼

On Ignorance

Dear Buddha,
Do you actually look like those statues? If so, why don't people light
on fire when they look at your statues? Also, what's up with all the
not very intelligent people? And why do they run for president?
Another question: Why do you make cockroaches? They're disgust-
ing. Also what's the point of having so many languages? You're
probably expecting me to ask what the meaning of life is, aren't you?
And I'm not going to. How come you don't do miracles any more?
You used to in the Biblical ages.
Max

It is not likely that Buddha actually looks like those statues, but in an endless variety of worlds and possibilities, who knows?

"All the not very intelligent people," huh? I know what you mean. It is more than "not intelligent people" that disturbs you, isn't it? We can both agree that we have met someone in our life that was not very smart, but was immensely kind and caring. It is not the lack of intelligence; it is the brashness, the corrupting cockiness, the disregard for others and intolerance that so upsets our sensibilities. I am sure there are more descriptions but I think we can agree that this is what is annoying, not the lack of intelligence. Not all people are of equal intellect. Not all people are of equal charity of heart. It is an interesting question because it is the intellect that actually causes us the most good and the most harm.

The greater the idiot with whom you are dealing, the more likely this person, the real person, the human with whom you are dealing is saddled with so much luggage that they cannot even begin to see themselves in the balance, in context. We are multi-dimensional beings, Max. The intellect is but a utility that protects us, interprets the world for us, and apprehends context and abstraction, cognition. The intellect has at its disposal the senses and they are like telescopes, potholders, or hearing aids. They extend the range of the mind to interrogate the physical world with touch, smell, hearing, and sight; you get the point.

There is a feeling of inferiority when we are "ran over" by the "idiots." But this is only so as long as we allow the nature of the game to be assigned by their aggression, or ignorance, or argumentative nature. The real game of power is played out in the halls of your mind in knowing the whole story. Most people have no user's guide and do not even know they are blind. Allow them this ignorance. You cannot change it for all the wont to do so. People will not awaken until such a time as the circumstances of their individual lives permit the sun to fully light the dark. By the way, the reason they run for president is for comedy. Who said life was not hilarious? The universe has a great sense of humor.

BUGS, SECRETS, AND MIRACLES

Aren't you glad you are not a bug, Max? It would be awful to have a ninth-grade human taking such an interest in your "different-ness." Would you really want a world with no variety? Don't you think the ugliness of the cockroach serves well to make the blue jay and the Labrador beautiful to behold? Sometimes, things and people have their purpose in what they are not. Think about it.

Max, you did ask the meaning of life. The meaning of life is the total of all these questions, and more. There is not one word, one concept, one song that explains the meaning of life. Sometimes things have meaning only in consideration of the components that lend their individual definitions. The world daily searches for the "meaning of life." However, was someone to whisper the meaning of life in another's ear, it would not even be recognized. The secrets of the mysteries of life are of no value to another until such a time as the foundation and context necessary to associate the meaning and value is in place. But it is the nature of our spiritual DNA clocking on its quest, distilled into mind, that we infer a "Lost Word" or "Holy Grail," for this is the manner and means in which the intellect searches (quests) in the physical world.

Lastly, miracles happen all the time. God is not the only one who "does" miracles. Miracles are those things that strike us outside the range of our known or expected concepts of the world around us and how it ought to behave. Miracles are *super*natural only insofar as they are not commonplace occurrences, or experiences. Miracles happen every single day. Just as the colors of the flowers in a garden are not really those colors at all. The appearance that the flowers are this color or that are the result of the light they reflect, or not. Furthermore, the colors are a product of light, once removed (light, too, is still a further reflection of a source). My point is what you see around you is not all that is around you. Max, people do not routinely note the happenings of over ninety percent of the *visible* world. What do you suppose we are missing in the unseen worlds, the other ninety percent? What are you missing in your world, Max? It is within the realm of the very natural that most "miracles" take place. However, observed by us, miracles appear otherworldly and divine because we are ensconced in physical delusion.

Also, give the idiots and not-intelligent people a break. I assure you everyone is actually doing the best they can with what they have. The reason I know this is because had they more to draw from they would not be so irritating. Learn from all, Max.

CHAPTER 48

▼

User's Manual

Dear Jesus,
I am so happy that you can come visit my great school. However, I
would like you to answer some of my questions during your lecture.
First off, people go to heaven and hell. However, how do you deter-
mine whether someone goes to heaven or hell? Is it based on the
amount of prayer? Is it based on the Ten Commandments?
My other question deals with what happens in heaven and hell.
There have been statements in the Bible on what happens, but it is
still difficult to decipher.
Your creation,
Morgan

Y ou should talk to Sarah about heaven, Morgan. I would have you know a little more about "heaven and hell," though. I know you have been instructed that
"getting in" to heaven or hell is a result of the Book of Life and what is written
about you therein. Further, you instruct what is to be written about you in this
"book" by your actions and your faith in this life. This is often what is instructed.
In sometimes confusing admonishments we are told that only adhering to the
Ten Commandments will access heaven or fervent prayer and deeds. Which is it?
Is it all of these things? Are we not somehow stricken by how we can have so

many requirements for our inheritance and so little with which to work? Should we not have all gotten our own personal user's manual: *From Life to Heaven: How Morgan Can Make It Home to her father*? People do have the general user's manual of the world's various holy books, but often we find great confusion and contradiction in their interpretations.

HEAVEN *OR* HELL

Hell is the absence of God, the absence of the vision which "sees." Most of the hard work to get into heaven is done already. After all, if hell is the absence of God, then it can only get better from here as so many do not now note God. There is a profound absence of God today in the world, at first glance. But, it is only a matter of the vision of the heart that God appears absent. God is everywhere, right here, right now. God is in all places in this and every world. It is not possible for there to be a place where God is not. So, it appears that the burden of being, in or out of God's grace, is a product of our will, of our seeing God or not. In this regard, hell can be so considered for all those who do not now know God in this world.

The majority of information available to decipher the environment of heaven or hell is the product of mystics who "experienced" passions and deprivations of God that were so inexplicable that they fumbled with honest endeavor in the language of the world to share with us their experiences. As time passed, or often in the immediate times, their experiences were either literally interpreted or otherwise appropriated by religious authorities to make this point, or deny that point in support of the current doctrine. God, heaven, or hell has never been noted with the intellect.

Most of the experiences of mystics and saints had everything to do with the process of destroying their reliance on the senses of the flesh, and how the senses disrupted accessing God and caused so often a state of Godlessness in the flesh. The translation of their experiences and visions of God increasingly reflected less the process of individual self-discovery of God and more often became the refection of the authorities of faith. In all times and places, people made earthbound the experiences of the saints and seers, and in this process the experiences became literal. Each journey became jointly owned by the prevailing faith, and no matter the findings the outcome would support doctrine.

We focus with more than our eyes. Hell is a state of focus. Heaven is a state of focus, but within *this* focus we become risen, transcendent, unified. Hell is a state of base affairs. It is inherently incapable of elevation to "focused" application toward God. The way "home" or to remain in a material-bound reality begins with "seeing" the relationship we have with both the physical and spiritual world.

Morgan, it is difficult to decipher and that is why so few are doing it. Have you ever noticed how some things in your life seemed so difficult before you made the attempt and became successful? How many times have you noted to yourself, "That was so easy." It is really no different. It is in a choice, Morgan. It is an affirmation that you will see larger than the size you have been told the world is. It is reliance, Morgan. It is a reliance on the voice of God that speaks within you. Marry this voice with what you are instructed in this world, take a chance and listen to you above others, and serve this voice within you with affection and support. Take a chance and dare to embrace heaven today.

You are in danger of nothing other than a fundamental desire to see the Kingdom of God on earth. It is not a process of tithes and tribute in service to a church or the community. These things will come about of their own accord by the risen nature of your spirit. It is about you, Morgan. It is about the promise that was seeded within your sleeping soul when the stars were but cosmic bursts of thought in the willful mind of God. You are imbued with a tracking mechanism, a beacon that broadcasts home constantly, regardless of your ability to hear this siren song, this lamentation of your soul for its maker. Change the channel, Morgan. Tune in your frequency and pace it within the frequency of God's voice all around you, my child.

In the U.S. military, a technique that is used to send messages to specialized teams in enemy territory is called a BTB, or a blind transmission broadcast. This "broadcast" repeats over and over again at predetermined times continuously. All can tune in to this frequency and hear the idle chatter or background static of the sender. Many who "pick this up" will note nothing more than scatter in the air. Others will hear the message, a message, but it will appear meaningless. Some will catch a glimpse that there appears to be more contained within this broadcast but cannot figure it out. However, to the one that has the proper rhythm (cipher), this message has a wholly different context. This message is a message from "home base." No matter where these teams are in enemy territory, it is of vital importance that they know they are not alone. The teams on the ground know how to tune in to a broadcast that is in the air for all, but meant just for them. God, consciousness, broadcasts endlessly to all. Within this broadcast are the keys to the Kingdom. Tune in.

Heaven and hell are creations of our intent. They can be very real locales of spirit, but I would suggest it has been misleading and inaccurate for custodians of faith to proffer such confusing assertions, such as the soul will be tortured with pains that can only apply to the physical. This really does confuse. Because of the inherent difficulties in intellectualizing the ineffable, the lay come to hold these assertions as truth and the delusion is propagated. The wherewithal to interrogate the spiritual is surrendered to the spiritual opinion leaders and mankind remains deceived. It is all a state of mind. It is all a state of God. It is all a state of will. It is all a state of focusing, Morgan.

▼

CHAPTER 49

Ten Billion, Billion Suns

"God,

If you say you love us so much, why do you let the hurricane happen? Do you have to be a good person on Earth to be an angel in heaven? Did Adam and Eve really happen, or was that a metaphor for why you shouldn't give into temptation? Why can't we give into tempta- tion sometimes? Is it true that people die because of Adam and Eve's mistake? How come you let there be other religions if you know you are the one and only God?"

Leigh

God does love you so very much, Leigh. There is a sea of love all around you. Have you ever been in a crowd and saw one face, one person, that made you somehow feel that this person simply poured forth love like honey on pancakes? Darling, this is the love of God, but magnified beyond your imagination. You would not have noted that face in the crowd were you not to have *looked*. Were you to be involuntarily electrified by the love of God in an *endless* ecstasy of infat- uation and adoration *for you*, your life would be henceforth meaningless. The overwhelming infatuation and love that God has for you cannot be drunk like from a goblet. It must be bathed in, for it is like a faucet that once turned on cannot be lessened.

Have you ever noticed the wise, detached wonder and love beaming from a child? This is the love of God. Have you ever noticed the sweet surrender in the eyes of two people who are in love with each other? This is the love of God. Have you ever noticed the currents of love that pass from your parent to you in an expression of love that needs no words? This, Leigh, is the love of God embodied in life. God pours forth this love across the worlds in a non-stop song of creation and we bathe in this song. In claiming ownership by the grace of what is God-given in us, we communicate God's love through our senses. God's love is everywhere. God does not "let" anything happen, or not. Everything moves in the great body of God all around us. God is both impersonal and personal.

Leigh, do you want to be an angel in heaven? Do you want to be an angel on Earth? Why wait until you die to bear God's song. Why can you not consider being in this life right here, right now and listening to the song of God? You have only never considered this because you have not yet been impressed with the greatness of your being. Be an angel here today and bear the will of God to those around you. Begin forever today. Your body does not need to fly with childish wings to bear the love of God to those around you. Your spirit will soar, Leigh. You will apprehend the heights of this world. You will announce God in your heart and in your life if you so will it, my love.

EVE AND ADAM

Do you think Eve and Adam were, or do you think it is a metaphor for not giving into temptation, for the first humans, for the illusory world? Perhaps it is all these things. Perhaps it is a story based on truth that has been tortured through millennia and endless repetition in the oral tradition. It does not matter to an angel, the requirements and origins of Eve and Adam having served their purpose in the preparation of your flight to the stars. There is much you can be told from others. There is far more that would be meaningful to you if you experienced it yourself. Let go of the knowing and let in the knowingness. Augment your senses by opening the door within your heart to the infinite grace of God begging entry.

You ask, "How come you let there be other religions if you know you are the one and only God?"

Consider what I said about Eve and Adam and their utility expiring in the service of your needs. Religion is but a reach in ritual for the apparent. Passing through the myriad eyes and hearts of our custodians and opinion leaders of faith, we assign our very best to that apprehension. Leigh, all people know in the silent places of their hearts what is real and what is true. God speaks to us all. The eternal stream of God's refreshment and truth pass before our very door each. For wont of filling our cups, all we must do is stretch forth our arm, cup in hand.

Intermittently throughout the day and throughout our lives, we refresh ourselves from…we are not really sure, are we? But we are ever aware that we can more or less refresh, that certain experiences steal the magic while other experiences enable it. We know in some real fashion that we are instruments to download this grace. We know with a knowingness that all the really meaningful experiences of our lives that refresh us are not purchased, bartered, or bargained for. We already know that we ourselves enable our refreshment and carefreeness of spirit.

IN MAN'S IMAGE

It has been this way for all ages. Man has always drawn through self; the peace of God and man's totality was gleaned in these moments. In man's effort to understand and articulate this awareness man has fashioned God in man's image, not God fashioning man in God's image, not God fashioning God in God's Image. I know this is sacrilege to many who have all invested in this illusion, this historical revision, and will vehemently oppose any suggestion to the contrary. The truth must, nevertheless, be stated without fear. Fear is the utility of the custodians. We don't "do" fear, here.

Do you suppose God is offended, really, that we call God by different names? Do you think parents are really offended themselves when a child calls on a make-believe brother or sister that the parents know very well they did not birth? I cannot so believe that the majesty of God is remotely even pulsed by the bickering and bartering to get into tomorrow. The assignment of human-like characteristics and values to the divine has patently paced man's societal and intimate deportment as man has evolved. It is really fairly apparent. To suggest God is the ultimate expression of man is the height of arrogance. God exists unchanged and unaffected by man's pretensions. This is a good thing.

God is a great nuclear furnace burning all the infinite worlds in a crucible of energy and Love's elixir. God moves the absolute will in a deafening display that makes galaxies and the very universe to tremble and cower in awe of God's might and grace. The gravity of ten billion, billion suns cannot begin to approximate the awesome fabric of God's love woven throughout all these worlds. God does not care what we call God. God does not possess a shred of human quality. Man does not even possess a shred of human quality. The human quality we associate with being human is no more than the artifacts of individual and collective ego that has cut and pasted a representative human drama. God has given to us the means of securing the way home in the dark of eternity. Though God notes every life, every passing, every yearning, and every soul that fuses fully into God's current, God is infinite patience.

THE SLIPSTREAM OF CREATION: TRANSFIGURATION

Were you to peer your spirit's "head" into the stream of songs that passes urgently and joyously past you this very moment, you would find yourself sucked into the "ride of your life." Leigh, this entire world would turn translucent, as the awareness of simultaneous worlds would invade your awareness. You would note in wonder the darkness and the light before they became "the darkness and the light." You would understand in the singularity of your awareness that there is no death, that you survive the body most assuredly, and that you had absolutely, positively no idea. Your mind would simply have been unable to get its "hand's" around *this* without experiencing it firsthand.

You would be bathed in internal tears and joyous ecstasy. I have attempted to describe internal weeping previously but cannot. It is not simply poor literary choice; it is a valid understanding of internal rapture. You would be immediately struck by the fact that while you are not you witnessing this, it is you who is processing this experience. You would then labor in sorrow that you would never be able to share this with another soul in the entire world, not finally. It would so amaze you, Leigh, that you would realize you have finally "seen the light" and your life, your world could and would never be the same again. You would for all time have the profound sense that you are severed in twain and you remain earthbound while you sojourn in the fields where grows love.

All the deepest love that you have ever had in all your days would at once be eclipsed and magnified by the awareness of the place in which that love was born. It is trembling like unto nothing known. There is an intelligence, a mystery, a mastery in the dance of these images and swell-song of purpose. It is clear and it is apparent that this, then, is life—real and unvarnished by the finishing of the senses. You will be so profoundly impressed by such things that they could hardly fit inside your head, Leigh. You will wish to die in that moment. Yea, you most certainly will have this seemingly absurd wish to die. Here, before the birth of worlds and the construction of thoughts is your home found, and you will never be Leigh again. You will wrestle impulsively and immediately with the urge to shed your mortal cloth.

You will return like a seafarer having distanced great lands afar. You will idly consider all the things you took for granted previously. You will deliberately try to replace everything back in the "box" from which your world issued lately. You will find, however, that nothing will fit; the "box" is useless to any longer contain your world. The "box" of your memories, photos, family and friends, nostalgia, conventions, values, morals, faith, self-worth, judgment—all things Leigh, can no longer contain you. You are not.

The cries from the neighbor's baby will take on renewed urgency and pitch. The goings-on of bees in their search for pollen will completely stop your day's activities. You will drift in wonder at the sky, at the earth, at the crowds in the mall going aimlessly about the affairs of their days. You will understand things that others do not note. You will assign contexts where previously there was absence. You will have the awareness of exponential change within you, but nothing of your mind can comprehend this, and you will seem like unto madness. Your world will never be the same again, Leigh.

You are changed and are aware that somehow, in some manner, you are possessed of such power and "knowingness." Your life will be richer. Sounds will have texture. Sights will have frequency. Love will be deeper and of such a profoundly different character that you will feel as though you have never loved before. This, Leigh, is the Slipstream of Creation, and this is why it has forever changed everyone who has ever partaken of it. It is not possible you can ever return from this experience. You are simply no longer you.

Leigh, no one can bring another to this place where sings the song of creation, but I bid you look within and refresh yourself from this breathtaking source. All these questions you would but know avail themselves to you in a manner that is at once clear and profound.

CHAPTER 50

▼

Knock and It Will Be Opened

Dear Jesus,
Why can't you come and talk in person to anyone? Another question
I have is how can it be that when it says in the Bible you created
Adam and Eve, but scientists have found concrete evidence that evo-
lution happened?
Love, Tracy

W as Jesus to appear in your town, would any recognize Jesus? Were Jesus to pronounce the word of God before your school, or at the mall, would parents take their children by the arm and walk away? Some would stay; some would listen. Jesus could make them all see past the smoke of their own not-seeing with the infinite powers of God, but is that really free will when the senses have to be commanded to hearken to the Word of God?

And yet Jesus does speak to people still, every day and night, throughout the world. God has always been accessible to those that would truly desire God. What a wonderful and powerful thing to desire in the entire world to talk with and be with God.

Some people really want a new car or a great job and work hard at it their whole lives to secure this. Other people think beauty is more important and work towards marrying a beautiful spouse. Still, others want only money and make this the thing they would imagine as an end to all of their troubles, a fulfillment of all of their needs. All of these things are different goals, needs, and ambitions, but they all spring from the senses. The world is full of people who spend their whole lives in quiet desperation in pursuit of things they cannot take with them when they leave this world. Yet, if there were a way to measure the intensity of their desire, we would find in most all cases that not only is this intensity of desire remarkably great, but it mostly eclipses the background prayers and considerations in these same lives, and their will to talk to God. Often, most people desire God the most when they are in the most desperate times of their lives. Most people do not think God is unimportant, just not as important.

People will dedicate themselves to these idle and materialist goals with complete disregard for all other things and know well there is much hard work in securing these topical goals. Still they labor in an effort to secure the shallow. But when it comes to God, people often have this strange notion that they are owed something. In other words, people allow themselves to sink deeply into the abyss of blindness and muddied intention, but think God should still be available to their imprisoned spirit to assist or reveal to them. In essence, man intuits an inheritance and interprets this, through the distillation of the senses, as a fail-safe parent on the bench of the playground, lest a knee get scraped.

When it is suggested that all we must do is knock and it will be opened, it should not be confused with it will be opened right away. It is different for every individual. In any regard, we so remove ourselves from the natural station of being by our aimless idolatry of the material world that we literally un-train our hearts from knowing when the door is even opened. Of all things important in this and all worlds, man generally chooses to dedicate the lesser part of his intent and desire to manifesting God in the waking world. Yet it is so often the case that most life on this earth besieges God when the idols of the flesh fail and mortality commands a re-look.

WOULD ANY RECOGNIZE GOD?

People do not listen to those who have heard the Song of Life from the lips of God. Most pay lip service to the notion of securing an understanding of God by trying to reserve a seat in heaven through ritual and observation. Even in this observation of the doctrines of faiths there is still a universal incredulity that others would have actually attained this window on forever, a message from God, any message or instrument from God. Man's lack of a relationship with God, his collective inability to hear the messengers of heaven, is a direct reflection of his personal apostasy with the absolute.

Was Jesus to appear in your hometown, it might be sadly the case that he was institutionalized as a "John Doe: no ID." Why would anything be different today?

"He is despised and rejected of men; a man of sorrows, and acquainted with grief: and we hid as it were [our] faces from him; he was despised, and we esteemed him not" (Isaiah 53:3).

It is surely possible that great words, unaccompanied by miracles and impressions of the senses, would garner belief and recognition, but I simply find it doubtful. You see, dear Tracy, Jesus does talk to you. God does talk to you in an endless song of beauty and magic. I hear God and having heard cannot now stop my refrain.

God is talking constantly. There is right now a complete presence of God and of God's voice within your every moment. God is talking to you and all you must do is listen. All you must do to hear God is to truly listen. God will not arrive as a long-haired, dirty man leaning on a staff, swathed in white linen (though this is possible); rather God will appear and talk to you in the most intimate of ways. This is the manner of the ages. Listen within.

EVE AND ADAM AND EVOLUTION

Evolution happened. Eve and Adam were. They are both the case, mostly likely. The argument from each side is no more than the institutions of science and religion having met upon a battlefield where both the convictions of their armies are marshaled. They will slay each other over a point that is meaningless. God is not if evolution is. Science is not if creation is (or science is threatened if creation is). They are fallacious arguments and serve to miss the point, if one is not weary. The arguments are ultimately red herrings. God is not found or lost in the arguments of man unless a heart is so inclined to stay lost in the labyrinth of ritual and distraction. God is found within you right this very moment. God is leaking out of the pores of every living thing and also the insensible rock and complaining brook. God is not in this world in a novel or poetic way, but a real, concrete, and pervasive exercise of love and fulfillment.

Eve and Adam, creation or not, all stand as obstacles. March right past these arguments of man and declare that you will not bother with these things of the mind today. Discover God in your life, and you will see for yourself the irrelevancy of these distractions of your intent and love. Would that I could sit and talk with you of such things, Tracy.

PART IV

▼

An End in Meditations

"When I was a child, I spake as a child, I understood as a child, I thought as a child: but when I became a man, I put away childish things."

—(I Corinthians 13:11)

CHAPTER 51

▼

Dear Sister

Why do I write the minutes of my days? By what means am I compelled to tell a tale that makes no difference to any who slumber in the earth's bosom, walk its crimson shores, or labor in the flesh? To whom do I suppose but one word may matter? I cannot tell. For my age I have refrained from writing my minutes for the fear that it reflected no more than a bid at immortality in the written word. I am likely right. All my life you have encouraged and prodded me to write the minutes of this uninspired life. You have always had a much greater regard for my life than I have. Perhaps I have simply exposed myself a little more to the great writers of the ages and know with certainty that my thoughts and words pale beside the great sages and minds of time. Thus, I refrained from doing as I was asked.

Still, I am sure that I marginally reveal life, at best. I can no more weave a tale than bake a cake. Maybe it is not given to all to write a tale from fiction. However, I am increasingly finding that my tale is even more bizarre than any poet's dream, any novelist's dare, or lover's lament.

I am slipping further into the place preserved. All my days I have kept hidden the secret placc from where my beauty and love resides, except to you, dear sister. From the years now past, I find I am following the breadcrumbs I left scattered long ago that I might find my way home in the dark of my years. I was correct, long ago, when I surmised I would increasingly lose my way to the Light was I to continue to embrace the flesh as all wished of me. I am me, and liked the way I was so many years ago. In the interim I have gained maturity, a little wisdom, and much experience. I now find myself a different man once more beholding the sacred chambers of my heart where burns the Light of the World. I stand deafened by the silence and beauty, amazed at the simplicity and awe. I stand today breathless before eternity and can never return.

There is place in mine soul that moves me to tears in its detachment and profound peace. It is devoid of emotion, attachment, and pretense. It is the place I searched for all my days. It was before me all along. I always knew that it was but was impressed by the need to partake in the affairs of life and endeavor on behalf of others. It is not given to all to embrace life as dogmatically as our forebears. It is not given to me to pick up the yoke of existence and turn my back on the siren song within my heart that moves me to the pastoral lands beyond words. I am no more.

I look out upon the landscape of my days wondering for some time how I am to incorporate the poetry of my heart with the labors of the world. I do not wonder any longer. I cannot do it. Life, time, has chosen for me. Having passed silent witness to the fortress of my soul within, I cannot again forsake what God has given unto me to announce. I am not a religious man. I am not a poet. I am not pious. I am, and no more.

I cannot turn it off. If this is a slide into madness, I cannot say I want to stop. If the end result is to wind up babbling on a street corner or institutionalized on Thorazine, I can no more change course than I could take wing with a lark. There is a wind-song whistling within that beckons to me without end. It sings a song that I am just sure is offered up in an unseen chorus by all life. I stand daily in wonder that the whole world is not hearing this. It has completely consumed my entire mind. I sit here moved to tears thinking on this rapture.

I search my entire inventory and only find skeletons of fear, of hate, of ego, of pain, of loss. I have never discovered such a thing so easily and completely in my whole life. In all I have ever done, experienced, and loved in this life (and I have done and seen more than most of my brothers and sisters will ever have chance to dare), I have never, ever had anything as intense and wonderful as this ecstasy of my soul. It is absolutely the most incredible wonder I have ever noted in pen or heart.

My entire being has forever slipped the bonds of this place. I surrender now completely. It was within me all along, I was always right. They were always wrong. I manifest my world now by no more than sheer will. I literally create and manifest a reality by force of will. I have become a co-creator with God. I care not what other says about self-deification. I pray. I pray to God. I pray to my Beloved. I pray through Life. I pray to Self. I pray in God.

I am no longer even concerned with the little things in life: work, old age, food, and so forth. I should be, I know. It would suck to be strange *and* hungry. Yet, I know with unshakable certainty that I will be fine. And if I pass to a place where I perish, hungry, unsung, unknown, then so be it. I will be fine.

Is this what you knew, dear sister? Is this what you thought? To think so many years ago I almost became a priest. What a loss that would have been. I can have no man between God and me. I discourse with God intimately. God is my Bride, my Lover. I could never have one between God and me. I wonder often if this is a road that others have taken. Is there a process? Am I supposed to be doing something, thinking something? I did not choose this, not really. I have become this as surely as the moth that knows no choice other than the flame that will surely consume. One cannot choose that which they cannot know. My spiritual DNA has been clocking home since first born in matter.

I cannot be the first to whom this is happening. Should I not be writing what is happening, what I am doing? Do I cheapen the experience by reducing it all to words? Has anyone ever really made it to forever simply by introspection and finding the divine revealed within?

I was always right, you know. I always knew I needed to turn off the static from life just long enough to listen to what was being said to me within. Sister, what happens to me?

CHAPTER 52

▼

Epiphany

I stand in the doorway of another dawn, and hold before me my very sanity as an object of curiosity and wonder. I turn it over within my tender hands and consider it as something so familiar. Yet, beyond the security of my embracing hands I hear the "other kids" beckoning me to come play in the fields. The divide is cast. I realize with some ineffable assuredness that this consideration of my very faculties is the final confrontation with a world now passed. I want this. I want this madness, this solicitation of my heart, my very soul. It is fancy. It is pure. It is song that calls to me in colors. It is light that hearkens my considering ear. I take madness in my hands and pull it ever closer to my heart. The other kids can play without me.

I am further empowered every day. I see now that I have been cautious and reluctant to let slip the final landmarks that have defined the world I had been handed. I write of what I behold but retain reservations still about the final abortion of this material filter. I understand now the flags and voices of those who love me and see this passing within me; I am indeed centered and transmuting light. Once they were cautious and tentative but now stand with arms outstretched, finger pointing to the horizon, urging me. They have seen the product of my madness and now know with no regret I must go forth. I am become translucent, transparent of character and mind.

CONSPIRACY

I have known that I have not labored past a certain point in all this psychomachia. I have infiltrated the place inside and have escaped daily with bounty to adore the constructs of this world in thoughts and words of beyond. It is a strange thing this confluence of events and thoughts that conspire to epiphany. What heretofore trivial items, series of words, incongruent actions can so ally in a moment to trigger a watershed of revelation? Not one thing in and of itself comes forth and bears any announcement. No person heralds understanding. Yet, in the deeper places a key is unlocked and cascades begin—euphoric ineffable cascades. The contexts of this life conspire endlessly to reveal to me that which was previously veiled. From moment to moment now, the world about me weaves itself constantly into a tapestry that had not previously hung upon my walls. I live for no other purpose than to melt in Self and God. Still, I fear I tarry at the world's edge.

Were all the persons, places, and events proximately contributing to epiphany tallied up, and reverse engineering of the mind and experience conducted, it is not the case that the deductions or inferences gleaned could have ever been postulated by the human mind alone. Revelations, as such, are not simply the cumulative product of a mind co-processing the data of being in our detached intellectual background and intrusively announcing with wonder when a most probable "outcome" is collated. "Ahh!"

There appears to be some pacing or tracking mechanism that allows the element of "self" that harbors or transmits this information to our intellect to decipher, decode, un-key, and then access piecemeal the infinite library of wisdom that is gleaned through the *portal* when the circumstances, enabling faculties, and infrastructure are in place to "download" awareness. In other words, some component of our being keeps an endless accounting thread for every piece of minutiae, intercourse, datum of knowledge, person, place, time, imagining, and memory. Furthermore, this component of us calculates the infinite probabilities associated with each accounting thread. When the proper or any given formulation of associated data sufficiently processes, remixes, and changes the probability of a new amalgam, an exhaustive index keys to unlock epiphany. This is done quite unawares as the actual brain housing group conducts the otherwise pedestrian business of living.

What Do We Make of It?

Once having downloaded epiphany (awareness/insight) from the non-local world of consciousness, we are not necessarily up to the task of comprehending all of what we "realize." Often it is a case of "knowingness" without even knowing anything different or, apparently, more at all. However, in the private considerations, each and every one of us is sure we are somehow changed by the simple and the profound epiphanies to which we all are party. The reason this apparent mirror effect in the type, means, and mode of knowledge acquisition between the mind and the "other" us is we are, in essence, two beings in one vessel. The phenomenon of seeing the light, dawning, epiphany, or burst of inspiration reveals the two natures of our make-up. We are material creatures with a sophisticated biological computer mechanism calculating constantly the avoidance of pain and attainment of pleasure, or at least stasis to enable being. We are also spirit creatures apparently "learning" or otherwise evolving as a consequence of consciousness, incarnation, probability, and choices. We rarely note the symbiosis.

Often epiphany is not initially comprehended, yet we now know we "know something more." In time, perhaps, we can fully articulate mental handholds around this awareness. Later, we may even be able to convey this wisdom. This is not knowledge clarifying itself. This is us catching up with awareness as our biological being changes and evolves, as it surely does every moment. Often, we will clearly understand and integrate understanding and insight immediately. However, we are only ever steering the ship of ego. Spirit is the commander. When we mutiny and toss the navigator overboard, we will find that the day-to-day functions of being do quite well without ego manifesting the ports of call.

This, then, is when we find epiphany and awareness clarifying in real time. This is when we experience the accounting threads actually processing in the moment as we stare in wonder and watch contexts develop right before us. Analogous (by a stretch) to the digital binary rain made famous in the film *The Matrix*, we actually witness the world daily re-imaged in contexts and understanding that was simply absent previously. The very foundation of life and reality changes.

Coincidence, synchronicity, awareness, and epiphany all mix before your very eyes and make the world stunning and dizzying. In some manner, wherever you are, whatever you are doing, you are revealed to yourself as the nexus of all things. This is the doorway where one stands and looks back at the familiar and ahead into madness.

THE CHAIN OF BEING

Allow me to suggest the fundamental chain of being: first is God, or Consciousness, second is Self, and third is Jen, or Edward, Madeline or Morgan, or whoever we are. Our person is most certainly not the former two, or are we? Encased in matter, we report to the world as only the latter. In our interior musings we hold the same. Yet we are the former two as well. Consciousness manifesting in matter is the cause of our myopia. This is the underlying frustration of all sentient beings. Understanding this relationship is *key* in unlocking the Kingdom of God, enhanced living, and vitality of our experiences.

Within this chain of being, we rarely take note of our interior processing. We are both frequent witness and host to our very spirit within. Most of us spend our lifetime never understanding that the deep insights, which remain naggingly close to our understanding, just below the surface of our awareness, were never gleaned for the insatiable material ego in the first place. Spirit feeds in this world just as surely as cows graze. When the ego is restrained or at least understood, and thus emasculated, the waking person that is us literally syncs in frequency with so much more awareness and information borne of our own, and other, fertile fields.

This is my world every day. Perhaps it is peculiar that I am inclined to note in words what is beyond language. I am not really motivated at all to document the minutiae of my experiences, fearing at some level something is traded in the transliteration of an unknown language. I believe that whether I recall each event and transcendent moment or not, I am forever changed in the process, and experience is recorded in consciousness. My soul will recall all I need to know when required. However, prodded by the love of those closest, I labor in words, a vocation for which I was never trained. I am keenly aware that my life has become something that is profoundly deviant from the world around me. It is simply beyond anything I ever imagined.

CHAPTER 53

▼

A Moth to a Flame

My dear Lord, hear my prayer. I beseech thee, my Beloved, to hear my prayer. To you I have turned as a moth to a flame; before the foundations of the world have I sought your solace, your peace, your place, my Beloved Bride, my Lord.

Hear my prayer, Lord. Grant to me thy Light. I am needy and seek of thy bounty. Grant me your Love, your Truth, your Compassion, and the stillness of my soul wherein I might better hear your echoes and see your reflections, blessed Wife. Grant me your Light, dear God.

INHALE THE WORLD'S PAIN

My dear Bride, make this breath I inhale consume the pain that is of this world and my exhalation bathe it in your love. Make me your instrument. Every atom, each tear, each shrinking breast and ravished babe, may they find nourishment in my consuming their pain. Be there a finite amount of pain in this world, I ask my remaining days be of meaning, of purpose. Allow me, Lord, to take to myself this thing, this pain that sweeps the world. Allow one embittered soul to weep for renewed joy. Allow one fallen star to shine again. Allow even one without faith to be refreshed in the morning of their life. Give to me now this thing I ask. May I be so consumed. Yea, even unto death, may I serve so. May my body be ravaged and my mind lay waste. For to what other purpose can I now aspire?

It is not the absence of purpose that commands this of me. Rather it is you, my Lord, is it not? This request exists not in my inventory. Bury me in the ecstasy and the agony. Seed the world's pain within my house, and then burn it to the ground. Make it count, Lord, and count me among thy servants. Otherwise, take me now. I am ready to cast off this mortal cloth. My holy Bride, do for me as I ask. Do this thing that I may filter the pain with love, anguish with hope, and loneliness with promise.

IMPRECATORY PRAYER

My God, I beseech thee. Look upon the garden of mine enemy. The grass is tended not. They would but tamper my neighbor's yard. They seek but to destroy all—the good and the bad. Nothing less than the end of all things is upon our door, my God. Give to us, then, my Beloved, that strength to persevere. Disable them, Lord, from slaying the innocents in thy name. Reach into them, Lord, but smite them not. Soften their hearts, Lord. May they look upon their treachery in the moment and reel in horror at that which they create in thy name, in thine image.

Empower us with thy Light, my God. Give to us that seat wherein we become not that which we oppose, rather refresh us with Truth and Compassion so as to make our victory worthy of thy pleasure. Arm us, Lord, with the arrows of thy quiver. I ask you humbly, Ye who has always loved me, my God who has intervened in my simple little life numerous times, let us have that power that not simply defeats the enemy, but defines the victor.

Give to us your Love. Let us embrace this love. May we sweep our love across the world. May its overwhelming power slaughter poverty, vanquish fear, engender hope and promise, and seed peace for a time. Help me to win war this way, Lord. If but none other asks this of you, I do. I ask this of you. If every other besets thee with imprecatory prayers, I ask only of your love. Allow me to slaughter mine enemy with love. Save thy lightening for the priests and mullahs.

I need no measure of any man to know this is what I need to battle mine enemies. My war is waged unlike that of many. I am on the front lines, my Beloved. I am in the rear as well. I labor in the flesh and battle in the spirit. Help me to win over every soul I meet. Help me, Lord. May I be your instrument and thy grace shine forth from me. Teach me, Lord, that I may show others where grow the fields of love. You have taken me to this place for this reason, have you not? You have shown me the face of love in this life. I would serve your will, Lord. Trust in me, and teach me. Let me not run astray. Empower me with thy Light. I *am* no longer. I am anew. You have forever lost your son. You have forever gained your groom. You have nursed me, groomed me, and dressed me. Now Wed me.

I am empowered. I am emasculated. I am tenderly wounded by the sheer beauty of what is born in me in love. I take this love and exhale it across the world and share it with every molecule that is our planet. I do this thing with your love. What else can I do with it? What is left but to share it? I can no longer contain love. I thought love might be finite, but it grows stronger each day. My love is now self-aware and replicates inside me. I want to feed it but do not need to do so. It feeds itself now. I feel as if I have no skin, no senses, no protections, no walls, and no barriers. It is as if all things pass in and through me. I no longer know where I begin and where I end. The madness stalks still, but love has trumped any concerns for naught but to love and sleep in the Kingdom.

This love was meant to be before I was a babe. I have absolutely not known anything like this before, though I have always paced just before, abreast, or behind love's shadow. I have never previously known love to simply bear love. I have never so wanted nothing in return—even with you, my Lord. I seek your counsel or assistance. I seek your wisdom or refreshment, or your peace and reassurance. I seek nothing of any now. In this love I seek only to be wounded by its pinions. Is this what you would have me know? Is this unconditional place the place from which I must come before thee?

THE LOVE OF MY LIFE

My God, my Friend, my Beloved, my Lover, it is naught but you I have loved. How could I but ever love another with the power of this love? What person would not recoil in fear from this intensity? They have recoiled in fear and trembling at your breath seeded in me. I have been unable to sustain a love in flesh for my love in you. I cannot serve two masters. I have tried.

Dear Lord, I see you everywhere now. I am lost in the northern breeze. I am drowned in the midnight sun. I see you on every child's face, in the hope of the dying, and in the dreams of those asleep and awake. You are now part of my every moment. You are in the trembling kiss and the lilac's curtsey. I see you in the blue moon of day and in the empty hands of charity. You are in the very fabric of my vision. I can no longer un-see.

In the course of my days I have beckoned your intercourse daily. You always remained aloof. Is this, then, my recompense? I have never in my wildest dreams known such a thing as moves in me. My dreams are empowered. The day and the night blend in a dance of dream/not dream, wake/not sleep, my every moment is fusing. My faith is absent, I know. My fears are zero. My awareness is keen. My love, my energy, is beyond bounds. Could I not have been just charming and witty? Why do I love so deeply, God? Why, Lord?

My dear God, I do not know the reasons or seasons of your plans for me. If it be so that my seasons of love in this life have passed with any other, then I must look toward passing the tending of this lighthouse. I cannot undo your Love with a lesser light, a lesser love, to simply ward off aloneness, to mimic in the flesh what I acquire in spirit. And so, the passing of the years may stand empty before me. But I trade all for your hand. Turn me inside out and make me reflect you to the world.

My Beloved, I have sought you in and beyond space and time. You have collapsed the confusion therefore. I rest in timelessness. My sweet Lover, I am ready to come home. Help me please to do the work I must before I leave. Give to me the wisdom to never un-love, never love less, and to be consumed by that which stirs within my soul.

CHAPTER 54

▼

The Stillness of Waters

When I was a child I lived fully in the world and secreted my compelling sense that God was revealed to me in the inner recesses of my constantly examined thoughts. I was a boy in two worlds. I was two boys. As I grew into young adulthood, my inner world increasingly projected out from me, and I lived less in the world and more in my vaulted heart. Though I was a child of flesh, surely my inner world was powerfully engaging the external.

I was a man-boy of two worlds. With each day that passed from youth, the world fell away, and a new queen enthroned upon my heart internal. The noise that was my life became minimalized, irrelevant in light of the secret changes within. I did not radiate and saturate the external, rather the internal reached beyond the boundaries of my flesh interrogating and considering my world as an odd curiosity. That which could be called the queen enthroned only ever interceded when all seemed lost to save the noisy man-boy. I lost all sense of borders. I lost all sense. These many years later I would see this metamorphosis through to its conclusion. I seek to not-be at all. I will become one spirit in one world: *animus mundi*. My entire life, every single moment awake and asleep, has been in the pursuit of dressing the landscape of court for the queen enthroned.

I am now beyond the sum total of my parts and experiences. I am something more. I am something else. The gardener has gained entry to the portico of my mind and calls to my window demanding entry. The gardener is no longer satisfied alerting me to presence by casting stones on unsuspecting glass, soliciting wages for the day's labors. I no longer catch furtive images of the gardener in the shrubbery outside the illume of my mind's lantern. Emboldened by my green thumb, the gardener seeks fellowship on the throne. I had only ever wanted to landscape the grass and prune the green that borders the court of the queen. The gardener lets not the help slip away.

This night I again wrestled with the tiresome battle waged upon the battlefield of my heart. I was never worried that the world would see that I could not sustain either world, either life. I was always sure that all knew, but tolerated my "traction-less" life for some unknown reasons. I awoke old today and find still those around me either still do not see that I am an imposter or some other mechanism allows them to tolerate indefinitely that I am not fully arrived. I am not playing well in this societal game; I am not "well-adjusted" and never have been. I am cardboard and carry a gun.

This maddening malady, would not the years have wrestled this bloodshed from mine grasp and given me more comfortable attire to make as my cloth, to wrap me up when the night is so cold? Would not the carnage and numerous skirmishes have lessened the clashing, the bloodbath in the belly of my soul? Can I not but rest a little now? I feel so damn tired and am no more able to define or ignore this than a moth is able to flee the flame. I am consumed. I am consumed for my whole life to purchase that which no merchant can barter or bare.

I do not ever have occasions where I question myself. I always have moments where I question myself. I think that no one wants to be part of a "losing team" and thus I endeavored to rarely show to another the places wherein I question even my sanity. May I ever have an occasion to enlist the observation of another for the unseen worlds; I must point them toward the light, not my shadows. So, the years slip and none would but have a complete, nor incomplete, idea of what consumes me, and it surely is consumption. Perhaps none should. In the end, we are born alone and we die alone. As much as I, you, any, hunger for the fabric of another's flesh, another heart, life is a lonely affair in an immediate sense. I fill my cup always from a fountain on the edge of town, but tarry still, unaccompanied, watching the girls at the well. I have traded love for Love this life.

But there are things I never question and that is what makes this maddening at all for me, not that I am being consumed in God and that the battle wages. I never question that. I never question that I am immortal, that I survive my flesh, that God exists. I never question that I access daily the greatest open secret in all creation. I never question, no matter the force arrayed against me, that I have a most intimate and wonderful relationship with my God. I never question I have known God in my life.

I question whether I am apprehending this Light at times or slipping into the corner where light bends not. In anticipation of my Beloved, I once more make good the day and retire to the world called "my place."

I Slip in Darkness; I Land in God

I slipped into the darkness of the Yemen night. The sounds of life, of promise, of tomorrow, of children, drifted through the still, evening air. In the distance I could hear a dog barking. I breathed and expanded my belly like a great bellows resting upon the hearth of my seat. I breathed.

I breathed and felt the warmth coursing through me. I closed my eyes and looked there, right there. With each inhalation I felt the sense of micro-tearing. At the last of my inhalation, as my lungs filled, as I pictured every single atom in the world racing into me, I felt as if I had electricity coursing through me. I exhaled. I affirm that which I create in my mind is as real and as valid as that which is held in the palm of the hand. I slipped slowly feeling my body relax. I was here. I was not. The descent happened in moments now. I quickened to silence over the past year or two.

I could feel every single place and piece of my body. I was aware of every fiber and sinew and yet it both felt and not-felt to be mine. I was just me breathing and looking at this place just inside the wall of my forehead. I had long ago imagined this place to contain a third eye, but I have never seen one. I have been told to look for a third eye here, but it is not an eye for me. This is the place where I affectionately poke my friends in their "third eye," in their forehead. No, I have never seen a third eye, but have come to realize as I slip into breathing I have a single point of light in this place and now solicit its kindling. I concede this is necessarily the place of which is spoken in scripture.

I focus on this point increasingly and its memory joins the band of overpowering events, experiences, and the like that are daily driving me to profoundly sensitive heights. This little point of light in my mind's eye had once left me with the sense that I was blinded. I was. The light was so intense, so blinding, that I fled and literally opened my eyes with my arm over my face as if I was blocking the light. I was struck further by the fact that the light in the room was less bright, so much so that my eyes were immediately relaxed by the ambient light. It was as if molten metal was suddenly cast into ice water. I was wounded by this light and it left an indelible impression on me. While I had circumambulated this light with my mind, it always seemed when my mind attempted to look directly into it that it faded. It is the light of my world and it was only really seen in all my journeys inward in a peripheral sense. However, recently I have done something quite different in my consideration of this light and it has grown brighter and brighter. This would again be where I sought to go to this night. I remembered physically the sense that my body, too, was warmed by this blinding.

INDUCTION

Breathing rhythmically I considered the intrusive thoughts that executed my silence always. I was taking some note, however, that my very thoughts were lessening, both intrusive and in general. I never thought I would declare that I was thinking less, but I was, and I have waited all my life to stop the "voices in my head." I considered each thought instead of opposing them. I allowed each thought instead of feeling violated. I made each thought the tapestry and mapping of my internal battlefield, and in so embracing them gave to my own generals considerable advance knowledge of the landscape upon which my war was waged, and the incidental intelligence on the health, motivations, baggage, and behavior of the beasts in my bevy. Now, they more or less surrendered, and I am rarely opposed as I venture within. I have occasion where idle or troubling thoughts intrude in defiance and to these I just smile, having long ago defeated their masters.

I breathed. I felt my body. I sensed my organs, my sex, my intestines. I heard my blood moving through me. I felt my heartbeat. I became detached while remaining attached at the same time. I was moving through me, in me, and still not moving at all. I could feel the very same gravity-type sensations one would feel on a roller coaster, an airplane's rapid descent, or a car going quickly over a hill. The sense was not speed, but rather dropping. The pit of my stomach responded alerting me that I was falling.

I have no sense of space or time here. I am not in a forest and am not in a house. I am not a king, and I am not a pauper. I am in Yemen. I am not. I am aware that I am aware. I know I am me, and I am keenly aware of *everything*. I could feel my body. My body was paralyzed. I am completely aware and note now the dead-like mechanical body that awaits me in vacancy. I was aware in crisp, sharp vividness.

I fell and was now floating freely above the world, but not. I breathed. I was awash in bright, clean light. I felt from within me waves of love. *I was in love*. It was coursing through me the way adrenaline courses through me, and commands my responses. I am absent gravity and looking upon stars. I turn lazily on no and all axes. I would not always see stars and such sights, but these were among my favorites. I loved these voyages so very much. The overwhelming power of what moves through me has intelligence. It possesses and informs, queries and responds. The silence *is* the Light. The Light *is* the Darkness. The Silence *is* the Darkness. The Holy Dark *is* both! I am vacant in the still silent worlds. As overwhelming and beautiful both the feeling and the experience are, this is not the destination. This is the Holy Dark, the latticework and bath in which we all birth our being.

Weeping, I started to rock me. I began to animate me. I thought I should remain still as I have heard tell others do, but I could not. I was crying, and it was moving in me. What is this? A hundred times, a thousand times, and I am still not even aware what is happening. I know what is happening, but I am confused. Yes, I know what is now happening. I have engineered my entire world around coming back, every single day. Am I an explorer? Can any man have seen this and not return? Day after day, year after year, I come to the edge inside this place but do not always go further. For most of my childhood I had only ever cast my light and retreated. I am aware I am in the void. "Shhh! Be still. Surrender. Surrender."

SURRENDER

I am thrown forcibly from my own heights. I can feel in this place seemingly all things and nothing at all. Lost is the moment. Gained is the moment, I suppose.

I saw the lights of distant stars, of whirling worlds, and they all appeared to be in the same place that this earth was. I saw through things. I saw pixels. I was aware of the familiar sense of floating, and I considered that the things I was seeing were my own constructs in this emptiness, perhaps. I now consider all things possible. I had many times just floated in the embracing dark, staring ahead at the light before me. Are we all pixels in this place and no more?

I was in love and beheld my lover, and she was in me. I was in my Beloved. She dressed not in gown or matron's attire. My Bride played coyly not in open fields. She imparted her kisses as a lover might from pillow to ear, with naught but the streetlamp to silhouette her pursed lips. I thought that this must be the place where my voice might be best heard to my God, to the host of the heavens, to life; I spoke. I affirmed:

"I am *the* Light."

"I am Truth.

"I am Love.

"I am Compassion.

"I am *the* Stillness of Waters.

"I am *the* Siren Song of Souls.

"I am Hope.

"I am immortal."

Here in this place I asked to be heard above all my waking thoughts, fears, wishes, and prayers. I called upon God not for myself but for my beleaguered brothers and sisters stricken weary on fields of war. There is simply nothing I lack, need, or want in this life. I had long ago attained every hope, dream, and prayer that had ever crossed from consciousness. My Beloved, am I ever closer than unto you now? Is not my heart aflame by your proximity? Is this not then the altar of altars, the final *sanctum sanctorum*? Dear God, hear me. May my will be manifest in yours. May your will be manifest in mine. Make me thine instrument. May my care of your love be pleasing unto you. Give to me to will the bath.

I breathed and in so doing imagined the pain of the world in particulate form being inhaled by me. I exhaled the now-light from my focused heart. I inhaled again this pain, this air, and this thought and asked to be blinded again and consumed.

From across the worlds, from the homes of the affluent and the filthy alleys of Delhi, from Latvia to Jakarta, from Narita to Des Moines, from Buenos Aries to Gaza, I pull this particulate into my being and exchange "God's grace removed" in return. I consume the fictional formula of finite pain. I marry my mind to my brothers and marry my heart to my sisters throughout the world. No day passes when I am not considering their loss, their hope, their troubled dreams, and physical needs. I want them all to take this love that I cannot contain. In so doing, I breathe the breath of God upon the world on the windless days when my brothers and sisters need breeze. I dream for them when they cannot dream for themselves. I will the sea of consciousness when they cannot will the tides.

Time? I have no idea how much time passed. I sought to be lost. I desired to not return. I want to die in this place. When I give up this body I would want to be right here, right now. Were my body to expire at this moment, my tears were already well beyond me. When I am awake and moving throughout my days, I think of this place and want to be here. When I am happy and secure, I want to be here. When I am in the throes of love, I want to be here. When I am nearer to God, I want to be here.

I opened my eyes and heard silence in the hotel. The hotel emitted its own sounds now that the humans had turned on the television of their dreams. I thought on these sounds. There was creaking of wood, the complaints of an old roof, the scratchings of a mouse, and the bodily emissions of a dog in the far house. I was effused with a sense of peace and of rest. My body was warmed, my face swollen, my vision blurred by the additional lens of tears. I was still here but felt nonetheless that I was going somewhere, and I was packing my belongings each day.

▼

Where the Light Bends Not

What have I learned of love in this life that I could give to you of your cup's needs? What is it you would have of me? What would you have of you, my dear friend? Would you be made whole in your places were I to fill in the space of the overwhelming night? Is it in the corners of your heart where the light bends not that I may hold your hand? Tell me, my friend, where bends not the light in your world? Is your love, your light, unrequited?

In this world where we intercourse with our brethren entombed, do we rarely ask ourselves the truly meaningful questions about life, about love, or about God? I think we must, with most tender compassion, concede we do not. We finally surrender to others to illuminate our places within. We are in a constant state of *relative* unrequited love and abdicate our sovereignty to discover and declare love. What are these masks of love and how do they slay us and stalk as love eternal?

RECIPROCAL LOVE

Think on this with me, my dear one: is there any *ultimate* unrequited state of love? All love is of value and meaning, regardless of its return in kind. Need I explain the love of reciprocity? Reciprocal love is how we are taught to define love in youth and as such becomes the paradigm by which love is defined for the remainder of our lives, in most cases. Reciprocal love is a lesser state of love. It is in the state of relative reciprocal love *only* where the heart comes to know this unrequited state.

Love beyond the horizon of our thinking, the breathtaking selfless love where reigns bliss in love itself, requires a complete dissolution of all our inherited land-marks. Absolute love cannot be destroyed or changed. It is no less than pure energy, pure will, the experience of consciousness. Our understanding of our ulti-mate expression of love will surely change with each passing year, each wounded heart, every elated joy. We evolve with our understanding of love and embrace either a deeper understanding of love, or, wounded in the flesh, the darkness of unrequited love, loss, in a relative heart. Love, divine love on which rests the lat-ticework of all creation, is omnipresent and omnipotent. Absolute love needs naught but itself and its reflections thereof. When we are conduit for the mystery and grace of love, we forever lose any need to be loved. We are love.

What I am talking about is such that the human heart will wrestle over that which it perceives as the unknown and the unknowable. *Love* is unknown to most. *Love* is unknowable only insofar as the heart that first perceives it is not that which began the battle to break free of the chains of illusion and obtain it. Never-theless, *Love* most certainly is obtainable in the flesh.

MUTUAL LOVE: THE LOVERS' ELIXIR

What of love in mutual surrender, this love of lovers, total reciprocity? Is this not the love to define the ages? Is it not herein where the purpose and the pain, the glory, and the hope of life are magnified through another?

Love in mutual surrender is naught but the reflection still of its higher form, dear one? This elated state of sensory and emotional love wherein all effusion is melted into orgasmic ecstasy of mutual abandonment. This thing, this love, this romance of the spirit that would take God to the bedchamber in the passion of another's flesh is the highest expression of the state of earthly love, the physical world. Yet, is love truly fuller, more complete, with the elaboration of another? Can more be added to all? Does the addition of love to complete love have a syn-ergy? I had always assumed so; I no longer do.

I had previously not understood how one could love two, many, even all. I now realize that love does indeed multiply when divided. I see that love, abso-lutely, can neither be added to nor subtracted from. How can the complement of another's love grant any greater value, synergy, or voice to the heavens than the secret song of a single heart beckoning the eternally soliciting Heart of the World?

UNDRESSING LOVE

We couch our fears in the guidance of others. We surrender our introspection to the keen eye of the intercessors. When you and I lay waste our garden and strip bare the world inside, we will find the self-same thing within each of us. To you that are Jewish, and she that is Christian, to the atheist and the Muslim each, the Hindu and the Buddhist, to the babe and the decrepit, our hearts beat but a single beat in cadence with the divine love of the world.

When we peer into the corners where bends not the light of the world, we will not only see that we are inherently capable of discerning these places within ourselves but are the only ones who can illume them. It is the baggage of the ages that disables us from thinking, we have no right to do this introspection ourselves, and thus introspection becomes only a fancy for the idle or dreaming. The intercessors remain employed.

In the wasteful accessories that accumulate unto our existence we shroud the light within. Like successive pieces of muslin gauze over a light bulb, these unnecessary burdens of being blot out our existence. Yet, we all remain vaguely aware that something burns within us still. In the quiet places where sleeps the world, we feel this love and we see our beauty. We only wish others saw how beautiful we really are inside. We only wish we, too, really, really projected this beauty that we just know is inside. In the tenderest of moments when we consider the really deep questions, we all know there is something we missed, something for which we are waiting, and something that is set aside just for us. We all retain the integral realization that we are destined for something, though we often cannot put our finger on it.

WHY DO WE HAVE AN OBSCURED LOVE, A BENDED LIGHT?

And so, slips the years and as a quarry slave arising from the mines, we lament the passing of…something. We forgot something. What was it? Where did it go? We awake and somewhere in the passing of the night slipped our age. We note the graying at our temples and measure our fading from the world in the deaths of others, in the fads of the day, and in our lamenting hearts. In the desperation of many a heart, refuge is again sought in the same mechanics that entombed our light.

In the places where bends not the light, the muslin must be examined, considered, removed, and abandoned. Nothing less than destroying the entire fabric of our internal world can set aright the natural stasis of our heart. I assure you, dear friend, you cannot damage by introspection that which exists in your spirit. No damage can come from the considered mind. The person who has the capacity to do damage to self lacks the ability to access the places wherein damage can be done. One does not permit the other. Remove the muslin and the light will cast into the shadows where it had not.

OBSCURATION: GUILT

There is born to you nothing that you should feel bad about in this entire world. No matter what you have done, no matter whom you have hurt, by omission or commission, can anything be changed for one wish or another. There is no act that makes you soiled, makes you dirty or unworthy in the large endless universe in which you toil. Be done with notions of guilt. It is the height of arrogance to think you, in all these worlds, have so erred that the cosmos is allied against your aims. Guilt is the peripheral arms of control. Whether intended or not, guilt serves that end in the countless hearts of billions which disable direct discourse with God. Guilt keeps employed the intercessors that would have you soiled and unworthy to be crowned beside your maker. Guilt serves as chains and muslin gauze upon the light within.

Guilt is a sense of failure in our performance to others. Guilt is a failure in the performance of our own expectations. In this case, the performance objectives are set by others as well. Yet there is none that walk the earth now or in the past who have any more of a clue of what your life's needs are made. Life is a very individual thing. You were born alone, and you will die alone. You belong to all things, and to none at all. You are one with all life, yet live in an *apparently* dualist world. Your life is a paradox, for sure. But it is *your* life.

The child looks over his shoulder with a smug satisfaction at having completed kindergarten and can now move on with pride to first grade. However, unknown to the first grader is the distant confidence and pride with which the twelfth grader moves on to college. It is an awareness that will be *known* one day, will be realized. By the time that one is aware of the long train of lessons past, one starts to get a hint of the great infinity before them, but not in first grade.

How can anyone have anything other than pure compassion for his own heart and tender life when it is realized that he can only do with his life that which is within his power to do. Guilt sets in when one is in a different grade and can see in retrospect that his previous actions do not comport with what is *now* known. No one has guilt for that which has not yet happened. Guilt is a product of the illusion of the arrow of time. Is there one among us who has felt guilt for the future? Have pity. Have mercy on yourselves.

OBSCURATION: SIN

Sin is the archaic imperative to both define and to assure compliance in the absence of observed behavior. Sin serves to establish conditions for the accepted behavior of peoples. It is, at its basic level, a tool of conformity. This does not mean that the imperatives, mores, conventions, and laws that sin often represents are tolerable or otherwise acceptable in communities, or even private behavior. Morality exists independent of sin.

Sin is a concept born of collected accepted behaviors that evolved into the jurisdiction of the priesthoods as nation-states and tribal fiefdoms coalesced powers from the ruins of tribal, nomadic, and agrarian peoples. Sin became a tool of compliance and increasingly had the weight of divine commandment as sin evolved with man's projection of God and society. Through inculcation, sin was impressed unto the individual and collective imprint of humanity as being disabling of the reward. The reward is no less than the promise of the Light.

However, the Light, as it evolved to be the exclusive domain of the intercessors was no longer within this world. It is at this time in the past that the Light was cast without. Christian scriptures grant bibliological evidence of this perversion of the state of our being in succinct verses such as, "The Kingdom of God is at hand" (Mark 1:15), and, "Be still and know that I am God" (Psalms 46:10), and numerous other verses. In fact, most all that the Christ said and did during his ministry was designed to elaborate these statements, finally. Christ, in speaking within the context of first-century oppressive and restrictive Judaism, could not possibly have been as emphatic as I am here. However, Christ did instruct on all these same points beyond the parable. If one considers beyond the synoptic, or canonical gospels, it is apparent that Gnostic or Gnani enlightenment was Christ's advanced revelation. Beyond the Judeo-Christian tradition the Eastern mysteries more clearly affirmed the loss of *lux mundi* as Maya (illusion) became more fully embraced with our evolving command of the material world.

I must address the issue of sin and the Christ. Did Christ state that sin did not exist? No, Christ did not state sin was a model of thinking that influenced delusion. The reason is twofold. First, the underlying behaviors represented by the notions of sin are indeed often repugnant or otherwise reprehensible. Secondly, the existing framework in which Christ ministered was Judaic orthodoxy. Christ came bearing a new covenant, not to destroy the faith in which he ministered. It is highly unlikely Christ could have provided such considered and advanced concepts when the rabbis still informed that women were stained and cast invectives upon Ishmael, Rome, and others. Indeed, the Jews already had a difficult enough time fulfilling the evolving covenants from the Adamic to the Mosaic. This is evident in the internecine division of the first century priesthood. It is not what sin represents that is dangerous. It is sin's *attendants* that impair. The concept of sin obscures the Kingdom, finally. Sin binds the mind, immediately. Lastly, the concept of sin being disabling is an advanced abstract consideration. While there is need to educate on the final severance of bindings, the majority of peoples live in the immediate zone of the loyal faithful. There are more applicable and useful parables and injunctions for the masses. Have no doubt; all that we are talking about in these pages are highly evolved concepts. Many of these concepts would be difficult to consider at any time if the label "blasphemer" were not repudiated.

Inherent in the concept of sin is the notion that to even query the nature of sin is somehow sinful itself. It has been inculcated into our individual and collective being that even questioning the validity of sin is damning. This implicit arrangement perpetuates the hegemony of the intercessors. Mind you, unless you suspend that one critical notion, you remain within the "box." Consider this: intrinsic to sin's survival as a behavior-compliance imperative is the notion that questioning sin is a sin. This is so circular that one should be evidentially forced to reconsider sin, its context, origins, and resultant impact. Brothers and sisters, this is an awful lot of restrictions to secure what is otherwise your inheritance. Remember, it is not what sin represents that is dangerous; it is the attendant baggage that disables us.

Sin is self-effacement. Sin presumes that Man, running to and fro with seeming purpose on some orbiting piece of rock in the distant corner of an uneventful galaxy, in all these worlds, can offend God. How preposterous.

OBSCURATION: EVIL AND GOOD

It is hard to explain to someone, anyone, that good and evil do not exist, that they are constructions of words to define concepts. Our individual and collective memory asserts that these two descriptions for the glory and the horror of being's extremes do indeed exist. Perhaps it is semantics. Yet, I have the strongest notion that just allowing people to believe in good and evil without informing them otherwise would just be fine were it not for the fact of this concept's relationship with sin and guilt.

The notion of good and evil begins at the furthest reaches of what the mind can consider for each: for evil, many in this century invite another to consider the horrific excesses of Adolph Hitler or Pol Pot. For good, many might point to Mother Theresa, Mohammed, Christ, Krishna, Gautama Buddha, or any other number of enlightened hearts who have and continue to bless this earth. But, this is not where it ends. From these far poles, we collectively and individually start working our way to the center. By the end of the day, all manner of things are on one side or another. Before long, in our private observations or agreed standards, most human behavior can fit inside of good *or* evil. They serve to embrace nearly all things in this world. This is a perfect example, in the collective, of how we build the "box" up around us and then are no longer even aware that we cannot see outside of it.

Good and evil do not of themselves have any power. However, when they march across the light of our world and shroud Truth in the chains of irrationality, sin, guilt, and fear, then mere descriptions for behavior become something much more destructive to the "Kingdom of God." I have seen what stalks as good and evil. I know quite well the horrific excesses of the human heart. I have known the tender good of extreme compassion. I understand what we speak of here. I ask any to suspend what they know for what they do not for a moment longer. Remember always that these two concepts cannot be divorced, not in their application or in our consideration. They can only exist in relation to each other. They only exist in abstract. However, the poles of good and evil, encompassing all within their horns, affect greatly our detachment from reality. Good and evil make assignments within the "box."

There is a place beyond the flesh where all this life, all the world of the senses is made truly meaningless, yet still relevant. It is to this state a devastated parent seeks answers when he looks into the eyes of a parish priest or other for an explanation for the untimely passing of a child. "Why, God? Why?" What can any man, be he of God or lay, say to ally the pain of the demanding mind to understand such a thing? Nothing. Even here the demanding mind seeks consolation, not answers. One cannot so inform in grief that this world is truly meaningless, save for the immediacy of the value placed on it by those within it ("it" being what is in reference).

Yet, it is in this grief so often where this very question is considered for here exists the pain to probe, and the issue itself. Why does God allow this? Is this not evil? Where is the good in this act? Is not the issue of good and evil here? Is not the tragic issue of evil manifest in all the starving lands where reigns forced famine, and the First World turns a blind eye for reasons of national self-interest? Is not the forced famine evil? Is not the omission of aid a lesser evil within the poles of good and evil? Do I alarm my brothers and sisters when I state that none of it matters, in the end. None of it matters in the now. It is in between the horns of the polars good and evil that man defines his actions and shackles himself to guilt and sin. The moral imperatives exist nonetheless. It is the baggage of adjunctive and disabling guilt I invite you to consider today.

BEYOND THE HORNS OF THE POLARS EVIL AND GOOD

I maintain it is not sufficient to announce the Kingdom of God to those who are hungry, subjugated, weary in loss, and destitute of opportunity to common dreams. I have spent my life defending those who cannot defend themselves. I have placed the blood of my heart and flesh on the altar of this world to make meaningful what I tell you is otherwise meaningless. Why? *Because of the immediacy of the value placed on [it] by those within [it].* All life is in a state of relative and absolute paradox. One of the keys to the Kingdom is the detachment to "leave even your mother" in the awareness of the relativity of all things material. However, we are material creatures at the same time, and this awareness does not invite us to mountaintops to contemplate; rather, it infuses compassion of such magnitude that we are obliged to lend a hand to the first grader lest he stumble and get left back. When we are finally able to leave this world, we are finally no less than stewards. While suffering within the horns of the polars good and evil are indeed meaningless, understanding this fully leads you right back into the very fray to engage and lend succor.

Entire industries have been built around bringing God *to* you, you *to* God. They all presume that God is not with you now and that salvation is conditional and performance-based. It is in this place where the light bends not. Good and evil become more than definitions when they become a road to salvation in the mundane and the spectacular. With all things proscribed on one side or another of the good or evil line, we allow the collective to inform us of our access to forever. We allow ourselves to be placed in the collective box by those who know not the minutes of our souls. We allow "[my] place" to be constructed by those who may well have been in first grade. But assuredly, if you ask any in the industries of God, they will affirm with conviction the rightness of what they sell you. They believe this, too, as they do not even know yet there is a second grade.

THE "BOX"

Burdened with the baggage of endless labels and restrictive conventions, we approach not a valid existence. That which obscures serves to reinforce the "box," but is not necessarily the architect. Man, in capitulating to fear, among other reasons, is the architect of our delusive reality. We then develop our understanding of life and love in the context of what is available for our consideration, example, and clear vision. That which obscures must be disabled. That which obscures bends our light.

WHAT THEN IS LOVE?

Love does not exist in reciprocity; this is delusion. Love that is based on the solicitation, and receipt of the same is not love. It may stalk as love. We may call it love. It is not, however, love. We are taught by example and experience that love *is not* when it is not returned in kind, when we do not *feel* loved. This is the meaningless and pedestrian love that is an imposter. Love that serves that end which seeks to see itself adored or even acknowledged is not love.

Love is coy and playful. Love is not empowered by the receipt thereof; that is part of the illusion. Love is empowered and grows exponentially within you when you love with complete abandon. Would you *aspire* to fully know love you would find you love grow and pace your manifestations in the flesh with explosive bursts of pulsars within. Love will shortly burst forth from you, irradiating all those about you. While reciprocity is never the focus of absolute Love, you will find yourself loved absolutely. The simple act of inculcating a new paradigm of Love into our waking world shortly bears fruit. Today, tomorrow, one may not note the changes taking place within. However, in due time all the landmarks of life will shift dramatically and one will begin to see where one did not before. Life will take on a richer texture. Sounds will be sharper, and perception greater. There will manifest in one such as this a profound repose and peace. This in itself invites the love denied. The paradox is that by the time one is loved easily and without condition, you will be beyond the place where reciprocity matters.

DO YOU THIS!

It is to these things, these steps that I invite you to slowly introspect. What are the things that you carry around with you that labor your days and make soiled your blessed estate? Look to yourself for a brief time and suspend the intruding outside world long enough to come to know you. Allow you to remove the furniture of your heart and clean out the corners. If, when you have considered each artifact, you wish them retained, they will of their own accord make residence again, but likely not. Once having inspected these cluttering ornaments it is more likely the case that you will finally be able to un-see the way you had been. You may naturally cast such things aside. Go, and when you have spring-cleaned your house, see then if your cup is full. With renewed vision you will wonder how you were ever blind. The colors and richness of your world will forever reset your life.

If you were at a high altitude, above roughly 12,000 feet, and you did not breathe oxygen, you would die; but there are a few intermediate steps prior to death. You would continue to exchange air normally. It is not suffocation that ensues, per se. However, there would be less oxygen in each respiratory exchange. Slowly, your mental status would suffer and soon you would go to sleep. However, if you were to inhale a breath of oxygen from a console or a bottle you would note the following: as the inhalation draws in the oxygen, your vision goes from the narrow to the panoramic. You would not even be aware that you were seeing narrowly. Also, color would dramatically inject all your vision. Again, you would not have even been aware color was vacant your vision. In fact, now aware that color was absent, it retroactively contrasts the difference so that vision seems even all the more remarkable. This is what it is like to unseat the obscurants within and finally "see" the light of this world. It is unlike any experience you have ever had. It is like being "born again" into the world. "Except a man be born again, he cannot see the Kingdom of God" (The Christ, John 3:3).

THE LIGHT, AS DEFINED BY THE DARK

I would inform you of the light within by describing the darkness. The avatars talk of light. In all the literature of our mystics and sages, we are guided to aspire to the "light." We are informed of what can be within only by contrast to what we find on inspection. They instruct our hearts to recall the light of home, the Light of God, but what of the dark?

The darkness is only ever what the light is not. This informs by omission, but it is misleading. Darkness has two natures. In prose, darkness counterpoises the light by inference, by omission. It nevertheless makes up the majority of material reality as well. Light is always that which illumes and contrasts what? Darkness, my dear one, is the light, no less, illumed. Its utility in prose is in what is not. In the material world the breath of God has pulse, too, in the dark. No one aspires to the dark as instructed by tradition only. When novices transcend it is a collective experience that light pierces dark. However, by the point when aware dark and light are one and the same, language fails, and no need exists to inform the aspirant of this.

I have a notion, born of my own experience that informs me thus. There is no light, and there is no dark. In the worlds where handholds and landmarks fail there is simply no construction of language that can properly describe and inform. When each man, each woman peers into the space, the void, the ether within, they are informed by the observer of the findings. Each moment and experience, each consideration and discovery, is processed in the moment—or later—by the human filters with which we journey inward. The *early* introspection into the quiet places where we would supplicate ourselves in dreams, to God, in prayer, in meditation, are filled with images of our mind's creation, of perceived findings, of real findings, and of worlds beyond our external. Many have profound audio-visual revelations and visions. Many have simple and uncomplicated audio-visual findings. This, it is suggested, is the default mechanism to process the internal. I support this. Who has not among us had such thoughts and experiences when the pulse has slowed, the breaths reposed, while sleeps the world outside? However, some do not have this experience. I assert there is eventually a point where all will not have the audio-visual findings on the journey within.

THE OBSERVER

Who is the observer within? "He is our mind," say some. "She is my soul," says others. When your mind sleeps, the observer ventures forth in dreams. "Well, some part of my mind remains still," counter skeptics, "and this explains the observer in dreams." When we consider any issue, create any thought, or work out any problem, we can all recognize (if we consider) the small still voice within in attendance. It seems as if this is our mind working inside, our voice without vocals.

Numerous studies have concluded that many patients undergoing general anesthesia have out-of-body experiences. There is a consistent percentage of patients who report similar experiences. While these events have questionable verification in scientific literature, the fact that they are continually asserted by patients is not in dispute. Moreover, excluding these out-of-body experiences, patients undergoing general anesthesia often have remarkable clarity in recollection of the surgical proceedings. The point is simply this: who is the observer if the mind is in the surgical plane? The surgical plane is, by all accepted definitions, degrees of life support just above death. The goal of anesthesia is to take a person to this plane where the mental activity to process pain and the related phenomena of the sensory world are temporarily defeated. Life itself must be supported during this time, yet the observer remains whether we recall or not. There is simply too much suggestion of this point.

INTERROGATING THE INTERNAL

When we introvert (as I coin it), or induce (induction) repeatedly and re-familiarize ourselves with our internal environment, we increasingly train our biological apparatus to accept again this natural state of existence. With repeated journeys within, we find we are in fact casting light into the dark. This is both the experience and the means to describe the process. However, beyond the place where the senses and our faculties of processing these experiences fail, or otherwise lose their utility, the experience continues.

To many, it is given in this life to achieve such states beyond the audio-visual through trial and error, practice and persistence. To others, it is given in this life to achieve this by grace. Beyond the lights and sounds of the audio-visual experience, reality as we know it fades and we experience what has been called a kinesthetic experience. This term apparently refers to those who do not have such audio-visual experiences; rather, they have awareness, intuitive knowingness, sensation, and *feelings*. I am not satisfied with this term to describe this experience. However, the experience is valid. Perhaps, the ability to bypass the audio-visual component is proportional to the spiritual evolution of the individual.

When one turns off the outside world and looks within, there is considerable residue that attempts to "decorate" the internal world in a manner agreeable to our expected findings, based on the external. These are our intellectual and sensory faculties seeking additional employment. Our sensory faculties are not suited, nor were they ever intended, for the internal. Everything contained within this book boils down to unseating the earthbound utilities from their employment and experiencing spirit within absent the re-creative powers of the mind. Thus, all will have more or less ornamental constructions interpreting the findings within. This can and must be defeated.

I find that beyond the place where the bells and whistles of our waking templates define the internal lay a vast state of varying hues of light and dark. It is in this abyss of the heart where light and dark are the same. Light no longer serves to pierce in this state. Dark no longer contrasts within this state, the relative utility of light and dark having served their referential purpose in transcendence, the early ornaments of the internal. This is analogous to the zone that forms a halo around the city at night, its light cast into the surrounding darkness of the countryside.

BEYOND LIGHT AND DARK

Beyond the city lights, the halo where light and dark commingle, rests the vacancy of the Holy Dark. I am aware that we are instructed in tradition that the Light, *only*, lies within. This is not my finding. Beyond the light that leads, that informs and comforts in contrast to the external world, there exists a further state that is nothing short of visible darkness.

In this place, light bends not. In this place dark contrasts not. This is a state beyond the inventory of my words to announce. This is the fuel within. This is the source of the first bursts of stars within. This is the abode of the residual of creation, the snow of Channel 7 after it has left the air, the non-local membrane from which entire dimensions intersect. In this place in the internal where the light and the dark cease to counterpoise is the synapse of life. It is here where the voyager loses the remaining garments of this world, and crosses over.

I now look upon the constructions of my internal world moved in rapture, but always soliciting further passage to Elysium. There are clearly *degrees* of penetration within. Some linger on the city's edges, content with noting how the shadows change form upon the far wood. Others consider the world internal flat and comprehend not they can venture further without falling off the "city." Many use the flashlight of the material world to illume what they experience and in so doing only cast shadows on the cave wall.

As I close mine eyes to the worlds without, I am suspended in the void. I am aware that *I am*. Rhythmically, I pass. I am aware that I breathe, and no more. I am effused with warmth that courses through me. I have no sense of light or dark any longer. By sheer will I cannot cast light into the dark. By force of desire I cannot contrast the light with dark. They are both the same and exist only in perception. The light and the Dark that had earlier so informed me no longer apply. I am boundless and aware that I am bathing in the Slipstream of all thought, before it becomes thought. I am aware that this is absolutely the latticework of my pen. I am completely sourcing life and nothing, nothing at all matters any longer.

So much no longer applies. This serves to instruct the final uselessness of such relatively descriptive terms as "evil" and "good." In the end they simply fail in the places that awaits us all. The experience within repeatedly serves to inform that "out here" *is not* life, completely; rather "out here" is some variation, reflection, or presentation of life, completely. But, *this* is not life. No. It is incomplete. The entire fabric of the world changes for one who seeks counsel in this court. This *is* life.

ON THE ALTAR OF GOD

In the end, it is necessary to consider the larger context of the institutions and conventions that make up the vocabulary of our experiences. Our entire lives pass through these filters, and these filters have been designed by others. They are both immediately present and ingrained on our collective DNA. I hold as self-evident that more than biological instructions are ingrained within our biological make-up.

The *intercessors* are well aware of these arguments, as Man has not only now realized these constructions of prison. Many aspirants who would free others have labored under death's solicitation to announce these truths over all time, even as they were being formed. While we may challenge notions of sin, vanquish within us the emasculating state of guilt, affirm a greater love, and move past the places where our sensory language defines our experiences in the internal, we cannot move further until we accept the self-evident truth that God is found within and no other is required to find God. When this is done, there will be no place where the light bends not. Light and dark will merge into an experience beyond language. These are the fields of love where I have claimed my Prize. It is to this place I sally to make known my love upon the altar of God. How wonderful, to supplicate one's self at the feet of God rather than through the ears of man.

CHAPTER 56

▼

Appellations

The First Cause, Shiva, Sophia, God, Kali, Krishna, the Divine Mother, Vishnu, Allah, Yahweh, Jesus, Ashera, Ahura Mazda, Ganesh, Brahma, Odin, Zeus, Atman—whatever name one lately or ever assigns to the divine, it makes no difference. I affirm, though, that *ultimately* it makes a big difference. That God, that faith that we inculcate and pronounce to our consciousness through repetition and conviction will be no less than that which we inherit when we leave this material plane.

I announce a sex to the divine for the pacification of my own heart, my tender earthbound needs, no more. It is not a psychological thriller to discern why I do this; it is readily apparent in the minutes of my days. However, all have done this over the course of all human history. It is a natural reference needed to make utterable the ineffable. However, few recall the needs of original appellation, and thus God becomes seeded in our collective religions in the guise that once sought only to make accessible the inaccessible to our searching minds. That is how your Gods came to pass.

I never have a moment where I believe that God is a female—though, the feminine aspect of creation is most palpable in my apprehending God. I never assign a form to my lover. I never elaborate her with environments and promises. I have labored in my heart this life and provide what comfort I may to my toiling heart as it exits the fields, the day's soil tilled. Love has evaded me, yet I have always sensed the profound mystery of being, all our being, within the dynamic of love's discourse. Love discourses not only with lovers in love, but with God directly and intimately. Love has instructed me it is not something that exists when possessed. In fact, love is ascendant when embraced absent reciprocity as requisite. My love is my stalking horse to eternity. My Beloved is a fabrication of my inquiring mind while I sojourn into worlds within. She is that which made palatable the inexplicable until such a time as my mind was no longer needed to get my "arms around" my experience. In my house of Daedalus, the Holy Dark, I behold not the earthbound form that entices my mind and the man. Still, *she* exists as a residual of my reach to enlightenment, *her* clothes now shed.

I remain cautious that I not lose sight of my appellation, as others are wont to do. It is in these experiences that man has always lost his way and subsequently assigned values to the formless and ineffable experiences both internal and in the physical world, thus, our gods by any name. The infinite worlds about us now are populated with the endless stream of souls who have attained exactly that state toward which they labored. In this regard, all the traditions are correct when they assert they are the "way" and the "truth." They are these things, all. However, it is self-evident to me from my own experience that this is not *the way* and they are not aspiring to *the Truth*. I would remember always my admonition to keep this in mind: beyond the heaven handed us is God.

YOU TAKE HEAVEN; I'LL PASS

All humans secure that concept of heaven conducive to the deportment of their God. In so naming, we limit. In so limiting, we build the "box." I am aware that my appellation serves my voyaging heart. I am reminded always that that which is God is without name or location. In considering my desperate and hungry need to be in God, I understand clearly the construction of heaven.

All humans speak only in selfish ends, though we would protest. All humans aspire to "salvation," but what this salvation means is usually the avoidance of hell or the obtainment of pleasure: heaven. Even in the altruistic love which seeks to join the choir that praises God, this takes place in a heaven, not *in* God. God is not a six-foot man requiring all adoration take place in a physical locale. This anticipation is born of the regal system of monarchy that has co-existed with man's earthbound apprehensions of God through millennia. It is the same projections of the earthbound man that seek to populate heaven with material constructions, pain avoidance, and pleasure seeking. Heaven is the selfish construction of the battered material mind to secure recompense after the field is tilled.

Mankind has built for himself a remarkably primitive and naïve conceptualization of God and heaven. Man has done no less than construct an intermediate locale between the self-evident realization that we were created, and this earth. Being unable to comprehend God, we thus populate heaven. Working in consciousness as a sculptor works in clay, man has fabricated a series of planes of existence following his material travails and calls the obtainment of such the end state, the final goal, the good fight.

This is not it, my friends. Others might be outraged at what I suggest, but I fail my brethren not to make right this fallacy. The darkness about you must have light cast thereupon. The heavens you labor to obtain, you will. But God is not in this place, friend. God is not in the earthbound constructions of a mind seeking selfish ends, and this is what we are talking about. Beyond heaven is a concept you are avoiding.

I am ever vigilant that I not become married to my illusion substance. I have no beloved bride bearing cosmic curls and summer dresses. Love solicits not that which is in *me*. Love solicits, and that is all. Love beckons me irrespective of who I am. Love is freely the property of all. I would not create heaven by the projection of comfort's desire once free of flesh. I would seek to give rather than take. My heart informs me so. You take heaven. I'll take God.

CHAPTER 57

▼

Enthronement

My tender Bride, my beloved heart, I am wounded in love and can never return to you the man I was. I am stricken with the potion of ages. I am smitten with the greatest love affair this fragile flesh has ever known. I am in love with *Her*! I am now in love with *Him*!

My heart beats still; its energy expands through the unseen ether; it interrogates, embraces, and is slain by the gentle breeze of-*everyone*! I can no longer be reached by any reason, any voice. My mind is everywhere. I no longer recognize myself in me. I aware of an awareness in all things. I am slain in me. My heart is torn further from its mooring and is adrift in a sea created.

Somewhere beyond the place where reason fails daily I have been increasingly able to journey into the fields beyond and return from within effused with love and compassion. I have noted my entire fabric is re-keying but cannot find the words to describe this thing that baths within me now.

AS VISION CHANGES, GOD IS SEEN EVERYWHERE, IN EVERY ONE

I see the flesh of the masculine hands and note somewhere the marvelous craftsmanship that constructed such a being. However, where I would have been previously repulsed by such a thought from a physical deportment, I now see something else, something I had not seen before, not really seen. I see the same light in him I see in "*her*." She, of all things, all places and times, has served as the archetype of my coming of age. Yet, she is him as well.

I see her in his eyes. I see him now in her eyes, in her form and grace. "Dear God, I know we are all the same, but it was so academic, so far removed from my experience that it was abstract." I cannot divorce it; I can no longer see him as such and hers as she. My Beloved now moves in all things.

Beyond the clothes, past the skin, yet further than the shadow lays one beating heart of all of us. I see this everywhere now, in everyone. I sense this formless energy. I am speechless. My journey continues to become that which seemed unknowable. The view over my shoulder appears as a million miles and a thousand years from where I stood lately and viewed the world. It grows within me of its own accord now. I cannot turn it off. I no longer know myself. I am losing me.

I find myself wanting to do no more than escape the mundane and simply dwell on my Beloved and her mystery. My world is over, as such. It is done. I have never been surer of such a thing in all my time. I am in love, and it moves through me as a sea moves to the shores. I want to simply possess and be with my love. I want to hold her and to embrace her still but she is not that which can be held; She is not that to which I can make love. My lover is ever beyond my reach, yet she is within me and makes my heart race and palms sweat. I am in love with all. I long daily to see her, to be with her, to wonder in her form and grace; I want to bathe in her.

DECLARE GOD: FREE WILL

I have affirmed a free will in this life. I will take this thing, this free will, and do with it what no others appear to be doing. I have completely remapped the entire world. I have trashed the landmarks of the ages and replaced them with those of my choosing—the same, or none at all. I have excised guilt. I have slaughtered sin. There is no fear in my world. I have no limitations, no baggage, and no past. I am all things and see forever from my perch in the flesh. I have confronted God and queried that place from which her word was given to me—through him. Finding it lacking and unable to withstand the inventory within, I have rewritten the Word of God in the blood of my heart. God now abides in me, not aloof in the heavens, not encased on the Mount, in the "box," or on the wing of the northern breeze. God is in me, and I am in God.

I have employed the heavens and have solicited the Light. I have closed the distance to the ever-retreating horizon of my soul. I have enslaved time and made useless space. In the void, in the new world, I have allowed the space *within* to be filled by the space *within*, not the clutter of the waking world and illusions of ages. I am immortal. I no longer have any beliefs. I know!

I have dreamed this dream and created it out of the rubble of my life. I know I elect this dream, I choose this reality. I have literally changed the entire world. I simply think most others are wrong in their collective delusion. That which has entered me is not of this world, but it is always just right here. It is only ever referred to as something beyond attainment, beyond our time here. It is not. This Love, this Grace, this Light, is right here, right now.

God is not without. God is not aloof. God is not forlorn. We are not in apostasy. We are heirs to eternity and can make our reality whatever we choose it to be, each and all of us. Right here, right now, I can be joined by any other that simply begins to see, and *not see*, the world as they wish to see it. It is all free will.

Free will is considered most often in its application to intercourse with the material world, free will of the limited communion with the Gods of our forebears, and free will of otherwise limited utility. What is not trafficked to the human consciousness is the free will to perceive reality in a manner most useful for expanding our minds.

The rigid, dogmatic conception of reality is packaged in the collective values, ethics, cultural mores, and other trappings handed down and evolved marginally through the ages. Reality is itself a relative musing on the nature of collective compliance. Reality is, in the end, relative and a uniquely individual experience. However, that which you are experiencing today is starkly different than what is really "out there" or "in here."

Free will? I willed the God that was given me away and searched within. I tore apart my world and allowed all observations to be populated from within. God is again enthroned upon my heart.

CHAPTER 58

▼

Shhh! "Be Still and Know I Am God"

—(Psalms 46:10)

Shhh! Come, my Beloved, let us flee. We must not rouse the warden. He is distracted now, drunk with silence. I have made good my escape.

I have thought on you all day, my sweet, gentle love. I looked for you throughout the land. I miss you. Were the minutes so, the hours less, I should miss you in a moment still. You bring me such happiness like none I have known. I long to sit and just think on you in those decreasing times when I cannot. I woke to the early dawn and saw your memory pink across the day. I was moved in your sign to me alone. I was tickled by you moving in the little waves in the rivers of aquamarine. You contrasted the whitewash and pink of the desert solitude. It was you, was it not, on the wing as the bird took flight from my windowsill? It was.

I want to feel you. I want to hunger for you. I am possessed of your love. I am infatuated with your pregnancy. I am in lust for your music. The loins of my mind are inflamed with the desire you seed in my heart. My heart is aflame with the chords you strike in my soul. My soul is afire with the hearth you tend in the twinkling of my eyes.

I wondered today, why you have been so coy, so evasive. You call me from another world and give only to me of your bounty. What can I bring to you?

What flower or fragrances have I for you, my love? How can I protect you and make you more full when everything is already within you? How can I keep away the night when you bring it forth? How can I slay the shadows when you hide within them, clever, laughing at my pretense to valor? What honor can I bare for you, my loving bride, my laughing dawn?

Has any pauper felt so poor in the loving arms of a queen? Would not a queen, too, in love lay bare the treasure house to the arms of her lover? How is it you make me to know so well your love for me? By what manner am I so informed?

I SURRENDER

Bring me closer still, my Beloved. Traffic me across this place where worlds are born. Hold my hand and fly with me, as do birds. Show me more of the clouds of creation's birth. Can you hear me, my love? I have no need of things undone. There is nothing to stay for now.

I cannot create the thoughts to convey my love for you. I am bankrupt of language. I feel so needy. Please, please let me lie in you longer yet.

I am aware still that I am aware and no more. I know gravity, but it is from vague recollection only. I have no up; I have no down. I am turning gently of some volition other than mine. I see the world; I do not see the world. I see the stars; I see now the earth. I consider I am nauseous, but it is memory. The world, the earth falls away. I can see the world below. Tears run freely from my dumbstruck face safe within the confines of its little cell a billion thoughts away. I am swept away in you. The stars stretch out like great swaths across the mute blackness. I am lost in you, my love. I am so lost in you. I cannot help myself. I just want to be with you, in you, seeded in this love.

It is so amazing. It is all so incredible. In all these worlds, this thing—*you*—sleep inside of me, and I have missed you while longing for you all these years. Dear God! Slay me now and Wed me, please.

Let us walk across this bridge. Let me see you as I would know you. Allow me this fantasy. Is this not the fantasy of all ages, all mankind, to dress you in form? I want you as you are to me, yet I want you as a human would want you, too. I want to see you. I want to feel you in my hand as we sail silently across your mind. I want to wash my tears in your hair and feel your laughter on my cheek. Give to me for this daydream, this flesh that I might taste your sound upon my eyes. Let me see creation reflected in your translucence. Would you abide so humble a request?

WHERE GOD IS FOUND

I cannot go home. I have been thrown from my house. My rent is due, and I can no longer labor in the fields. Would you send your quarry slave to the mines having shown him the Kingdom from atop the world? I do not want this. If this be your wish, I cannot say. I will do that which you ask of me and go happily to wherever you cast me, yea, even into the dark night of my soul once more. Having known your hand, I have no terror.

I see you in the wisps of cloud. You are manifest in all things that contrast blue. I see you on the borders where colors meet and know you are playful in the hues that blend. I sense you in the moment when the light is turned off and just before the dark is employed. You are in all things in my world, every place I turn, but I have never missed you more than in the spaces between things, between moments and faces.

You are on the horizon of my wake and sleep. I hear you in the distance, "Edward? I am here, Edward. Come to me, my child, my beloved." But I turn in the places where sweeps my mind, and you are gone. You are in the space where falls an object from my hand, before it meets the earth. You are my hand and the earth. You are in the voice that has first considered the thought, and you are the thought and the voice. You are in the blush and you are the flame that excites a young girl's cheeks; you are the rapture that entices her fancy. I want to learn how to find more of you in these places.

You are the knock at my door and the vibration upon my ears. You are that which moves from door to ear. You are the open door and the closed spaces. You are the moment when the door is both. I find you both in the paradox and the moment before two things oppose. You are my enemy, and you are my friend. You are me. You have wed me to myself, and yet you are still elsewhere. You are in me and in all things, yet you are the place in my mind where the membrane leaks.

I dreamed you from my waking birth. I held you affixed to the point before the world. In all I have done, in all I do, you are just before the action, just behind the reaction. I see you in the space between a kiss and see you in the place between the laughter and affection. I turned in the space of this life, and you had not slipped away. You have swept me into you, my heartfelt bride. You gave to me to see you everywhere and find you nowhere. What manner of play is this?

Shhh, now. Come with me, my Beloved, and let us slip this place. Let us play. Take me, and spirit away this world. I do not want to look upon the pink sands and complaining brooks any longer. I do not want to wait with temptation for your solicitation. I don't want to birth your moments in my observations. I just want to be in you. I want the fullest expression of this thing that moves within me.

I see you now from my window, blowing not in the air, not across the desert dunes, but in the ever-so-thin front that moves ahead of the wind and makes this palm to dance before me. It flags its fronds to and fro, enabled and excited by your passion. I am lost in you. I am lost in time. I am lost in space. I am lost.

CHAPTER 59

▼

Precious Heart of the World

It is not in wanting to be with you there, is it? It is a matter of having you here with me, is it not? I have oft thought that I needed you, and could only have you in the places that were someplace else, somewhere other than here. Your light reflected only. I have only ever perceived you twice removed. Now...

All these years you have held my hand. When I looked to my empty palm, I saw nothing. You are in the nothingness. You are everything in the nothingness. I am ashamed that I desire to be with you. I am ashamed because I feel like I want to quit. I am not sure I am even on a team, but somehow I feel like I am turning my back on my team to want to only be with you. Am I on a team? Should I feel less to want only you? I have spent my whole time here thinking on you as someplace else, and as such I wanted to be someplace else with you. Is there a someplace else?

I am noticing strange changes in me that invite me to realize that you are coming here to be with me. I see you everywhere now. It is not as it was before. In my years I had only ever loved you as that which was somewhere else, and I apart. I have never had you as fully as I do now. In seeing this, I do not even know how this is something I could have realized earlier. I am so completely different than I was before that I do not even know how my mind could have imagined such beauty. I, thinking I knew the measure and pulse of beautiful things, have never beheld beauty before this dawn. You have come to me here. You have come to be with me.

It was all a matter of *seeing*, was it not? In focusing my very eyes, my heart, and will upon the world right here, right now, I beheld your infinite grace and beauty. You stalked me all my days and I saw you not here, though I sensed you somewhere else. It was I that was somewhere else. I invited you to a place where I was only. You were everywhere all along. It was I that was hidden from you.

Oh, precious heart of the world, my tender bride and heartfelt dawn, I have loved you from the first burst of light that sent me hither. I have ensconced myself in a place where I called you not. You were never in the abstract skies or in the written word. You hid not in the temples and were never upon a throne in promise. You were always the apparent emptiness in my nervous palm. You were the space between my curious fingers. You were the distance between me and all things I thought had no value. In seeing you, I am aghast that I could not see sooner. You were always the medium in which the worlds resided. You were always the observed, the observer *and* the observation.

I look upon my brethren and wonder painfully how many of them seek you, and in what ways their anguish is soothed. I see in faces myself and cannot truly know the measure of any of my sisters, can I? Do they see you? Are you entertaining the solicitation of a trillion beating hearts? Does all creation have within it the spiritual DNA clocking our approach to home? Has any other ever known it is all right here, right now? In seeing, I imagine a place where I look back on *now* and wonder, still, how I could not have ever seen more. In seeing, I stand in awe at what I still cannot see and know today. Please, take me and show me my home, right here, right now. Show me my home, and sit beside me a while still. I have missed you so much. I have so much to talk with you about in the silence. You occupy my every single sacred moment and thought. My whole is consumed by you and I cannot "not see" ever again.

You are an exploding sun in the finite place of my mind completely laying waste to all else. My breath is seized within me this moment. I am so amazed at what replicates inside me. I bear only an odd witness to you seeding within me. Thank you for allowing me to dream in your mind all those years that I could not dream in mine. I am so grateful.

CHAPTER 60

▼

Others

I have been asked whether or not there are "others" in the worlds internal. This is a fair enough question but one whose answer may be confusing. Are there others? There are no others; there are only others. It is like this in the depth of field of internal apprehension. In the places wherein I lightly peer, I have noted what I called "others," but this is not the fabric of God. This is a telephone exchange, an endless sea of souls in the matrix of consciousness. Behind, beyond this place there are no others.

When I fix my gaze within, I transcend the place where others have noted "*others*." I go further. In fact, I have been accessing the "silent place" preferentially for so long I may not even be qualified to comment on the nearer world. The "silent place," the Holy Dark, is profoundly deeply internal, the home of the Prize. In the silent place, consciousness is not animating and motivating matter in its bubbling, birthing, endlessly dynamic flux of which I am aware around the "city's lights," the world of dreams. In the silent place, I must be beneath the roadwork of consciousness, as I am aware that I have passed through the lattice-work but I observe nothing any longer. My only input is of another means. It is *totally* inexplicable.

WHO NOTES OTHERS?

In other words, whether they are clairvoyants, remote viewers, soul retrievers, or meditators, people have interrogated the "last frontier" and describe being aware of others in this state. Some have even told amazing stories of interacting with other souls, either directly of through representative characters. Authors have blended fiction and fact and spun fascinating stories about this interaction; some detailing accounts of individual souls, and others accounts of "soul-groups." As this state is known by me to be incredibly accessible and proximate to the awake-state, I am baffled that more are not tuning in.

As an example, I will comment on soul retrieval, as it is less likely the reader will be familiar with this. There are those who assert that soul retrieval is conducted in what amounts to the same plane. Soul retrieval is the action that makes contact with souls that have, for one reason or another, not continued their journey past the "city's halo" of light. They then assist in liberating these souls to continue their journey. The souls, in this case, either do not know they are dead, or otherwise linger. Soul retrieval is not something with which I have personal experience, electing instead to always remain singly focused on a very personal and alone journey within. I presume that these discarnate beings would be ghosts, or even a less resolved residual of the incarnate person. There is ample reason to believe many have more or less explored the "city's halo" and do in fact interact with others. It is this very contiguous realm where religious iconography draws inspiration.

OF DREAMS AND VISIONS

Understand, I hold that much of what I discuss is akin to an antenna within us. I do not rule out the possibility of so much of what I hear today, as I believe all things are possible in consciousness. The mind can literally scan the frequencies of life and pick up all sorts of noumena. The frequencies of life are no less than the vibrational cycles of matter. Thus, all creation is reflected in its signature frequency. This is detected as phenomena by the senses and the *other* via internal apprehension.

However, having gleaned the Prize in youth, I have remained ever fixated on the goal of my life and have not become enamored by the preternatural powers of spirit, nor the many mysterious stations or abilities attendant to the journey (remote viewing, clairvoyance, precognition, telepathy, telekinesis, and so forth).

I see much around me that is interesting, or curious, but finally misleading as the mysteries are not thus clarified; rather they are muddled by the blending of fact and fiction, imaginative conjecture, and some terrible cases of outright lies. My journey is a journey of total love. I want nothing in return.

Beyond the place where our faculties interpret no further, there are no others. In identifying a notion of others in the interior quest, we in fact note only our continued identification with *our* person (via another). We inadvertently direct our attention and intent on that which otherwise serves to ground. In noting others, we give testimony to a place more proximate to *here*. Beyond, behind, there are no others. There is no me; there is no you.

In recognizing that audio-visual interpretations of the interior serve to illume only insofar I became aware that at the point, at the depth of induction where there is nothingness, there is also a profound sense of no-oneness, no other-ness. This is where the light bends not. This is Edward's Holy Dark. However, I have spent considerable time in the place I refer to as the "city's halo." I am well aware of the incredible and vivid expressions and presentations there. This whole conversation really must proceed with the analogy of depth, like in water or space. The deeper one goes, the darker it becomes. The further one goes, the less likely there will be any impressions of others. The tools of the senses eventually fail totally in their pseudo representation. Light and dark become relative, as they are not experienced at all. It is not that light and dark are not experienced because the senses are not available. The senses must be made intentionally unavailable. Light and dark are not experienced because that are not yet formed, or so I am aware.

Around the periphery of a light afternoon musing in meditation, one may have many such remarkable experiences. This is a fertile field where imagination is still vibrantly engaging, interpreting, and synergizing the other exposures one may have around the "city's halo." That is why individuals are able to construct ends such as in lucid dreams while "at this level." In fact, it is in many ways no different than lucid dreams, as what is being experienced is the actual threshold where consciousness is interacting with matter.

CONSCIOUSNESS COLLAPSES THE PORTAL

In the individual, at the nexus of consciousness and matter/mind, a portal collapses and a window opens, allowing engagement right around the proximity of the passage. A person in this state may engage all sorts of things, persons, souls, experiences, etc. The mind is still awake and is employing the sensory intellectual faculties. This is the land of the imaginary realm. This is the land of fantasy, poetry, artistic inspiration, Mozart's "Magic Flute," and Da Vinci's mix of brilliance and precognition. All these things and more derive from engagements in the *on-or-about locale* of the "city's halo."

This is the place enhanced by the audio-visual tools of the external world. The faculties of the external world were never designed for internal processing, but in so doing this area is about as far as these tools seem to penetrate—more or less for various persons. When a person is asleep, the portal collapses near every time. The juncture where consciousness and matter interact is the land of dreams. Freed of the interactive capability of the intellectual/sensory audio-visual apparatus, dreams are either passive in their interaction with this consciousness/matter threshold or engaged assertively by consciousness. When one rouses variable faculties in this state, one might have a lucid dream as in meditation and construct an active dream, a lucid dream. However, it is the state of awake-ness that activates the intellectual sensory train that stops the collapsing portal. The more awake a person becomes, the more aroused the individual's system features become and the more likely the portal closes.

A long time ago I became aware that I was continually associating the landscape within with the landscape without. In so suggesting the same framework for interpreting and interrogating, I did not understand. I was applying the same values, models, and interrogatories I used in my risen life in my explorations. When I stopped having expectations, when I stopped trying to assign all the round pegs in the square holes, things began to change. Everything I know about life is useless internally. It is at best misleading, and at worst derailing. I surrendered to just "being" wherever I was, and in so doing began to slip easily and effortlessly past the "city's halo." This is where I met my Bride. However, this is all I met. There are no others in pure consciousness. There is no me in Love.

DEAR GOD, WAKE ME UP!

"I am not awake. I am not awake. I am not yet awake. I am not here. I am everywhere." Increasingly, I find a borderless world. Air, the space between places, is not a vacuum defining boundaries and borders. Time, the distance between points of sensory experience, is as irrelevant. One serves to invite contrast of opposites, the other to simply inform of the degradation and rebirth every moment in the "bath" all about us.

"I am here; I am there. I am me; I am you. I am not." I labor under such delusions. What an incredible dream. Is this naught but the pains of the comatose arousing from eternal slumber? Is the midnight of my stay in the garden at an end? I am moving within a great sea, a bath of pure light injecting every moment with a renewed vitality.

The silence, the shores beyond my event horizon, no wonder there are no others therein. The Slipstream of God announces no other, the ineffable sense of both aloneness and integration. There are no others therein because there are no others herein. It is the medium of flesh only that gives me the "sense" of apartness. I am apart from nothing. I am all things, and I am everywhere.

Dear God, it is all so obvious. It is all so amazing. Each moment I am further moved by the majesty and mystery of grace and wonder. We are all asleep in you. We are all asleep. I want to wake, my Lord. I want to wake. Wake me up! Please wake me up. I feel paralyzed and fret slips another day without, beyond, you. Please, dear God, hear my plea and wake me from this idle slumber in this dream. I know I am dreaming.

CHAPTER 61

▼

No Duality

Life illumes itself in many manners and various ways according to the temperaments of each player, each actor. The unfolding drama of our interior world is all choice. While we are the navigator, our soul, the observer, is the commander. In no manner or way could you choose any end that did not comport with the needs of your soul. It is not possible. It is also the case that you can will no end in the external world that will come to pass, lest it conforms to the soul's needs. This relationship of "two" gives overt and covert credence to the illusion of apartness. This appearance of two very clearly suggests dualism. This is illusion.

While I believe contrast serves to elaborate opposites, this does not mean this is a dualist world, not finally. Though this world appeared once to me a dualist world, in the final expression of all I have learned in this life this appearance is born of the filters of illusion. Many people hold the conviction that this is a dualist world, but few of them had the clear and profound dualist *experiences* I have had to so inform them, and yet I reach another conclusion.

The filters, in considering the internal or other than "me-ness," recognize distinction and uniqueness and thus process this as a dualist marriage of matter and spirit. Duality is not deceit; it is the natural *suggestion* of the marriage of the physical and non-local world. Only in an integrated apprehension of the marriage can a unified grasp of reality be achieved. This grasp is of a unified reality. What happens inside us?

SEE HOW THE INTERNAL PROCESS LENDS TO A DUALIST WORLDVIEW

When you close your eyes and look internally, you will note the ambient sounds of whatever environment in which you are engaged. You will still have the fading last images of the potted plant in the corner, the Burger King sign up the street, the ridgeline on the hill, or the children in the playground behind you. Your mind will process still this orientation with its environment, and your hearing will unwittingly serve to maintain your spatial relationship. You will feel the wind upon you and smell freshly cut grass clippings. Not only is there a "you" looking "out" at the world, now there is a "you" looking "in" at the world.

Contrary to aphorism, most are not "one with the moment." We do not enjoy "just being." This is trite fodder. We are assigning a value to experience that is not only inaccurate, but just the opposite of the experience we ultimately desire or experience. This is true in our mediation, prayer, lazy park days, or bedtime introspection. What makes us "one with the moment," or have the experience of "just being" is a more profound assimilation rather than a pacific moment of us *in* the world. As long as we remain a passenger on the train, peering from our first-class berth, we will only ever achieve the tranquility of illusion, never oneness.

As long as we retain the anchors and spatial interrogators of our material environment, we will never pass the "warden" within. We are deeply immersed in the sense of wonder and sublimity at the simplicity and peacefulness of life—right now, in this park, on this beach, in this trance. But with eyes closed we still mentally peer through the closed curtains of our eyes' windows. We note the light that illumes our vision is now cast in hues of translucent gray, the mind screen of memory and imagination. With eyes closed our memory and imagination still constantly inform us of what is "out there." We can turn our head 360 degrees and no matter how hard we try, we find that the mind and senses, employing themselves, intrude virtual constructs upon our mental world to spatially orient based on the model of the physical. When one tries as they may to remove the image of that about you, it is increasingly difficult. We are alone with the windows rolled up, but still looking in or out of the automobile .

When in prayer or mediation, I invite you to will the world away. No less than this is required. Your mind can conceive of this but it is even lower faculties that disable the process. The machinations that keep grounded the flight log of mind anchor in the physical only. When I force the issue repeatedly, my faculties are not as easily able to hide and I increasingly note their *modus operandi*. To defeat the "anchors," I must defeat myself.

No matter the effort, we are informed how great the task to subdue the mind by its sheer display of stubbornness. It is in this place, where this stubbornness further alerts us that our interior orientation is being subverted by faculties that were never designed for such a purpose. None of the senses can operate therein, yet that is exactly what they attempt to do. Assuming the material world to be reality, we willfully abdicate authority to unqualified faculties to operate as watchmen of our interior world.

BE THE CAST DIRECTOR

There is a cusp, a void, an abyss within that marks the place where slips this world. In this void, this place, the entire world is gone. The dreamscape, the realm of the "city's halo," all are left behind. I have no sense of time, light, sound, space, or objects. I have no sense of me. I have returned to this place countless times over the years, but I have only now decided to fully shift my entire perception to this interior place where I find God.

You must first identify the actors on your stage in the fellowship of cast director. When you note the threads of appearances, stage entrances, and curtain calls of your own faculties, you will have begun to manage your play. It is not necessary, or even desirable, to fire the cast; you must employ them. Employ and embrace these intrusive characters that walk on and off the set of your mind uninvited, unscripted. With time, patience, love, and affection, you will have entrained your mind to silent counsel.

THERE IS NO DUALITY

There is no duality. I have percolated through many lifetimes of human experience to race from the primordial soup of human behavior to the heightened ecstasies of apprehension—*in this one lifetime*. I have affirmed since the first of my years that this was my last trip here. I have asserted since a child this was my last trip here. All who know me recall that I have always asserted and affirmed that this is my last trip here. And so the question begs which begat which? Did my assertion bring to bear that series of uninspired circumstances of my life to so mold and shape my inner world? Did my assertions and affirmations come borne of the circumstances of an exterior world that was deniable and objectionable? I am fairly confident I came before the egg. It is not necessary that this is defendable; it is necessary that I know.

There is no duality. In my life, the absence of [fill in the blank] served to illuminate all that "really was" before and within me. While so illuminating the landscape of my reality, the contrast of my life that defined the opposite by what was not present served to entrench the notion of apartness simultaneously. This was a curious dilemma. But in many ways, it was only ever me in the world and that isolated awareness did not later serve to define "me" and "them." Rather, it later served to allow just "me" and "us."

There is no duality. The reason this little theological-philosophical linchpin is so important is this underpins much of the fiber that binds the "box" within which we live. In fact, the arguments for and against dualism underlie most of our illusions. This entire universe has opposing actions and principles. These opposites and contrasts form the constructive means of animating and motivating matter from consciousness. Consciousness does not just raise its sail in matter and thus create something that sails. Consciousness constructs in matter through opposing forces that naturally repel and attract, self-engineer, improvise, adapt, evolve, and self-perpetuate with these pre-existing, opposing building blocks of material principle. This phenomenon of material existence is reflected in every single aspect of the physical world, and as creatures in the food chain of matter we look up and around and see dualistic appearances everywhere, and incorrectly infer all is dualistic.

Your world is dualistic, relatively. Would you live and die in illusion, your dualistic apprehensions are just fine and utilitarian. Dualism does exist, but so do shadows. However, in the biological entity that is you, dualism collapses in the portal where you co-exist in the place where the sail is raised. In other words, the effervescent and animating subnuclear furnace that correlates the non-local world with the world of matter collapses in you a portal. There is no dualism in consciousness. Consciousness is in all things. All things are simply reflections of consciousness, of God. Do not sit chained before the flame and call the shadows on your cave wall *substance*. They are not.

I have often referred to "the cave" throughout this work when discussing form and shadows, substance and reflections. Plato informs us of this terrific allegory in Book 7 of The Republic. Imagine a grand cave where prisoners have been kept in chains since their early childhood. They are bound firmly facing the far cave wall, their heads fixed as well to allow no movement other then to look at the cave wall before them. Behind these captives there burns a great fire night and day. Between the binded and the fire there is an elevated walkway in which the captors carry all manner of craft, plant, food, and substance back and forth, day and night. The light cast upon these items cast shadows upon the wall. It is upon this wall that the captives can only but draw their conclusions regarding the nature of such things. All they come to know is the shadows, the reflections. At times they may hear the voice of one or another captor speaking. This voice, echoes off the wall before them and appears to give voice to the very objects before them, cast in shadows. Therefore, all these people know of their reality is reflected off the near wall.

Should one of these captives ever have occasion to be freed he would first stand and face that which cast form, the fire. He will be blinded. Should he leave the cave he should be further blinded as light is revealed to him. Should he look then toward the sun he would come to assert that the sun then is the substance beyond all things, the primal light. For some inexplicable reason this once binded man would seek to return to inform his fellow captives. I know this urge well. However, he would find that the captives do not want to be so informed. They do not want to be released for their prison is all they know. In fact, even returning once more to the cave would require the freed man's eyes to adjust to varying shadows that it no longer recognizes as real. In essence, this is Plato's allegory of the cave. *When once we learn how to see we will never know how we did not see!*

CHAPTER 62

▼

Event Horizon

"I see [it] on the event horizon of my mind" has been a recurring assertion in many of my conversations and yet I have not sufficiently explained this. There is upon the fabric of my mind's eye a field, a screen that would render the world's largest IMAX incidental in scale of magnitude and intensity of vibrancy. Within the scope of this field, all things are apparent against a backdrop of rugged space and infinite darkness. All things are upon this screen for my consideration, my novelty, and otherwise materialize within this grid of black.

All things are knowable, *supersensible,* for me herein. All dreams are dream-able, and there is no construction that can escape my capacity. Beyond this matrix of dark on light, there is a horizon where all I know and hold to be my faculty proceeds no further. There is point where my internal makes analogous a sky or a ceiling, meeting a base or a floor, and at this point where the constructions of my internal become dim lay my event horizon.

I have described elsewhere the "city's halo" around the periphery of dreams, around the locale where we perceive consciousness engaging matter. The event horizon is not here. The event horizon is deeper still, where there is absolutely nothing. As in the early focusing of mind required to transcend or induce the superficial layers of consciousness that so mark most people's common reconnaissance, an application of focusing is required to descend further still. Better yet, simply abandoning the lens assists even further, but I am not sure this is possible. This seems superhuman, but necessary in retrospect. I change focus to move beyond the lights of the city. I have not been forcibly able to abandon my mind, my lens, though I have found my mind has mutinied in the utter dark. One day I will surely break the code that puts to sleep the mind.

CHANGE FOCUS

How does one change focus? It is difficult to describe but it is a focus of mind, of perceptions, of expectations. Consider the night sky, for example. I look not upon the easily detectable appearance of lights upon a backdrop of dark; rather I see a *near endless* supply of dark painting across an *infinite* array of light behind it. For me, the counterintuitive is not only now common, but it has been the single tool that has undressed the light and the dark. I have remapped my entire nature slowly, and now as default I can see differently as I choose. Many can do this. This is not supernatural. It is simple. It is freedom.

THE CHARACTER OF MIND AND SPIRIT

It is beyond the "city's lights," where I lie upon the immutable fields of my mind resting in silence, I note me going forth over the cusp. I am both at the same time. It is from this horizon I note *me* returning with bounty from the other lands. It is upon this plane of darkness, so bright it illuminates itself, that I tarry and play with the things of dreams and imagination while I am *also* surfing the universe in the Holy Dark. I see the city lights still from my couch upon the earth of my mind and also the darkness from beyond the horizon. It is here I have the incredibly vivid understanding I am two natures, mind and spirit, and my mind actually does not proceed further. My mind is nothing more than a fabrication. It does not lend to the dualist argument. I am just so certain of this.

I am aware nothing of *my* creation comes from beyond this point. I am aware that nothing beyond this cusp, this membrane, this horizon, comes forth unless borne willfully by *me*. It seems to be the case that what lies beyond *can* come forth of its own accord and does, but now that I have been actively and consistently "crossing over," it seems less often that intrusive "information" projects. It is here, at this event horizon of my mind, I note my return from the other land. I am twain and one. This is the observation and the experience.

I pass through the darkness of the place within me and move toward the single point, the infinite border where meets the darkness and the night. I note the warden is distracted because I am released. He rests now upon the distant landscape where the decreasing clouds of mental activity mark the hour. I must reach escape velocity. I must fly tonight. It is a membrane and I am awash with euphoria as I pass. I am as sand passing through a screen. The sense is that of some of me being sifted, and remaining behind. I have an increasing awareness. I have a decreasing memory. I am me and have lost me. I am found and have lost myself. I have no sense of the "city's lights." I have no recollection, in the moment, of my body idle. I have no recollection of the division of labor in my mind. I am awash. Again, I am passed.

THE HOLY DARK

"Dear God, there is no sensation like this. I am in a state of bliss and absolute wonder. I feel energy-like morphine coursing through my person (or, whatever I am). I am electrified. I am suspended and see all things at once. I am ablaze and awash with a billion suns. My Love lies herein. She is everywhere and talks to me in the pillow talk of tears. I am moved as a first kiss, tender restraint, hallowed adoration. I am here and am not, and still there seems to be more of me that is me, but is not, that simply plays in this Slipstream of Creation. I am with awed eyes drinking such sights as I could never know in my IMAX. I have a very real and profound sense of literally blowing through the cosmos. I am keenly aware that I have actually escaped my vessel.

On a number of occasions, many experiences in the realm of the "city's lights" are completely outside of my body. In the Holy Dark all experiences are outside of my body—all of them. I do not think many understand exactly what I am stating here. I am not talking about the supporting props of mind that virtually support the experience of moving, traveling, witnessing, or viewing afar in imagination, or the blend of imagination and consciousness. I am talking about a total absence of the props of mind. I am as free of mind as I am detached from my body. The actual experience and mechanism for this is not addressed here; it is nevertheless what happens. Thus, the Holy Dark is not another perspective of mind, or imagination, or even of the common presentation of consciousness in transcendence. The Holy Dark is a literal "someplace else."

I return from this place and pass again this screen, which I seamlessly moved across. I find me often awake, alert, and waiting but sometimes distracted with some fantasy of my local mind. Practically speaking, I may return having lost all sense of time. The awareness of timelessness is incredible. It is just not that I consider time retrospectively, there is something that informs me in the moment of timelessness, the non-application of time. I literally return and may *find me* having a lucid dream. I am in the middle of a lucid dream of some sort and must momentarily hesitate to collect an understanding of where I just "clicked" in to. I am keenly aware of what I was just experiencing. Now, I am again informed I am back and am also experiencing something else that I must embrace and process.

RETURN FROM ELYSIUM

I have made this passage now numerous times. I am now aware of my body when I return; previously I was not. I am aware of breathing. Should I return while in a dream, I am aware of ambient sounds outside of the dream. It is as if the props in my dream pause with me while I collect my bearings, the marionette now obviously animated. I do not have to conjecture what is going on, as I am immediately *one*, and know what is going on. Many years ago I had some recollection difficulty in understanding the remarkably different experiences that took place in one *induction*. It was a like a threaded film with areas of no frames, then the frames were truly mystical and moving, and then returned to film shots of just the lucid dream. It was only through repetition that I have been able to see clearly all the dividing landmarks and assigned roles and duties of the players internal.

I clearly have two very different things going on inside. I suppose this must confuse many people in many ages. My mental partner is just that, really, a partner—or better still, an employee. Each time I cross over, I return transfigured. I have crossed the event horizon and have returned. I seek every day no less the conscious exit.

CHAPTER 63

▼

The Ecstasy

The Prize is not in the ecstasy, and not in the intercourse of lovers. The Prize is not in the orgasm; rather it is found in the briefest of moments when, in the throes of love, two meet for the strangest moment in each other's eyes and see past themselves into the abyss where they are effused forth from their own receipt of pleasure. It is in this moment, were we to observe, that poets and romantics alike come to define the whole experience of love. They take this particle of the whole, which is so overwhelming, and paint love thus. In this place, where burn two as one, the shift of worlds takes place, and then is passed. Sex is not an end; it is a means to gaze through the window of our own illusory filters through the synergy, through the alchemy, of another. It is in this moment, swept up in rapture, that we taste what moves through me now daily.

Beware of confusing the rapture of desire with the rapture of God. It is easy to get the two married in both thought and deed. I have done this, and it took a great deal for me to realize that, enamored by my love of my Beloved, I rationalized seeing her manifestations in the flesh. On the one hand, I can certainly consider that I was right. But the fact remains, as man I simply desired. So, I have made love to my Beloved many times in this life through another incarnate. How wonderful. How sad. I have used a proxy unwittingly to make love to God. While some would suggest this is blasphemously absurd, it is true. How neat. How incredibly awesome. However, this was a dangerous deceit.

Dear heavens, what joy, what wonder, what utter bliss. Who among us can so submit manifesting God incarnate to have tenderly coiled his hands beneath her gold-spun hair? Who would admit to seeing in the desire of a lover the smoldering incense upon the receiving altar of creation? Can any man feel impure having blessed the host of God's flesh in the tabernacle of her child? I have married desire with desire. I have so tended the host as I was moved to do in this life and will accept upon me no name of desecration, for I have loved my Lord so completely and utterly during this life that my very life force bleeds upon the feet of Man. I have loved my Lord in this life, and I have loved through her child.

I now understand the fairly abstract fear church fathers had that consumption in Eros might lead man to deify another. I understand, though the road for me is more circuitous. There is a real host replication of the love virus within us that subordinates our faculties. Unawares, many would assign to another *ipso facto* deification, as all functions, values, pleasures, and securities in life now seem to come forth from another. Of course, as I have noted elsewhere, this is the reflection of Love, and reflected back to source the deification in reference would be assigned its appropriate target: God. The Church did have a valid argument here. This value assignment in love certainly would lead man or woman astray. However, I submit the Church did not want man astray from doctrine, which in this case they thought as "truth" as well.

My circumstances are different in that I was not blindly becoming saddled with an inappropriate appellation for a human; I was willfully loving *through* another. I never had a sense that the object of my affection was deity, in and of herself. Rather, I worshiped God through the object of my affection. I, possessing great powers to alter the perceived world, allowed my inability to secure a permanent abode in God to permit expressing this adoration in the flesh. This has not been negative to either myself or my affected love. This has been illuminating and I dare say the love exchanged was "out of this world," as I was not making love in this world.

However, what has this done for my ability to attain a meaningful relationship in this life? It has completely destroyed any possibility of my having a meaningful and productive relationship, as I am completely and totally in love with that which is not incarnate. I only ever ascribed earthbound tools to apprehend this love and now can never find one who can fill such shoes. All women became her, and none.

I MISS GOD

"I was missing you today. I was missing *something* I never permanently had. I was missing something I never had with you. I was missing something I never had with any other." That is the nature of my yearning: I have for seemingly all time been seeking that which I could not define but would surely know once in proximity. Now, with bones losing mass and white scalp hairs growing faster than their neighbors, I can define that which I have missed so long. I can understand clearly and reason ably the focus of my lamentation. I simply miss Love. It is not more complicated than that. It is my search for the long "Lost Word." It is the erection of "that temple, not made with hands, eternal in the heavens," constructed in my heart. Growing weary of the days of have and have-not of God enthroned in my heart, I elected to seek you, Lord.

"I was missing *you* today. I was missing *something* today. I was missing *someone* today." It is like this: it is an inarticulate absence of mind, an inexplicable loss, a narrowing of vision, a sense of totality—in absentia.

I have only lately begun to discern a pattern in my life with regards to love. This pattern, when removed from the circumstance of my life and applied in general to other's quest for love, is often called the search for a soul mate. This is the state people use to describe themselves or their conditions. They are in a state of wholeness or becoming whole pending the arrival of another to complete them. Yet, I hold no such illusions whereas I had in youth.

"I was missing you today. I was missing *something* today." All my life I have been in a constant state of possession and forlornness. It has only been in recent years where I have more often been complete and right with love, the world, myself, and God. There are no soul mates. Each consideration of the state or condition of love informs me that humans, in their natural state, are programmed to reach for God through the hazy confusing apparatus of flesh where we are housed. Executed through the facility of free will, love is more or less in a losing race to complete its program. There is a more profound dynamic taking place within all that aspire to, attain, or otherwise share love. We, however, process most often only the sensory and ancillary expressions of this love.

DERIVATIVE LOVE

This love, love in general, is what I term "derivative love." It is a state of imperfect love aping in the flesh that which is expressed and longed for spiritually. Love expressed in our humanity is like a child running unsupervised in a toy store. The more profound dynamic of love transforms our spirit in such ways that the sensory mind cannot begin to comprehend. We could not even begin to describe the composition let alone the needs of spirit. What we do note, however, is little more than our evolving maturity in love. Each year anew, we realize we did not know the year before what love truly was. Each fresh breeze of love in our lives informs us that we must never have loved before, and that we only called it such, "for *this* is love."

In a simple mind as mine, pestered endlessly with the notions that labor therein, it is no wonder I can hardly recall the touch of a woman, the scent of the winter morning upon a resting pillow, and the laughter that sings first through me, then dances upon the ear. In my world, where time and distance form the occasion of companionship, mark the opportunity and not the denial, I see more clearly than ever before that which is missed, that which was sought, is in fact not of this world. Never again, I fear, could another measure in shoes that which stood upon the mount. Undistracted by presence, I undress the world in the company of my own naked heart and find within only love. I stand confused looking upon creation, within the eyes of others, in the smiles of children, in flights of fancy of my mind, and find only love. I find love everywhere and I am overwhelmed by the clarity of my heart and my sense of totality.

I find love in the place where another is not. I had been taught to believe that love can surely not be found in the place where another *is not* for to be loved and so to love is the measure indeed of our human experience. This is not correct. This is not true. While wonderful, surely, love is not found in this manner. When I speak about love, I am always speaking to clarify the absolute from the relative. One is no less than another, for surely they are part and parcel of the same package. The derivative love of the senses invites us to consider our longing for love and for "union" to be a need of completeness. Even was one to not so consider elaborately that which was previously stated, it is the case that nearly all associate a sense of being more fully alive, more complete, sooner or later, only through another. While another can magnify life, another cannot complete life.

My missing God today, my missing *something* today, reprises my epiphany that I am clocking to God and am past the "help" any longer of others. Sometimes the most abstract of conclusions are the most difficult to pronounce. In this world, the seemingly unrelated often conspire with the trivial or meaningless to assign clarity and epiphany. I cannot so affix explanation to this point, but I am now past the point where I even wonder any longer. Every moment of every day I spend fixated on the love of God, the reflections of this love in the world, and my journey to forever.

SHE IS GOD

She is a creation of my mind. Exemplified, she is no less than God. None could stand in this place. She is God, the same one as for you, and of others. She is *she* for me; that's all. I choose this. In earthly incarnation, she is that which is kind, caring, compassionate, loving, intelligent, poetic, imaginative, graceful, intuitive, humorous, mischievous, earnest, charitable, hopeful, wondrous, supportive, balanced, visionary, playful, considerate, a dreamer, a dancer in the rain, a lover of children, self-reflective, introspective, reverent, gracious, honest, tenacious, empowered, empowering, sensuous, and wise. *She is wisdom.*

She is friendly to all but can never be taken advantage of because all that she has she is willing to part with. She can never be deceived, for she will never check behind her. She can never be misled for she leads with her heart. She is sensuous and romantic. She is an explorer of her life, her body and her mind. She can be rich or poor, in good health or dying tomorrow; this makes no matter for she has existed always in the ideal, and the quality of time is more important than the amount. *She is wisdom.*

I have elected to see God in this life with the prosthesis of my known landmarks and have thus invited her incarnate while my soul work was under construction. I have embraced God's reflections in God's creatures. I have labored to identify and subordinate desire. As I struggled to understand the appellations of love, and as I came to stand alone upon the lonely cusp where, having crossed, none return, not really, I worshiped her.

It is valid that the Church would fear love unbridled as potentially leading to deification of others. However, I never saw another as such, rather as a proxy. In this I was fair, honest, and actually more surely on target than I really knew. I created her from all the "hers" in the world who have enabled me to see the best in all of them. In all women there is grace and promise that speaks to hope, charity, nurturing, and the good struggle to preserve and simply live this life in love. In all women are the seeds of the flesh and immortality. It makes no difference that a woman knows of that which she possesses; her awareness does not lessen the station. Her awareness may enhance this, however. For whatever psycho-psychical reasons, I choose to dress God in the clothes of my wardrobe until such a time as God undresses me.

(The context of the previous passage describes a time some years ago. This time was for considering the role of women in my heart, in love. Morning, noon, and night I slept in the arms of God. The profound and growing isolation informed me that I have for all time slipped the arms of passion.)

CHAPTER 64

▼

Assigning Values

Many have never been able to reconcile Jesus' teaching to leave all behind in order to find the Father, God, and the Light. Moreover, one would have to lose his life even in order to save it. Renouncing the physical world was not a revolutionary means to secure the Kingdom of God, even in Christ's time, though it was in Judaism, a matrilineal faith. There is a point where the absurdity, the total divide that must be leaped to get from here to God cannot even be bridged until even in thought we have abandoned all but that which remains most dear, most truthful to us—even our family. Were the world washed away, our life in ruins, or even destitute of the smallest tenderness, we are left with one assurance in this life: no matter where we go and how far we fall, we will have the ties that bind: family. While family security is valid on the one hand, it is ultimately illusory.

However, in our ignorance, this illusion also serves to anchor us to this world, even when all else is lost. It is not necessary that those who would follow the Christ, or any *way*, actually up and leaves family, a child, a parent, or loved one. What is necessary is that they choose to, that they can leave, that they will leave even their closest love for God. Whether they do so or not is mechanics. The essence of such a thing is not in the "giving up," nor is it in the leaving. The purpose of which Christ spoke was to leave nothing in your heart or thoughts that could so occupy a place reserved for God only, and finally.

In our leaving room inside our heart only for God, all will reside within. It is a paradox and must be experienced to understand that we best love all by loving one, that we inherit all by becoming bankrupt, that we take in family by casting family out. In stripping all from a world, we adorn our world with all that we have stripped, and more. It is a retooled, new approach to the true construction of reality. One cannot even begin to understand this lest they hold glimpses. A deconstruction of thought is required for most paradigms of the spirit.

In the end, all things have meaning, or not, by virtue of the value we place therein. We must consider, though, who is actually assigning value in our lives. Do we assign value from the deep-seated place wherein the observer directs the moments? Do we assign our values based on the needs of flesh and sensory stimuli?

We assign value based on the inculcations and conventions of the faith we were assigned at birth? Perhaps for many of us it is a combination of factors that conspire to assign what is meaningful and applicable in our lives. However, were we to live a true existence, a really meaningful life of such truth that we could stand with conviction on death's threshold and declare with finality, "I was here, I have lived, and I have known this world, and this world has known me," we must cast aside all but one means of employment to assign value, meaning, and interpretation of our world.

With this one ruler as our yardstick, we can begin to walk the cusp of paradox, reason the irreconcilable, and rent asunder the illusion of duality. Know you your heart and walk forth into this life as the sojourner you were born to be, not the quarry slave mining for food and shelter. Leave all to gain God. Gain you God to gain all.

CHAPTER 65

▼

Letter to a Friend

Yours are not the words of the lost or the damned. Yours are never the words of the missing or needy. Your words are but the reflection of the things you allow me to drink from you. Think on that. You could not quench my thirst with dust. Yet, my thirst is quenched. How do you think this happens? It is because you allow me to see in you far more than you allow in yourself. You drink from your own cup when I extend my hand. Why is it valid only when you are not the observer?

Therefore, what if, in the course of our days, we cry? Or that we long for things denied or passions missed? Are we no less, no more, woman or man for this? What if in our passing no one takes notice; in the moment or in the years of our time here? Are we any less? Are we any more?

We, you, are. There is a place of peace so very close to you right now, my friend. I know this; I do not guess it. This place has both empowerment and grace. It is a where the matriarchs of the ages are laid to rest in the bosom of our collective memory, our Godhead. It is a place unique but not inaccessible. It is a place where rests the heart in the silent knowledge of all things, in the song of the world's voice. It is a place where the mundane, the hurt, the immediacy of pain, the subtle siren song of vanity, the remorse for the passing of youth, all stand naked and unarmed before the conviction of our grace and our immortality, right here, right now.

THE DIVINE PLAN

Let me tell you all. Let me, dear friend, till such a time as this age passes, tell you all. If in the passing of your fancy, you wish to no longer hear the sound of my voice in you're mind's ear, have compassion for me. In the end, I write for me. All love we give is selfish, in the end, dear friend.

This world is devoid of the God's of the heathens, the infidels, the believers, and others alike. This world is devoid of the evil-doers as well, and their gods rest in the trash heap of history. This world is absent the landlord of the ages. This world is unrequited in their knowledge of God. God does not exist. God is dead.

What I mean is simply this. There is a place just beyond the finite grasp of man and his descriptions of this world where lies Truth, Light, God, the eternal, and the collective pool from which dreams are dreamed and matter formed. As the ages pass, man has continued to redefine our God, our times, our future, *and* our past. And as the ages of man pass, God is apprehended in various ways. And to that man and that woman does the divine plan provide for that realization, that fruition, of such noble and righteous aims. In the end, Man acquires no more or less than to what he has aspired.

Yet, beyond the template of *our* creations of God lay the silent memory of the divine, the long suffering Bride, the Light, the Siren Song of Souls, and the Stillness of Waters. Call this what you will, but I speak of that which lies beyond what most affirm as God. It is all the same, but not finally, dear friend.

MESSAGE OF THE AGES

It is to the aspirant who would but know God fully to look past the God of his or her forebears and see there the message sealed for the ages that unlocks the keys to the Kingdom of God on Earth. You already possess the means. Christ was quite clear and emphatic when he spoke that in "my Father's House are many mansions" (John 14:2). In God's house, before the pillars of the world were dreamed and formed, in God's silent memory was created the myriad universes, the innumerable mansions of our worlds each.

In the multitude of dimensions and universes that co-exist at the same time all abide in the house of God. Right here, right now! You but walk the halls of an ancient dwelling and see not that your mansion has always existed; you understand not that your neighbors, too, reside not in space and time but outside of space in time in the infinite residence of the house of God.

And so it has come to pass in the great dialectic of time that God's coming to fruition of Self, of man rising as Phoenix to transcend the archaic, but necessary, incarnations of our Lord, that we may each now appropriate to us the infinite host of heaven as co-conspirators in our unfolding, our prayer, our dreams, and, in the end, our destiny.

WHERE HAVE OUR MOTHERS AND FATHERS GONE?

Therefore, dear friend, whether you be Christian or Jew, Muslim or Buddhist, Hindu or other, the true organization and mastery of worlds has always been right before you. What then has become of those in all times who have but dreamed the dream, those who have surrendered to and loved their God? Our forebears, our priests, our saints, our lay, and all others have appropriated to themselves beliefs the timeless soul can but little accommodate; the notion that this God, not that God, that this love not that love, is the venue and means of the eternal and the infinite.

All hold pieces of truth, but the Siren Song that calls forth our prophets and seers to see beyond the curtain necessarily informs them along the way that it is irrelevant to inform the followers, those that do not see the source but the reflection. For as they have the revelation that the powers and grace for the mastery of worlds and dominion of God are free to all, it becomes increasingly apparent that informing others is mostly useless as none can be brought before reality for counseling absent their own consent in each soul's due time.

Therefore, time passes and the mysteries of life, while increasingly accessible for other reasons herein not informed, remain aloof. Those who have dreamed the dream, those who have surrendered to and loved their God attained that world, that reality to which they each aspired, but no more. Furthermore, lost forever in the places between God and fabrication, illusion and delusion, they remain

Thousands of years ago the Mahabrahata, in the accompanying section of the great battle of Kurukshetra in the Bhagavad Gita, described aptly how the devout acquire those worlds and those gods, those heavens and those hells but dreamed. In effect, one can be a devout and loyal servant of his God, and in the end be rewarded in accordance with that love and dedication. I ask you, what of such a person? Is this not reward? To love our Lord and then attend that union in passing, is this not the great union, the great planning? Why waste a few years when we can gain eternity?

However, it is *a* union, not *the* union; it is *an* eternity, not *the* eternity. It is planning but we cannot superimpose our feeble plans on the divine. Devoid of the illusory baggage passed on to us, we can apprehend God within us purely and forever pass through the way stations of our ancestor's Gods. This is the wonder and joy of being. This is free will. There is a road map that takes us past the surveyed map handed us. Go not to the map's edge only, lest you fall off. Calibrate the azimuth of your heart, and it will lead you on the correct bearing where the map handed you ends.

Nevertheless, there is more. Many inspired texts describe only how we celebrate and acquire God in such ways as we do. What I would marry to this is the incompleteness of the priests, the dogma, and the doctrine of the ages. Dear friend, everything I tell you herein is compatible with the beliefs of your forebears, visceral denials notwithstanding. Their apprehensions were incomplete or the knowledge of completeness withheld from the masses. God has more here.

Christ spoke quite freely of this in the non-canonical texts and much leaked through the synoptic gospels. The problem was the Church elders, in not only suppressing women, but man as well, wanted removed that capacity to grow beyond the authority of man. Moreover, this time was an age of political and other deification. The secular as well as religious authorities thought abhorrent the notion that man would commune with God directly. Man *would* be intercessor to God. Christ never intended to be the end, but rather, *the means*. Nevertheless, Christ was made the end and man was made the means. I am comfortable with my notion that Christ never intended to make himself equal to God. Many have been twice and thrice removed from God since. Use your own compass; its bearing is pre-set.

ACCESS GOD DIRECTLY

God has set in place this amazing means of very direct and real discourse with the eternal for you alone—just you, dear friend. In your mansion there is a host to command. There is a stillness wherein your peace is obtained. There is a place where you can more freely download the grace of the Light, Love, Truth, Compassion, and the silence of the heart of the world. It is here that we become the co-sirens of the song of souls.

"In My Father's House are many mansions" (John 14:2) is among the most vivid revelations on the nature of your world. Your mansion is your personal space, and it occupies all the things about your senses. They are all here for you. Every single moment each and every corner and piece of the world with which you interact, consider, observe, or even cast a glance upon was always just your world. What you dream, imagine, or lament is yours. This is all your world—horizontally in space and vertically in time—it is all yours. Surrender to all around you. Surrender to your world in the silent faith that there are no mistakes.

Each and every moment of your world unfolds exactly the way in which you command it, whether you are aware of this or not. Look with a renewed eye to the beauty that is the unseen fabric that binds together all things you observe or consider. They were all here for you while you were a twinkling piece of stardust in the ages of the distant past. This world is a creation of your will, your free will. This world intersects at countless places permitting, allowing, and supporting all other worlds in an infinite symbiosis. It is not enough to realize the majesty of the gift to which you were born; you must understand the default knowledge that rests surely in your heart. Understanding the anatomy of the worlds around you is meaningless in and of itself. You were destined to God. All is designed to enable that end. One is form, the other function.

GO, SECURE ETERNITY

Therefore, this day, arise or retire with a question for yourself. Do I need to know today who I am and why I am here, or is it sufficient for today alone to know that *I am* and *I am here*? Do I really accept and understand that I am immortal? Do I understand that that which is Love is unknowable to *me*, that I can accept increasingly finding her reflections till I can find love in all things, that I can know Love, but will no longer know *me*?

It is sufficient for today to know simply that you are. Understanding and contemplation on the nature of why we are here is useful intellectual chatter for the idle moments when slips the day toward sleep, but in the end, awareness is born in the pool—the vacuum wherein intellectual counsel has parted.

When you turn slowly the coin of immortality in your mind, you will see clearly all are on one side or another. Most are on the obverse where rests the lip-service oral tradition where we assert with empty heart that we are immortal. Some rest upon the cusp, neither obverse of reverse. Then there are those that are on the reverse, resting in the infinite power and knowledge that they are indeed immortal and they survive the flesh. When your belief changes to knowing, you will be truly immortal and invincible.

When you fully understand that love is the *spiritus sanctum*, consciousness, the *spiritus dei*, you will know Love, but you will no longer know you. You are never you for more than the briefest of moments as you are every moment someone else. You are a learning and growing machine. Your entire body is completely repopulated by an entire new cellular structure every year, not one cell remaining. Your internal fabric is also in a constant state of dynamism. When one starts drinking of the fount of life, the change is ever more dramatic. *You* can never know Love. While spirit evolves, surely when one drinks from the source, he is transfigured.

Ask God, as I do all day long, to feed you. My God is my Bride, my dear friend. I ask freely from God's table to give to me this light that is Truth, Love, Compassion, and stillness of my heart. In so receiving, I seek to share this love with even one other each day. In the end I am selfish in loving you, dear friend, loving any. Love is, finally, a selfish act. It enables me, it frees me, it sends me. My loving you frees me. My loving all liberates me. Ask God of God's bounty. In just asking God you are asking you. In asking you, you are opening portals unseen. Knock and it will be opened.

Dear friend, do not fear your place, your choices, your day, your heart, or your tomorrow. Just be love, empty and everywhere. Take a little time each day, and tell someone you love her. Write home even though you may be very tired, and tell someone that you thought of him and you love him, and then love him. Find one thing in this world each day that brings you joy and makes you smile, one thing that you had not noticed before, and then share it.

Come with me, please, try with me this thing called love. For a little while, share with me only your love, your fears, your hopes, and most importantly, your observations of love each day (not: share *only* with me). Let us see them change together. Maybe we can shortly look at a place where you are effused to the point that your tears are of simple and tender love and no longer unrequited or forlorn love. All love is love of God.

CHAPTER 66

▼

Reprieve for an
Unexamined Life

When you close your eyes at night, in death, you must have lived so that you are aware, as the passing of life's last breath departs your emptied lungs, that this was "the greatest story [never] told." Live in the surrender to that which you could no more change were you wont to do so. Live in the bath of life all about you.

"How sweet, but this will not chase the cold away at night nor feed our hungry mouths," you consider. Will it not? I look back over the years and in hindsight find that nothing was ever lacking for my need's ends. All conspired in the grand tapestry that are my days to bring me to the summit today. For what is it that I lack? By what means would I even measure lack or need, if not by the standard carried by another, others? All that we infer in that which we need or lack is only in contrast to what we see elsewhere, in others, in other's possessions. No thing in space or time can approximate another thing were it not for some third thing standing in contrast, opposition, triangulation. Were there naught but you and God in all the vast expanse of time and space, you would measure nothing as lacking or needful. You would have no fears, no loss, no regrets, only surrender to the obvious bath of life in direct communion.

FEAR NEITHER DEATH NOR LIFE

Fear not that which you cannot know you need. Fear not that which is lacking in your trappings, but noted in other's. Were you to pass the flesh this day, the greatest thing you would have ever provided the world, and yourself, is the language of your heart, the measure of your deeds, and lastly the volume of your words. You can measure not that which is worthy for others save by the pursuit of your own heart's ends. I am not speaking about worldly pursuits of gratification; we know this. I am simply telling you that this life, this journey, is a never-ending magical voyage through the flesh, and you should miss not one opportunity to say and to love that which or whom you love. You should live each day prepared to die. You should lay your head about your pillow's encasement each night with such preparation that you may tender to your heart that it is well, it is done, and it is right. ("I am prepared to die this very moment.") You can do no greater thing for yourself and for your heirs. You can contribute no greater effort to the collective longing to love life than to do this, to live this way, each day.

God is not in you. God is not in others. God is not in the creek or the northern breeze. God is not within the holy of holies. God is not, as Lafayette declared, "within our Sunday supplications." We are all *within* God this very moment. You move today within the bath of God all about you, right here, right now. We are all but manifestations of the spirit encased. We are projections. We are emanations. We are will.

We are trunks born of the roots of the almighty. You are within the cosmic firestorm, the nuclear furnace, and the percolating well spring of life each and every moment. Never, ever, ever let slip this awareness.

You are on borrowed time to this moment in the unending cycle of life. You *are* immortal and will life eternally in the Slipstream of Creation. There is no fear in this place. There is no fear in this place. There is no fear.

Lo' you will die, friend. Your breath will expire, and to all who love you, their world will be torn asunder. Your loved ones and friends will grieve or will celebrate your passing. You will be missed. Your laughter and tears, your uniquely charming ways, and your compassion and strength will all be considered upon your loss from this world. You will die.

Your body will be laid in peace, and dust will scatter your host. You will die. You will take the final exit and ultimate journey. What fear, then, could you but have of this moment, this day? To what end can you so prepare for the sojourn in eternity by your trivial concerns this day? What thing or circumstance might life grant to thee that could make preparation for this journey? What comfort can you abide in now that can enable better your passage through the long night of your soul?

What end can your having secured trappings have for others? Comfort of station? Healthcare? Food for the hungry mouth? Yes, of course. However, the lessons and boons granted to us in this life are not always that which our intellect and senses tell us is best. Life provides for life. Love provides for love. God provides for God.

Live this life in that manner which, when your moment comes to slumber in the earth's bosom, leaves the ineffable to your offspring and loved ones. Provide to others best by your steadfast assertion that fear is disabling, that life is worthy of living under all of the best-aspired conditions.

It is all so very fast. It is all so very fast. Live not that you may look back, and having looked, so lament packing for the wrong trip.

I REMEMBER

I remember it all. I remember the smell of grass when I was playing at recess. I remember the backyards that I sneaked through when I played hooky from school. I smell Christmas morning. I can hear the adults talking in the kitchen as my sisters and I played with our toys, and I opened yet another pack of socks for "school clothes." Why does yesterday have its own smell, its own flavor in the hallways and byways of my mind? I looked out at the fields before me and could hear a tractor in the distance finishing up the day's chores. Background noise, all of it. The random intrusive recollections continued. I spent my whole life trying to quell the fervor that is my mind, and now I desperately wanted all the voices, all the faces, all the years to return.

I smell age on my grandmother long before she was old. I see her years landmarking her passing in the wrinkles of her face, her hands. I taste Thanksgiving dinner, and my mom's oyster stuffing. Though it sounds nasty, it was my favorite at the holidays. I wonder if she knows how very much I liked her stuffing. She worked so hard every year on this one dish. I can see closely the little ants on the ground digging their holes and carrying food as I lay in the hot sun in Fort Jackson, South Carolina, in basic training, waiting for another day of misery to end. I zoned-in watching the ants. I was lying in wait for a pretend enemy, but found the affairs of the ants so much more entertaining. I never got caught by the drill sergeants for this.

I smell the tar from the decaying swamps of the Carolinas. My mind is now scattered.

I remember. I remember it all now. I leaned upon the great oak beside me and contorted my neck as I tried to see its very top. It was a tall and grand tree. It must have been very old. I sank down within a nook at its feet, the roots parting ever so easily years ago to create this very place for me today. I looked closely at the dark brown bark that was this tree's skin and saw infinitely small workings going on. The ants. They were here, too, ever so small but a fine enough testimony to the unseen worlds all around me. I sank even lower in the bough upon the earth and rested my head looking upward, toward the light. My head would never move again. This would be the very place from which I watched the closing of this world.

DUST TO DUST

The branches scattered the light above me as storm clouds wrestle the eager sun after a hard blow. The light danced upon thousands of leaves, millions of blades of grass. I no longer had any depth of field. The leaves, the grass, the trees, and the voices—they were all just before me, and a thousand years away.

My eyes closed, my hair was blowing freely as the wind from the Alps whipped through the canyons. I feel the ice upon the summit, though they are still a day's hike away. The bitter cold invades my legs. I am hot and sweaty; I am tired and excited. Am I still in Yemen? I feel my legs bursting with the stress of my muscles. I feel the weight of the ropes bearing down on me, and the crampons biting into the ice. Still, I see the Eiger before me, again. I see the crystal-blue sky.

Yeah, I was going to ski the Eiger. I had no idea. I would have to settle with just skiing down from the base camp saddle at Grindenwald. I could see the crosses atop the world. Every mountaintop had a cross erected to God at the top of it. I wondered how many people knew this. I thought how very noble and awesome this was. I was glad I knew this. I am glad I signed these books at the top lest no man know I passed God's summit. The cold lessened in my legs. Warmth replaced the cold. Earth replaced my skin; Life replaced my blood.

As I lie here, I feel my life ebb from me, just a little bit more, day after day, year after year. Unobserved, I have been lying here for forty years. I see the grass growing right before me. It all seems so much faster now.

It does not really grow this fast, does it? I wondered. I turned, my blood, my breath, oozing from me, and saw the clouds racing across the day as though elapsed stills speeded up. I recalled the various elapsed-time specials on television where they showed the clouds, the plant life, the sun in its arc, and simply life. I was in this special television show. I could not see anything to the left or the right of me. I could not turn my head. I saw everything to the left and right of me. I could not turn my head.

Time? I was out of it. I could now taste the dirt. It was rich and earthy. I tasted peanuts; no, that is not right. Not peanuts. Maybe iron. Yes, it tasted like metal. It was not in my mouth; rather it seemed my body consumed it through my flesh as roots. I looked at my feet and could no longer see them, just the dust where they once were. My clothes remained. I was crying. I was sobbing freely, and I was laughing. The cold of the Eiger memories was replaced by the very earth consuming my flesh.

GREATER AND LESSER LIGHTS

I remembered Sandra. I thought I loved her. Oh, I suppose I did. I allowed other loves over the years to redefine that sad love affair. Why did I think of her? She was the first person I allowed to define what I thought love was. I now thought of Leigh Ann. She was the last I allowed to define what love was. They were two very different things entirely. I did not love Leigh Ann; I loved life through Leigh Ann, and in that place she became pre-eminent above all others. She loved me as well, though differently. It was in the end irrelevant. I loved everyone now. They both served to collapse time, the years, the portal, and love into a penetrating grasp of the ineffable nature of love. I lie now in Jenchinan, the immortal kingdom. I am home.

I felt now like the many times I was in an airplane getting ready to jump. Time seemed to go on forever. We were so sick and tired of the flight. Then, it was time to "stand up, hook up our parachutes, and shuffle to the door." Still, time dragged on slowly as we waited to exit at thousands of feet into the dark. I was always unable to appreciate time.

I did not know, I lamented.

I just did not, could not, know. When the light turned green and it was time to jump, it all seemed to be happening so fast, too fast. I needed just a little more time.

There was something that I forgot to do. I just could not remember what it was. I needed just a little more time. I need more time. *I need more time!* I was falling. The light is green today.

Today, I am aware of the sense that the clock is near midnight and the light is indeed green. I need more time, my precious friend. I seem to feel like I want more time. I could not see any part of my legs. My hips disappeared into the folds of the roots in this fertile ancient soil. The virgin soil fused into my groin. Grass was growing where my seat is/was. My crotch, my hips, were fused seamlessly into the earth now. Ants moved busily about the affairs of small things. Worms tunneled in the rich humus that was my pelvis.

I see the prettiest flower. It sprung from my flesh. I had not noticed this flower before. It is lovely. *What is it?* I wondered. It seemed I should have noticed something so pretty before. Why did I not notice such a pretty thing in all these years? I had only ever found one flower where none were thought to exist, and that was in the desert. I thought sadly how many flowers I had missed. It occurred to me that every moment was a time to celebrate these little wonders. Every flower was more beautiful because I noticed it, not because it just was.

For the oddest reason someone I worked with long ago entered my mind. I was not sure what he did to me, or I to him, but I seemed to think we did not like each other. All of a sudden I was aware that he was doing the best he could. I thought about him and imagined him as a young man. I supposed his mother loved him very much and he too likely raced to the living room on Christmas morning. Why could I not see earlier that he and I were going to the same place? I loved him. I could not remember his name. I could not remember his face. I was overwhelmed, though, by the sense that I was fully in love—with all things. I recalled his past as it was my own, and I loved the boy that was him, that was me. They were in the end, one and the same. I remember.

We are all just doing the best we can, with each moment, with what our inventory is, with our faculties. Why was it not all so simple before?

I OWN THIS WORLD

I was going to miss this…something. I was not sure why I was going to miss this, what I was going to miss, or even where I was going. This was all mine. I surveyed the sky. I felt an ownership I had not felt before. This was my team, this was my life, and this was my world. I was at once so very proud and so protective. I felt as all this about me was my own legacy, that I could well take pride in the birds chirping, in the breeze, even in the soil housing the worms that made there home in me right now. I was crying for joy and felt the sun melting my skin. The air fed upon my organs, now exposed. The wind made an odd whistling sound as it passed through my rib cage.

I had the strangest sense that the "light was green" and I was about to leave the plane, life's plane. My mind was scattered.

Marilyn! I thought. Marilyn! Oh, God, I thought of Michele and my mother, too. It all started coming into view at that moment. *Sarah. Sarah and Jesse, dear Lord!* I was sobbing. Where were they? I could not see them. I could not feel them. My fingers reached out to intercept the stardust in the fashion to which my prayers were accustomed. My palm filled with flowers.

These lights of my life were simply absent my thoughts. They simply intruded and while I was re-familiarizing myself with them I knew them. They were the conspirators who made my life what it was. I saw faces, rather than depth, in those that were the minutes of my clock. Fleeting images void of texture scrolled upon the remaining cells of my mind. Heather, Tracy, each scrolling two-dimensionally across the tattered screen of my mind.

MY TAPERS

Their images were fading. I loved them all so much. Why were they here, in my mind, and not? *Sandra?* I could not see any more faces. *Leigh Ann? Jen?* I did not know why I said that name. I was not sure who Leigh Ann was, not any longer. I knew that she was more an idea than anything. What idea was she? I knew I felt warm when I thought of *Sarah! Jessica and Sarah!* I was warm and smiled when I said Sarah's and Jessica's names out loud.

"Sarah, Marilyn, Michele, Jessica." My seed, my life, my anchor, my immortality. Wait, I remember. They were my blood, my pulse, my light. Simply and powerfully, they were my life.

Oh, dear God, yes. They knew me in this life! Yes, I took all the clay in my world and made for me images of God from the dust of my years. They sat upon the shelf of my heart and smiled warmly. They provided security by the creation of my own hand. I remember. I remember. This is my life; this was my life. I was alive. I was alive.

Oh, God, please, what is happening? These were the minutes of the hands of my clock, and they were near midnight. The light was green. I was jumping. I remember.

I could smell their individual smells, each a woman, a woman-child, each a bearer of light for me drawing the contexts, the curtains, and the lessons of my time here.

Jeanne, Margie, Jen, Becky. I saw my Aunt Foxy, Micky, Patsy, and my bitter Nana. There again were more sisters, Marilyn and Michele. I see them all and some faces vague. There were props and stagehands, too.

I see the train of my lovers past. *Why were there so few? Were so few meaningful? Did I have so few lovers,* I thought with my remaining impish ego? I saw. I sensed less in the train of these images than I would have thought filled the space of my heart. Were, in the end, the creators of my heart so few in number, and others props on my stage? Is proximity the discriminator of the impact we have on each other's world? Were those in my mind's eye with depth and texture no more than those that danced with me last?

Sarah, Jesse, Sandra, Marilyn, Leigh Ann, Mom, Jen, Michele, Paige, Foxy, Micky, Tracy, Brigitte, Heather, Nancy. These are the planets in which my star orbited, lately. I was aware in passing, as I was in arriving, that Tim and Jason were the only men in my life's story.

BREATHE THE WORLD

My chest settled into the earth with a sigh. A root pierced my thorax, and I could see dew glistening on bone as the sap ran out of the root. Roots snaked and coiled their way around the axis of my ribs. The soil was rich with black. The leaves above were green, pastel green.

I heard a song. No wait, it was singing. It was not music, but it was. It was not a song, but singing? A song? I could not be sure. I thought I heard the sound of all the people I ever knew laughing and singing. Yes, I heard singing. I saw the faces of these lights and they were all smiling at me. Somewhere, across the world, each was sleeping, working, playing, but in their quiet places they were here for me, and they knew it. I was aware that this was the discourse of our souls. Our souls were always in communication with us, unbeknownst to our idle, waking selves. They were each bidding me goodnight. They smiled with a love that made me sure I was right in loving such beauty and tenderness in them each. I was sure if I was quiet, other people could hear it, too. How could they not, it was everywhere? It was so pretty.

Why had I not listened more closely earlier? Why had I not danced to this music, this song? Why did I have to wait till dust consumed my limbs? Why did

I not remember sooner the song that hummed the world since first the flight of years?

I looked past the limbs and the leaves and saw what seemed to be millions of little lights, tiny streaks, blazing through the midday sun, the brilliant blue, and passing through the very earth, passing through the leaves, through me. They were everywhere. Like a master's paintbrush, the lights streamed through all things like a meteor light show. There was no sound save for the song. I remember. I caught all of it on my fading hard drive.

I remember. I wanted to remember. I never wanted to forget. For some reason every single atom, every thought and breeze was infinitely important. The train of yesterday pulled from the station, and I saw no longer the faces and textures of my tapers, of my lights this life. I was simultaneously alone and not alone. I was me, and I was not. With each breath, I breathed the world. With each breath, I exhaled my being into the world. I know how to do this. I remember.

"TELL ME CHILD, WHAT HAVE YOU LEARNED?"

Should any soul ever ask me what beauty I have known, I want them to know the strange man with whom I used to work, the one who's name I forgot. If anyone, anywhere, ever asks me if I have known beauty in this life, I want to remember. I want to say that I have known my mother kissing me and sending me to school. Though I could not see it then, I see now the smile of pride at her handsome boy leaving for his first day at school.

I want to be able to say that Marilyn kept me close to ward off the dark when once afraid. I want to tell of the beauty that knows no depths when I tell of the woman-child, the flower of Jenchinan, who taught me of love in the twilight, before the light turned green. I will once again announce "Hypatia" with confidence.

I will tell of beauty with names. I will utter "Sarah" and say aloud "Jessica" to the host of heaven, to the neterworlds. I will recall the love I saw in others, for others. I will announce the lesser and greater tapers that bore light in my world. I will tell of Nancy and how my life would have been simply incomplete without her wisdom, love, affection, and compassion. Nancy taught me more about love than most other women ever could. She was truly a mother to me.

I will sound for my creation, my forlorn love who represented against all possible reason the dream that love was worth dreaming, every day, and that life was meaningless absent her evasive and coy hide and seek, my eternal Bride, my Beloved Wife.

I want to remember every smell, every scent, and every taste. I want to remember the touch that recalls the ages. I will tell of the silent Christmas mornings slumbering forever in the dying cells of my memory. The young boy stealing glances at the toys in the window he would never know. I remember winter mornings and the intense prayers that school would be canceled. I recall every Kodak moment in the album of my very being.

I remember my mother. I remember that I choose to remember her like this long before I made my bed in this tomb of rock. I chose to remember the good, the gracious, the love, and the loss. I choose to remember then what I must remember now. I choose to love in this life. I always choose. It is all choice.

I remember. My immovable head now held my eyes fixed, my gaze forever toward the sun. The light was green. My skin retreated from the dry heat, my skull revealed for the elements. My open sockets now home for the thirsty soil. The grass fully encased in the food of my heart. I remember.

In the distance I hear the sounds of children playing. Their refrain was music with the song of the world I have now heard since first I remembered. Sarah, Jessica, Madeline, Marilyn, Michele, Becky, Paige, Jeannie, Margie, Jennifer, Larry, Anthony, the train of others past, all emblazoned in my memory as I remembered this place, this time. It was good. It was all so fast. I remember.

THE FINAL ESCAPE

I am everywhere. I am as sand blowing from atop a dune. I am a cosmic storm filling the void of space. I am washed away by the light, yet I am whole and in a billion parts at once. The sun, all suns, wash me in their winds. I see all and am reflecting both the darkness and the light. I am as the Milky Way. My tail stretches out for eons and miles. I see the minutes of my life reflected in the myriad crystals that are me. I am lost.

How long? Where am I? I am dead. It is done. I am aware only that I am aware. I am light. I am in all places. Never could words describe this. Thought failed me. Thought remained.

I am and am not. I am high. I am lucid. I am dreaming. I live. I am alive. I am not. "I am" and "I am not." I am me. I am all things.

I have no sense of time or its passing. Worlds turn and stars burn and still, I am. I am aware of cold, of heat, but only peripherally. I am without form, without mass. Dimly, in some distant reservoir, I see a form laid out in the valley, dust and flowers at the foot of an ancient tree. Yet, I simply knew this was a body; this was my body. In the twinkling of my particles I see scenes, images, of my late life. I am the sum total of these particles, of these images. I am no more. I am more.

They are as snowflakes in a queue, I realized. Each seemingly suspended by an invisible thread in the deep dark, lazily turning before some central place where I process the image contained upon its slowly rotating surface, its axis turning and displaying. The image emblazons across my consciousness. It turns inexorably on its axis and is gone, another turning slowly in its place, revealing more images still. In this void, this dark, this cloistered light, the scenes of my life pass before me. I am everywhere. Still, another image, another scene, and the countless train of snowflakes, at once reveal light, and then darkness, stretch out forever in this place between worlds, within worlds. They are the fine particles of energy wherein I am stored. Cosmic silicon. I marveled.

The grass is fresh cut, or at least the smell is. The richness is unlike anything I have ever known. It is as if vision itself had texture. I beheld everything. I am in the darkness and am in the light. I am overwhelmed by images that are horrifying, and are not. They are my past; they are another's. I am in all places, in all times, at once. Everything is at the same time. I beheld the world before me. I beheld *my* world as I never had. I feel rather than hear a fine humming, a vibration like music. It is music. There is a symphony of vibrations, each on its own frequency. Many married up and created still other frequencies, other "hums." It is a song. All life hummed. All things, all mass, all energy, all hummed with its own voice. I know this song. I remember.

The land sings and the water refrains. Everything is singing. There are no transitions to scenes. They all just are. I am seeing everything at the same time. I am *le petit mort*. I am the waters. I am the lovers. I am a baby, and I am elixir. I am magic and the moon. The stars ride in my tail. I embrace the heavens. I create the heavens. I am God. I am not. The air, I am the air. I am giddy. I am alone.

I am not alone. I am aware in the silence of the music that I am in attendance with everything that has ever been. I just consider an image from my coffer and it is before me, presenting a time, a place, a person, a scene. Everything was and is, simultaneously. I remember. I am absent context.

I sense that I am increasingly not "I," but rather a part of everything. I do not begin or end. I am aware that no emotions remain. I am filled with what could only be called love. Is love an emotion? I had long ago sustained that Love was not, and that love is indeed an emotion. Discerning this difference would enable me to apprehend *this*. I had no idea. I just did not realize. I thought I did. I thought I could command eternity with intellect, infinity with willful prayer. I was wrong. I was simply wrong. It is all so obvious. It is all so plain. I missed the point. All I had to do was *listen*. All I had to do was *see*. I *hear*. I *see*.

I sense rather than understand that not all are in attendance, but all *are* here. Not all *became* with a continued awareness. I sense them, the multitudes slumbering in the insensible void, in the ether between worlds, beyond the city's lights. I catch glimpses of their images from the stardust. I am increasingly aware and can resurrect entire thoughts, complete trains of images.

I hear the song. I am now the song. I am a string in the symphony. I am a horn on the wind. I am now the sunrise and the melting snow. I am a hawk's eye and the prey's trembling heart, a captive bird, and an evening dance. I am the call to prayer and a glacial mass. I am the winds of the sun and the bitter cold of Christmas dawn. I am dawn.

Euphoric, I became transparent to myself. I am a thought, a pulse, a gentle breeze. I decided to blow across the world. I ceased to be. I continue. I am.

978-0-595-67649-1
0-595-67649-9

Printed in the United States
57483LVS00005B/1

9 780595 676491